D1548192

Samuel Wilderspin
and the Infant School Movement

PHILLIP McCANN AND FRANCIS A. YOUNG

CROOM HELM
London & Canberra

© 1982 Phillip McCann and Francis A. Young
Croom Helm Ltd, Provident House, Burrell Row,
Beckenham, Kent BR3 1AT

British Library Cataloguing in Publication Data

McCann, Phillip
    Samuel Wilderspin and the infant school movement.
    1. Wilderspin, Samuel
    2. Education, Elementary – Great Britain
    I. Title   II. Young, Francis A.
    372.941   LA633

    ISBN 0-7099-2903-X

Printed and bound in Great Britain by
Biddles Ltd, Guildford and King's Lynn

CONTENTS

ILLUSTRATIONS

Plate I Samuel Wilderspin.
(From the portrait by J.R. Herbert, R.A., by courtesy of Mrs. T.N. Buell, California, U.S.A.).

Plate II James Buchanan.
(From R.R. Rusk, *A History of Infant Education* (London 1933), by courtesy of the University of London Press).

David Goyder.
(From the *New Church Magazine,* Vol. XXIV, No. 406, Oct. 1915, by courtesy of the Trustees of the British Library).

J.P. Greaves.
(From A. Campbell (Ed.), *Letters and Extracts from the Manuscript Writings of James Pierpoint Greaves* (London, 2 vol., 1845), by courtesy of the Trustees of the British Library).

Plate III The Interior of Bristol Infant School, Meadow Street.
(From D.G. Goyder, *A Manual of the System of Instruction Pursued at the Infant School, Meadow Street, Bristol* (London, 3rd ed., 1824), by courtesy of the Trustees of the British Library).

Plate IV The Interior of Walthamstow Infant School.
(By courtesy of the Museum of Local History, Old Vestry House, London Borough of Waltham Forest).

Plate V Drygate Infant School, Glasgow.
(By courtesy of the Mitchell Library, Glasgow).

Plate VI Cheltenham Infant School, St. James' Square.
(From the painting by T. Westall, by courtesy of Cheltenham Art Gallery).

Plate VII Dublin Model Infant School.
(From T.U. Young, *The Teacher's Manual for Infant Schools and Preparatory Classes* (Dublin 1850), by courtesy of Mrs. K.Y. McNamara, New York, U.S.A.).

Thomas Urry and Sarah Anne Young, (By courtesy of John A. Young, Vermont, U.S.A.).

Plate VIII "Baby-Lonian University", by George Cruikshank.
(From the *Comic Almanack, 1843* (London 1843), by courtesy of the Trustees of the British Library).

Lines to a Great Philanthropist.

Oh Wilderspin! I would attune the harp
Of sweetest poesy to tell thee how,
With heart and spirit, I esteem the work
And labour of thy life! no harsher sound
Than softest music will befit the theme—
No tone less 'trancing than the poet's lyre.
Kind friend of Infants! who in early life,
Amidst the haunts and dwellings of the poor,
Looking around thee, saw them left to roam
In paths of wickedness, untrained, untaught,
Save in the deeds of ill; and with a heart
Of tender care, a mind resolved to act,
Didst love and pity them; — with deepest thought
And observation piercing and intense,
Didst keenly study all the mystic laws
Of mind unfolding in the infant breast.

Teacher of babes! thy cause, when in its rise,
Drew friends around, who fostered it with care,
Endured a little time, and then fell off.
Alone, undaunted, in the face of scorn,
Of opposition, slander, ridicule,
And all that most can sink the heart of man
And baffle perseverance, thou didst still,
Upheld by strength imparted from on high,
With boldness persevere, and plead the cause
Of helpless infancy around the land,
And work unceasing for its lasting good
With untired ardour.

T.J. Terrington, *Christmas at the Hall* (1853).

PREFACE

Though this book is in every sense a collaboration, Dr. McCann is responsible for chapters 2, 3, 4, 5, 9, 10, 11, 12, 13 and 14, and Dr. Young for 1, 6, 7, 8, 15 and 16. To Dr. McCann has also fallen the task of organising, editing and preparing the text for publication.

Our list of acknowledgements is a lengthy one. First we would like to thank the Canada Council, whose grant, covering the years 1971-75, enabled the greater part of the research to be carried out; in addition we are grateful to Memorial University of Newfoundland for a large grant in aid of printing and for several smaller grants from the Vice-President's Fund, and to the Dean of Education for additional financial assistance to cover printing costs. We are indebted to John A. Young of Wolcott, Vermont, a great-great grandson of Samuel Wilderspin, for allowing us the unfettered use of the papers of Wilderspin and of Thomas Urry Young in his possession; to Theodora Niven Buell, Elizabeth Knox Ahlm and Patricia Wilderspin Sewall, of California, great-great grand-daughters of Wilderspin, for the loan of correspondence and for allowing us to photograph the Herbert portrait; to Katherine Young McNamara of Staten Island, N.Y., another great-great grand-daughter, for the loan of rare copies of Wilderspin's works.

With respect to research, we were particularly fortunate to have as research assistant during 1971-72 Miss Sylvia Hodder (now Mrs. Worrall), whose energy and resourcefulness in discovering and collecting material in all parts of the British Isles laid the foundations for the book. We also wish to thank the following for assistance of various kinds: Hyacinth Douglas, Maryvonne Plessis-Fraissard, Kay McCormick and Leslie Zweigman for help with research; Dr. Herbert Jackson and Mrs. Helen Jones for translation services; Brian G.C. Brooks, of Brooks and Simpson Ltd., for genealogical research; Rex Russell, of Barton-on-Humber, for permission to use his unpublished Ms. on Wilderspin in Lincolnshire; Harold Speak and Mrs. Jean Forrester, of Wakefield Historical Society, for information on Wilderspin's residence in Wakefield; John Goodchild, of Wakefield Public Library, for permission to use material in his private collection; J.E. Whitaker, Hon. Secretary of the City of Wakefield Golf Club, for access to the clubhouse, formerly Lupset Hall; A.C. Dunsmore, Publicity Manager of the Gourock Ropework Co., for information from the New Lanark Visitors' Books; Rev. H. Edwards, vicar of St. Michael's, Highgate, for searches in local parish registers; J.N. Baldry, Headmaster of Hackney Free and Parochial Secondary School, for access to minute books in possession of the school; Miss G.P. Collins, former Principal of Saffron Walden College of Education, for access to rare works on infant education; S.J.D. Gegg, of Spirax Sarco Ltd., Cheltenham, the present occupiers of the former Alpha House, for information concerning Wilderspin's tenancy of the building; W. and R. Chambers Ltd., publishers, for supplying letters of Wilderspin from their archives; Jacky Grayson, of Birmingham University, for making available material in her possession on Worcestershire Infant Schools; John and

Margaret Crump, of Bristol, for help in locating letters of Wilderspin and in providing references to Wilderspin in the Combe Papers; Trevor Hearl, of St. Paul's College, Cheltenham, for assistance in locating sites associated with Wilderspin in Cheltenham; Rev. A.F. Munden, of Newcastle-upon-Tyne, formerly of Cheltenham, for making available copies of the works of Rev. F. Close in his possession and for other assistance re the early history of Cheltenham infant schools; Miss D.M. Edwards, of the *Brechin Advertiser,* for access to minute books in her possession; Peter Lineham, of New Zealand, for help and advice regarding various aspects of Swedenborgian theology; Dr. Otto Vag, of Budapest, for information concerning Wilderspin's influence in Europe. We owe a special debt of gratitude to Madeline Waters, secretary, and A.S. Wainscot, librarian, of the Swedenborg Society, London, whose courtesy and kindness to one of the authors over a period of several years made research there a pleasure. In addition, the Rev. D. Duckworth and the Rev. C.H. Presland, ministers of the General Conference of the New Church, freely placed at our disposal rare manuscript material in their possession.

We are also indebted to the officials and librarians of the following institutions: the British Library; the Public Record Office, London; the National Library of Scotland; the National Library of Ireland, the Irish Record Office and the Irish State Paper Office, Dublin; the Library of Congress, Washington, D.C.; the Bibliothèque Nationale, Paris; the National Bibliotek, Vienna. The following University libraries have been particularly useful: the Houghton Library, Harvard University; the Bodleian, Oxford; the University Library, Cambridge; the Goldsmiths' Library of the University of London; the Library of University College London, and those of the Universities of Edinburgh, Birmingham, Hull and Leeds. Of the many specialised libraries in which we have worked, the following are those to which we are mainly indebted: the Department of Education and Science Library; the Guildhall Library; the Society of Friends' Library; Dr. Williams' Library; the Library of Swedenborg House, London; the Methodist Archives; the National Society of the Church of England Library; Vestry House Museum, Waltham Forest; William Salt Library, Stafford; Fruitlands Museum, Massachusetts; the New Church Library, Bryn Athyn, Pennsylvania. Finally, our grateful thanks are due to the archivists and librarians of the many County Record Offices, County Libraries and local Public Libraries in all parts of the British Isles, too numerous to mention individually, whose unfailing courtesy in answering queries and placing their records at our disposal did much to make the research both successful and pleasurable. Finally, we are grateful to Harold Silver, Susan Parkes, Marjorie Cruickshank, Phyllis Annis, David Hamilton, Jim Alexander, Victor Jones and Rosanne McCann, who read parts of the manuscript and made helpful comments and criticisms. To the Supervisor and staff in the General Office of the Faculty of Education, Memorial University and to Miss Maureen Kent, who typed the final draft of the manuscript, our special thanks.

ABBREVIATIONS

Wilderspin's works.

Wilderspin's main works on infant education went through many editions, each containing new material and with varying titles. The titles of all his books have been abbreviated according to the main wording and the date of publication of the book or edition added.

Infant Poor (1823)
S. Wilderspin, *On the Importance of Educating the Infant Children of the Poor* (London 1823).

Infant Poor (Dublin 1823)
S. Wilderspin, *On the Importance of Educating the Infant Children of the Poor* (Dublin 1823).

Infant Poor (1824)
S. Wilderspin, *On the Importance of Educating the Infant Poor* (London, 2nd ed., 1824).

Infant Education (1825)
S. Wilderspin, *Infant Education; or, Remarks on the Importance of Educating the Infant Poor* (London, 3rd ed., 1825).

Infant Education (1829)
S. Wilderspin, *Infant Education; or, Practical Remarks on the Importance of Educating the Infant Poor* (London, 4th ed., 1829).

Infant System (1832)
S. Wilderspin, *The Infant System, for Developing the Physical, Intellectual and Moral Powers of All Children, from One to Seven Years of Age* (London, 5th ed., 1832).

Early Discipline (1832)
S. Wilderspin, *Early Discipline Illustrated; or, the Infant System Progressing and Successful* (London 1832).

Early Discipline (1834)
S. Wilderspin, *Early Discipline Illustrated; or, the Infant System Progressing and Successful* (London, 2nd ed., 1834).

Infant System (1834)
S. Wilderspin, *The Infant System, for Developing the Physical, Intellectual and Moral Powers of All Children, from One to Seven Years of Age* (London, 6th ed., 1834).

National Education (1837)
S. Wilderspin, *A Reply to the Various Speeches, Delivered at a Meeting, held at the Assembly Rooms, Cheltenham, on Friday October 27th, on the Subject of National Education* (Cheltenham 1837).

Infant System (1840)
S. Wilderspin, *The Infant System, for Developing the Intellectual and Moral Powers of All Children, from One to Seven Years of Age* (London, 7th ed., 1840).

Early Discipline (1840)
S. Wilderspin, *Early Discipline Illustrated, or, the Infant System Progressing and Successful* (London, 3rd ed., 1840).

System of Education (1840)
S. Wilderspin, *A System of Education for the Young* (London 1840).

Manual of Instruction (1845)	S. Wilderspin and T.J. Terrington, *A Manual, for the Religious and Moral Instruction of Young Children in the Nursery and Infant School* (London 1845).
Infant System (1852)	S. Wilderspin, *The Infant System, for Developing the Intellectual and Moral Powers of All Children from One to Seven Years of Age* (London, 8th ed., 1852).

* * * * *

B.M.Add.Mss.	British Museum Additional Manuscripts.
B.R.O.	Bristol Record Office.
D.N.B.	Dictionary of National Biography.
E.I.S.S.	Edinburgh Infant School Society.
G.I.S.S.	Glasgow Infant School Society.
G.L.	Guildhall Library.
G.L.C.R.O.	Greater London Council Record Office.
H.R.O.	Hampshire Record Office.
J.R.U.L.M.	John Rylands University Library Manchester.
L.R.O.	Liverpool Record Office.
N.L.S.	National Library of Scotland.
Owen, *Life.*	*The Life of Robert Owen, Written by Himself* (London, 2 vol., 1857-58). Owen's autobiography is in two volumes. Vol. 1 contains the narrative, and *A New View of Society*. Vol. 1A consists entirely of reports, addresses and memorials, including "Report to the County of Lanark".
Parl.Deb.	Parliamentary Debates.
P.P.	Parliamentary Papers.
P.R.O.	Public Record Office.
S.P.O.D.	State Paper Office Dublin.
P.R.O.I.	Public Record Office Ireland.
U.C.L.	University College London.
W.M.I.	Wakefield Mechanics' Institution.

INTRODUCTION

Samuel Wilderspin, the self-styled founder of the Infant School System, became a household name in his own lifetime. Befriended by Dickens, lampooned by Cruikshank, his achievements discussed in Parliament, he was one of the best known educators of the 1830s and 40s. "When we set forward WILDERSPIN, we set back FAGIN", wrote the *Daily News* in an editorial in 1846, assuming that its readers would be as familiar with the one name as with the other. At the end of his career he was praised as "a heaven-born genius" and compared with Pestalozzi himself. After his retirement in 1847, however, a reaction set in and his reputation both as a practical educator and as a theorist declined. Ten years after his death in 1866, Professor Leitch included him, together with Locke, Pestalozzi, Herbert Spencer and David Stow, in his *Practical Educationists,* and sensing the neglect into which Wilderspin's reputation was falling, hoped that the name of "this patriarch of infant teaching" would not be allowed to go down to oblivion. Leitch's statement that the dates of Wilderspin's birth and death were unknown was, however, indicative of the prevailing lack of interest in his life and work.

Wilderspin's place in educational history has been considered secondary to that of Owen, to whom the accolade as the originator and organiser of infant schools (according to the wording of the memorial over his grave) has traditionally been given. Furthermore, Wilderspin's consistent and often bitter opposition to denominational education (especially the Church of England variety) and his liberal views and associations gave the Establishment little cause to keep his name alive. The State also, when it began to administer education in 1839, ignored the possible contribution he might have made in a practical or advisory capacity, though he was only forty-eight at the time; because of this, his ideas and practices were not formally associated with the State system, though they exercised, in various ways, a great influence on the development of infant schools in general.

Wilderspin's reputation as an infant educator has, however, survived; he is usually given a paragraph or two in the standard works on English educational history and sometimes even a chapter in the relatively few accounts of the development of infant schools. Ironically, however, it is the most formal and least creative aspects of his work which are given prominence; he is almost invariably depicted as concerned wholly or mainly with memory work. Distortion of his kind probably reached its peak in T. Raymont's *History of the Education of Young Children.* Seizing on a ten-letter word, Raymont described Wilderspin as a "psittacist of the first order", whose sole conception of education was to force children into parrot-like repetition of long words syllable by syllable in chorus.

Much of this, of course, was and is due to an ignorance of Wilderspin's writings. Raymont, for instance, was under the impression that Wilderspin's first book on infant education represented all that he had to say on the subject, and appeared to have little knowledge of the contents of the subsequent dozen editions and new titles. Admittedly, Wilderspin's works are hard to come by; no institution, not even the British Library, possesses a complete set. Furthermore his correspondence and papers were assumed to have been destroyed by fire in the United States, which seems to have discouraged attempts to construct a detailed account of his career.

Wilderspin's papers were, in fact, in possession of his descendants in the U.S.A. and were utilised by his great-great grandson Francis A. Young, co-author of this book, in his 1949 Harvard doctorate. The present study incorporates a great deal of new material from British sources, particularly the numerous accounts of Wilderspin's lectures and public examinations of infants to be found in Scottish, Irish and English provincial newspapers. This has enabled us to reconstruct much of the chronology of Wilderspin's travels to found infant schools, which occupied the central part of his career, and to give a more detailed account of his other interests and activities. These were largely concerned with the struggle for a non-denominational system of education. Wilderspin played an important role in the Liverpool Corporation's experiment on these lines in the 1830s and also assisted in the development of the Irish National System of education. In later life he interested himself in the adult education movement, taking part in the work of Mechanics' Institutes and the development of their lecture programmes.

Wilderspin's greatest achievement, however, was his work in founding, or helping to found, several hundred infant schools in all parts of the British Isles. Without his labours the infant school might well have remained little more than a curiosity associated with the names of a few seemingly-eccentric early nineteenth century philanthropists. In addition, he was the first English educationist to attempt to propound a theory of child development and an associated teaching method on which a viable system for the education of young children might be founded. His conception of infant teaching, though it had certain negative features, was greatly in advance of his time and anticipated many of the methods associated with modern "progressive" education; he can, in fact, be seen as the fountain head of the tradition which survived to flower in the much-admired British infant schools of today.

Wilderspin, of course, built upon the foundation established by Robert Owen in the famous infant school opened at New Lanark in 1816. But though Wilderspin adopted several Owenite ideas and practices, he brought to infant education many insights and concepts derived from rather different sources. As a member of the Church of the New Jerusalem, founded on the theological writings of Emanuel Swedenborg, he was familiar with many of the Swedish mystic's views on infancy and education. Several of the first group of infant school teachers were, in fact, Swedenborgians, and the exploration of their influence opens up a hitherto-neglected area in the development of early nineteenth century education. In addition to Swedenborgianism, Wilderspin was interested in the ideas of the Swiss educational reformer Pestalozzi and in the theories of the Scottish phrenologists. From this diverse intellectual heritage

Wilderspin, an untiring innovator and experimenter, developed a pedagogical system which he felt was peculiarly his own.

Like many syncretists, however, he failed to unite discrete and sometimes refractory elements into a satisfactory whole. He was unable to make a synthesis between the empiricism of Locke, with the emphasis on "practice" which he felt it entailed, and the esoteric continental theories to which he was irresistibly attracted. Consequently he was unable to develop a self-consistent theory of infant education which would have placed him in the front rank of British educational reformers. In addition, in his practical work as an educational missionary and organiser of schools and institutions he sometimes allowed his combative nature to gain the upper hand. Ideally suited to overcoming opposition and to hard work in the face of adversity, he found it difficult to exercise tact and diplomacy in dealing with those who did not share his views or his zeal for reform; consequently, in the latter part of his career, he found himself embroiled in a series of controversies and disputes, with both former associates and those he regarded as his enemies, which seriously lessened his effectiveness and finally helped to put an end to his active work as an educator.

Nothing, however, could take from Wilderspin the honour of having founded, by his own industry and initiative, a network of several hundred infant schools which were, at their best, the most advanced and sophisticated educational institutions in England. Despite his shortcomings, he remains one of the most interesting and controversial figures among the radical-liberal educationists of the early nineteenth century. His model of the infant school also spread to the continent of Europe and to the United States of America, where it exercised an influence on the development of early childhood education. This book, the first on Wilderspin to be published, is primarily a biography; as far as the subject's life and public career is concerned, it is as complete as seven years of research can make it. Detailed local investigation, of course, may modify or enrich some points, but failing the discovery of a large cache of new material will probably not change the basic story. The infant school movement outside Wilderspin's orbit has, however, been treated in somewhat less detail and mainly from the point of view of light it can throw on Wilderspin's own achievements. We hope that this study will not only restore Wilderspin to his rightful place as a pioneer of infant education but also add an historical dimension to the study of early childhood and the development of an education most appropriate to those years.

CHAPTER 1

EARLY INFLUENCES: NATURE AND THE NEW CHURCH

Samuel Wilderspin was born on 23 March 1791 in Hornsey, near London, the son of Alexander and Ann Wilderspin.[1] His mother dedicated him, her only child to live, to some special work for humanity.[2] He was baptised on 10 April 1791 in the Swedenborgian Chapel in Great East Cheap, London. The beautiful cap he wore at the christening was made by his mother, who, according to family tradition, also made his other clothes, except for his shoes, which were made by his father.[3]

Although baptised in London, Wilderspin spent his infancy in idyllic surroundings in Hornsey along the banks of the New River, its channel now straightened by the hand of man, but then a meandering stream which came down from Hertfordshire to provide London with its principal water supply. On approaching Hornsey the river swung in a wide arc, enclosing the village on three sides with a border of trees and grassy banks which added much to its rural charm. After skirting the old parish church with its ivy-covered tower (the only part of the building still standing today) the river turned southward again, passing east of Hornsey Wood before making its final run to Islington and the reservoirs of Clerkenwell.[4]

This wild and beautiful stretch of the river became Wilderspin's playground. He recalls that as an only child he was thrown much upon his own resources and thus had to find his principal pleasures in exploring his environment. "I beheld a beautiful world around me, he relates, "full of everything to admire and win attention".[5] The countryside was indeed a cornucopia of plants and animals, fruits and flowers, rocks and minerals. In addition, his father and mother took a constant and affectionate interest in his welfare and instruction, interpreting his growing world of experience and inspiring, by reference to the book of nature, his first religious thoughts. His mother, he said, taught him that all things came from God, who made heaven and earth as proof of his wonderful existence. Wilderspin disclaimed having a well-formed notion of God at so early an age, but said that he was led through

---

[1]P.R.O. R.G.4/4239, Register of Baptisms, Friar's Street New Jersualem Church, 1787-1825, which includes the baptismal records of the Great East Cheap Society of Swedenborgians. *D.N.B.* has '1792?' as the date of his birth and this has been followed in most accounts of his life. There is no documentary evidence for Hornsey as the place of Wilderspin's birth other than his own statements, e.g., in the information supplied to the 1851 Census return (P.R.O. H.O.107/2328, Census 1851, Alverthorpe with Thornes parish).

[2]Alice Paterson, Samuel Wilderspin and the Infant System, thesis for the degree of Doctor of Philosophy, Jena 1906, p. 9 (English translation). Paterson's source was Miss Young, a grand-daughter of Wilderspin.

[3]Private information from L. Franz, a great grand-daughter of Wilderspin.

[4]A. Ford. *Springs, Streams and Spas of London* (New York, n.d.), p. 311; J.H. Lloyd. *History, Topography and Antiquities of Highgate* (Highgate 1888), p. 95; pp. 294-99.

[5]*Infant System* (1852), p. 1.

the visible world to recognise an invisible presence which he could feel within but could not see.[6]

While he was still a young child, Wilderspin's parents allowed him to wander freely in the neighbourhood. On the south side of Hornsey, a footpath led to Hornsey Wood and to a network of other pathways, one of which followed closely the course of the New River, making in less than a mile four crossings of the stream. Describing his juvenile excursions, Wilderspin wrote:

> The world and the wonders in it formed as it were a heaven to me... In the beautiful fields and wild coppices about Hornsey, as yet unencroached upon by suburban extension; and by the side of the then solitary banks of the New River I was always to be found... Small live animals were my constant companions; they taught me that love begets love. I did love and delight in them, and when they died I mourned their loss.[7]

Wilderspin was thus nurtured, like Rousseau's Emile, in the lap of nature, and the care which his parents took in his early instruction and their methods of teaching were enlightened and unorthodox, and may have been influenced by the teachings of the New Church, of which his father was a member.[8] His mother, he said, in addition to playing childish games with him, was his oracle during the first six years of his life, resolving his difficulties and answering his questions.[9] His grandmother and other relatives related "simple tales of the Bible", which, he remembered, filled him with delight.[10] There were no set tasks; instead he learned his first lessons from the world of things, his parents waiting until he asked for information and then perfecting his impressions. Only later was the alphabet mastered and spelling, reading and simple arithmetic begun. "My mind *being thus previously filled with ideas",* he later explained, "the acquirement of words and abstract terms became less irksome and I cannot remember that...it cost me any trouble, much less pain".[11]

Finding learning a delight, the young Wilderspin could not understand why children cried on their way to school. He soon ceased to wonder when he was sent there himself. At his first school, he recalled, he learned nothing, but often had "raps with the cane on the head, across the shoulders, and on the hand...for

---

[6]*Ibid.,* p. 2.

[7]*Ibid.,* pp. 2-3.

[8]An article in the *New-Jerusalem Magazine,* No. II, 1 Feb. 1790. pp. 64-9, entitled "Thoughts on Education", stated that it was the duty of the parents to superintend and instruct children, and that this task should not be given to a tutor. The mother should direct the child in the moral sphere, the father should provide instruction and wisdom. Children were endowed with "rationality" (the power of forming ideas via the senses) and "liberty" (the power of making free choice). Ideas should be clear and self-evident and the parents should not compel children to believe but induce conviction by well-chosen examples. Whether or not the Wilderspins were aware of this particular article, their methods were strikingly similar.

[9]*Infant System* (1852), p. 3; p. 13.

[10]*System of Education* (1840), p. 329.

[11]*Infant System* (1852), p. 3.

not learning what the teacher had *forgotten to teach me"*. The master and mistress soon became "objects of terror"; the "dislike and pain" he experienced at school, in comparison with his previous happy existence, affected him so much that his parents removed him and resumed their own informal teaching, an enlightened act which involved obligations they did not seek to evade. "My father...became my teacher as before", he wrote, "the world being my great book".[12]

Alexander Wilderspin was well fitted for the task. "My father", his son recalled, "always in the evening took great pains to explain things to me; he nurtured but never crammed; he knew when to teach and when to leave alone".[13] The close relationship which existed between Samuel and his father is evidenced by the son's care in preserving a fragment of his father's handwriting in which the elder Wilderspin, writing to friends, thanked them for their "kindness to my dear and only son Samuel, who is worthy of that endearing name from me, and whom I shall always with love and pleasure acknowledge". Coming across this memento in later life, Wilderspin put it in an envelope which he marked "Sacred to the memory of my Father", dating it "Jan'y. 30, 1860". Below he wrote, "This envelope contains the handwriting of my simple-minded, Christian, humble, yet learned father. I do not know how I came by or possessed of it but, now, to me it is above all price".[14]

It is evident from this surviving sample of his handwriting, as well as from his signature on New Church records, that Alexander Wilderspin was a fine penman, much better in fact than his son became, and that he had had some formal schooling. Moreover, he could scarcely have become "a learned man" without a taste for reading and he communicated his love of books to his son. "I was delighted with *Robinson Crusoe"*, Wilderspin recalled, "and this work became my companion, and to which was added the *Pilgrim's Progress.* After these, my great favourite was Buffon's *Natural History"*. "I used to go alone", he added, "taking a volume at a time to read amongst the pleasant country around, but most frequently in the quiet nooks and retreats of Hornsey Wood". His mother, not unlike Emile's tutor, kept an unobtrusive watch on these excursions "and whenever danger was near she generally appeared, but never otherwise, so that I had perfect freedom in these matters".[15]

In these reminiscences, written long after the event, Wilderspin seems to be idealising his childhood and attributing to his parents some of the pedagogical insights he arrived at in later life, but there is no reason to doubt their essential truth. "I have every reason to believe", he concluded, "that the first seven years of

---

[12]*Infant System* (1852), p. 4. Wilderspin does not state what type of school he attended. He makes reference in another work to having attended a dame school (Ms. Revisions, *Early Discipline* (1840), p. 151). It is unlikely, however, that this would have been conducted by a master and mistress.

[13]*Infant System* (1852), p. 3.

[14]Wilderspin Papers, fragment of a letter of Alexander Wilderspin addressed to his "Dear Friends" (n.d.).

[15]*Infant System* (1852), p. 4.

my life laid the basis of all I know that is worth knowing and led to the formation of my character and future career in life".[16] A distaste for the formalities of the traditional classroom and an appreciation of the desirability of freedom and activity on the part of the pupil were undoubtedly the legacies of his early childhood, and when he looked back after half a century he was convinced that the roots of his infant system could be traced to these years.[17]

This idyllic phase of Wilderspin's childhood came abruptly to an end at the age of seven. "Through very peculiar circumstances", he states, "I was removed from the immediate care and superintendence of both parents...and, at an age the most dangerous, was left to grapple nearly alone with the wide world..."[18] Wilderspin's careful wording suggests that it was separation rather than death which was the cause of the break-up of the family, and some evidence survives to support this view. The fragment of Alexander Wilderspin's letter to his friends, which, as we have noted, his son preserved with such care, seems to bear upon the episode. After referring to his "dear and only son", Alexander complains of his wife's temper and the harsh treatment he received at her hands. One grievance was "not suffering me to eat any victuals more than she pleased", a readily-available form of wifely discipline; the other was "by being of a turbulent, dominating spirit and temper, not resting without my entire submission to her will and thereby destroying all happiness in the marriage state" (though this does not seem to have been apparent to the son). He then claimed that he tried his best to mollify his wife, adding "but for the sake of peace (which I am very fond of) I submitted and agreed that she should have one-half (in times past) of my earnings". Another possible cause of marital disharmony was the religious difference between the partners. Ann Wilderspin was, and apparently remained, a member of the Church of England;[19] Alexander was one of the earliest converts to the Church of the New Jerusalem, founded upon the doctrines of Emanuel Swedenborg, the Swedish mystic. In view of Wilderspin's regard for his father and the influence which Swedenborgianism had on his later life and educational theories, it will be appropriate to outline here what is known of Alexander Wilderspin and his involvement with the New Church.

Alexander Wilderspin's forebears were said to have come to England from Holland in the seventeenth century to work on the drainage of the Lincolnshire fens and later to have settled in Cambridgeshire.[20] Efforts to learn more about

[16]*Ibid.,* pp. 4-5.

[17]*Ibid.,* p. 5.

[18]*Ibid.,* p. 3.

[19]In 1850 Wilderspin, conducting a public argument with supporters of the Catholic Church in Wakefield, referred to the Church of England as "the church of my mother, who taught me in infancy some of its truths and who expressed a hope I should abide in them..." (*Wakefield and West Riding Examiner,* 14 Dec. 1850.)

[20]Wilderspin Papers, Ms. entitled "Memoir of Samuel Wilderspin: Founder and Promoter of Infant Schools" (n.d.); *Notes and Queries,* 9th Sers., Vol. I, 1898, p. 332. According to the latter, the Wilderspins were said to be related to the De Witts. The name Wilderspin appears frequently in the parish registers of Cambridge, Earith, Over and Swavesey throughout the eighteenth century.

Alexander's ancestry, birth and early life have yielded little. In the early 1790s, according to a later report, he was employed at Clerkenwell in the printing shop of Robert Hindmarsh, one of the earliest followers of Swedenborg.[21] The Swedish theologian had, of course, settled in London and become a familiar figure there (he was known as "the New Jerusalem gentleman"), dying in modest lodgings in Clerkenwell in 1772, in his eighty-fifth year. Hindmarsh, a master printer and classical scholar, had become interested in Swedenborg's writings (which he read in the original Latin) in 1782, and he subsequently associated with other Swedenborgians to form in 1787, after several reorganisations, The Society for Promoting the Heavenly Doctrines of the New Jerusalem Church. After several meetings at the houses of members and at temporary quarters in New Court, Middle Temple, the Society rented a chapel in Great East Cheap and it opened for public worship on 27 January 1788.[22]

The Great East Cheap Society of the New Church was one of the many "competing sects and seceding chapels" — chiefly the Methodists and Unitarians, but also such relatively obscure denominations as the Sandemanians and Muggletons — which flourished during the turbulent years of the late eighteenth and early nineteenth centuries, when the old social and religious certainties were beginning to crumble under the impact of the vast increase of population, the growth of large cities, the emergence of new social relationships inherent in the spread of the factory system, and the fears and inspirations bred by war and revolution abroad. Swedenborgians believed that the Church of the New Jerusalem was the successor to the existing Christian Church. They differed from members of other millenarian sects of the period, who looked forward to some future transformation of existing society, in their belief not only that the millenium would be a spiritual one but also that it was already arising. They shared, however, in the general optimistic and forward-looking spirit of millenarianism, as also in a certain separation from the imperatives of existing society which these beliefs involved.[23]

The New Church proved especially attractive to the artisan class, of which Alexander Wilderspin may be taken as a fairly typical member, providing those of adventurous mind with "intellectual and mystical millenial beliefs" based upon a radical and challenging re-interpretation of the Scriptures.[24] When Robert Southey visited a Swedenborgian Chapel some twenty years after the New Church was founded, he noted that the worshippers were "chiefly respectable tradesmen".[25] Although Southey's observation is confirmed by the

[21] *Intellectual Repository*, Vol. VIII, Nov. 1847, p. 438.

[22] C.T. Odhner, *Robert Hindmarsh: A Biography* (Philadelphia 1895), *passim;* R. Hindmarsh, *Rise and Progress of the New Jerusalem Church* (London 1861), p. 56; p. 60.

[23] Cf. E.P. Thompson, *The Making of the English Working Class* (London 1963), p. 51; C. Garrett, *Respectable Folly: Millenarians and the French Revolution in France and England* (Baltimore 1975), p. 155 ff.

[24] Thompson, *English Working Class,* pp. 48-9.

[25] R. Southey, *Letters from England* (London, 3 vol., 1807), III, p. 144.

baptismal records of the New Church after it was well established, Swedenborg's vision of a new heaven and earth was also taken up by a group of cosmopolitan intellectuals and artists, including Benedict Chastanier, a French emigré surgeon, Henry Servanté, a political refugee from France, Francis Barthelemon, composer and friend of Haydn, and the Swedes Augustus Nordenskjold and Charles Berns Wadstrom, the latter an anti-slavery agitator and projector of colonial projects in Africa. William Blake and the sculptor Flaxman were also attracted to the New Church in its early days.[26]

Alexander Wilderspin's interest in Swedenborgianism pre-dated his formal entry into the New Church. He is credited with introducing Manoah Sibly, who later became a New Church minister, to members of the sect "in the latter end of the year 1787", at a time when they were meeting on Sunday evenings in each other's houses.[27] Sibly, however, was the first to join the Great East Cheap Society, being admitted on 3 March 1788, the day that Wilderspin was proposed as a member.[28] Wilderspin was formally admitted to the Society on 7 April[29] and was baptised into the church on 8 June.[30]

During his recorded membership of the Society (which lasted until at least May 1789)[31] Alexander Wilderspin was more than ordinarily active; he attended about half the meetings, was chosen by lot as one of 12 to help ordain two new ministers,[32] was present at the funeral of J. Rayner, a deceased member[33] and on 7 December 1788 signed a letter to the Rev. John Clowes attempting to justify the separatism of the congregation.[34] This activity came to an end, however, sometime in the latter half of 1789, when he was one of the six members of the Society from whom the Church felt the necessity of "withdrawing herself"; Hindmarsh, Servanté, Wadstrom, Nordenskjold and George Robinson (who had seconded Wilderspin's admission to the Society) were the others.[35] The

---

[26]Blake was not baptised into the New Church; the evidence for his interest in Swedenborgianism rests upon his attendance at a general conference in 1789 and his signature to a circular emanating therefrom approving the establishment of the New Church, his reading and critical annotation of several of Swedenborg's works and certain Swedenborgian influences in his poetry. Cf. D.V. Erdman, "Blake's Early Swedenborgianism, a Twentieth Century Legend", *Comparative Literature,* Vol. V, No. 3, 1953, pp. 247-57.

[27]*New Jerusalem Magazine,* Vol. 1, No. 1, Jan. 1826, p. 2.

[28]Minute Book of the Society for Promoting the Heavenly Doctrines of the New Jerusalem Church. East Cheap, London, 7 May 1787 to 7 Nov. 1791; Minutes, 3 Mar. 1788.

[29]Minutes, 7 Apr. 1788.

[30]P.R.O. R.G.4/4239, Register of Baptisms, Friar's Street New Jerusalem Church, 1787-1825.

[31]Minutes, 4 May 1789, record his last attendance, but there is a year's gap in the minutes after this date.

[32]Minutes, 1 June 1788.

[33]Minutes, 23 July 1788.

[34]*Reasons for Separating From the Old Church, in Answer to a Letter Received From Certain Persons in Manchester, who Profess to Believe in the Heavenly Doctrines of the New Jerusalem Church.* By the members of the New Jerusalem Church who Assemble in Great East Cheap, London (London 1788). Clowes, a Manchester clergyman, argued for the purification of the Established Church from within rather than the setting up of a separate organization.

[35]Odhner, *Robert Hindmarsh,* p. 26, citing "An Address" by Manoah Sibly to the Friar's Street Society in 1839.

society had been rent by disputes over Swedenborg's liberal, though carefully circumscribed, doctrine of concubinage; the six had apparently supported the interpretation that a single man could take a mistress if he could not marry, and a Swedenborgian husband was permitted a concubine if the wife rejected the New Doctrine.[36] There are few details (the minutes are missing for a year following 4 May 1789)[37] and the dispute may have been a purely academic one. It is not known to what extent the Church's ban was effective or how long it lasted; Robert Hindmarsh certainly resumed activity in 1790,[38] and it may be inferred that Alexander Wilderspin kept up a connection with the Society in view of his son's baptism in 1791 and the latter's own subsequent activity as a Swedenborgian.[39] Question marks must remain, however, against other aspects of Alexander Wilderspin's life. Was his support for the doctrine of concubinage occasioned by his wife's religious beliefs? To what extent, if at all, did it affect their subseqent marital relationship? What was the reason for his move from London to Hornsey? (At the time of his entry into the Church he was living at 2 Old Street Square in the City).[40] One point may, however, be made with confidence: Alexander Wilderspin was revered by his son, and the lessons of early childhood and the Swedenborgian atmosphere in which he grew up were to leave indelible impressions on his outlook and activities.

* * * * *

After the separation from his parents Wilderspin lived in London; he was brought up in the city, he stated in his first book, and later referred to himself as "a true Cockney".[41] His schooling there, he recalled, "was the usual routine such as others had",[42] though in a later book he seems to imply that he studied the classical languages.[43] If he did study Latin and Greek, it had little influence upon his subsequent writing style, for his books were poorly constructed and marred

---

[36]*Ibid.*, pp. 29-31; the doctrine was valid only if the situation were reported to the Church, which alone could sanction action on the matter.

[37]Odhner, *Robert Hindmarsh* (p. 27), states that the pages of the minute book were 'torn out'. It is not possible to confirm this as the volume in possession of the New Church Conference is apparently a copy of the original.

[38]Hindmarsh was present at a meeting of the Great East Cheap Society in May of that year (Minutes, 3 May 1790); cf. also Hindmarsh, *New Jerusalem Church*, p. 112; p. 155.

[39]C. Higham, "Samuel Wilderspin", *New Church Magazine*, Vol. XXXIV, No. 399, Mar. 1915, pp. 109-10, makes this point, which seems reasonable. The elder Wilderspin is also reported as picking up some sheets of Swedenborg's *Conjugial Love* while working as a printer for Hindmarsh, and reading them to some acquaintances, converting at least one family. *Conjugial Love* was published in 1794, which suggests (if the story is true) that he was an active Swedenborgian at this date.

[40]Minutes, 3 Mar. 1788.

[41]*Infant Poor* (1823), p. 112; *Educational Magazine*, Vol. II, Aug. 1835, p. 150.

[42]*Infant System* (1852), p. 5.

[43]*System of Education* (1840), pp. 305-06.

by frequent violations of grammatical and stylistic rules. He was always aware of his educational deficiencies; at the age of fifty he felt constrained to turn down a request to become a tutor to Sir Francis MacKenzie's sons because, as he pointed out, "my own education has been too circumscribed to qualify me for so precious a charge..."[44] He had learned much, however, from the school of life. He had taken part in such boyish pranks as robbing orchards and had become familiar with "the snares and dangers that the children of the poor are liable to fall into".[45] His years in London helped him to develop the qualities of courage, self-reliance and combativeness that were evident in later life.

Though Wilderspin may have lacked parental care during adolescence, he enjoyed many advantages unavailable to the very poorest classes. He was born, his obituary reminds us, "not in poverty...but in a lowly rank";[46] in keeping with this status he was, he wrote later, "destined for business, and served the usual apprenticeship to become qualified for it".[47] By "business" Wilderspin meant a trade, and he presumably commenced his apprenticeship at fourteen, in 1805. Much uncertainty has persisted about the precise nature of Wilderspin's training and employment as a young man; the matter can now be clarified on the basis of his children's baptismal records. That of his eldest daughter, Sarah Anne, in the Parish Register of St. Giles Church, Cripplegate, identifies Wilderspin as "a calico printer" living in Tenter Alley, Moorfields,[48] one of the centres of the London textile trade.[49] The entries for his five other children, who were baptised in the New Jerusalem Chapels in St. George's Fields and Waterloo Road, specify that up to 1819 Wilderspin was "a calenderer".[50] The *New Oxford Dictionary* defines a calenderer as "one whose business it is to calender cloth" and a calender as "a machine in which cloth, paper, etc., is pressed under rollers for the purpose of smoothing or glazing; also for watering or giving a wavy appearance, etc". Wilderspin was thus a skilled tradesman and there is no reason to doubt that he worked in his trade for at least eight years before becoming an infant school teacher in 1820.

Some confusion exists insofar as Wilderspin himself stated that he spent a short period in business "on my own account"[51]; furthermore, a trustworthy biographical source states that he was working as a clerk in a counting house when he left to take up teaching,[52] and he was certainly employed in the City and

[44] Wilderspin Papers, Wilderspin to Sir Francis MacKenzie (n.d.?1839).

[45] *Infant Poor,* (1823), p. 112; *System of Education* (1840), p. 305.

[46] *Wakefield Free Press,* 17 Mar. 1866.

[47] *Infant Education* (1852), p. 5.

[48] Parish Register, St. Giles' Church, Cripplegate.

[49] In 1817 Tenter Alley contained three firms specialising as calenderers. *(Johnstone's London Commercial Guide, and Street Dictionary* (London 1817), col. 481).

[50] P.R.O. R.G. 4/4501, Register of Baptisms, New Jerusalem Chapel, St. George's Fields, 1816-34.

[51] *Infant Education* (1852), pp. 5-6

[52] W. and R. Chambers (Eds.), *Infant Education* (Edinburgh 1836), p. 3.

living in City Road at this time.[53] It is possible that he had graduated to become a clerk in a calico firm;[54] nevertheless, up to December 1819 he was content to record his occupation as a calenderer in the New Church records.[55]

Wilderspin had married in 1811, in his twentieth year, probably just after finishing his apprenticeship. His wife, Sarah Anne, was not a Swedenborgian but a Wesleyan Methodist, and was independent enough to inform her fiancé that she was unlikely to change her religion, and that if he would not consent to her continuing in it the marriage would not take place. The young couple solved the problem by agreeing to continue attending their respective churches after marriage.[56] Sarah Anne Wilderspin had been born in Lambeth in 1787, and was thus some four years older than her husband. Her education was probably superior to others of her sex and position in life, as it was said that "her parents gave her the best education within their power",[57] an opportunity not often provided for girls. After her marriage she was gradually reconciled to her husband's faith, her membership in the New Church dating from 10 September 1815, when she was baptised by the Rev. Thomas F. Churchill, in the chapel in Lisle Street, Leicester Square.[58] Her conversion was described by the writer of her obituary in somewhat extravagant terms; it gives, however, an inkling of the appeal which the New Church doctrine might have:

> As she was naturally fond of reading, she soon began to examine some of the doctrines of the New Church, and upon reading them was forcibly struck with the clear and bright views of eternity which they exhibited to her mind; from that time she became a cordial receiver of the doctrines of the New Church, and frequently returned thanks to Almighty God for having permitted her to see those glorious truths which so clearly unfold to the mind the bright realities of another and better world.[59]

The obituary notice, which was obviously based on first-hand information, states that Samuel Wilderspin was a member of the New Jerusalem Church at the time of his marriage in 1811 and implies that Swedenborgian literature was readily available in the home. There is no reason to doubt Wilderspin's active connection with the Church of his father early in life but it is not known for certain which particular chapel he attended, though it is probable that he was connected with the Lisle Street congregation to which his wife belonged. A

[53] He spoke of his employment in the City in a speech at a later date *(New Moral World,* Vol. I, 3rd Sers., No. 19, 17 Nov. 1840, p. 291). His last address before moving to Spitalfields was at City Road, Middlesex, (P.R.O. R.G.4/4501, Register of Baptisms, New Jerusalem Chapel, St. George's Fields, 1816-34).

[54] *D.N.B.* states that "he began life as a clerk in a merchant's office", but this is clearly an error.

[55] His daughter Jane was baptised on 26 December 1819; the entry for the baptism of his next child Emma, on 10 February 1822, describes him as a school master. (P.R.O. R.G.4/4501, Register of Baptisms, New Jerusalem Chapel, St. George's Fields, 1816-34).

[56] *Dawn of Light and Theological Inspector,* No. 1, Jan. 1825, p. 32.

[57] *Dawn of Light, loc. cit.*

[58] P.R.O. R.G.4/4399, Register of Baptisms, New Jerusalem Temple, Cross Street, Hatton Garden, 1797-1837.

[59] *Dawn of Light, loc. cit,* p. 33.

section of this congregation united with a group from Soho; from this body another society was formed in Obelisk Yard, near the Obelisk in St. George's Fields, just south of the Thames at Waterloo.[60] Within a year the first minister had resigned; Thomas Goyder took over as a probationer in March 1816 and was ordained on 20 July 1817.[61]

Wilderspin moved with his family to Obelisk Yard at the end of 1815,[62] and at some unspecified date, but presumably after July 1817, became clerk to the minister Thomas Goyder,[63] a position he retained until his move to Spitalfields in 1820.[64] Wilderspin's duties were "to assist in the celebration of Divine Worship, in the usual manner, and to proclaim all public notices ordered by the Committee".[65] Under the leadership of Goyder, studious and introspective,[66] and Wilderspin, active and extrovert, the chapel prospered; by 1819 the congregation had increased to 80 members, which necessitated a move to larger premises. On 30 May 1819 a new temple, designed to hold several hundred people, was opened in nearby Waterloo Road,[67] and Wilderspin was a subscriber to the fund opened by the committee of management.[68]

He was also active in the educational efforts of the Society. The New Church had always had an interest in education and from the turn of the century had fostered Sunday Schools in both London and the North.[69] In 1816 the congregation at St. George's Fields had opened a small Sunday School, which attracted some fifty children.[70] In 1817 Wilderspin was appointed, with two others, to visit parents with a view to improving attendance.[71] Thereafter he

[60]D.G. Goyder, *The Autobiography of a Phrenologist* (London 1857), p. 84; C. Higham, "The First New Church Society in South London", *New Church Magazine*, Vol. XIX, No. 224, Aug. 1900, pp. 337-38. Thomas Goyder, later minister at St. George's Fields, was a member of the Lisle Street church and thirty years later wrote to Wilderspin reminding him of their friendship there (Wilderspin Papers, T.G. Goyder to Wilderspin, 31 Jan. 1842).

[61]Higham, "The First New Church Society…", *loc. cit.*

[62]P.R.O. R.G.4/4501, Register of Baptisms, New Jerusalem Chapel, St. George's Fields, 1816-34. Wilderspin's second daughter was born at Obelisk Yard on 4 Nov. 1815.

[63]Goyder, *Autobiography*, p. 109.

[64]According to T. Bilby and R.B. Ridgway, Wilderspin was acting as clerk at the time of his engagement at Spitalfields Infant School. *(Educational Magazine*, Vol. II, Sept. 1835, p. 225.)

[65]Rules and Signatures of Members of the New Jerusalem Church, Waterloo Road, (1823).

[66]Cf. "Sketch of the Life of the Rev. Thomas Goyder", in D.G. Goyder (Ed.), *Miscellaneous Sermons of the Late Rev. Thomas Goyder* (London 1850), xxxii-xxxiv; Goyder's obituary in *Intellectual Repository*, Vol. I, No. 120, Dec. 1849, pp. 474-76.

[67]*New Church Magazine, loc. cit.*, pp. 339-40.

[68]Report of the Trustees and Committee Appointed to Manage the Affairs of the New Jerusalem Temple. Waterloo Road, Surrey (London 1821). p. 2. Wilderspin's subscription of £1 was made after his removal to Spitalfields.

[69]Hindmarsh, *New Jerusalem Church*, p. 107; p. 200; p. 216; p. 290.

[70]New Church Sunday School. Minute Book 1816. Minutes, 20 Aug. 1816; 17 Mar. 1817; Minutes of the Eleventh General Conference of the Ministers, Leaders and Delegates of the New Church (London 1818), p. 28.

[71]Sunday School Minutes, 10 Nov. 1817.

became a member of the school's committee, serving on and off till 1822.[72] Jane Peacock, who became Wilderspin's second wife a decade later, was one of the Sunday School teachers.[73]

On 17 September 1821, feeling that one day in seven was insufficient to counteract "the effect produced by moving in society with those whose principles and opinions are different and in many cases opposite", the members formed another committee, of which Wilderspin was a member, for the purpose of founding a permanent day school.[74] With the support of other London congregations this was accomplished, and the school opened in the premises of the former Sunday School in 1822.[75] Wilderspin was a member of the day school committee in 1822 and 1823,[76] and subscribed to its funds till 1827.[77] Wilderspin moved his residence to City Road, north of the river, some time in 1819[78] and to Spitalfields in the summer of 1820. It was indicative of his attachment to the New Church and its doctrines that he continued his activities in the religious and educational work of the Swedenborgians for over three years after his appointment to Quaker Street. In fact, his signature appears on the membership list of the Waterloo Road congregation on 23 March 1823.[79] It would appear that only when he began his travels to found infant schools did he relinquish his activities in the New Church.

Until he was nearly thirty, Wilderspin lived the life of a skilled London artisan, though he devoted his spare time to New Church activities rather than to radical politics as did many of his class in the turbulent post-war years after 1815. Only the fact that he "went into business on his own account", as he phrased it, pointed to any ambitions or abilities beyond those of others in his station in life. Of his future role as an educator there was, however, one significant indication beyond that of his involvement in the running of the New Church schools. In 1807, at the age of sixteen, he had begun to teach in a Sunday School;[80] at that period these schools were multiplying rapidly, and attracting as teachers the more intelligent members of the labouring population.

[72]Sunday School Minutes, 11 Dec. 1817; 4 July 1821; 28 Sept. 1821; 9 June 1822. The Sunday School moved to larger premises at the rear of the Waterloo Road Chapel in 1820 (Goyder, *Autobiography*, p. 108).

[73]Sunday School Minutes, 20 Aug. 1816.

[74]Sunday School Minutes, 17 Sept. 1821; *Plan for the Formation of a School, for the Education of Children in the Principles of the New Jerusalem Church* (London 1822), pp. 3-4; p. 8.

[75]C. Higham, "The First New Church Day School", *New Church Magazine*, Vol. XIX, No. 225, Sept. 1900, p. 286.

[76]Sunday School Minutes, 7 Aug. 1822; July 1823; First Annual Report of the Committee of the New Jerusalem Church Free School (London 1823), p. 3.

[77]The Committee of the new Jerusalem Church Free School in Account with Jervoise Bugby, Treasurer of the Said School (Ms.), *passim*. Wilderspin's wife (till 1825) and his eldest daughter were also subscribers.

[78]Rules and Signatures of Members of the New Jerusalem Church, Waterloo Road (1823).

[79]P.R.O. R.G. 4/4501, Register of Baptisms, New Jerusalem Chapel, St. George's Fields, 1816-34, His daughter Jane was born there on 14 November 1819.

[80]"I began the business of tuition at the age of 16", he stated in a speech many years later (*North Cheshire Reformer*, 20 Sept. 1839); "I had a fancy for teaching children when a mere child myself. Sunday Schools had, at that time, come into vogue", he recalled on another occasion *(New Moral World, loc. cit.)*.

"I being then a junior", he recalled, "it fell to my lot to have a class that knew little or nothing".[81] His duties were merely to teach the alphabet,[82] but he soon found that the children in his class required different treatment from those more advanced. "Thus I was forced", he said, "to simplify my mode of teaching to suit their state of apprehension, and now and then even to amuse them". This succeeded so well that in the end his class became the most popular in the school; the experience strengthened his growing conviction that very young children needed special methods of tuition.[83]

Wilderspin's views on education were thus already somewhat advanced when he made the acquaintance, quite by chance, of the very first infant school teacher in the British Isles — James Buchanan, formerly of Robert Owen's New Lanark Infant School. Buchanan, a former weaver, had opened the school in January 1816 and taught there until Owen had been persuaded by Henry Brougham and his associates to allow him to go to London to take charge of a second infant school, inspired by the Owenite model, which they had organised at Brewer's Green, Westminister.[84]

The date of Buchanan's arrival in London is not known, but it must have been shortly before the school opened in February 1819. The date and place of Wilderspin's meeting with Buchanan is likewise obscure; on later occasions Wilderspin gave two different locations for the encounter — at the house of a friend and accidentally in the street.[85] What is certain is that sometime during 1819 Buchanan was in contact with the Swedenborgian congregation at either St. George's Fields or, more likely, in the Waterloo Road chapel after its opening in May, for on 13 February 1820 he was baptised into the New Jerusalem Church at Waterloo Road by Thomas Goyder,[86] and became active in its affairs.[87]

As members of the same congregation Wilderspin and Buchanan had ample opportunities to meet and, under the inspiration of Buchanan, Wilderspin became intensely interested in the subject of infant education.[88] At the same time he missed no opportunity of observing young children "in the streets, in the dwellings of their parents, and in all the dame schools to which I could gain access".[89] Despite the fact that he was then living in City Road, several miles

[81] *Infant Education* (1852), p. 6.

[82] *New Moral World, loc. cit.*

[83] *Infant Education* (1852), p. 6.

[84] Cf. Chapter 3.

[85] *Early Discipline* (1832), p. 2: *New Moral World, loc. cit.* The former is the more likely; according to Bilby and Ridgway, Wilderspin was first introduced to Buchanan by Thomas Goyder (*Education Magazine*, Vol. II, Sept. 1835. p. 225).

[86] P.R.O. R.G. 4/4501, Register of Baptisms, New Jerusalem Chapel, St George's Fields, 1816-34.

[87] Buchanan became a member of the committee of management of the Temple in 1821 (Report of the Trustees. p. 8). He also taught in the Sunday School and served on its committee (Sunday School Minutes, 7 July 1820; 7 and 31 Aug. 1820; 27 May 1821).

[88] *Educational Magazine*, Vol. II. Aug. 1835. p. 148.

[89] *Early Discipline* (1832). p. 2.

north-east of Brewer's Green, he also frequently visited Westminister Infant School,[90] presumably in the spring and summer of 1820, and, according to David Goyder, was given instruction by Buchanan in all his methods.[91] It was at this time that Joseph Wilson, a Spitalfields silk merchant and a member of the committee of the school, was looking for a teacher for a similar institution he was about to open in his home parish. He asked Buchanan to recommend a suitable person and, according to Buchanan's son, he named Wilderspin "as one who seemed suited, and who, on visiting the school had expressed a desire to engage in such a work".[92]

"One day a gentleman called on me in the city where I was employed…and asked me if I thought I could undertake such a school as that at Brewer's Green", wrote Wilderspin, recalling the first step on the road to his subsequent career. He hurried home at dinner time to tell his wife the news that they were about to take charge of two hundred children. "It spoilt her dinner completely", he continued, "she always thought I had some strange visionary notions; and she said she had trouble enough with one!"[93] Despite his wife's misgivings, Wilderspin accepted the offer, struck by the coincidence of the request with his own wishes and feelings. He had a desire to teach, and some experience in a Sunday school; now an opportunity had occurred for him to do something practical and worthwhile for young children under six years of age who, too young to attend British or National schools, were forced to attend unsatisfactory dame schools or, more likely, to be left to run wild in the streets.[94] Above all, as we have seen, he had a strong though unformulated feeling that very young children needed a special kind of education. These considerations apart, the post offered the opportunity of a new and exciting career; New Lanark Infant School was at the height of its world fame, and the second school at Westminister was under the sponsorship of eminent parliamentarians and public men. In addition, there was an attractive salary and a rent-free house provided.[95] It was with these thoughts in mind that Wilderspin, together with his wife and family, moved to Quaker Street, Spitalfields, in the summer of 1820 to begin a new life.

---

[90] *New Moral World, loc. cit.*

[91] *Goyder, Autobiography*, p. 109.

[92] U.C.L. Brougham Mss., 26554, Buchanan to Brougham, 2 May 1851.

[93] *New Moral World, loc. cit.,* Wilderspin is sacrificing truth for the sake of a good anecdote; he had at this time at least 3 children living.

[94] *Early Discipline* (1832), pp. 2-3.

[95] Cf. Chapter 2.

CHAPTER 2

SPITALFIELDS INFANT SCHOOL

Quaker Street Infant School, Spitalfields, opened on 23 July 1820,[1] but according to Wilderspin's account it was not until 7 August that he and his wife were asked "to take the management of the concern".[2] It was later asserted by critics of Wilderspin that he had served the first fortnight as assistant to a female teacher.[3] He denied this, and it is possible that he had been approached by Wilson to succeed a previous teacher after the school had opened.

Whatever the circumstances of the first two weeks, by 7 August nearly all the original pupils had left the school, or been taken away by their parents, and the Wilderspins found themselves faced with a new batch of children 165 strong, all under seven years of age.[4] Wilderspin optimistically had covered the walls of the schoolroom with gaily-coloured alphabet cards, hoping that he could begin teaching reading right away.[5] But when the mothers left, the children huddled together, "not knowing what to make of it", as Wilderspin put it. One child, trying to open the door in order to escape, and failing, began to cry "Mammy"; in a few seconds the rest of the children began such a piercing and uncontrollable wailing that Mrs. Wilderspin exclaimed "Oh, my head — I can stand this no longer", and left the room. Wilderspin himself stayed behind, but in the end, exhausted by effort, anxiety and noise he was forced to follow suit leaving his unfortunate pupils "in one dense mass, crying, yelling and kicking against the door". Feeling that it was a presumptuous folly for any two people to believe they could control such a large number of infants, Wilderspin was tempted to dismiss them at once, but desisted solely because the mothers had begged him to keep the children until twelve o'clock, as the children would be unable to find their own way home.

The children were alarming the whole neighbourhood with their cries. In despair Wilderspin seized a cap of his wife's adorned with coloured ribbons, placed it on top of a clothes prop lying in the yard, and returned to flourish it in front of the children. This stopped their wailing and made the children laugh, but not for long. But Wilderspin now no longer despaired of being able to influence the children's behaviour and began to play games. "Now we will all play at 'Duck'", he cried, "and I will be the great duck". The children started crying "quack, quack", and when this had exhausted itself Wilderspin started a game of "hens and chickens", crying "cup-biddy, cup-biddy", and leading the children

[1] *Infant Poor* (1823), p. 7.

[2] *Ibid.,* p. 8.

[3] The suggestion was made by Bilby and Ridgway. (*Educational Magazine,* Vol. II, July 1835, p. 57; Aug. 1835, pp. 149-50).

[4] *New Moral World,* Vol. I, 3rd Sers., No. 19, 7 Nov. 1840, p. 291; *Early Discipline* (1832), p. 3.

[5] *New Moral World, loc. cit.*

around the room. To his relief he found it "succeeded to a miracle" and the morning was over before be realised it.[6]

The incident became a legend;[7] but the mothers of the children were not impressed. "Well Tommy, what book have you been reading in?" one asked. "We have not been reading in a book mother, but playing at 'ducks', and we have had such fun", was the reply. "I sent you here to read", exclaimed the astonished mother, "not to play at ducks". A group of mothers got together and waited on Wilderspin. "My boy says, Sir, he has been playing at 'duck' here", said the spokeswoman, "but I sent him to learn his book, and not to play at such nonsense". In vain did Wilderspin explain that he thought it necessary, since the children had been left with strangers in strange surroundings, to put them at their ease, to gain their confidence and to "make them happy", and this, he added, would probably take a week, not a morning. Many of the mothers thereupon removed their children from the school, exclaiming "We can send them to Mrs. So-and-So, where for 4d a week they will learn something". The attendance was halved and then went down to 50, and Wilderspin was publicly derided, being pelted with filth in the street and mocked with cries of "There goes the Baby Professor".[8]

It was a discouraging beginning, and the Wilderspins found the educational attainments of the children who remained equally depressing. When they began to organise the children into groups under monitors for teaching the alphabet, they found that only six children knew it.[9] But this merely reflected the prevailing destitution, intellectual and physical, of the whole area. A survey of Quaker Street taken eight years previously had shown that only 3 of the 90 children investigated could read, and that half the adults were illiterate; the child literacy rate for the surrounding area was a mere 5%.[10] A similar investigation of 1816 estimated that seven-eighths of the very poorest stratum of children were entirely uneducated.[11]

The physical condition of the children was also deplorable; some came to school without breakfast, others without shoes, unwashed or only half-dressed. In many cases both parents had to go out to work because the father's earnings were insufficient to support the family. Girl child-minders were sometimes employed, but these were from families poorer still, and often totally

---

[6]These paragraphs are based on Wilderspin's retrospective accounts in *New Moral World, loc. cit.; Albion* (Liverpool), 5 Sept. 1836; *Early Discipline* (1832), pp. 3-4.

[7]As late as 1871 it was referred to as an example of a "curious mode of teaching", though the date was given as 1836 and the place as Islington. (G.C.T. Bartley, *The Schools for the People* (London 1871), p. 110).

[8]*New Moral World, loc. cit.; Albion, loc. cit.;* P.P. 1835 VII, Report from the Select Committee on Education in England and Wales, p. 18.

[9]*Infant Poor* (1923), p. 8.

[10]*Philanthropist,* Vol. II, 1812, p. 189.

[11]P.P. 1816 IV, Report from Select Committee on the Education of the Lower Orders in the Metropolis, Second Report, p. 190.

uneducated, passing on to their charges "deceit, lying, pilfering, and extreme filthiness". Dangerous living conditions in Spitalfields, where garrets were often three or four storeys high, were a cause of frequent accidents to children and "a dead weight" of concern to parents; children ran wild in the streets, were run over by coaches, burnt themselves in fires, and fell out of windows, down garret stairs and into ponds with alarming frequency, in addition to succumbing in large numbers to measles, whooping cough, small pox and various kinds of fever. While at Spitalfields Wilderspin lost two of his own children in one epidemic of measles. Child labour was common; many girls were sent to work at 7 or 8 years of age for a shilling per week, which may have accounted, Wilderspin thought, for the preponderance of boys in almost every London school.[12]

The poverty and illiteracy of Spitalfields, the traditional centre of the silk-weaving industry, lying to the north-east of the City,[13] can be traced to the violent economic and social dislocations of the period. Between 1811 and 1831 the population mushroomed from 59,000 to 90,000, largely by immigration of the poor from the City districts, and periodic crises in the silk trade threw many weavers and others out of work. The per capita taxable income of the Tower Division, of which Spitalfields was a part, was a mere £5, in comparison with £16 for Westminster and £54 for the City of London; two-thirds of the population were manual workers, of whom only 10% could be classed as skilled.[14]

The old Huguenot-based culture of the eighteenth century, fated to die almost as soon as it had bloomed, was hardly more than a memory, and little remained of the intellectual life represented by the many local learned societies — historical, mathematical, entomological and the like — or the delight which the inhabitants took in gardens, fields and the growing of flowers.[15] Middle-class observers regarded it as a "rough" neighbourhood where bulldog-fighting and bull-baiting in the streets were common[16] and where the genteel — as a visitor to Quaker Street School was to discover — might expect to be jeered at, robbed, or hit by flying stones.[17] In September 1819 Fowell Buxton M.P., the Evangelical brewer associated with the local firm of Truman and Hanbury's was, with Spitalfields in mind, moved to declare that "we could not have believed, that, in this enlightened city. . .*such* depravity could have been so long hidden from the public notice".[18]

[12]*Infant Poor* (1823), p. 3; p. 12; p. 33; pp. 92-3; pp. 101-02; p. 108, pp. 123-24; pp. 128-29.

[13]Spitalfields was the name given to the parishes of Christ Church Spitalfields and St. Matthew Bethnal Green, the "hamlet" of Mile End New Town and the "liberties" of Norton Folgate and the Old Artillery Ground (P.P. 1816 IV, Education, p. 208; P.P. 1817 VII, Committee on the State of the Police in the Metropolis, p. 109).

[14]P. McCann, "Popular Education, Socialization and Social Control: Spitalfields 1812-1824", in P. McCann (Ed.), *Popular Education and Socialization in the Nineteenth Century* (London 1977), pp. 1-49, *passim.*

[15]P.P. 1840 XXIII, Hand-Loom Weavers: Reports from Assistant Hand-Loom. Weavers' Commissioners, Pt. II. J. Mitchell, Spitalfields, pp. 215-17.

[16]*Ibid.,* p. 246; p. 250.

[17]F. Hill, *National Education: Its Present State and Prospects* (London 2 vol., 1836), I, pp. 194-95. Hill was describing conditions in the early 1820s.

[18]*British Statesman,* 16 Sept. 1819.

When Wilderspin arrived in the district, the people of Spitalfields were being subjected to a process of social control virtually without parallel in the rest of the country. The small local bourgeoisie, no more than 6% of the total population, with the memory of the Spitalfields Outrages of the 1760s and 1770s still within living memory, and alarmed at the possibility of a spark from the radical politicial activity of the working classes in the post-1815 period igniting a social conflagration in Spitalfields, called in the aid of sympathetic bankers, financiers and merchants from the City. Largely Quaker and Evangelical in religion, they organised a vast programme of relief and moral exhortation, which included the provision of money, food and clothing, the sale of cheap soup, the distribution of Bibles and tracts, and a comprehensive series of house visits; in addition they inspired a programme of school building which gave Spitalfields seven new schools in the dozen years between 1812 and 1824.[19]

In one sense, Quaker Street Infant School was part of this process of winning the hearts and minds of the citizens of Spitalfields for a policy of social stability, sobriety, and subordination; Joseph Wilson, the patron of the institution, was a member of a family of Evangelical silk manufacturers long established in Spitalfields,[20] and had taken a prominent part in the foundation of Spitalfields National School, opened in Quaker Street in May 1819.[21] On the other hand the infant schools could not be classified with the other schools of the district. Wilson was a member of the Westminster Infant School Committee and thus familiar with an institution based on Robert Owen's plan. In addition he was, at this period, one of the more liberal-minded Evangelicals, willing, for instance, to overlook Wilderspin's Swedenborgian beliefs in the interest of good teaching.[22] Born in Milk Street, Cheapside, Wilson was a prominent member of the London Weavers' Company.[23] He used his wealth in the service of many Evangelical causes, subscribing to 22 Evangelical societies and holding office in several,[24] and was perhaps best known as the founder, in 1831, of the Lord's Day

---

[19]McCann, "Popular Education, Socialization and Social Control", *loc. cit.,* for a detailed analysis of the movement.

[20]Joseph Wilson was the son of William Wilson of Cheapside, brother of William Wilson, Vicar of Walthamstow (who later founded an important infant school) cousin of Daniel Wilson, later Bishop of Calcutta, and cousin of Stephen Wilson, silk manufacturer, who led the campaign against the Spitalfields Acts, which regulated wages in the silk trade.

[21]*British Statesman,* 7 July 1819; J.H. Scott, *A Short History of Spitalfields* (London 1894), p. 31. Scott incorrectly gives the date as 1820.

[22]*Infant Poor* (1823), p. 178. The *Christian Observer,* the Evangelical organ, was strongly opposed to the New Church.

[23]Wilson was apprenticed as a silk weaver in 1799, became a freeman of the Company in 1807, renter bailiff in 1818, and upper bailiff in 1820 (G.L. MS. 4655/19, London Weavers' Company. Court Minute Books 1786-1824, *passim*).

[24]F.K. Brown, *Fathers of the Victorians* (Cambridge 1961), p. 355.

Observance Society, whose secretary he remained until his death in 1855.[25]

Quaker Street is a narrow, slightly crooked thoroughfare, today lined with factories and blocks of flats, but in Wilderspin's time containing numerous small houses, many occupied by weavers.[26] Surprisingly little is known about the infant school, despite the fame Wilderspin was to bring to it. It was situated on the opposite side of the street to the National School[27] and had been converted from an existing building on the site.[28] Apparently it had a house or dwelling attached[29] and an enclosed playground paved with brick containing vines, trees and a border of flowers planted by Wilderspin himself; in the centre were flower pots containing "geraniums, auriculas and other choice plants".[30] Wilderspin's eldest daughter Sarah Anne, in later life, recalled that when the day's work was done and her sisters in bed, she would steal out "into the little playground behind the school to watch the few flowers...or as the twilight deepened into night to contemplate the stars whose light struggled through the murky atmosphere".[31]

Wilderspin estimated that the whole institution cost Wilson some £120 per year to run; this included rent, the teachers' salaries of some £80 per annum, coal and incidental expenses. During the first five years there were no fees; later 1d. per week was charged, but the total income from this source never amounted to more than £40 per annum.[32] Apparently there were others besides Wilson who contributed to the funds. Wilderspin spoke of "gentlemen who patronised the school",[33] and in later life received a communication from a lady who described her father, John Hinton of Wheler Street, with whom Wilderspin and the Rev. Wheldale had many conversations, as "I believe, one of the subscribers".[34]

The patrons of the school, recognizing the peculiar difficulties of the situation, had agreed to allow six months to elapse before visiting Quaker Street. But within three months, according to Wilderspin, "they found ample matter of astonishment";[35] carriages began to appear at the door and the conversation of eminent men, Sarah Anne remembered, began to form part of her education.[36]

[25]Society for Promoting the Due Observance of the Lord's Day. *Quarterly Publication,* No. 50, July 1855, p. 510; No. 53, July 1856, p. 555.

[26]In 1812 an investigation carried out by local philanthropists showed that 19 of the 34 families interviewed in Quaker Street were weavers. *(Philanthropist,* Vol. II, 1812, pp. 186-89).

[27]S. Lewis, *A Topographical Dictionary of England* (London, 2nd ed., 4 vol., 1833), IV: entry 'Spitalfields'.

[28]P.P. 1835 VII, Education, p. 30.

[29]*Early Discipline* (1832), pp. 3-4; *New Moral World, loc. cit.;* Lewis, *Dictionary, loc. cit.*

[30]*Infant Poor* (1823), pp. 35-36, p. 130; *Early Discipline* (1832), p. 26; Lewis, *Dictionary, loc. cit.*

[31]Young Papers, T.U. Young, "Memoir of the Late Mrs. Young" (Ms. I).

[32]*Infant Education* (1825), p. 196.

[33]*Bath and Cheltenham Gazette,* 24 May 1831, reporting a speech by Wilderspin.

[34]Wilderspin Papers, Elizabeth Hinton to Wilderspin, 28 Feb. 1843.

[35]*Bath and Cheltenham Gazette,* 24 May 1831.

[36]Young Papers, T.U. Young, "Memoir of the Late Mrs. Young" (Ms.II).

In the beginning some of those who came to inspect the school "could not see the use of it" Wilderspin admitted; among those who approved was Robert Owen, "the first to perceive its utility, and the first to treat me as a gentleman, and take me into his carriage".[37]

Wilderspin's account of his early teaching days stressed the important effect of the first morning's experience. It convinced him, he asserted, of two things: first, that if he were to succeed, the senses of the children had to be engaged; second, that the secret of teaching was to descend to the level of the pupils and become a child oneself. "Practically to act on this conclusion", he admitted, "was however, a matter of no small difficulty", and the accounts of his subsequent trials and errors bear this out.[38] David Stow, the Scottish infant school pioneer, visited Quaker Street in the first few weeks of its existence, and found Wilderspin in the midst of an attempt to control nearly two hundred children by keeping them within chalk lines on the floor, and drilling them "quite *a la militaire*".[39] It seems likely that Wilderspin's attempt to "become a child" was not a spontaneous process (as it was with Buchanan), but required a conscious effort on his part. The subsequent visits of Owen taught him a great deal, as he made clear in his first book. James Buchanan, according to his grand-daughter, also assisted Wilderspin in his early days, walking from Westminster to Spitalfields in the early morning to help open the school and start Wilderspin on the day's work.[40]

The whole question of the relationship of Owen and Buchanan to the development of Spitalfields Infant School, and also the influence of Swedenborgianism on the ideas and practices of the early English infant schools, will be examined in subsequent chapters. At this point, however, it will be instructive to describe Wilderspin (and his wife) in action at Quaker Street School, using the first three editions of his book *On the Importance of Educating the Infant Children of the Poor* as a guide.

* * * * *

All types of schools at this period essentially consisted of a single large room and Quaker Street was no exception; it was almost certainly rectangular in shape, probably some eighty feet long and twenty feet wide.[41] It had benches around the walls, a stove in the middle, a master's desk at one end, a large inclined gallery at the other, and classrooms leading off the side.[42] At the

[37] *New Moral World, loc. cit.*

[38] *Early Discipline* (1832), p. 4.

[39] D. Stow, *The Training System* (Glasgow 1836), pp. 5-6.

[40] B.I. Buchanan, *Buchanan Family Records* (Cape Town 1923), p. 8.

[41] These are the dimensions recommended by Wilderspin in a "Plan for an Infant School, Playground and Master's House" which formed the frontispiece to *Infant Education* (1825); Quaker Street Infant School, however, may well have been smaller.

[42] *Infant Poor* (1823), p. 10; pp. 16-17; p. 95; *Albion,* 5 Sept. 1836.

appointed hour in the morning a hundred and fifty or more children would crowd in, some dirty, raggedly dressed and without shoes, but most of them washed and combed in accordance with the rules of the school. "The children at first were sent more like sweeps than anything else", admitted Wilderspin, "but afterwards they were sent with clean hands and faces, not very tidy, for the parents had not the money to buy the clothes".[43] The rules, which differed little from those common to traditional charity schools,[44] were given to parents on a large piece of pasteboard for them to hang in their homes; the parents were enjoined to send their children to school washed, with their hair cut and neatly combed and with clothes well mended, to ensure their punctuality and regular attendance, to submit them to the governance of the master and mistress, and to accustom them to family prayer.[45]

Once inside the school, the children were assembled in order and inspected by the Wilderspins and the monitors, and those with dirty hands and faces were sent home to be washed. Then the children knelt down to repeat prayers and to sing hymns. Latecomers were refused admittance, and sent home again for the morning. The school was then divided into sixteen classes of about ten children each, with two monitors in charge; these shared the work of instructing the children individually in the alphabet, using National School reading cards placed in tins around the room. Monitors were used sparingly, but a general monitor walked about to supervise the others and Mrs. Wilderspin was in charge of the whole operation. When every child in the school had "said his lesson", each class in turn went into the classroom, where under Wilderspin's supervision they spelled out in unison up to a hundred words. Apart from being a change of scene, and a "kind of play", this procedure also helped to correct bad pronunciation.[46]

As a change from the routine of alphabet learning, Wilderspin placed letter cards "or raised letters such as are used for shop fronts" on the end of a stick and held them up before the assembled school for the children to recognise and name, occasionally interspersing the picture of an animal or a bird to keep the children on their toes; sometimes he placed printed words on a special slide at the end of the stick. This method he used only at the children's request, believing this stimulated their learning capacity. Another variation was to ask the children to bring to the teacher letter cards or raised letters placed in different parts of the room. After one or other of these lessons the children were allowed to go into the

[43]P.P. 1835 VII, Education, p. 19. Soon after the school opened Wilson had installed a trough in which the children could wash, but the antics of the children, criticism from the parents and the exasperation of the Wilderspins at an unsatisfactory state of affiars caused it to be given up. (*Infant Poor* (1823), pp. 76-9).

[44]Cf. Hackney Libraries Archives Dept. P/J/C/2. Hackney Charity School, Minute Book, Vols. 3 and 4, 1787-1834, entry for 4 May 1789. These rules urged the parents to send the children to school on time "with their hands and face clean washed, their hair combed and their clothes sound", to see they attended school regularly, obeyed the rules and prayed night and morning.

[45]*Infant Poor* (1823), pp. 10-15.

[46]*Infant Poor* (1823), p. 10; pp. 17-20; p. 79.

playground to "divert themselves", because Wilderspin believed that short lessons and frequent changes of scene were best suited to very young children.[47]

The older children, those aged five and above, were given slates on which the whole alphabet was inscribed in copperplate script and were shown how to put their pencil in the engraving and to follow the shape of the letter; they learned the shapes of numerals in a similar way by tracing raised figures fixed on the wall. After diversion in the playground, the children returned for arithmetic, dividing into classes and entering the classroom in turn where they learnt the elementary principles of addition, subtraction and multiplication by the arrangement and rearrangement on a table of inch cubes of wood. Much "patience, attention and trouble" on the part of the teachers were needed, thought Wilderspin, if the children were to gain the necessary insights into numerical processes by this method.[48]

Interspersed with the basic subjects were lessons on natural history; brightly-coloured pictures of birds, beasts, fishes, flowers, insects and so on were displayed, and the children encouraged to ask questions about them which the teacher answered.[49] Nature itself was not neglected, however; the plants and flowers in the playground were also made the subject of the pupils' queries. In addition general knowledge — of public buildings, trades such as weaving, building, shoemaking, etc. — was given by means of illustrations. The inspiration or support for this method came from the life of Dr. Doddridge, the theologian whose mother had taught him, as a child, the history of the Old and New Testaments with the aid of some Dutch tiles in the chimney of the room where they usually sat.[50]

Pictures were also used in religious instruction, which Wilderspin attempted to adapt to the capacities of infants. He rejected Bible reading on the ground that the text was above the comprehension of infants, and the learning of a catechism because it would limit the intake to children of the approving denomination. Instead, he covered the walls of the schoolroom with brightly-coloured engravings of some of the more striking scenes from Biblical history. The children then gathered around each picture in turn, and the questions they asked were utilised as a means of conveying simple Scriptural facts and moral stories.[51] The danger lay in the temptation on the teacher's part to convey too much inert or esoteric knowledge, a danger Wilderspin did not always avoid,[52]

---

[47] *Infant Poor* (1823), pp. 21-4; pp. 25-7.

[48] *Ibid.*, pp. 28-31.

[49] *Ibid.*, pp. 41-2. Wilderspin "searched the print shops in the metropolis" for these pictures, and also made use of drawings supplied by friends (*Infant System* (1852), p. 12).

[50] *Infant Poor* (1823), pp. 41- 2n; pp. 42-3; p. 131.

[51] *Infant Poor* (1823), p. 44; pp. 139-42; P.P. 1835 VII, Education, p. 26.

[52] In the second and third editions of his book he printed sets of questions and answers relating to Biblical incidents; it is not clear whether these were based on Wilderspin's own lessons or whether he included them as guides for the use of teachers.

though he was capable of flashes of inspiration; in a lesson on "Joseph's Dream" he asked the class to relate examples of their own dreams.[53]

Wilderspin was not, however, attached to pictures on principle, preferring where possible the objects of nature themselves.[54] Mostly he used everyday examples that came easily to hand; a piece of coal, for instance, would be picked up and its origin investigated and its use in heating the school or in the production of gas would be outlined; pieces of wood were treated in a similar manner. The processes involved in the production of common, man-made articles such as bricks, knives and forks or children's toys were also investigated, and Mrs. Wilderspin's workbox was searched for off-lengths of thread and pieces of cotton, calico, silk and velvet and the manufacture and use of each discussed. Instruction in elementary geography, with the aid of maps and a painted compass, was also introduced.[55]

Conveying factual information on Biblical history, natural history and everyday things was obviously an important part of the educational process at Spitalfields. Former pupils, returning to see Wilderspin, complained that the National School (on the opposite side of Quaker Street) did not teach them natural history or geography.[56] The children's interest in, and mastery of, those subjects added greatly to the effect which the school had upon the public. A visiting clergyman, the Rev. J.A. Janes, was astonished to find that children of four and five could give him a detailed account of butterflies and beans, and that others were knowledgeable on such diverse subjects as bridge building and scripture history.[57]

Much of the school day, however, was spent in activity. "As an infant school may very properly be called a combination of the school and the nursery", Wilderspin pointed out, "the art of pleasing forms a prominent part in the system". This applied especially to the very youngest children. Short lessons, and a change of scene he believed to be essential; keeping young children at one task for too long blunted their liveliness, made them unfit to learn, and bred distaste for the school. At intervals he would direct the children in arm or leg exercises, or let them play on rope swings in the classroom, while they chanted number tables or rhymes of his own devising[58]. The latter are today of greater sociological than pedagogical interest:

[53]*Infant Poor* (1824), pp. 61-4.

[54]*Infant Poor* (1823), p. 138.

[55]*Early Discipline* (1832), p. 6; p. 8.

[56]P.P. 1835 VII, Education, p. 22.

[57]J.J., "Infant Day Schools", *Sabbath School Magazine for Scotland,* Vol. IV, No. XXI, Sept. 1824, pp. 113-14.

[58]*Infant Poor* (1823), p. 31; pp. 34-5.

Twenty pence are One and Eightpence,
That we can't afford to lose;
Thirty pence are Two-and-sixpence,
That will buy a pair of shoes.
Forty pence are Three and Fourpence,
That sum's paid for certain fees;
Fifty pence are Four and Twopence,
That will buy five pounds of cheese.[59]

The swing, he felt, had several advantages — it allowed children to develop not only courage and dexterity, but also self-discipline while awaiting their turn in an orderly manner.[60]

In fine weather the children danced around the trees in the playground, each class having its own particular tree, singing or chanting the alphabet, arithmetical tables or hymns. "Thus the children are gradually improved and delighted", observed Wilderspin, "for they call it play, and it matters little what they call it, as long as they are edified, exercised, pleased and made happy".[61]

At first Wilderspin and his wife had introduced toys into the playground; a supply of balls, battledores, shuttlecocks, tops, whips, skipping ropes, sticks and wheelbarrows was procured. "This must produce universal happiness" they thought, but

> ...balls frequently bounced over the wall, — the players not being able to throw them with the precision of Spartan children, sometimes struck their comrades, perhaps on the eye, — if we could succeed in quieting the sufferer by a kiss and a sugar plum, the ear was immediately afterwards saluted with the cry of "O my chin, my chin", from some hapless wight having been star-gazing, and another, anxious for as many strokes as possible, mistaking that part for the bottom of his shuttlecock, — while this would be followed by "O my leg' from the untoward movement of a stick or a barrow...and what with the accidents that arose, and the tops without strings, and the strings without tops, and hoops without sticks, and the sticks without hoops, the seizure of the favourite toy by one, and the inability of another to get anything, it was evident that we were wrong...[62]

The toys were withdrawn and replaced by wooden bricks, 4" long, 1½" thick and 2½" wide, with which the children were encouraged to build walls and houses and to construct bridges, using the principle of the arch.[63]

* * * * *

[59] *Ibid.*, p. 37.

[60] *Ibid.*, pp. 36-41. The swings had first been used by James Buchanan at Westminster.

[61] *Infant Poor* (1823), pp. 35-6.

[62] *Infant System* (1834), pp. 99-100.

[63] *Infant Poor* (1824), p. 208; *Infant System* (1834), p. 100.

The curriculum and related activities represented only one side of Wilderspin's efforts at Spitalfields. Equally important were his attempts at what today we would call socialization — the inculcation in the local children of habits and moral values acceptable to society or, more specifically, to that stratum of society to which he belonged, the respectable artisan class with aspirations to upward mobility. Both fascinated and repelled by the children of the urban proletariat, whose activities contrasted so sharply with those of his own rustic childhood, he spent much of his spare time in gaining a first-hand knowledge of conditions of life in Spitalfields, often in difficult and dangerous circumstances.[64]

Spitalfields children, he felt, were in a lamentable state, much given to swearing and blasphemy, sexually precocious, and inured to the fact of death. They wasted their time at fairs and pantomimes, begged in the streets with the aid of grottos or indulged in petty thefts — trinkets and ribbons from genteel children, silk handkerchiefs from respectable gentlemen, goods from shops, brass knockers from doors, and so on.[65] Wilderspin became convinced that juvenile delinquency was one of the major obstacles to youthful development, and increasingly laid emphasis on the infant school as the moral spearhead of the fight against the evil.

The process of moral training was a complex one and involved efforts to correct the neglect or aberrations of parents as well as to adopt counter-measures against the physical and moral dangers of the neighbourhood. It began when the child, perhaps not much more than one year old, entered the school. The young pupil was first instructed in obedience and order, then taught delicacy, cleanliness, kindness, self-control and self-respect before more formal teaching was commenced.[66] The child's physical health was also looked after — Wilderspin insisted on vaccinating all his pupils against smallpox, sending home children with coughs or indispositions and taking reasonable precautions against accidents in the school.[67] More positive action was taken in the utilisation of the playground as a species of moral laboratory; the children were urged not to pick the fruit or pluck the flowers out of respect for the property of others. This exercise in honesty apparently was successful, for Wilderspin noticed that children who came to school hungry never touched the food boxes of those who stayed to dinner.[68]

The child's mental health was also a concern. He rejected the psychological terror with which ignorant parents frightened children into acquiescence — threats to put children in "the black hole" or get the sweep to take them away

[64]He sometimes disguised himself as a labourer, with a beard, dirty face and shabby jacket, in order to mingle with the poor undetected. At other times his investigations resulted in physical clashes with thieves. (P.P. 1835 VII, Education, p. 35; *Infant Poor* (1823), pp. 136-38).

[65]*Infant Poor* (1823), pp. 134-50; *Infant Poor* (1824), pp. 129-33; p. 217.

[66]P.P. 1835 VII, Education, p. 20.

[67]*Infant Poor* (1823), pp. 91-7.

[68]*Infant Poor* (1823), pp. 131-32; *Infant Poor* (1824), p. 138.

(which caused one of Wilderspin's pupils to flee in terror when a sweep passed the school), or stories about "mysterious ghosts and hobgoblins" indulged in by many gossips in poor neighbourhoods.[69]

He was convinced by several incidents in which children upbraided him for not carrying out promises he had made — to return a confiscated whistle, to make a paper boat — that he had, as a teacher, to set an example on every moral issue, or the children would pay little attention to what he said.[70] To this end he devised a set of "rules for teachers" which forbade them to correct a child in anger, to break a promise or to deprive children of any possession without returning it again.[71]

Despite this attempt to modify the customary authority of the teacher, Wilderspin somewhat inconsistently made use of both physical and psychological punishments. These were largely based upon Lancaster's methods of shaming. If children made themselves dirty on the way to school, they were either given "a pat on the hand" with "a small twig" or shamed into cleanliness by having ink put on their faces and paraded round the school whilst the other children cried "sweep, sweep, sweep, chimney sweep". Liars were made to carry a broom around the school to the cry of "told a lie, old brooms" and truants had a piece of green baize tied to their backs while the rest called out "green-tail, played the truant, green-tail"; on one occasion a particularly persistent truant and thief was placed in the cage-like fire guard, to be mocked by the other children.[72]

In the light of Wilderspin's attempts to understand child behaviour and to create an atmosphere of mutual trust and happiness among the pupils, these practices stand out as a glaring aberration; they were, however, abandoned before he left Quaker Street, following strong public criticism.[73] That they were tried at all was probably due to the intractable nature of some of the children with whom he had to deal, and the difficulty of getting parental co-operation in the socialization process.

He hoped, in fact, that the children whose morals were reformed in the school would be one of the means whereby the behaviour of parents would be improved. The idea was Evangelical in inspiration,[74] and much in vogue in the Sunday School movement. He sometimes found that the most obdurate parent — he gives an example of one who kept bulldogs for fighting purposes — could be moved by his children's attitude.[75] He related many anecdotes on these lines

[69] *Infant Poor* (1823), pp. 85-90.

[70] *Infant Poor* (1823), pp. 148-50; *Infant Education* (1825), p. 172.

[71] *Infant Poor* (1823), p. 16.

[72] *Ibid.,* p. 61; pp. 68-71; pp. 75-6.

[73] Cf. Chapter 3.

[74] Joseph Wilson's cousin, Daniel, had put it forward in a sermon on the opening of Spitalfields National School. (Rev. D. Wilson, *The National Schools a National Blessing, A Sermon Preached at Christ Church, Middlesex. . .in aid of the Spitalfields Schools* (London 1819), pp. 32-3).

[75] P.P. 1835 VII, Education, p. 19.

— one, for instance, of an infant whose interest in the Scripture pictures on the school wall induced a laggard and uncouth father to open the illustrated family Bible, and absorb its contents for the first time in his life.[76]

Wilderspin was convinced that his efforts at improving morals and behaviour had yielded some results. He noticed, for instance, that the general appearance and behaviour of his scholars when out of school had improved and swearing was on the decrease.[77] These judgements were endorsed by David Stow, who felt that from the beginning Wilderspin had made a "mighty difference" in the aspect of the pupils compared with those who did not attend; in addition, even the youngest had a distinct impression of right and wrong, truth and falsehood.[78] A resident of Spitalfields later recalled the delight it gave her to see "that happy school",[79] and the editor of the *Morning Chronicle* found the children happy and contented.[80] What excited visitors was the obvious difference between Wilderspin's pupils and those they saw in the streets or in attendance at dame, charity or Sunday Schools. Here was a man who could take nearly two hundred infants of the poorest class of society, and within a matter of weeks or months transform them into an obedient, orderly and happy group, eager to learn and to attend school. One visitor felt that the grand feature of the school was precisely its success in arousing interest in the lessons among two- and three-year-olds to the extent that they actually preferred school to home.[81] The Rev. J.A. Janes was "humbled and astonished at the almost unnatural intelligence and decided principle evinced by infants under six years old", following tuition by "the pious, vigilant and able Mr. Wilderspin, and his worthy wife".[82]

It was all very different from the conning of lessons on the benches of a dame school, the uninspired drudgery of a charity school or the mechanical rote learning of the monitorial system. Those who saw Spitalfields Infant School in action felt that Wilderspin was breaking new ground and was doing so in very unfavourable conditions. A newspaper reporter who had visited the school in Wilderspin's time summed up, many years later, the impact which his work had made on the public:

> The idea of such a school, and almost every part of the plan pursued, was then a novelty. The chant and march were novelties. The substitution of affection and enjoyment for restraint and punishment were novelties. The gallery, with the

---

[76]W.H. Watson, *The First Fifty Years of the Sunday School* (London n.d.), p. 140, citing a speech by Wilderspin. For examples of the reformation of thieving and drunken parents, cf. P.P. 1835 VII, Education, p. 19.

[77]*Infant Poor* (1823), p. 104; p. 110; p. 139; P.P. 1835 VII, Education, p. 18; p. 20.

[78][D. Stow], "Infant Schools", in J. Cleland, *Enumeration of the Inhabitants of the City of Glasgow and County of Lanark* (Glasgow, 2nd ed., 1832), p. 39.

[79]Wilderspin Papers, Elizabeth Hinton to Wilderspin, 28 Feb. 1843.

[80]*Morning Chronicle,* 8 June 1824.

[81]*Christian Guardian,* Apr. 1823, p. 153.

[82]J.J., "Infant Day Schools,"*loc. cit.,* p. 107.

questioning, and rapid answers, and all its excitement, were novelties. And though before that time the world had heard of the Lanark Factory School, and ranked it with the beauties of that picturesque locality, yet the growth of similar beauty in the gloom of Spitalfields was a novelty.[83]

* * * * *

Not the least measure of Wilderspin's achievement was his success in winning over the initially hostile neighbourhood to an appreciation of his novel and advanced form of education. The people of Spitalfields ceased to remove their children from school on the grounds that they were not learning their lessons; on the contrary, in the summer of 1823, the attendance had reached a total of 214 and Wilderspin was forced to turn away the children of fifty parents who applied to have their children admitted[84]. The Wilderspins began to enjoy the affection and respect of the people of the district; even, Wilderspin noted, of "the most abandoned characters",[85] and on many a summer evening a dozen of the local children could be seen playing with the young Wilderspins in the playground, or returning in the dinner hour "with their bread and butter in their hands".[86]

Consistent with this success — and indeed a measure and indication of it — was the publication, in the spring of 1823, of Wilderspin's first book, *On The Importance of Educating the Infant Children of the Poor*. It was the first practical handbook on infant school education to be published in Britain and went through seven editions, with numerous changes of name and content, in the following three decades. Published and translated widely in Europe and the U.S.A., it gave Wilderspin both a national and an international reputation as an educator.

The book was also the first educational work to deal solely with the life and education of poor children at the grass-roots level. Contemporary treatises on infant training, the two most popular of which were Thomas Babington's *A Practical View of Christian Education in its Early Stages* (1814) and Louisa Hoare's *Hints for the Improvement of Early Education and Nursery Discipline* (which reached its eighth edition in 1824), were Evangelical in tone, and written for the middle classes. Essentially parents' manuals, advocating a benevolent but firm discipline and the formation of good habits which would preserve the child from evil influences, they foreshadowed many of the attitudes of the Victorian *paterfamilias*.

---

[83] Wilderspin Papers, leaflet (n.d.), reprinting unidentified extract from the *Daily News*, c. 1846.

[84] *Infant Poor* (1823), p. 109; *Infant Poor* (1824), p. 213.

[85] *Early Discipline* (1832), p. 25.

[86] *Infant Poor* (1823), p. 130; p. 173.

The *Infant Poor* was a moderate-sized volume of 184 pages, its appearance redolent of Browning's "scrofulous French novel, with grey pages and blunt type". Published by Thomas Goyder at five shillings, its contents were arranged haphazardly and it was written, as W.F. Lloyd (secretary of the Sunday School Union) pointed out in the preface, in a "plain and unvarnished style". Nevertheless it had a freshness and immediacy lacking in the more polished treatises of the period, and the children of Spitalfields spring to vigorous life in its pages. It is difficult to say at which audience it was aimed, though the fact that Wilderspin changed the title from the plain and informative *Improvements in the Education of Infant Children* to *On The Importance of Educating the Infant Children of the Poor*[87] suggests that he was attempting to remind wealthy philanthropists of their duty. Perhaps in deference to his patron, the book had a top dressing of quasi-Evangelical religiosity — Biblical texts on the title page, frequent mentions of the Bible, and a concluding prayer to God to protect the infant children of the poor; much of this was omitted in later editions.

The *Infant Poor* of 1823 also contained a tribute to Robert Owen and fulsome thanks for the help that he had rendered Wilderspin in the early days at Spitalfields. This raised an issue which is crucial to the understanding not only of the development of the first English infant schools, but also to an appreciation of Wilderspin's own methods and practices: the degree to which Spitalfields (and also Westminster) were branches of the tree that first flourished at New Lanark.

---

[87] G.L.C.R.O. P83/MRY1/289, leaflet entitled "Improvements in the Education of Infant Children" (n.d.).

CHAPTER 3

THE ENGLISH INFANT SCHOOL:
BUCHANAN AND OWEN

The founding of infant schools at Westminster and Spitalfields marked the transfer of a new type of educational institution from the exceptional conditions of a Scottish industrial village to the densely-populated working-class districts of the English capital. Ostensibly, the succession was direct; Owen's teacher was transferred to Westminster and he in turn set Wilderspin on the same road. Owen, however, came to see the situation in a different light. In the 1830s, after his return from the United States and his subsequent involvement in the British labour movement, he alleged in some detail that Wilderspin had been responsible for the establishment of an "English" type of infant school, fundamentally different from the New Lanark original.

Owen based his allegations on the supposedly weak link at Westminster. In the pages of the *New Moral World* in 1836, and later in his *Life,* Owen alleged that Westminster Infant School was a "lame attempt" to imitate New Lanark and that Wilderspin, though "aided by the frequent hints which he thankfully received from me", derived his first notions of an infant school from the "inferior model" at Westminster.[1] Educational historians have tended to follow, and elaborate on, Owen's views. We need examine here only two of the most recent and representative examples of the genre — Harold Silver's *The Concept of Popular Education* (1965) and Nanette Whitbread's *The Evolution of the Nursery-Infant School* (1972).[2] Essentially they make two points. On the one hand New Lanark Infant School is depicted as a highly informal institution, in which marching to music, dancing, fife-playing, amusement and exercise in the playground are virtually the only activities and from which both religious teaching and books are excluded. On the other hand the English infant school is alleged to be (in Whitbread's words) "a much more rigid instrument for instruction and discipline" than the New Lanark original, and Wilderspin in particular is represented as deliberately turning away from Owen's concept of education to "something much more rigid and theology-centred" (as Silver puts it), with a concentration on formal curriculum, words rather than things, "books, lessons and apparatus" and the premature development of the intellectual powers.

No serious account of the origin and early history of infant schools, or of Wilderspin's work as one of the pioneers, can dismiss these assessments out of hand. But it should be recognised that these views, based largely on a

[1] *New Moral World,* Vol. II, No. 64, 16 Jan. 1836, p. 94, in a letter to Messrs. W. and R. Chambers; Owen, *Life,* 1, p. 153. Similar charges were made in other works (cf. *Robert Owen's Journal,* Vol. 1, No. 5, 30 Nov. 1850, pp. 38-9).

[2] H. Silver, *The Concept of Popular Education* (London 1965), pp. 139-41; Nanette Whitbread, *The Evolution of the Nursery-Infant School* (London 1972), pp. 12-14.

comparison between Owen's ideals and a discrete selection of Wilderspin's prescriptions and aspirations,[3] tend to distort the issue. The relationship between Owen and Wilderspin is not to be discovered by inferences drawn from statements of intention and belief. It can be found only by a comparison of the methods and practices at New Lanark, Westminster and Spitalfields between the years 1819 to 1824, when the three schools were in operation under the stewardship of Owen, Buchanan and Wilderspin themselves. The regime at Spitalfields has already been described in detail. We can now turn to Owen's conception of the infant school and the way in which the institution, when established, functioned under the superintendence of James Buchanan and his successor, a young man named Dunn.

* * * * *

The village of New Lanark consisted of a number of large cotton mills and tall, solidly-built tenements of the traditional Scottish type, spaced on the steep, wooded slopes of a beautiful valley adjacent to the Falls of Clyde. It stands today virtually as Owen left it, a breathtaking monument to the early Industrial Revolution. But neither in the matter of buildings nor of welfare facilities did Owen start with a *tabula rasa*. He built on the foundation left by his father-in-law David Dale, a member of a quietist religious sect descended from the Moravians,[4] who had provided improved physical conditions and rudimentary infant schools for the pauper children on whose labour the mills depended.[5]

Owen, however, went far beyond Dale. His schemes of social amelioration were based on an attempt to solve the most important social problem of the period — the poverty, unemployment and consequent misery of the poor.[6] His educational plans were formed on the conviction that social improvement depended on the prevention of "bad and vicious" habits among the children of the poor and the provision of "good and useful" ones in their place. The first step was to prohibit child labour under the age of ten.[7] The second, based on his belief that the child's disposition was largely formed by the end of its second year,[8] was to remove children between the ages of two and six from the care of their parents

[3]Silver's account of Wilderspin is entirely from secondary sources; these cite his *Infant Poor* (1823) and his evidence to the Select Committee of 1835. Neither Silver nor Whitbread include any of Wilderspin's works in their bibliographies.

[4]Cf. E. Halévy, *The Birth of Methodism in England* (Chicago 1971), p. 74.

[5]W.A.C. Stewart and W.P. McCann, *The Educational Innovators 1750-1880* (London 1967), pp. 64-5, for a more detailed description. Owen, in his appraisal of Dale's work, does not mention these infant schools. Cf. *New View of Society,* Second Essay, Owen, *Life,* 1, pp. 276-77; "New Lanark Address" (1816), Owen, *Life,* 1, p. 339. Owen, in fact, denied that "an infant school" existed during the last years of Dale's operations (*New Moral World,* Vol. 1, No. 3, Nov. 1834, p. 21).

[6]For the Poor Law problem as the context of Owen's schemes of practical philanthropy, cf. J.F.C. Harrison, *Robert Owen and the Owenites in Britain and America* (London 1969), p. 13 ff.

[7]*New View of Society,* Second Essay, Owen, *Life,* 1, pp. 277-78, for his arguments on this point.

[8]Owen, *Life,* 1, p. 288.

during the day and place them in an infant school, the first stage of a comprehensive and graded system of education.

Owen founded his philosophy, as recent studies have shown, on a synthesis of ideas derived from millenarianism, philanthropy, socialism and communitarianism, whose frame of reference was the eighteenth-century Enlightenment.[9] From this source Owen derived the theoretical foundations of New Lanark Infant School. It is possible (though unproven) that Owen's views on the nature of an infant school may also have been influenced, or at least reinforced, by the ideas of his sometime partner Jeremy Bentham and by the fiction of Maria Edgeworth, daughter of his friend R.L. Edgeworth. In the 1790s Bentham had speculated on the possibility of an infant nursery, with a wide curriculum, exercise and recreation, as part of his plans for a Panopticon.[10] In 1812 Maria Edgeworth had published *Madame de Fleury,* a fictionalised but accurate account of her friend Mme. de Pastoret's Paris school for children under six.[11]

The theoretical staples of Owen's institution were the doctrine of circumstance, encapsulated in the slogan "man's character is formed for him, not by him" and issuing in the belief that children could be trained to acquire "any language, sentiments, belief, or any bodily habits and manners, not contrary to human nature"; and the commitment to happiness, the object of all human exertions whose prerequisites were "health, real knowledge and wealth".[12] If the infants were to become "active, cheerful and happy, fond of the school and of their instructors",[13] the latter had to be carefully chosen. Owen selected James Buchanan, a former weaver of thirty-two years of age and an ex-soldier of the Scottish militia, and Molly Young, a seventeen-year old local girl. The school occupied the rooms immediately to the right and left of the Ionic columns which flank the entrance to the Institute; the level grassy space in front of the building immediately below the main thoroughfare of the village formed the playground (now used as a parking area for vehicles of a local metal firm). The bucolic

[9]Harrison, *Robert Owen,* pp. 78-87; pp. 139-47. The extent and manner of Owen's commitment to Enlightenment ideas has always been a problem. His acquaintanceship with members of the Manchester Philosophical Society, with Godwin and R.L. Edgeworth, and with the Scottish school of moral philosophers should all be taken into account. M.A. Jullien, the French educationist, stated in 1822 that Owen was influenced by his reading of Mme. de Genlis' *Adèle et Théodore,* which contained several verbatim extracts from Rousseau's *Emile* (M.A. Jullien, "Sur la Colonie Industrielle de New-Lanark, en Ecosse, fondée par M. Robert Owen", *Revue Encyclopédique,* Tome XVIII, Avril 1823, p. 16).

[10]U.C.L. Bentham Mss., CVII/53-61, Paedotrophium (1792; 1794); CXXXIII/1 Paedotrophium (c. 1794).

[11]Miss Edgeworth, *Madame de Fleury,* in *Tales of Fashionable Life* (London, 3 vol., 1809-12) Maria Edgeworth had visited Paris in late 1802 and met Mme. de Pastoret, who gave her the details of the school. (F.A. Edgeworth, *A Memoir of Maria Edgeworth* (London, 3 vol., 1867), I, pp. 130-39; p. 156n.). Mme. de Pastoret knew of Oberlin's school in the Ban de la Roche, founded in 1767 and generally considered to be the first European infant school, through her friend Baron de Gérando (D. Deasey, *Education Under Six* (London 1978), pp. 17-20.)

[12]*New View of Society,* First Essay, Owen, *Life,* 1, p. 267; "Letter Published in the London Newspapers of August 9th, 1817", Owen, *Life,* 1A, p. 83.

[13]P.P. 1816 IV, Select Committee on the Education of the Lower Orders of the Metropolis, p. 240.

setting, the air of innocent gaiety engendered by Buchanan's personality and methods, attracted visitors from Britain and many parts of the world. European royalty and aristocracy (including the Grand Duke Nicholas of Russia, later Tsar), ambassadors, politicians and educationists, as well as, in the words of a critic, "benevolent individuals and committees of philanthropic societies, speculative regenerators of mankind, gossiping justices and jail-gadding ladies..." journeyed in thousands to the banks of the Clyde.[14]

* * * * *

Among the visitors were John Smith, banker and associate of the Evangelical party, and William Allen, the Quaker chemist and one of Owen's London partners. On their return they gave accounts of the infant school to Henry Brougham, the Whig spokesman on education, and to James Mill, the Utilitarian educationist, stimulating an interest in infant education which led them to consider (in Brougham's words) "attempting some general application in England of the same principles".[15] The decision to act came in December 1818, when Brougham had several long conversations with Owen on the latter's return from his European tour. "Brougham", wrote James Mill to Ricardo on 7 December, "has become strongly impressed with an idea of the importance of Owen's *infant* school...It is part of his schemes on the education subject, which seems to be engrossing his whole mind". Brougham hoped to establish in London an institution "for taking the children from the parents during the day, after three years of age — when they can be trained in good habits, and under the exercise of reason, instead of being trained in bad habits, under gusts of passion, irrascible and sympathetic, in the hands of poor parents". Brougham and Mill, after discussing the project "a great many times", agreed that the time was not ripe to bring the matter before Parliament"; a show school however, would favourably influence the public mind.[16] A committee was then brought together, £1,000 collected from members of the committee and sympathisers (including the Evangelicals Fowell Buxton and Wilberforce),[17] James Buchanan secured as master and the school established.

If the infant school was born in Scotland as a response to the conditions created by the factory system of the Industrial Revolution, it was transplanted to England as an attempt to counter the effects of expanding industrialism in urban areas, particularly the capital, where juvenile delinquency, crime and political unrest were particularly visible to legislators. The post-war agricultural and

---

[14]J. Aiton, *Mr. Owen's Objections to Christianity, and New View of Society and Education, Refuted, by a Plain Statement of Facts* (Edinburgh, 2nd ed., 1824), p. 13.

[15]*New Moral World,* Vol. I, No. 3, 15 Nov. 1834, p. 21, citing a letter from Brougham to Owen.

[16]P. Sraffa and M.H. Dobb (Eds.), *The Works and Correspondence of David Ricardo* (Cambridge, 10 vol., 1951-73), VII, pp. 355-56.

[17]According to Brougham in a speech twenty-seven years later (Parl. Deb., 3rd Sers., LXXXVIII, 3 Aug. 1846, 274).

industrial slump resulted in widespread unemployment and poverty; strikes and riots in the factory districts, radical political activity and the circulation of "seditious" and "infidel" literature alarmed the Tory government. They replied with a policy of repression: the suspension of Habeas Corpus, Sidmouth's Gagging Acts of 1817, which severely restricted political activity, the Peterloo Massacre of August 1819 and the subsequent Six Acts, which virtually ended free speech, free assembly and the free dissemination of ideas. The atmosphere was highly charged and if reactionaries turned to repression, liberals looked to moderate reform, particularly the provision of education. Brougham felt that the education of the poor was "the best security for the morals, the subordination, and the peace of countries";[18] John Smith believed it would cool the fires of revolt by revealing to the poor their "true interests". With the recent Smithfield Riots in mind he wrote to Brougham in August 1819:

> ...the great majority of those who attended the two meetings in Smithfield were persons of the very lowest description in the Metropolis, and consequently uneducated. Instigated by such a man as Hunt they are capable of any mischief, and so long as we suffer the poor to be untaught, and ignorant of their true interests we shall be in perpetual jeopardy from these troublesome and tumultuous assemblies.[19]

New Lanark appeared to provide practical proof that education could, in fact, provide a peaceful solution to pressing social problems. Several of the Westminster Committee had connections with Owen or admired the New Lanark experiment. The members of the committee were, in addition to Brougham, Lord Lansdowne, John Smith, Sir Thomas Baring (another pro-Evangelical banker) and Thomas Babington and Zachary Macaulay, members of the Clapham Sect; Henry Hase, cashier of the Bank of England, a particular friend of Owen and a frequent visitor to his house at Braxfield; John Walker, one of Owen's Quaker partners at New Lanark, the Philosophical Radical James Mill; Benjamin Leigh Smith, a Unitarian and a member of the radical Smith family; Lord Dacre, William Leake, M.P. and Joseph Wilson, the Evangelical silk merchant and later Wilderspin's patron, completed the number.[20]

Owen knew most of the committee. He had discussed educational issues with Brougham and James Mill for a decade,[21] was in partnership at different times with Bentham, Walker and William Allen and counted Zachary Macaulay and other Evangelicals, including William Wilberforce, to whom he dedicated the first Essay of *A New View of Society,* among his friends.[22] The Westminster group were part of a sizeable body of opinion which, impressed by the evidence

---

[18]Parl. Deb., N.S., II, 28 June 1820, 56.

[19]U.C.L. Brougham Mss., 30046, J. Smith to Brougham, 27 Aug. 1819.

[20]The membership of the committee has been compiled from three sources: Owen, *Life,* 1, p. 142; Wilderspin, *Infant Poor* (1824), p. 23, and B.I. Buchanan, *Buchanan Family Records* (Cape Town 1923), p. 7.

[21]*New Moral World,* Vol. I, No. 3, Nov. 1834, p. 22.

[22]Owen, *Life,* 1, p. 103.

of New Lanark, was prepared to experiment with some of the more radical solutions to the social problem propounded by Owen. Westminster Infant School was, in fact, merely one of a number of Owenite projects, indeed the only successful one, promoted by middle-class philanthropists in the post-war decade.

Others were the Association for the Relief of the Manufacturing Poor, founded in 1816, the committee of which included Owen himself, Thomas Babington, Sir Thomas Baring, Brougham, Macaulay, William Allen and Wilberforce;[23] the Committee to Report on Owen's Plan for Providing for the Poor (1819) with John Smith, M.P., as a member;[24] the British and Foreign Philanthropic Society (1822), supported by a large number of philanthropists (including Henry Hase) and twenty-nine M.Ps, among whom Brougham and Sir William de Crespigny were prominent,[25] and the Hibernian Philanthropic Society (1823).[26] The last three organisations each raised large sums for the establishment of Owenite communities, but none, as far as can be ascertained, were put into operation.

Those who supported these schemes were in no sense theoretical Owenites; in fact they went to great pains publicly to dissociate themselves from any adherence to the "speculative" or "visionary" aspects of Owen's philanthropy, i.e. any link with his philosophy of social change. Orthodoxy reserved all its venom, as Brougham pointed out, for "visionaries, speculatists, enthusiasts, to sum up all in one worst of words — theorists".[27] So we find W.H. Crook, of the Philanthropic Society, insisting that "Everything of a *speculative* nature has been rejected by the Committee, and we have confined ourselves to that which we know to be practicable and useful..."[28] Brougham, in the debate of December 1819, made a careful distinction between Owen's "plan", which in the main he supported, particularly in its educational aspects, and his "theory", which as a good Malthusian he found "wholly erroneous", being founded on a principle which he denied — that an increase of the population benefited the nation"; on the contrary, maintained Brougham, "the excess of population" was one of the great causes of the distress which then afflicted the country.[29]

[23]Cf. list of committee members in *The Times,* 30 July 1816.

[24]Owen, *Life,* 1A, pp. 237-49.

[25]Proceedings of the First General Meeting of the British and Foreign Philanthropic Society (London 1822), *passim.* The Committee hoped that its plans would relieve the affluent part of the community of "distressing expenditure" by reducing the Poor Rate (p. 6).

[26]R. Owen, *The New Existence of Man Upon the Earth* (London 1854), Pt. IV, App., xc-xci.

[27]Parl. Deb., N.S., II, 28 June 1820, 87-8.

[28]British and Foreign Philanthropic Society, pp. 39-40. Conservative opinion made the same distinction between Owen's practice, which could be accepted, and his "speculative opinions" which were rejected. (Cf. *Blackwood's Edinburgh Magazine,* No. XLIX, Vol. IX, Apr. 1821, pp. 85-92; No. LXXIV, Vol. XIII, Mar. 1823, pp. 338-42.

[29]Parl. Deb., XLI, 16 Dec. 1819, 1195.

The Malthusianism of Brougham (equally with that of Mill, buttressed by Ricardo),[30] provided a point of departure from Owenite ideology for the Westminster Infant School Committee and focused attention on one of the most visible effects of "the excess of population" — the crime and juvenile delinquency in the overcrowded working-class areas of the expanding cities, particulary London. Evangelicalism also was critical of Owenism; Wilberforce had repudiated his former welcome to Owen's principles following the latter's anti-religious statements in 1817.[31] John Smith was equally opposed to "Mr. Owen's unfortunate religious belief", but was willing to support his system, particularly as it apparently eliminated crime.[32]

Population increase and the attendant evil of juvenile delinquency thus cannot be ignored by those investigating the rise of the English infant school. The great upsurge of population, beginning in the latter half of the eighteenth century and continuing in the first decades of the nineteenth, reaching an increase of 15% in the years 1811-20, had, of course, resulted in a relatively sudden rise in the number of young children. The poverty and unemployment of the post-war years exacerbated the situation. The Juvenile Delinquency Committee of 1816 pointed to the frequent connection between indigence and crime,[33] and two years later the Society for the Improvement of Prison Discipline and the Reformation of Juvenile Offenders maintained that poverty and unemployment were among the reasons for "youthful aberration from the path of virtue".[34] Statistics were for the most part no more than intelligent guesses, but the figures impressed public opinion; Brougham in 1816 put the number of young thieves in London at 2,000-4,000[35] and five years later Thomas Fowell Buxton, M.P. was estimating the number of young offenders at between 8,000 and 10,000.[36] Several of the Westminster Infant School Committee concerned themselves with the problems of juvenile delinquency, illiteracy and poverty in the post-war years: Brougham as a member of the Committee on Criminal Laws of 1819 and as chairman of the Select Committee on the Education of the Lower Orders in the Metropolis, set up in 1816; Smith and

---

[30]Ricardo refused to associate himself with Westminster Infant School, believing that Brougham planned to feed and educate the children. He wrote to Mill, "I see the most serious objections to the plan, and I should be exceedingly inconsistent if I gave my countenance to it. I have invariably objected to the poor laws, and to every system which should give encouragement to excess of population" (Ricardo to Mill, 12 Dec. 1818, in Sraffa and Dobb, *Correspondence of Ricardo,* VII, pp. 359-60).

[31]Parl. Deb., XLI, 16 Dec. 1819, 1212.

[32]*Ibid.,* 1205.

[33]Report of the Committee for Investigating the Causes of the Alarming Increase of Juvenile Delinquency in the Metropolis (London 1816), p. 13.

[34]Report of the Committee of the Society for the Improvement of Prison Discipline and for the Reformation of Juvenile Offenders (London 1818), p. 13.

[35]Parl. Deb., XXXIV, 20 June 1816, 1230.

[36]*Severity of Punishment. Speech of Thomas Fowell Buxton, Esq., in the House of Commons, Wednesday, May 23rd, 1821* (London 1821), p. 5.

Babington as members of the latter committee; James Mill as a member of the Juvenile Delinquency Committee and Baring and John Smith as officials of the Prison Discipline Society.

A conviction as to the inability of working-class parents to bring up their children with the requisite attention and control permeated the outlook of the founders of the first English infant school. If they admired the practice of Owen, their intellectual background was formed by the theories of Bentham, Malthus and Chalmers, whose watchwords were regulation, restraint and indoctrination. The social diagnosis of Brougham and his associates, particularly that of the Evangelicals and Dissenters, rested on the moral unfitness of the poor; they may "exclaim against taxes and ill-government", wrote Brougham, "but the worst government is their own of themselves".[37] The cause of the social problem was thus transferred from the social and economic system (the starting point of Owen's argument) to the people themselves, and they were evaluated not on their own terms nor in the light of their own circumstances, but according to middle-class values.

The reformers' model of the child was that depicted in Thomas Babington's *Practical View of Christian Education* — one accustomed to a secure and stable environment and constantly watched over and guided by stern but just parental authority.[38] As Wilderspin observed, "the children of the rich have every possible care taken of them, being seldom or never left alone, and never suffered to go into the streets without a guide".[39] In contrast, the life of many of the children of the urban poor, with its familiarity with the adult world, its boisterous freedom of movement, its relative independence of parental control and its early commitment to earning a living, seemed unnatural to the middle-class and a threat to order and stability, and thus gave them an exaggerated fear of the consequences of allowing the situation to continue.[40] By the same criterion the parents were at fault; if the offspring were socially anarchic, their elders must lack the powers of care and control which the middle-class *paterfamilias* evidently possessed. The Juvenile Delinquency Committee of 1816, a creation of the reformers, characteristically stressed the weakening of "parental authority and love" among the poor as the main cause of juvenile crime, as did other similar organisations.[41] The corollary was stated by Brougham in 1816; if, as he took to be the case, poor parents were not only neglecting children, but actually

---

[37] H. Brougham, "Establishments at Hofwyl", *Edinburgh Review*, Vol. XXXII, No. LXIV, Oct. 1819, p. 497.

[38] T. Babington, *A Practical View of Christian Education in its Early Stages* (London 1814).

[39] *Infant Poor* (1823), p. 4.

[40] Margaret May, "Innocence and Experience, the Evolution of the Concept of Juvenile Delinquency in the Mid-Nineteenth Century", *Victorian Studies*, Vol. XVIII, No. 1, Sept. 1973, pp. 18-19, for an elaboration of this point.

[41] Report of Committee, pp. 11-13; the Committee included amongst its members W. Allen, T.F. Buxton, Samuel Hoare, James Mill, David Ricardo, and several members of the Quaker families of Barclay, Forster, Hanbury, Harris, Phillips and Sanderson; cf. also Society for the Improvement of Prison Discipline, Third Report, 1821, p. 49.

corrupting them by hiring them out to beggars, then it was in order to resort to "forcible interference" between parent and child.[42] The reformers thus envisaged (as Owen had done in different circumstances and for different reasons) that serious inroads would be made into the traditional jurisdiction of the patriarchal family.

Brougham's views on the education of the poor had been much influenced by his visit, in 1816, to the educational estate of the Swiss patrician Fellenberg. The Poor School there, run by Wehrli, had impressed Brougham as a type of infant school[43] and convinced him that attempts to form habits of industry and virtuous conduct among delinquent children should start "in their earliest years".[44] It is not surprising to find that his conception of the ideal infant school was a place where children could be amused and kept out of mischief; "Whether they learnt less or more was of little consequence. The moral discipline was the great consideration".[45] Paradoxically, and significantly, the master of the first English infant school was, in character, purpose and method, almost the antithesis of the type of teacher who would best have translated into practice the ideals of the Whig reformers.

* * * * *

The success of Westminster Infant School was largely due to Buchanan's ability to base the education of the young on a foundation of interest, amusement and activity. His son William, recalling his boyhood at New Lanark, remembered that his father had shown great ability in bringing noisy and unruly children to a state of order and obedience by means of "gentle arts".[46] William Rathbone, later Mayor of Liverpool and Wilderspin's employer, was struck by his "undeviating kindness in manner" and the "gaiety, playfulness and activity, with the freedom from quarreling (sic) or troublesome habits" displayed by the infants in his charge.[47] Barbara Buchanan, his grand-daughter, adds some details to the general picture. "At New Lanark in the beginning, Grandpa made the children march round the room to the strains of his flute. Then he marched them through the village, and allowed them to amuse themselves on the banks of the Clyde, and march back again". When the weather was bad he invented indoor amusements, beginning with "simple gymnastic movements, arm

---

[42]Parl. Deb., XXXIV, 20 June 1816, 1230.

[43]In the debate on Owen's Plan in the Commons in 1819, Brougham referred admiringly to "the plans of Mr. Fellenberg for infant education" (Parl. Deb., XLI, 16 Dec. 1819, 1197-98).

[44]P.P. 1818 IV, Select Committee on the Education of the Lower Orders, Second Report, p. 195.

[45]Parl. Deb., N.S., II, 28 June 1820, 87-8.

[46]U.C.L. Brougham Mss., 26554, W. Buchanan to Brougham, 2 May 1851.

[47]"Account of the New Lanark Schools Contributed by William Rathbone...", appended to J. Murphy, "Robert Owen in Liverpool", Transactions of the Historic Society of Lancashire and Cheshire, Vol. 112, 1960, pp. 79-103.

exercises, clapping the hands and counting the movements". Later he introduced the repetition or chanting of arithmetical tables, simple object lessons in which the children did most of the talking and learned to observe and describe. Buchanan also gave simple forms of religious instruction — repetition of the Lord's Prayer, the telling of Bible stories "which he filled with life and significance" and the singing of hymns from Watts' Divine and Moral Songs, accompanied by him on the flute.[48]

There seems no reason to doubt, from the evidence available, that Buchanan carried on at Westminister where he left off at New Lanark, for his grand-daughter describes his doing exactly the same things in the early days at Brewer's Green. In 1822 the school moved to new premises, provided by Benjamin Leigh Smith, at Vincent Square.[49] Equipment and facilities were much superior to those at Brewer's Green, and it was here that Buchanan was observed by Edward Baines, editor of the *Leeds Mercury,* who had been to New Lanark five years earlier. Visiting Westminster in the summer of 1824, Baines was delighted to find, in the yard which served for a playground, a scene of "uproarious mirth", with young children of three to four years running about, playing and dancing under the mild discipline of Buchanan, "a kind, patient intelligent man who studied and accommodated himself to the humours and understanding of the children". In the "airy" schoolroom large enough to take 140 infants, the younger children, supervised by Mrs. Buchanan, learned the alphabet under monitors, or talked to each other and played with toys, and the girls did sewing. The older children were taken by Buchanan to a separate classroom, where they learned the simple rules of arithmetic, wrote on slates or read short stories. Large letters of the alphabet and pictures of animals and flowers covered the walls and formed the basis of lessons. Marching, dancing and the singing of Watts' hymns completed the day.[50]

Owen's allegation that this school was an inferior copy of New Lanark rested on somewhat idiosyncratic grounds. In the first place he alleged that Westminster lacked real knowledge, sound practical morality and music and dancing of a superior kind. But the adjectives Owen used — "real", "sound", "superior" — are of so abstract and relative a nature as to render discussion of the subject pointless, quite apart from the fact that the music and dancing at New Lanark was provided by specialist teachers for the pupils of all the schools. Second, he argued that Buchanan formed the character of his charges into "believers and slaves of the system, founded on falsehood and supported solely by deception..." This, of course, tells us more about Owen's political attitudes during the 1830s than it does about Buchanan's activities in the early 1820s.[51]

---

[48]Buchanan, *Family Records,* pp. 3-4. Owen confirmed that the infants in Buchanan's day were given lessons from objects gathered in the gardens, fields and woods and also instructed from paintings and maps (Owen, *Life,* 1, p. 140).

[49]Buchanan, *Family Records,* pp. 5-7; p. 8; pp. 26-7.

[50]*Leeds Mercury,* 31 July 1824.

[51]These two charges were made in *New Moral World,* Vol. II, No. 64, 16 Jan. 1836, p. 94.

Third, and perhaps most seriously, Owen claimed to have discovered that corporal punishment was practised at Westminster. When visiting the school he found Mrs. Buchanan brandishing a whip in front of the children (whose dismayed faces struck Owen forcibly) while Buchanan was in another part of the room "as much subject to his wife as the children".[52] An incident of this sort could have happened; Mrs. Buchanan, though generally kind to the children, was known to have administered spankings to them if she thought it necessary.[53] But to generalise from this incident, as Owen does, distorts the picture; the main burden of the teaching fell on Buchanan who, according to Barbara Bodichon, Benjamin Leigh Smith's daughter, was the reverse of his wife and treated the children with "extraordinary patience and tenderness".[54]

Buchanan's unworldliness and his gift of identification with children did not always satisfy those with more orthodox images of a teacher. He was regarded by the majority of the Westminster Committee as a "queer fish"; this led to a lack of interest in the project on their part and precipitated the move to Vincent Square in 1822.[55] There is no doubt that Buchanan did have some of the defects of his virtues. Mrs. Bodichon was aware that he was "very unpractical, childlike and thriftless" and could act in an erratic manner; he would sometimes "study or dream away his time" or abruptly go off on holiday, leaving his wife to cope with the school as best she could. In her opinion he was "too uncertain" to have run a school entirely on his own.[56] Owen, though he recognised Buchanan's love for and patience with children, declared that "he was quite unequal to the organisation and management of a school".[57] But all other accounts agree that Buchanan had the heart of the matter in him. "He made infant schools what they ought to be", affirmed Sarah Austin, a frequent visitor to the school, "nurseries for the body and soul, and not exhibitions of learned babes".[58]

* * * * *

If Owen was critical of Buchanan he was much more favourably disposed towards Wilderspin. On his first visit to Spitalfields, Owen found him "very desirous and willing to learn, and much more teachable than my first master, having much more talent and tact for the business". Returning at Wilderspin's

---

[52]Owen, *Life*, 1, p. 152.

[53]Buchanan, *Family Records*, p. 14.

[54]*Ibid.*, p. 22.

[55]According to Barbara Bodichon (Buchanan, *Family Records*, p. 25).

[56]Buchanan, *Family Records*, p. 22; p. 27.

[57]*Robert Owen's Journal*, Vol. I, No. 5, 30 Nov. 1850, citing *The Revolution in the Mind and Practice of the Human Race*; Owen, *Life*, 1, p. 139.

[58]U.C.L. Brougham Mss., 2292, Sarah Austin to Brougham, 21 Feb. 1851. Mrs. Austin, wife of John Austin the jurist, spent a great deal of time at Brewer's Green at the request of James Mill.

request, Owen found great pleasure in giving him "general and minute instructions" on how to act with children and how to govern them "without punishment, by affection and undeviating kindness", noting that all his recommendations were "faithfully followed".[59] Owen's help was not confined to the early days of Spitalfields; in 1823 he bought 50 copies of *Educating the Infant Poor* and apparently revisited Spitalfields during the same year, bringing "many of the nobility and gentry" with him and requesting them to read the book.[60] Owen, in fact, always had a high opinion of Wilderspin's abilities and described him as "an apt disciple of the spirit and practice of the system, as far as the outward and material mode was concerned". Owen's one reservation about Wilderspin was that he had no powers of mind to comprehend the infant school "as a first step towards forming a rational character for a rational system of society"; but, he added magnanimously, "I did not attempt to advance his knowledge so as to unfit him to act under the patronage of his then supporters".[61]

Wilderspin, in his early writings, paid generous tribute to Owen's achievement at New Lanark and to the help he had proffered. He not only praised "that eminent philanthropist Mr. Owen" for the efforts he had made to keep his employees happy by finding them employment and providing buildings and teachers for the education of their children but also he begged "most humbly to thank him" for visiting Spitalfields School three or four times, expressing his approbation of the methods being developed there and for giving "many useful hints". Without this (and other) assistance, he admitted, the school could not have been brought to the state it had reached in 1823.[62]

There was obviously a large measure of agreement between Owen and Wilderspin as to how an infant school should be organised. But the model Owen had in mind could only have been New Lanark Infant School as it existed in 1820, under the superintendence of a young man named Dunn. Buchanan, in Owen's somewhat uncharitable opinion, had not been amenable to the instruction he had "drilled into him for years" and had produced his results "unconsciously". Young Dunn, on the other hand, was "the best instructor of infants I have ever seen in any part of the world" and had enabled a "rapid advance and improvement" to be made in the school.[63] Owen does not go into details, but contemporary accounts suggest that the improvements were in the direction of widening the curriculum and introducing a greater measure of order and organisation into the institution.

First, a rudimentary time-table was in operation throughout the schools, including the infant school, each teacher being given a list of the lessons his class

[59]Owen, *Life*, I, p. 153.

[60]*Educational Magazine*, Vol. II, Aug. 1835, p. 148.

[61]Owen, *Life*, I, p. 153.

[62]*Infant Poor* (1823), pp. 108-09.

[63]Owen, *Life*, I, pp. 141-43.

was to receive during the week "to prevent any confusion or irregularity".[64] Second, a precise classification was made; children from two to four years of age had a different programme from those from four to six, though all divided their time equally between lessons and play.[65] Third, the curriculum was at least as wide as that later developed by Wilderspin, and included a certain amount of repetitive work. The younger division began by learning, in small groups, the alphabet and monosyllabic words, while children from four to six years had, in addition, "short and easy lessons".[66] These lessons, according to M.A. Jullien, a French visitor, involved reading from books.[67] Natural history was learned from objects, supplemented by drawings, and the division of the natural world into animal, vegetable and mineral kingdoms was always brought out.[68] Geography, consisting of knowledge of the form of the earth and information about foreign countries was also taught to the infants.[69] Singing (both "the scale of the gamut" and formal songs),[70] dancing, marching and military drill were taught by specialist teachers attached to the institution and took in all age groups, though Robert Dale Owen stated that singing did not begin before five or six years of age.[71]

Fourth, religious instruction was given at New Lanark, though those who form their picture of the infant school from a reading of Owen's *Life* might be pardoned for failing to notice it. Non-denominational Bible study in the schools was part of the 1813 Articles of Partnership, zealously enforced by William Allen.[72] The children, Owen stated in 1816, had the same religious instruction as in other schools in Scotland, including Church attendance and examination by the minister.[73] The headmaster at New Lanark stated in 1819 that Friday was set aside for religious exercises and catechising and that on Sunday "sacred music,

---

[64]R.D. Owen, *An Outline of the System of Education at New Lanark* (Glasgow 1824), pp. 71-2. Though this work was written in 1823, it is retrospective in character and describes the school after Buchanan's departure.

[65]*Ibid.*, p. 32.

[66]"Daily Routine of the New Lanark Institution" (25 Sept. 1819) in H.G. MacNab, *The New Views of Mr. Owen of Lanark Impartially Examined* (London 1819), p. 221-22.

[67]M.A. Jullien, "Sur la Colonie Industrielle de New-Lanark, en Ecosse, fondée par M. Robert Owen", *Revue Encyclopédique,* Tome XVIII, Avril 1823, p. 16. According to R.D. Owen, the "younger classes" were taught reading (*Education at New Lanark*, p. 30).

[68]Owen, *Education at New Lanark*, pp. 44-5.

[69]*Ibid.*, p. 30; pp. 47-8.

[70]"Visit to New Lanark, August 1822", in *Report of the Proceedings at the Several Public Meetings Held in Dublin, by Robert Owen, Esq.* (Dublin 1823), pp. 92-9.

[71]Owen, *Education at New Lanark*, pp. 30-1; pp. 69-71.

[72]Letter signed 'B' in *Christian Observer*, Vol. XVIII, No. 216, Dec. 1819, p. 790. For Allen's activities in this respect cf. *Life of William Allen, with Selections from his Correspondence* (London, 3 vol., 1846-47), I, p. 209; p. 215; pp. 244-48; p. 324-5; p. 344-53; II, p. 237; p. 366.

[73]P.P. 1816 III, Report of the...Select Committee on the State of Children Employed in the Manufactories of the United Kingdom, p. 26. R.D. Owen stated that religious instruction was given in deference to the liberty of conscience of the parents (*Education at New Lanark*, p. 68).

reading and expounding the Holy Scriptures, and prayer" was the business of the day.[74] One visitor noticed that children learned to read from the Bible,[75] and another confirmed that children as young as four could "read well in the Testament".[76] Whether or not Owen informed Wilderspin of the religious instruction at New Lanark is not recorded.

It is clear that much of the so-called organisation and rigidity, not to mention the theology, which critics have ascribed to Spitalfields Infant School was present also at New Lanark.[77] This, however, had not undermined the happy atmosphere that had existed under the Buchanan regime. The American educationist J. Griscom, who visited New Lanark in March 1819, found the infants "perfectly happy",[78] and the Quaker J. Smith, a year later, was impressed with the atmosphere of harmony and the lack of fear among the children.[79] If, in fact, we abstract the main features of New Lanark, Westminster and Spitalfields, we must recognize that the institutions were varieties of the same stock rather than plants of dissimilar species. All three had the following common characteristics: — the provision of a playground as a place for happy and healthful exercise; informal relationships between teacher and pupil; play and simple alphabet learning for the younger children while the older children were having lessons in writing and arithmetic; the teaching of natural history and general knowledge by means of objects; the singing or chanting of rhymes as a method of learning; the incidence of story-telling (including Bible stories), plus marching or dancing and singing.

That there were differences between the three schools cannot be disputed; but it was the similarities, rather than the differences, that impressed contemporaries. David Goyder, of Bristol Infant School, declared that there was nothing to be seen at Spitalfields that he had not seen at Westminster.[80] Griscom felt that Westminster and Bristol schools were formed upon "a similar plan" to that of New Lanark.[81] W.H. Crook of the Philanthropic Society was of the same opinion; in Spitalfields, Westminster and Bristol infant schools, Owen's principles "as far as circumstances allow", were adopted.[82]

* * * * *

[74]'Daily Routine', MacNab, New Views, pp. 221-24.

[75]Sir William de Crespigny, M.P., British and Foreign Philanthropic Society, p. 13.

[76]"The Report of a Deputy sent by the Town of Leeds, to Examine the New Lanark Establishment", MacNab, New Views, p. 106.

[77]Brian Simon's description of Wilderspin as a supporter of "orthodox religion" in education, and of Owen as an educator who presumably admitted no religion in his schools may need revision (B. Simon, Studies in the History of Education 1780-1870 (London 1960), p. 237).

[78]J. Griscom, A Year in Europe (New York, 2 vol., 1823), II, p. 385.

[79]J. Smith, Notes Taken During an Excursion in Scotland in the Year 1820 (Liverpool 1824), pp. 65-6.

[80]D.G. Goyder, The Autobiography of a Phrenologist (London 1858), p. 109.

[81]Griscom, A Year in Europe, II, p. 386n.

[82]British and Foreign Philanthropic Society, pp. 41-2.

The "circumstances" were primarily city life, and secondarily the personalities and outlooks of the teachers, and the differences between the English and Scottish schools have their origin in these areas. Wilderspin argued that conditions in East London necessitated certain modifications of New Lanark practice. Owen, he exclaimed, had not "one tenth part of the difficulties to contend with at New Lanark that we encounter in London", nor were the children exposed to so many dangers. Owen's control of the mills and the comparative orderliness of the parents, Wilderspin argued, gave him a much freer hand to experiment without endangering the stability of his school, whereas in London the parents worked for many different employers, were more independent, and would even refuse to send their children to school unless the teaching met with their approbation; "...what might answer very well at Lanark", Wilderspin concluded, "would require some alteration to be adapted for London, and to be accommodated to the inhabitants therein".[83]

Wilderspin did not specify the alterations he had in mind. One of them was obviously the introduction of corporal punishment; on this issue he disregarded the "minute instructions" which Owen had given him. Owen was opposed to corporal punishment because he felt it undermined his objectives with regard to character formation,[84] whereas Wilderspin, as we have seen, believed punishment, both physical and psychological, to be the ultimate sanction in keeping order among the minority of obstreperous children he had to deal with. As the Quaker William Allen's journal the *Inquirer* pointed out, however, nothing but ill-will among the pupils could result from children being made (as in shaming) the instrument of inflicting punishment upon one another.[85] Wilderspin, admitting he was not taking "the popular side of the question", was showered with criticism. In 1823 Thomas Pole, the Quaker author of *Observations Relative to Infant Schools,* condemned its use;[86] Brougham, in the same year, called for "unsparing condemnation of these barbarous and absurd inventions"[87]; David Goyder added his criticism.[88] Wilderspin, who defended the use of punishment on the grounds that order could be preserved in no other way, and even somewhat despairingly quoted Scripture in support,[89] eventually bowed to the storm and in 1825 abolished shaming; the pat on the hand, however, was retained for use in cases of disobedience, occasionally found when a child first entered the school.[90]

[83]*Infant Poor* (1823), pp. 106-07; *Infant Poor* (1824), p. 180.

[84]*Report of the Proceedings...in Dublin,* pp. 78-9.

[85]*Inquirer,* Vol. II, Apr. 1823, p. 350.

[86]T. Pole, *Observations Relative to Infant Schools* (Bristol 1823), p. 49 ff.

[87]H.Brougham, "Early Moral Education", *Edinburgh Review,* Nov. LXXVI, May 1823, p. 448.

[88]D.G. Goyder, *A Manual of the System of Instruction Pursued at the Infant School, Meadow Street, Bristol* (London, 4th ed., 1825), pp. 117-25, *passim.*

[89]*Infant Poor* (1823), pp. 64-5. He was countered by Pole, who produced a similar number of Biblical texts which condemned corporal punishment (Pole, *Infant Schools,* p. 49).

[90]*Infant Poor* (1825), p. 208.

Another change was the use of monitors, which do not appear to have been used at New Lanark Infant School,[91] and which Wilderspin adopted from the beginning; perhaps he was following the example of Buchanan, though monitors were, of course, in universal use in National and British schools, to which they gave a generic name. Monitors were also a response to a large number of children, and though New Lanark Infant School contained over 100 children in its early days.[92] Owen was theoretically in favour of small numbers, holding that it was impossible "for one master to do justice to children when they attempt to educate a great number without proper assistance".[93] Wilderspin accepted large numbers as normal and indeed boasted that his system enabled a man and a wife simultaneously to teach two hundred infants.[94] Some, at least, of his practices — the gallery is a case in point — stemmed from the assumption that large numbers were a normal feature of infant schools.

A further difference centred on religious teaching. Owen treated its use in infant schools as an unavoidable necessity, whereas Wilderspin included it in the curriculum as a matter of principle. Owen, as we have seen, introduced religious teaching in deference to the wishes of the parents and his partners; his own views, particularly after 1817, were highly critical of Christianity. In August 1817 he had publicly declared it to be, with all other religions, a divisive force in society which ran counter to efforts at unity and co-operation.[95] Wilderspin, on the other hand, believed religion to be an essential part of education, though the morality he inculcated via Bible illustrations was closer to Owen's "sound practical morality" than the theological instruction later given in Church infant schools and with the adoption of which Wilderspin has been saddled by modern historians of education.[96]

One final difference concerned the status of the teacher. Owen, as a paternalistic proprietor, believed that the ideal infant teacher was one who would uncomplainingly take orders and carry them out to the letter. Whenever he left New Lanark for any period of time it was Owen's practice to give his teachers explicit orders and to check on their implementation on his return.[97] He was unable to perceive that this kind of "teacher training" would severely limit the number of rational infant schools that might be established. In fact he appears to argue that a thorough training from Owen himself, plus an ability to comprehend his science of society, were the essential equipment for the rational

---

[91]Cf. Smith, *Excursion in Scotland,* p. 63.

[92]According to the report of the Leeds delegation (*Leeds Mercury,* 4 Sept. 1819).

[93]P.P. 1816 IV, Education of the Lower Orders, p. 241.

[94]P.P. 1835 VII, Report from the Select Committee on Education in England and Wales, p. 29.

[95]Cf. esp. "Address Delivered at the City of London Tavern on Thursday, August 21st. . .1817", Owen, *Life,* 1A, pp. 115-16.

[96]*Infant Poor* (1824), p. 11; *Infant Education* (1825), p. 274.

[97]Owen, *Life,* 1, p. 138.

infant school teacher and hence the necessary basis for the formation of infant schools on the New Lanark model. Wilderspin, on the other hand, as a practising teacher, took the view that those in charge of infant schools should be persons of special abilities and distinction of personality. One of his most important contributions to infant education was his insistence on the fundamental importance of the character of the teacher.[98]

Wilderspin, despite his early connections with Owen and his willingness to construct his infant school on broadly Owenite lines, was no Owenite. "I must here candidly express my dissent from the theoretical and religious opinions of this gentleman", he wrote in 1829.[99] Nor, despite his presence in the Broughamite educational camp, was he a Malthusian or a Benthamite. Essentially he was a Swedenborgian and though Owen's "plan" remained the foundation of the English infant school, Swedenborg's educational theories provided much of the scaffolding around which he and Buchanan built their model. Swedenborg also opened the door to the ideas of Pestalozzi, which were to have a significant effect on Wilderspin's theory and practice. The following chapter will explore these themes.

[98] Cf. Chapter 10.

[99] *Infant Education* (1829), p. 51n.

CHAPTER 4

THE ENGLISH INFANT SCHOOL:
SWEDENBORG AND PESTALOZZI

One of the most interesting aspects of the English infant school movement is the preponderance of Swedenborgians among the first infant teachers. In addition to Buchanan and Wilderspin, the most important was David Goyder, a former printer, and brother of the minister at St. George's Fields Temple; a considerable but neglected figure in the early infant school movement, Goyder became superintendent of the third English infant school opened at Bristol in 1821. James Slade, a former brazier from Reading, and a member of St. George's Fields' congregation in Wilderspin's time, went to Bristol as master of Temple Infant School in 1825. William Carter, who began life as a Rutlandshire labourer, also found his way to St. George's Fields, where he was baptised a Swedenborgian in 1816 at the age of 23, taught in the Sunday school there and later took over an infant school in Chelmsford. These teachers retained close links with each other throughout the 1820s and all had their children baptised at St. George's Fields, despite their residence elsewhere.[1] J. Chalklen, who taught in London, was another New Churchman[2] and C.F. Lewis, first master of Alstone Infant School and later Wilderspin's agent, was at least exceedingly sympathetic to the doctrines of the sect.[3]

The attraction which infant teaching had for Swedenborgians can best be appreciated within the context of the millenarian movement which swept Britain during the half-century between 1790 and 1840. Millenarians of all shades of opinion looked forward to the second coming of Christ and the thousand-year reign of the saints on earth. Swedenborg, whose followers founded one of the strongest and most durable sects, believed he had been divinely commissioned to act as agent of a final revelation from God to mankind, the establishment on earth of the fifth or New Church, superseding what he termed the Most Ancient, Ancient, Hebraic and Christian Churches.[4] The Last Judgement, Swedenborg dramatically declared, had taken place in 1757; it was, however, a spiritual event, marking the end of the old, corrupt dispensation and the advent of the Church of the New Jerusalem and its Heavenly Doctrine. Similarly, the Second Coming was envisaged as occurring not in Person but in the Word, the unfolding to believers of new spiritual truths rather than the onset of terrestrial upheaval.[5]

[1] For biographical details of Goyder, Slade and Carter, cf. P.R.O. R.G. 4/4501, Register of Baptisms, New Jerusalem Chapel, St. George's Fields, 1816-34.

[2] According to J. Bayley, *New Church Worthies* (London 1884), p. 32.

[3] Wilderspin Papers, C.F. Lewis, *Letter to Mr. Thomas Bowller* (Cheltenham 1838).

[4] Cf. *Manual of the Doctrines of the New Church* (London 1879), p. 109; E. Swedenborg, *A Treatise Concerning Heaven and Hell* (London 1778), 327n. The number refers to the paragraph cited, as in all Swedenborg's works. Wherever possible, the first English edition is used.

[5] E. Swedenborg, *The New Jerusalem and Its Heavenly Doctrine* (London, 4th ed., 1792), 1-7; G. Trobridge, *Swedenborg: Life and Teaching* (London, 4th ed., 1945), pp. 135-38.

Swedenborgians thus felt themselves to be both part of the still-existing material world and also as experiencing the Millenium in spiritual form. In Swedenborg's words, "Man was created to be in both the spiritual and the natural world at the same time".[6]

The appeal of millenarianism, J.F.C. Harrison has argued, was on several levels.[7] It attracted, in particular, members of the artisan and lower middle-class (in Weber's view the *locus classicus* of religious radicalism) who, in a period of economic, political and social upheaval, might experience various forms of deprivation and insecurity, often in a personal manner. Dissatisfied with the ability of traditional social or religious dispensations to deal with the crises of the period, they turned to ideologies which promised a transformation of the world and the establishment of a purer, more humane socio-religious order. Intertwined with millenarianism were elements of popular religious belief concerned with signs, wonders and portents, a strain of "madness" which, Harrison suggests, was a form of repudiation of the rationalism of the Enlightenment espoused by established opinion. In the case of William Blake, influenced as he was by Swedenborg, it expressed itself in opposition to the unholy trinity of Bacon, Newton and Locke.

Blake's position was not without an element of irony. Swedenborg, a scientist and engineer in early life, embraced within his philosophy elements of seventeenth and early-eighteenth century rationalism and empiricism as well as the idealist cosmology of the later period. This reconciliation of the material and the spiritual originated in Swedenborg's own intellectual history.[8] In his studies at the University of Uppsala, from which he graduated in 1709 at the age of twenty-one, Swedenborg was strongly influenced by the philosophy of Descartes and the prevailing tendency to interpret the world in terms of mathematics and science. He spent the next fifteen years of his life studying the natural sciences in the leading countries of Western Europe and even after assuming his grandfather's post as Assessor of the Board of Mines in Sweden in 1724, he continued his studies in science and philosophy, publishing many books and treatises. He was, however, becoming increasingly dissatisfied with mechanistic science and more appreciative of the idealist theories of Malebranche and Leibniz; he began to transform the Cartesian machine into a spiritual organism and to give the concept of the soul increasing importance.

After his spiritual illumination in 1745 he abandoned his scientific interests and devoted the rest of his long life to the study of the Bible and the interpretation of the Scriptures on which his fame rests. His concern with the world and his encyclopaedic knowledge of the science and philosophy of the first half of the eighteenth century did not, however, wholly disappear in a cloud of

---

[6]Swedenborg, *New Jerusalem*, 36.

[7]This paragraph is based on J.F.C. Harrison, *The Second Coming* (London 1979), Chapter 8.

[8]The following paragraphs are based on Inge Jonsson, *Emanuel Swedenborg* (New York 1971), Chapters 1-6, *passim*.

angelic fantasies. His religion was related to life and many of his doctrines, particularly those pertaining to education, incorporate materialistic, mechanistic or empirical elements common to Enlightenment thought.[9] He divided all existing phenomena into the natural, the spiritual-rational and the divine[10] and, with an echo of the Cartesian dualities, postulated a correspondence between the natural and the spiritual world, not only in general but also in every particular. All natural things in the animal, vegetable and mineral kingdoms corresponded to "spiritual things in heaven".[11]

Early nineteenth-century critics of the New Church, particularly Robert Southey, tended to concentrate their attention on the more fantastic aspects of Swedenborg's spiritual experiences — his conversations with angels, his visits to the planets, his conception of Heaven as the Grand Man, and the like — and on these grounds to pronounce him mentally deranged. They also drew attention to the "splendid temples, vestments and modes of worship" which distinguished the New Church. They recognised, however, that the members considered these as of relatively minor importance and that the theology was the main attraction, appealing both to those who rejected the Christian (or Protestant) doctrines of evil, holiness, propitiation, predestination and justification by faith, and to those who sought a "love of the marvellous" or visions of futurity.[12]

The first infant teachers were cases in point. Buchanan was attracted by the grandeur and sweep of Swedenborg's visions and the bizarre symbolism which permeated his theology. Sarah Austin, wife of John Austin the jurist, who knew Buchanan well, spoke of his "innocent and holy dreams of Swedenborgian-ism".[13] He looked upon children as angels and saw evidence of Swedenborg's system of correspondence on country walks. "A straight fir", recalled Barbara Bodichon, "was the subject of a long discourse on a righteous man". Living much in the world of imagination, he would often "rush away to the land of dreams or alchemy", returning with "some copper chains which he asserted were gold because they had been seven times in the fire after some receipt in the Cabala".[14] David Goyder was attracted to the ritual of the New Church; from an early age, he manifested "the strongest desire to wear a surplice"[15] and eventually became a Swedenborgian minister. Wilderspin, though less demonstrative in his allegiance, did not always conceal his attachment to the millenarian ideal. In 1840 he wrote:

[9]Jonsson, *Swedenborg,* p. 131.

[10]*Ibid.,* p. 81.

[11]Swedenborg, *Heaven and Hell,* 104-10.

[12]R. Southey, *Letters from England* (London, 3 vol., 1807), III, Letter LXII; D. Bogue and J. Bennett, *History of Dissenters* (London, 4 vol., 1812), IV, Section II.

[13]U.C.L. Brougham Mss., 2292, Sarah Austin to Brougham, 21 Feb. 1851.

[14]B.I. Buchanan, *Buchanan Family Records* (Cape Town 1923), pp. 23-4.

[15]Obituary of D.G. Goyder, *Intellectual Repository,* Vol. XXV, No. 296, 1 Aug. 1878, p. 406.

There are some who think that this iron age is to be succeeded by the golden one, and much purification may be necessay on the surface of the earth, prior to its glorious commencement; it is to the young we must look to be the prime actors in these matters, and it is our duty in every point of view...to fit them for the mighty works which God will make them the mediums to perform.[16]

Nothing specific, however, is known of the extent of their knowledge of "the writings", as they were called, though we may surmise that their reading included those works by Swedenborg which were translated and published in their lifetimes. During the thirty years or so following the foundation of the New Church in the late 1780s, the works of Swedenborg in English translation enjoyed a minor boom; observers put their circulation at some 16,000 copies before 1812.[17] *Arcana Coelestia,* Swedenborg's major work, in which most of his observations and teachings on childhood were made, had appeared in translation during the years 1783-1806. *The Doctrine of Life* had reached five editions by 1810, *Conjugial Love* had twice been published by 1811, *Heaven and Hell* had gone through six editions up to 1817, and *The True Christian Religion* five by 1819; in addition there were numerous other editions of selections and minor works. One of Buchanan's favourite books was reputed to be by Swedenborg, though the title is not known.[18] Goyder came into the New Church following "a course of reading and diligent inquiry" concerning its doctrines,[19] and Wilderspin's position as clerk to a New Church minister had given him a unique opportunity to absorb the faith. It is possible that both Goyder and Wilderspin attended a course of lectures at the York Street chapel about the year 1808, given by Rev. J. Proud, in which he reiterated Swedenborg's views on child nature and the learning process; the printed version was certainly circulating in the New Church in the following years.[20]

Swedenborg's educational views reflected his philosophical position. His learning theory united elements of Lockean empiricism — sensory impressions of the natural world as the basis of knowledge — with the theories of speculative rationalism regarding the soul. He envisaged the educational process as developmental, proceeding from the blank mind via the principles of order, knowledge and truth to wisdom in God. The progression was broadly in line with Enlightenment theory; Swedenborg, however, added the concept of the soul, to which, he held, the sensory life aspires and which transformed sense data into ideas.[21] He believed that young children were basically innocent, as did Helvétius, Rousseau and others, though he regarded this innocence not as

---

[16] *System of Education* (1840), pp. 234-35.

[17] Bogue and Bennett, *History of Dissenters,* IV, p. 143.

[18] Buchanan, *Family Records,* p. 23.

[19] Goyder, Obituary, *loc. cit.,* p. 405.

[20] J. Proud, *Six Discourses Delivered to Young Men and Women* (London 1810), p. 15.

[21] Jonsson, *Swedenborg,* pp. 82-4; p. 131.

natural but as a gift from the Lord. There was, however, sufficient ballast of Enlightenment empiricism in Swedenborg's educational theories to provide a counterweight to the orthodox Christian position and to allow his followers to regard him as having affinities with Pestalozzi.

This provides the point of departure for an evaluation of his influence on the infant school movement in general and on Wilderspin in particular. On the question of the nature of the child, Swedenborg, in contradiction to the orthodox Christian view that human nature was tainted with sin by the fall of Adam, and to the harder Evangelical line that children were "beings who brought into the world a corrupt nature and evil dispositions",[22] maintained that infancy, the period from birth to five years, was a state of innocence and ignorance. One of the most striking aspects of Swedenborg's writings is the amount of attention he devoted to infancy and infants, and the sympathy and benevolence with which he regarded them, a circumstance that might go some way to explain the attraction of infant teaching for members of the New Church. The young child, in Swedenborg's system of correspondence, was the symbol of innocence.[23] A whole chapter in *Conjugial Love* was devoted to the theme "of the Conjunction of Conjugial Love with the love of infants".[24] The concept of infancy in *Heaven and Hell,* probably Swedenborg's most popular work, foreshadows that found in the poems of Blake rather than in Protestant treatises (especially the Evangelical variety) of the early nineteenth century.[25] Swedenborg's young children display innocence in their "looks, action and prattle"; they possess "no design or reflection", know "neither good nor evil", nor what is true or false, and have no love of self or the world, confining their affections to their parents, nurses or little companions.[26]

Swedenborg did not deny the presence of evil, but held that it existed in the world rather than in the nature of man. He maintained that man was acted upon by both good and evil influences; his rationality enabled him to discriminate between them, and his will was free to choose either. He could direct his energies towards living the good life in charity with his fellow men and with the love of God, or he chould choose to give rein to his self-love, sin against God, and embrace the evils of the world.[27] The potential for evil is present in the heredity of the child in the sense that a love of self and the world could be derived from the parents; but God had placed "celestial things" within the infant, who was

---

[22] H. More, *Strictures on the Modern System of Female Education* (London, 2 vol., 1799), I, p. 57. This work went through 11 editions in 12 years.

[23] E. Swedenborg, *Arcana Coelestia* (London, 12 vol., 1783-1806), 430.

[24] E. Swedenborg, *The Delights of Wisdom concerning Conjugial Love* (London 1794), 365-82.

[25] Cf. H. Melvill, *Religious Education: A Sermon* (London 1838), for a lugubrious account of the Evangelical attitude to infancy.

[26] Swedenborg, *Heaven and Hell,* 277.

[27] E. Swedenborg, *The Doctrine of Life for the New Jerusalem* (London, 4th ed., 1791), 19; *New Jerusalem,* 249; *Manual,* p. 35.

"withheld from evil and preserved in good by the Lord". Evil thus lay quiescent, as long as the child loved its parents and loved other children; innocence "remained" in the child's disposition until he grew up, when he was enabled to resist the evil of the world and to understand and practise the good and truth in civil and moral life.[28].

This powerful exposition of the innocence of childhood acted like a magnet on Swedenborgian teachers, drawing them irresistibly into opposition to the traditional Christian view and positively affecting their treatment of children. As Owen's son Robert Dale Owen observed, a child's nature was inherently imbued with neither wickedness nor rationality, but capable of displaying either according to the treatment he received from adults; the teacher who believed infants to be depraved and irrational would act in a way that would produce children whose behaviour would support his beliefs.[29] Buchanan and Wilderspin's professed love of children, and their attitude to them in the classroom, were sufficient evidence that they were animated by an outlook very different from the "intemperate religious zeal" of many teachers, which R.D. Owen saw as originating in Calvinism.[30]

In Wilderspin's case there is documentary evidence of his familiarity with Swedenborg's educational views. The most unequivocal Swedenborgian passage in his works is in the second (1834) edition of *Early Discipline*.[31] Incongruously inserted amid accounts of his travels, it provides strong evidence that not only did Swedenborg's ideas underlie his position on the upbringing of children, but also that he was a theoretical Swedenborgian during the height of his fame as an independent educator.

In a long passage addressed to mothers, Wilderspin uses the Swedenborgian doctrines of good and evil to argue for an education through the medium of the feelings. The dependence of the child on maternal love, and the mutual feelings it engendered was, he stated, "a beneficent disposition of Providence, designed at once to supply feelings of the purest and most intense delight, and form an indissoluble bond of love between the parent and offspring". He urged mothers not to neglect the development of their children's faculties in favour of an interest in pretty clothes or mental adornments. Children were active, thinking and feeling beings. The bodily powers of sight, touch and hearing were the instruments of superior faculties which we call the intellectual; mental powers were, however, but agents "acting under the influence of a yet higher impulse, that of the spiritual principle". This formulation echoed Swedenborg's account of the progression of man under

---

[28]Swedenborg, *Arcana Coelestia,* 164; 530; 561; 661; 1050; 1906; 2307; 4317; *New Jerusalem,* 175; cf. also W.D. Pendleton, *Foundations of New Church Education* (Bryn Athyn 1957), p. 74.

[29]R.D. Owen, *An Outline of the System of Education at New Lanark* (Glasgow 1824), pp. 66-8.

[30]*Ibid.,* pp. 65-6.

[31]*Early Discipline* (1834), pp. 171-75.

instruction from natural truths to intellectual truths and thence to celestial truths.[32] The highest state of the human character, Wilderspin continued, is found where the spiritual principle, directing the inferior powers, acts under the influence of what he termed Divine Light.

Taking Swedenborg's position on the question of evil, Wilderspin argued that man could exercise his faculties for good or for ill, and that only the misdirection of the affections could lead to moral evil; this was not essence, i.e. was not innate, for if it were, no good could be accomplished.[33] But the fruits of goodness could be produced only if "a germ of good were...placed by the Divine Power in the heart". Even so, "improper treatment" and "ungenial influences" could prevent the germ from fructifying. Only "sympathetical development", i.e. kindness and love, could achieve the aim. It was a principle of great possibilities for education. Hitherto, vain attempts had been made to operate on the feelings through the mind; now it was proposed "to operate on the mind through the medium of the feelings"; kindness and love would educate the head and the hand.

In his first book, which had traces of Evangelical terminology, Wilderspin had written that human beings were, "by nature", more inclined to evil than to good, and that children had "hereditary propensities" towards wrongdoing or vice.[34] Even so, he uses these terms in their Swedenborgian rather than their traditional sense. Children's evil inclinations, he argued, derived "hereditarily" from parents — he had seen children in the cradle imbibing "vicious principles" by imitating adult behaviour.[35] He points out, however, that children were equally capable of imitating good actions, and examples of virtuous behaviour — propriety, temperance, the provision of innocent amusement — by parent or teacher were the best antidotes to anti-social tendencies in children.[36] With the Doctrine of Remains in mind, Wilderspin postulated the existence of "a certain natural principle implanted even in the babe by the Creator", which he termed "the internal Conscience" and which, if fostered by parent or teacher, enabled the child to perceive the difference between right and wrong.[37] On several occasions he was to declare that children were basically good rather than evil,[38] and late in life he reflected that he had always had "a very favourable idea of poor human nature..."[39]

Swedenborg's theological position also played an important part in

---

[32] Swedenborg, *Arcana Coelestia*, 1495.

[33] The Christian answer was that the grace of God led to salvation, a doctrine the Swedenborgians repudiated.

[34] *Infant Poor* (1823), pp. 3-4; p. 122; p. 171.

[35] *Infant Poor* (1824), p. 82; p. 86.

[36] *Infant Poor* (1823), pp. 121-22.

[37] P.P. 1835 VII, Report of the Select Committee on Education in England and Wales, pp. 17-18.

[38] *Infant Education* (1829), pp. 142-43; P.P. 1835 VII, Education, p. 18; *System of Education* (1840), p. 24.

[39] *Wakefield and West Riding Examiner*, 20 Oct. 1849.

insulating the Swedenborgian teachers from Protestantism in any of its forms, and in providing them with an alternative orientation to that of their Christian patrons. At the same time, since Swedenborg claimed to have expounded "The True Christian Religion", it was difficult to depict them as anti-Christian. There were, however, important differences. Swedenborg's theological position hinged on his concept of the One Divine Person, Trinity in Unity, rather than that of Father, Son and Holy Spirit.[40] It followed that this necessitated a restatement of the doctrine of Atonement, for if there were not three persons in the Trinity, one could not offer himself as sacrifice to another. The concept of salvation was also called in question. Salvation, for Swedenborg, involved reformation of character, i.e. the replacement of external or natural man, devoted to the love of self and the world, by the internal or spiritual man, loving God and his neighbour in accordance with the precepts of faith; the only way this reversal could be affected was by regeneration from the Lord.[41] But as man had absolute spiritual freedom to choose good or evil (whose influence was held in perfect equilibrium by the Lord) salvation could not be attained without man's voluntary co-operation[42] — a view totally at variance with the orthodox Christian teaching of salvation of sinners by the grace of God. Swedenborg condemned hope of reward in heaven and fear of punishment in hell — so heavily stressed by Evangelicals — as impulses to salvation, as he did the adherence to priestly imperative and dogma.[43] "No one is reformed", he declared, "in states that are not of rationality and liberty".[44] The life that led to Heaven was not founded merely on compliance with Church ritual or withdrawal from the world, but one which led a person to a life of charity, which consisted of "acting honestly and justly in every employment, in every business and in every work".[45]

Wilderspin's general openness on religious matters, his benign view of the nature of young children, the omission from his writings and speeches of all reference to the Trinity, the Atonement, Redemption, Salvation and Sin (and the inclusion of only a few formal mentions of Jesus Christ as Saviour), his emphasis on the need for charity and love to one's neighbour, his rejection of "externals and trappings" and his insistence on good action and good conduct as the criteria of religion — all pointed to the permanent mark which Swedenborgianism had made on his thinking and beliefs. His insistence on non-denominational religious teaching also found support in Swedenborg,[46] though it is unlikely that Swedenborg was the sole inspiration.

[40] E. Swedenborg, *The True Christian Religion* (London, 2 vol., 1781), 1-15; Swedenborg, *New Jerusalem,* 288-90.

[41] Swedenborg, *New Jerusalem,* 161, 173, 179, 182.

[42] *Ibid.,* 143; *True Christian Religion,* 475-78; *Manual,* pp. 34-7.

[43] Swedenborg, *Arcana Coelestia,* 6478; 7318; *New Jerusalem,* 316; Trobridge, *Swedenborg,* p. 133.

[44] E. Swedenborg, *The Wisdom of Angels Concerning the Divine Providence* (London 1790), 138.

[45] Swedenborg, *New Jerusalem,* 123-24; *Heaven and Hell,* 535.

[46] Cf. *Manual,* iv.

Though Swedenborg's educational views, as will be shown in Chapter 9 and elsewhere, affected all aspects of Wilderspin's theory and practice, he never (as far as can be ascertained) admitted in public his New Church allegiance. Swedenborgianism was unacceptable to the Church and to the Evangelicals in particular,[47] and in 1818 the New Church had received unfavourable publicity when a person who had attended one of its temples was involved in a notorious murder case.[48] It is probable that Wilderspin felt that new methods of teaching, together with maintenance of non-denominationalism in religious instruction, was about as far as he could go and still maintain his position and his ambitions. In an age when the Anglican Church was striving to unite the nation and claiming the sole patent of educating the poor, even Dissenting teachers were under a cloud, and members of highly unorthodox religious sects even more at risk. James Brown, Wilderspin's brother-in-law, had been dismissed from the mastership of Brighton Infant School on the grounds that he was a Wesleyan Methodist preacher,[49] and according to Sarah Austin, James Buchanan's Swedenborgianism had lost him "the favour and countenance of the orthodox".[50] Wilderspin himself, despite his silence on the issue of Swedenborgianism found that his method of religious instruction brought him a sufficient amount of opposition, traduction and slander. "I well remember", he wrote later, "that when we invented our infant system it was said, that it was intended to undermine the established church".[51] Brougham, surveying over a quarter of a century of infant education, found that "the shadow of Westminster Abbey fell coldly on the dissenting teacher".[52] Wilderspin's attitude was always a prudent one; in 1825 he had felt it politic to state that he was a well-wisher towards the Established Church.[53] But prudence is not capitulation, and he maintained throughout his life a commitment to non-denominational education and an opposition to all religious dogmas and formularies.

* * * * *

The infusion of Owenite and Swedenborgian ideology had given the first English infant schools a direction which strongly attracted those groups and individuals who were themselves at odds with the orthodoxies of Church, state and social life or were members of minority religious sects or social movements. Until the mid-20s the Evangelicals, though striving for respectability, could be

[47]Bogue and Bennett, *History of Dissenters,* IV, p. 144.

[48]D.G. Goyder, *The Autobiography of a Phrenologist* (London 1857), p. 95 ff. Newspapers alleged that aspects of the Swedenborgian doctrine — "vile clay", "transitory world", etc. — had led to the murder.

[49]T.W. Mercer, *Co-operation's Prophet: the Life and Letters of Dr. William King of Brighton* (Manchester 1947), p. 176.

[50]U.C.L. Brougham Mss., 2292, Sarah Austin to Brougham, 21 Feb. 1851.

[51]*National Education* (1837), p. 37; cf. also *Stamford News,* 14 Jan. 1834.

[52]*Westminster and Foreign Quarterly Review,* Vol. LIV, Jan. 1851, p. 397.

[53]*Infant Education* (1825), vii.

included in the latter category, mainly because they were treated with hostility by the High Church. Certainly Zachary Macaulay, Thomas Babington and Joseph Wilson were willing to work with Dissenters and radicals of all kinds until the late 1820s.

Westminster and Spitalfields schools, financed respectively by a Unitarian and an Evangelical, set a precedent for sponsorship by the unorthodox. The third school at Bristol was superintended by a committee of ladies of various denominations, among whom were "several" Quakers and "many" Unitarians.[54] Dr. Lant Carpenter, the Unitarian divine, who was influenced by Pestalozzian ideas, and whose *Principles of Education,* published in 1820, incorporated some of the most advanced theories of the period,[55] was amongst the subscribers.[56] David Goyder's infant school at Liverpool, which he took over when he left Bristol in 1825, was organised and conducted by the Society of Friends.[57] The Evangelical clergyman William Wilson, Joseph's brother, founded a much-praised infant school at Walthamstow in 1824, organised and opened by Wilderspin. Shortly before this, Dr. William King, one of the earliest supporters of Co-operation, had brought Wilderspin to Brighton to set on foot a similar school.[58] In the same year Lady Powerscourt, a friend of the Irish Evangelical and Pestalozzian J.H. Synge (with whom she was to join in founding the Plymouth Brethren) opened an infant school on her estate in Ireland.[59] A member of the New Church, impressed by Spitalfields School, opened a similar one at Chelmsford in March 1825.[60] In 1824, James Pierpoint Greaves, a philosopher and mystic who subscribed to the theories of Swedenborg, Pestalozzi and Owen, had been appointed secretary of the newly formed Infant School Society.

Much of the publicity for infant schools in the early 1820s was also in the hands of individuals who stood outside the religious and educational mainstream. In this connection it is worth noting that all the reviews of Wilderspin's first book appeared in the Evangelical and Dissenting press.[61] Dr. Thomas Pole, author of *Observations Relating to Infant Schools,* published in

[54]Goyder, *Autobiography,* p. 113.

[55]Carpenter divided education into intellectual, moral and physical, based learning on sensation and perception, and argued that conduct was regulated by affections (L. Carpenter, *Principles of Education, Intellectual, Moral and Physical* (London 1820), *passim*).

[56]Second Annual Report of the Bristol Infant School (Bristol 1824), p. 6.

[57]J. Murphy, "The Rise of Public Elementary Education in Liverpool: Part Two, 1819-35", *Transactions of the Historic Society of Lancashire and Cheshire,* Vol. 118, 1966, p. 131.

[58]Cf. Chapter 5.

[59]Wilderspin Papers, Lady Powerscourt to Wilderspin, 29 June 1824.

[60]*Intellectual Repository,* N.S., Vol. I, No. VI, Apr. 1825, p. 517.

[61]*Evangelical Magazine,* Apr. 1823, p. 154; *Christian Guardian,* Apr. 1823, pp. 152-54; *Wesleyan Methodist Magazine,* 3rd Sers., Vol. II, Apr. 1823, p. 251; *Inquirer,* Vol. II, Apr. 1823, pp. 345-52; *Christian Observer,* Vol. XXIII, No. 5, May 1823, pp. 304-15; *Intellectual Repository,* Vol. VI, No. XLVII, July-Sept. 1823, pp. 466-71.

1823, a few months after Wilderspin's *Infant Poor,* was a Quaker physician at Bristol, and a friend of Brougham, William Allen and David Goyder, who published his book. The Evangelical Dr. Charles Mayo, who had taught at Pestalozzi's institution at Yverdon in the early 1820s, urged the importance of infant schools in speeches and pamphlets during the 1820s. A lesser-known but equally important publicist for infant education was Dr. Edward Biber, a young German refugee, a supporter of Pestalozzi and associate of Greaves. Another friend of Greaves, P.L.H. Higgins, who had taught at an infant school in the Hackney Road founded by David Goyder, wrote a Pestalozzian treatise on infant education which was published by Goyder and which previously had been printed (with some changes) by Wilderspin.[62] In 1826 the latter employed Martha Cowper, friend of Maria Edgeworth and later wife of the radical educational publicist Frederic Hill, to draw a series of charts on natural history for lecturing purposes.[63] Finally, Montague Burgoyne, a maverick Whig landowner, disciple of Pestalozzi and friend of Greaves, did much to establish and popularise infant schools in the mid-20s.

The early infant school movement thus attracted an unusually large number of "outsiders" — Evangelicals, Unitarians, Quakers, Plymouth Brethren, Swedenborgians, and progressives and radicals of various kinds, many of whom were also Pestalozzians.[64] They subscribed to, or were drawn along in the wake of, the many enthusiastic and millenarian sects who flourished in the period of evangelical awakening in the late eighteenth and early nineteenth century, not only in Britain but also, it is worth noting, in revolutionary France and westward-expanding U.S.A. Dissatisfied with the pieties of orthodox Christianity in an age of economic and social upheaval, they sought in various ways a purer and more absolute revelation. Those who looked forward to the sudden and total transformation of existing society by supernatural means, and the establishment of the Christian millenium on earth, formed part of a recognisable cultural milieu which embraced a number of ultra and unorthodox sects.[65]

[62]P.L.H. Higgins, *An Exposition of the Principles on which the Infant System of Education is Conducted* (London 1826).

[63]C. Hill, (Ed.), *Frederic Hill* (London 1894), pp. 190-91. Wilderspin's first contact with the Cowper family was in 1824 when a Mr. Cowper sent a present to Spitalfields Infant School which Wilderspin promised to use in his teaching. This could have been a drawing or poster. Wilderspin replied to "Mr. or the Misses Cowper" (J.R.U.L.M., English Ms. 386/3062, Wilderspin to the Cowpers, 24 May 1824).

[64]The infant school movement also attracted the "radical right" of millenarianism — Henry Drummond, who was a member of the committee of the Infant School Society, the Rev. Edward Irving who spoke at the first meeting of the Society and Lady Olivia Sparrow, who founded an infant school. They were all connected with Drummond's Albury Conferences (1826-1830) and their social and political sympathies were violently anti-progressive (cf. E. Miller, *The History and Doctrines of Irvingism* (London, 2 vol., 1878); A.L. Drummond, *Edward Irving and His Circle* (London, n.d.,? 1934); P.E. Shaw, *The Catholic Apostolic Church* (New York 1946).

[65]J.F.C. Harrison, *Robert Owen and the Owenites in Britain and America* (London 1969), p. 92 ff; C. Garrett, *Respectable Folly: Millenarians and the French Revolution in France and England* (Baltimore 1975), *passim*.

Many of the members of these sects and movements were what J.F.C. Harrison has called "spiritual entrepreneurs",[66] avid to sample heterodox philosophies and unusual modes of life. David Goyder, who began life as an Anglican, was converted to Swedenborgianism, took up in turn the ideas of Pestalozzi and the phrenologists, and ended up as a Freemason,[67] was a typical example, as was Greaves, exponent of Owenism, Swedenborgianism, Pestalozzianism and Transcendentalism, and who practised vegetarianism, communitarianism and the simple life. Wilderspin, though openly more conventional, also had a penchant for dabbling in unorthodox theories and for mixing with savants who subscribed to unfamiliar philosophies. Intellectual free trade between heterodox and millenarian groups was a characteristic feature of the period. United by a sense of dissatisfaction with existing society, each sect (the Evangelicals excluded) professed to find aspects of other philosophies with which they could identify. Thus Swedenborgians could admire Owen's principle that "love ought to be the connecting bond of human society and the influencing motive of human action".[68] Many New Churchmen found phrenology sufficiently attractive to enrol themselves among its "most efficient and strenuous supporters".[69] Some Owenites saw no fundamental difference between their outlook and those of the phrenologists.[70] David Goyder, when he joined the Freemasons at Accrington, found that the majority of the lodge were Swedenborgians.[71]

This alternative culture (as we would call it today) eddied and swirled around the early infant school movement, providing an ambience sharply different from orthodox pieties and at least one stage removed from the outlook of Brougham and his collaborators. Adherents of this culture, highly receptive to new ideas and movements and in sympathy with various aspects of social reform, saw in the infant school movement the beginning of a new era in education, based on a radical reassessment of child nature and pedagogical theory, and one which offered the possibility of social improvement by means of the transformation of the character of the individual child. Harrison has postulated a "commitment...to social change in some form" as a recurrent theme of millenarianism.[72] Simplistic theories which would view the establishment of infant schools merely as a movement to integrate sub-groups of

[66] Harrison, *Robert Owen*, p. 94.

[67] D.G. Goyder, *Lectures on Freemasonry* (London, 4th ed., 1864).

[68] *Intellectual Repository*, N.S., Vol. I, No. III, July 1824, p. 247.

[69] *New Jerusalem Magazine*, Vol. II, No. 8, Aug. 1827, pp. 243-44.

[70] W.H. Smith, "Remarks on the Application of Phrenology as a Test of the Practicability of Socialism", *Phrenological Journal*, N.S., Vol. 3, No. 10, 1840, p. 11-28.

[71] Goyder, *Autobiography*, pp. 216-17.

[72] Harrison, *Second Coming*, p. 222.

the population into the "national society",[73] must be questioned in the light of the above evidence. A significant group of supporters and teachers saw infant schools as the embodiment of philosophies of action and as a means of changing (if only partly) the existing situation.

* * * * *

Several supporters of the infant school movement in the early 1820s were, as we have seen, followers of Pestalozzi. The Swiss educator's influence on the early infant school movement, though apparent to contemporaries, has received little attention from educational historians; in particular, the extent to which Buchanan, Wilderspin and Goyder were affected by Pestalozzian theory has been overlooked. Yet each, in different ways, drew upon Pestalozzian ideas as a source of inspiration or as a reinforcement for existing practices. This becomes less surprising when we remember that the New Church was one of the earliest disseminators of Pestalozzian theory in Britain. As early as December 1818 the *Intellectual Repository* had published a long letter from J.P. Greaves, then teaching at Yverdon, which praised Pestalozzi's work, in particular his belief in the interior and exterior nature of man, the importance of the domestic circle, the education of the child's affections and the need to allow infants to develop according to their own nature.[74] This letter was the first of a number of pieces in the *Repository* which publicised the theories of Pestalozzi or drew attention to the similarity of his ideas to those of Swedenborg; "Further Confirmation of the Excellence of Pestalozzi's System of Education" (1821) may be taken as a typical title.[75]

Swedenborgian literature was, however, not the only channel for Pestalozzian ideas in the post-war years. With the lifting of impediments to European travel after 1815, a number of important educationists had visited Pestalozzi at Yverdon—Brougham, William Allen and Dr. Andrew Bell in 1816 and Robert Owen two years later. Only Allen, however, was sufficiently impressed to organize support for Pestalozzi's work on his return. The greatest contribution to the dissemination of the Swiss educator's theories and methods was made by a group of gentlemen Pestalozzians — John H. Synge, Dr. Charles Orpen and Dr. Charles Mayo among others — who were free enough or rich enough to travel to Yverdon, study the system and write about it on their return. The movement, if such it can be called, was confined to the unorthodox or eccentric, and never achieved the organisational level it was to do in the United

---

[73]Cf. the attempt to treat the contemporary Mechanics' Institute movement in this manner: I. Inkster, "The Social Context of an Educational Movement: A Revisionist Approach to the English Mechanics' Institutes, 1820-1850", *Oxford Review of Education*, Vol. 2, No. 3. 1976, pp. 277-307.

[74]*Intellectual Repository*, Vol. IV, No. XXVIII, Oct.-Dec. 1818, pp. 237-42.

[75]*Intellectual Repository*, N.S., Vol. IV, No. XXXII, Oct.-Dec. 1819, pp. 500-07; N.S., Vol. 5, No. XXXIII, Jan.-Mar. 1820, pp. 46-52; No. XXXVII, Jan.-Mar. 1821, pp. 303-04.

States, or became identified with nationalism and state education as in Prussia or the Netherlands.[76] As Synge noticed, Pestalozzi's theories met with "the prejudice which anything of this description is received from the continent by Englishmen".[77] In an effort to make Pestalozzi's ideas more palatable, both Orpen and Synge wrote imploring him to refute allegations that his system was not founded on Christianity and to state categorically that he considered children corrupt from birth.[78]

The writings of the Pestalozzians fell broadly into two categories: general expositions of theory, and manuals of method. The first included Synge's *Biographical Sketch* (1815), in which he drew attention to the use of the term "intuition" as a mode of learning, the threefold division of language, form and number as the basis of education and the way in which each could be taught concretely, proceeding from the simple to the complex;[79] a long and lucid article in the *Christian Observer* in July 1819, which demonstrated that Pestalozzi's method involved arranging and teaching a subject in accordance with the natural mode of apprehension of a child so that, motivated by his affection for his teacher, he was led to discover the truth as it presented itself;[80] and a number of other expository works by the Scotswoman Elizabeth Hamilton, Orpen, Mayo and others. The second category included Synge's own works on forms and on arithmetic (including Pestalozzi's number tables) and J.H. Pullen's rather desiccated sets of Pestalozzian exercises on the basic subjects.[81]

To later generations, familiar with Pestalozzi's own works and with detailed accounts of his theories, the strands of his thought available in the 1820s seem insubstantial as materials for adaptation to a theory of infant education, and the efforts of Buchanan, Goyder and Wilderspin must be appreciated in light of this. Some, at least, of this corpus of work must have been available to David Goyder when he was making himself "fully acquainted with the system of Pestalozzi" before opening Bristol Infant School. A teacher at the Swedenborgian Sunday School in St. George's Fields, Goyder was dissatisfied with his work as a printer, and was casting around for alternative employment, when he was informed by Buchanan that he might have the post of master at the infant school about to be built in Bristol; all that was necessary was one day per week training at Brewer's Green and "a careful study of Pestalozzi's works".[82] Goyder, a spiritual

---

[76]For a detailed account of the Pestalozzian movement in Britain, cf. K. Silber, *Pestalozzi: The Man and His Work* (London 1960), App. I, pp. 278-306; P.C. Williams, Pestalozzi John: a Study of the Life and Educational Work of John Synge, with Special Reference to the Introduction and Development of Pestalozzian Ideas in Ireland and England, unpublished Ph.D. thesis, Trinity College Dublin 1965.

[77]J.H. Synge, *A Biographical Sketch of the Struggles of Pestalozzi* (Dublin 1815), xvi.

[78]Silber, *Pestalozzi,* pp. 291-92.

[79]Synge, *Struggles of Pestalozzi, passim.*

[80]*Christian Observer,* Vol. XVIII, No. 7, July 1819, pp. 434-37.

[81]For a list of Pestalozzian works published in England at this period, cf. Appendix in Williams, Pestalozzi John.

[82]Goyder, *Autobiography,* p. 109; C. Higham, "The Rev. David Goyder's Work for Infant Education", *New Church Magazine,* Vol. XXIV, No. 406, Oct. 1915, pp. 445-50.

entrepreneur *par excellence,* not only mastered Pestalozzi,[83] but after opening Bristol Infant School in June 1821, spent his spare time in qualifying for the Swedenborgian ministry, attending lectures on phrenology and acquainting himself with the theories of Robert Owen.[84] His brother Thomas visited New Lanark in 1822,[85] and three years later he went himself, thereafter incorporating many of Owen's ideas into his teaching and declaring, with characteristic hyperbole, that he was indebted to Robert Dale Owen "for all the information I possess".[86]

To the standard features of the Buchanan-Wilderspin model — the wide curriculum,[87] teaching by alphabet cards and pictures, the chanting of tables, dancing, singing, the use of swings and toys, exercise in the playground (complete with flowers and trees) — Goyder added several features characteristic of his philosophical interests. From Swedenborg he took the aim of harmonising the will and the understanding; from Owen he borrowed military-style music as an aid to the "general formation of character"; he drew on phrenological analysis to guide him in the choice of monitors; and the influence of Pestalozzi — "my great model" — could be seen in the use of unit tables for teaching arithmetic and in the exercise of children's memories "by short conversations after the manner of Pestalozzi".[88] Bristol Infant School was undoubtedly a lively place, and visitors were rarely bored; some wept with emotion at the children's rendering of the Hallelujah Chorus,[89] while others were appalled by the noise and the dust.[90] But the school was an outstanding example of the new type of institution and from early 1822 Goyder began founding other schools in its image in the Midlands, the West Country and, in 1825, in Dublin; in 1826 he reorganized the Quaker Infant School in Liverpool, introducing many of the principles he had learned at New Lanark.[91]

It would have been difficult for Wilderspin to have escaped the influence of Pestalozzi. In addition to his friendship with Buchanan and Goyder, he was

---

[83]Goyder would have studied only the secondary literature, for he later declared that when he opened the Bristol school he had not seen or read a line of Pestalozzi's works. None, in fact, were available in translation in 1821. (R.E.D. (i.e. D.G. Goyder), "The Pestalozzian System of Education", *New Jerusalem Magazine,* No. 12, Dec. 1828, p. 378n).

[84]Goyder, *Autobiography,* pp. 109-13; Obituary, *loc.cit.,* pp. 404-08.

[85]R. Hindmarsh, *Rise and Progress of the New Jerusalem Church* (London 1861), p. 394.

[86]*Dawn of Light and Theological Inspector,* Mar. 1825, p. 92.

[87]D.G. Goyder, *A Treatise on the Management of Infant Schools* (London 1826), pp. 50-67. Astronomy was taught by observation, biography, history and natural history with the aid of pictures and geography by means of maps.

[88]D.G. Goyder, *A Manual of the System of Instruction Pursued at the Infant School, Meadow Street, Bristol* (London, 4th ed., 1825), v-vi; p. 29; *passim; Autobiography,* p. 114; p. 116; p. 120; p. 125.

[89]Goyder, *Manual,* p. 12 n.

[90]*Bath and Cheltenham Gazette,* 21 June 1825.

[91]Goyder, *Autobiography,* pp. 190-91.

acquainted with Brougham and Owen,[92] who had visited Yverdon, and with Mayo and Greaves who had taught there.[93] It was Greaves, however, from whom he took most of his ideas. He first met him in July 1824, when the newly-founded Infant School Society had informed the public that all applications for information should be addressed to Greaves at the School House, Quaker Street.[94] He spent at least part of his time there, on friendly terms with Wilderspin — they had a common interest in Swedenborgianism — and acting as secretary-cum-public relations officer for the Society.[95]

Greaves had been born in Merton, Surrey, in 1777, the son of a rich city merchant; he had given up his interest in commerce at the age of thirty following financial reverses and taken up the study of Swedenborg and Boehm. In 1817 or 1818 he came across some of Synge's works on Pestalozzi, was converted to his views and travelled to Switzerland where he became a teacher at Pestalozzi's school at Yverdon for five years. He later took up University posts at Basle and Tubingen, but in 1824 was ordered to leave by the Wurtemberg government, allegedly for spreading subversive doctrines among his students.[96] "He had some peculiar opinions", observed John Minter Morgan, the Owenite philanthropist, "resembling the German mystical and metaphysical speculations, hard to be understood, and to which few, in general, are willing to listen and still fewer to subscribe; but his sincerity and the kindness of his disposition always secured for him a patient hearing".[97]

The first sign of Greaves' influence on Wilderspin's thinking was in 1825, when he included in the third edition of his book *Infant Education* an appendix containing "Pestalozzian" answers to a set of "Questions That Have Been Asked Concerning Infant Schools".[98] Greaves' hand in the formulation of the answers is attested by the addition of his name to the virtually identical Pestalozzian catechism published by P.L.H. Higgins the following year, referred to in an earlier section. The new note was struck in the first question and answer. The use of an infant school was now declared to be the development of all the powers of the mind at a much earlier period than had hitherto been considered possible and thus to prepare the children for "moral progress". As the fundamental principle

---

[92]Owen thought that Pestalozzi's theory was good, but that his principles were those of the old system (Owen, *Life*, I, p. 177). The Pestalozzian influence on New Lanark Infant School is difficult to detect; his mental arithmetic was taught in the higher school in 1824 (Owen, *Outline*, p. 40). But Goyder felt that "everything" at New Lanark was Pestalozzian (Goyder, *Autobiography*, p. 188).

[93]For Wilderspin's acquaintanceship with Mayo, an early visitor to Spitalfields, cf. *Infant Education* (1852), p. 7.

[94]*Morning Chronicle*, 5 July 1824.

[95]*Infant Education* (1825), p. 171; *Early Discipline* (1832), p. 252.

[96]This account of Greaves' life is based on *D.N.B.;* F.E. Buisson, *Dictionaire de Pédagogie et D'Instruction Primaire* (Paris, 14 tome, 1882-87) 1er Partie, Tome Second, p. 3024; E. Martin, "Greaves, Un Disciple Anglais de Pestalozzi", *Revue Pédagogique*, N.S., Tome IX, No. 11, 15 Novembre 1886, pp. 430-41; Williams, *Pestalozzi John*, pp. 159-60; p. 188.

[97]J.M. Morgan, *Hampden in the Nineteenth Century* (London, 2 vol., 1834), II, p. 23.

[98]*Infant Education* (1825), App., pp. 273-85.

of the infant school was love, the children should be invited to regard the master as one desirous of promoting their happiness "by the most affectionate means" — chiefly by checking the growth of every evil tendency and encouraging the growth of all that is estimable, by banishing a fondness for "the delusive pleasures of the world" (a typical Greaves touch). There would be no rewards — children would find their chief delight in continually seeking their own improvement — and no punishment for disobedience, which would "sufficiently punish itself"; the only exception was "a trivial punishment" as mild as possible, if children were disobedient when they first entered the school (a typical Wilderspin reservation). Children were assumed to possess an "intuitive" power independent of outside circumstances. Young children, it was held, could best be educated by the use of "external natural objects", which would lead to habits of observation, thought and expression. Memory should not be the chief faculty employed and mutual instruction ought to be confined to the merely mechanical aspects of teaching.

Some of these formulations were expressive of views and practices that Wilderspin had already developed independently. But the manner of expression and the wording of many of the concepts were new and offered exciting prospects to the infant teacher. Wilderspin had merely attached the questions to the text in the 1825 edition of his book; four years later he was to include a far more sophisticated theory of learning in the text of the fourth edition, again under the influence of Greaves.[99] Meanwhile Greaves and his associates continued their work of adapting Pestalozzian ideas to infant education. In 1827 Greaves helped to produce the English edition of Pestalozzi's *Letters on Education* and the following year issued a prospectus for a Pestalozzian infant school to be established in Holborn,[100] and (with Montague Burgoyne of the Infant School Society and G.E. Biber) founded one in Shoreditch.[101] He helped Biber edit the *Contrasting Magazine,* which contained extensive extracts from the works of Owen, Swedenborg and Pestalozzi, and a number of quasi-Pestalozzian "Maxims for Infant Schools". Biber, also a former teacher at Yverdon,[102] arrived in England in 1826, became a tutor, interested himself in a newspaper, lectured on education, and issued a prospectus for a Pestalozzian Institution, using the address of the Infant School Society at 15 Bucklersbury.[103] In the later 1820s he published a Pestalozzian journal called the *Christian Monitor* and in 1831 the long and somewhat turgid *Henry Pestalozzi and His Plan of Education.*

[99] Cf. Chapter 9.

[100] *Co-operative Magazine,* Vol. 3, No. 2, Jan. 1828, pp. 29-31.

[101] *World,* 2 Jan. 1828.

[102] For details of Biber's life, cf. *D.N.B.*

[103] "New-Pestalozzian Institution". Prospectus dated 27 June 1827.

It is hardly surprising to find, before the end of the 1820s, a general feeling that the infant school movement was an embodiment of the ideas of the Swiss reformer. Dr. Mayo was writing that some of Pestalozzi's "fondest expectations" were being kindled in infant schools;[104] the *World,* a London newspaper, considered that the movement was carrying into effect the Pestalozzian system.[105] Wilderspin, in 1829, was also aware that many were saying that the infant school movement was Pestalozzian in inspiration.[106] The main negative effect was to arouse the hostility of Tory-Anglican opinion, a trend to which the Infant School Society was to succumb. Positively, however, the infusion of new ideas from the continent — those of Swedenborg no less than those of Pestalozzi — was evidence of the vitality of the infant school movement and its development along the lines laid down by Owen, and some way beyond. Once again it is necessary to query the view that the early English infant school was rigid, theological and intellectually oppressive.

[104]C. Mayo, *Memoir of Pestalozzi* (London, 2nd ed., 1828), p. 3.

[105]*World,* 28 Nov. 1827.

[106]*Infant Education* (1829), viii.

CHAPTER 5

THE INFANT SCHOOL SOCIETY

On 3 June 1824 an advertisement appeared in the *Morning Chronicle*, inserted by "a number of gentlemen", inviting those who supported "the care and education of the INFANT CHILDREN of the LABOURING CLASSES" to a general meeting for considering the best means of extending the system of infant schools. Ladies and gentlemen, it added, who were desirous of satisfying themselves about the nature and advantage of existing schools were invited to visit those at Quaker Street and Vincent Square.[1] The advertisement was also circulated in the form of a leaflet which was printed, obviously at Wilderspin's instigation, by the Philanthropic Society, St. George's Fields.[2]

The gathering was duly held on 7 June at the Freemasons' Tavern, Great Queen Street, the central meeting place of the philanthropic movement before the opening of Exeter Hall in the early 1830s. The hall was described by an American visitor, the Rev. Nathaniel Wheaton, as "an elegant apartment, capable of holding one thousand persons"; it had a gallery and organ at one end for concerts and a platform at the other.[3] "A very numerous and highly respectable meeting", observed the *Courier*, "among which were not less than seven or eight hundred elegantly dressed ladies".[4] Many of these, the *Chronicle* stated, were members of the Society of Friends.[5] The expenses of the meeting, according to Wilderspin, were covered by Joseph Wilson.[6]

"I never attended so interesting a meeting in the whole course of my life", declared Wilderspin somewhat hyperbolically,[7] impressed by the fact that some of the foremost orators and public men of the day were devoting attention to infant education. The speakers included Lord Lansdowne, who took the chair, Henry Brougham, John Smith, Sir James Mackintosh and William Wilberforce. The basic theme of the meeting was expressed by Lansdowne and elaborated by nearly all the other speakers: that infant schools would give the children of the poor "principles of virtue" and save them from growing up into perpetrators of "the most atrocious and injurious crimes". Separation of the children from their parents was justified on the grounds of the latter's supposed lack of the essential familial virtues. John Smith and William Allen, both of

[1] *Morning Chronicle*, 3 June 1824.

[2] J.R.U.L.M., English Ms. 386/3062, leaflet entitled "Infant Schools" (n.d.), attached to letter from Wilderspin to the Cowpers, 24 May 1824.

[3] N.S. Wheaton, *A Journal of a Residence During Several Months in London...in the Years 1823 and 1824* (Hartford 1839) p. 224.

[4] *Courier*, 8 June 1824.

[5] *Morning Chronicle*, 8 June 1824; the following paragraphs are based on this report.

[6] Ms. Revisions, *Early Discipline* (1840), p. 3.

[7] *Infant Education* (1825), p. 9.

whom had visited New Lanark, were the only speakers to touch upon the pedagogical aspects of the new institutions. Human character, they argued, was formed "much earlier than might be supposed"; therefore principles of human kindness and assistance were practised in order to destroy selfishness; the power of love would give the child confidence before its faculties were called into action.

At the end of the meeting a subscription of some £700 was collected (including contributions from Robert Owen and Dr. Charles Mayo)[8] and a committee of twenty-five elected, which had much the same complexion as that of the Westminster Infant School. Nine members of the Westminster committee were, in fact, elected to the new body: Henry Brougham, M.P., Sir Thomas Baring, M.P., Lord Dacre, Henry Hase, Zachary Macaulay, James Mill, Benjamin Smith, John Smith, M.P., and Joseph Wilson. The other members included William Allen, the Quaker chemist; Dr. George Birkbeck, founder with Brougham of the London Mechanics' Institute; John Bowring, Utilitarian, businessman and editor of the *Westminster Review;* the Evangelical Fowell Buxton, M.P., the Spitalfields brewer; the Evangelical Stephen Lushington, M.P., and Sir James Mackintosh, then a leader of the law reformers. The remainder of the committee, mostly City bankers, financiers and merchants, would appear to have been chosen as much for their potential financial contribution as for their interest in education: Henry Drummond (an Irvingite), Henry Entwistle, William Evans, M.P., the Quaker Samuel Gurney, George Hammersley, Samuel Hoare, Jr. (another Evangelical), Sir Gregory Lewin, Samuel Jones Loyd, M.P., Sir John Lubbock and John Abel Smith (son of John Smith).[9]

Ten of the committee were or had been prominent members of the societies concerned with the criminal laws or juvenile delinquency; twelve of the Committee were Evangelicals, Dissenters or members of unorthodox religious sects; eighteen were financiers, merchants, bankers or members of families with these connections.[10] In fact, so obvious was the City connection that the *Morning Chronicle* welcomed the formation of the Society with the observation that "a conviction seems to be fast gaining ground in this country that the well-being of the labouring classes is essential to the security of the rich".[11]

[8]*Morning Chronicle,* 5 July 1824.

[9]The list of the committee is given in *Morning Chronicle,* 24 June 1824.

[10]Information derived from *D.N.B.,* biographies and autobiographies, and reports of relevant societies. Changes in the Committee at the 1825 conference did not greatly alter the picture; Gurney, Hase, Hoare, Loyd and James Mill gave way to Thomas Spring Rice and Montague Burgoyne, Whig landowners, Richard Wellesley, banker, Henry Blanshard and James Morrison, merchants, and John Marshall, industrialist. (Wilderspin Papers, Infant School Society. The Annual Report read at the First Anniversary Meeting...June 4th, 1825, p. 3).

[11]*Morning Chronicle,* 8 June 1824. Cf. the observation of the Scottish educationist, Mrs. Elizabeth Hamilton, that "many of those who take no further interest in the education of the lower orders than as it affords additional security to property" and on whom higher motives would have had little influence, had become friendly to the education of the poor on this basis. (Elizabeth Hamilton, *Hints Addressed to the Patrons and Directors of Schools* (London 1815), pp. 144-45n).

The direction of the infant school movement was, in fact, in the hands of the alliance of advanced Whigs, Evangelicals, Dissenters and Utilitarians which had been active for a dozen or more years in various reform movements: in the extension of non-denominational education to the poor; in the reduction of crime by reform of the criminal law and of prison discipline; in the alleviation of poverty by practical philanthropy, and in the crusade against slavery and the slave trade. The social weight of this group was centred on the commercial and financial upper middle-class of the metropolis and their professional associates. In social origin, politics, religion and education they were outside the traditional ruling-class elite; they stood left of the line that divided merchant and financier from landed gentry, Evangelical and Dissenter from High Churchman, Whig or Radical from High Tory and the non-University man from the classically-educated Oxbridge graduate. They were well known to each other in the House of Commons and the City, accustomed to meet socially and in many cases connected by marriage.[12] William Allen's journal *The Philanthropist* (succeeded by *The Inquirer,* 1822-23) provided an informal forum for the group with articles on education, crime, philanthropy and the anti-slavery movement and contributions by or about figures as diverse as Owen, Wilberforce and Bentham.

The Society's Address to the Public, issued in July 1824, reflected an awareness of the conflict which faced the Society. On the one hand the Tories and High Church, averse to reform of the criminal law, uninterested in the tract and soup-kitchen brand of philanthropy, hostile to Dissent, and convinced that the Established Church was the sole agency for the education of the poor, could bring heavy artillery to bear against this kind of organisation. On the other, the radical pedagogues who permeated the infant school movement were advancing ideas and practices which could not be ignored. Thus the Address began with a picture of urban conditions no conservative could deny — "streets, lanes, and alleys...crowded with squalid children" left to acquire "habits of idleness, violence and vice" and virtually out of the control of harassed parents. The need for infant schools for children of the poor was then stressed; these institutions would relieve mothers of the "incumbrance" of the infants, allowing them greater liberty to pursue some gainful occupation for the benefit of the family.

The Address continued, however, with a laudatory description of the methods and practices found in the new schools. They would have greatly improved facilities and teaching methods, "an airy and spacious apartment", a playground and a properly-selected master and mistress whose qualities — patience, mildness, equability of temperament and so on — were considered at length; under guidance of these teachers would flourish "activity and amusement...intellectual improvement and moral discipline". Teaching methods would include the use of pictures, which stimulated curiosity and other faculties "without the necessity of resorting to any harsh measures or of

[12]Fowell Buxton and Samuel Gurney were brothers-in-law, as were Babington and Macaulay; Hoare married into the Gurney family; the Hanburys linked William Allen and Fowell Buxton in both marriage and business.

imposing *any strain* on their faculties", an issue on which some criticism had been levelled against infant schools; play, it was pointed out, would occupy the larger part of the infants' time.

But to give attention to educational innovation alone was to sail dangerously close to Owenite waters and to the position of appearing to advocate too rich an educational diet for the children of the poor. So the address made a tack in the direction of religious instruction, adroitly avoiding the rock of undenominationalism that stood in the way. Useful knowledge, it was asserted, and the temporal advantages to be derived from education, were less important than the elimination of "vicious propensities" and the formation of the temper and moral character of the children, which comprehended the habits of "cleanliness and decorum, of cheerful and ready subordination, of courtesy, kindness and forbearance, and of abstinence from everything impure or profane". These qualities would be "rendered permanent" by principles of religion — reverence towards the Creator, acquaintance with the leading truths of revealed religion and examples of piety and benevolence in the Scriptures. The Address ended on a practical note:

> The special object for which this Society has been formed is to establish, in some central part of the metropolis, an infant school which may exemplify the principles now explained; and which, while it dispenses its benefits to the adjoining population, may also serve as a model of imitation with respect to its mechanism, and as a seminary for training and qualifying masters and mistresses to form and superintend similar institutions.[13]

Despite its relative caution and the somewhat incongruous juxtaposition of Benthamite and Evangelical ideas with the progressive pedagogy of the Owen-Buchanan-Wilderspin type, the Address on the whole marked an advance in English educational thought. It recognised the importance of the early childhood years, the possibility of a new type of education for this age group, the need for teachers of a special quality, the provision of activity, amusement, creative learning and moral instruction, and the desirability of non-denominational religious instruction. In doing so, it went far beyond the perspectives of all previous types of schools for the poor.

The freshness of many of the Society's educational principles, the calibre of its sponsors and its more-than-adequate financial support, seemed to augur a promising future. Yet within four years of its foundation it had succumbed to the powerful opposition it aroused, deserted by its leading figures, its coffers empty, its secretary dismissed and its objectives, particularly that of the establishment of a central model school, unfulfilled. The story of the decline and fall of the Infant School Society, unexplored by educational historians, is important not only for the effect it was to have on Samuel Wilderspin's career, but also in relation to the developing structure and content of English education. Furthermore, the

---

[13]H.R.O. Calthorpe Papers, 26M62 F/C 852, leaflet entitled "Infant School Society", dated 16 July 1824. The Address was reproduced in the *Christian Observer,* Vol. XXIV, No. 8, Aug. 1824, pp. 522-24.

opposition it encountered gives some indication of the lengths to which those who hated or feared a "progressive" breakthrough in the education of the poor were prepared to go.

* * * * *

When the Infant School Society, on its formation, was looking for a person "to go into the country, at the request of any lady or gentleman, to open schools according to the method now in practice",[14] the choice naturally fell upon Wilderspin. The post was in accord with his aspirations. After only a few years in East London, he had begun to regard himself less as a teacher employed by a wealthy patron and more as the originator of a system of infant education which could be applied on the widest scale. One reason for this had been the number of requests he had received to open schools similar to Spitalfields. The first request was from William Allen, whose school at Stoke Newington Wilderspin opened on 1 April 1822.[15] Invitations followed from Hackney, Peckham, Camberwell and other places.[16] Early in 1824 he organised a school in Brighton for William King, the Co-operator,[17] followed by one at Walthamstow for his patron's brother, the Rev. William Wilson.[18] Lord Calthorpe and Sir John Lubbock also made use of his services at their country seats in the same year.[19] Another reason, as we have seen, had been the publication of his first book *On The Importance of Educating the Infant Children of the Poor* in 1823.

During his absences in the country, the burden of running the school, and receiving the numerous visitors, fell upon his wife Sarah, assisted by their eldest daughter.[20] The strain proved too much, however, and worn out by the combined effects of housework, school supervision and the bearing and raising of a large family — six children were born between 1813 and 1824 — Sarah Wilderspin died on 4 October 1824, aged only 37, shortly after the birth of her son Samuel.[21] A thousand of the local inhabitants attended the funeral, many of the women wearing black ribbons in their bonnets, and almost every house on Quaker Street was closed for the occasion.[22] The death of his wife, followed at

[14]The wording was in a footnote to the Address of 1824.

[15][W. Allen], *Life of William Allen* (London, 2 vol., 1857), II, p. 30.

[16]*Early Discipline* (1832), p. 9.

[17]T.W. Mercer (Ed.), *Dr. William King and the Co-operator, 1828-1830* (Manchester 1922), xii-xx; T.W. Mercer, *Co-operation's Prophet: The Life and Letters of Dr. William King of Brighton* (Manchester 1947), p. 5; *Early Discipline* (1832), p. 18.

[18]*Early Discipline* (1832), pp. 20-21. The Walthamstow school was opened in March 1824 (P.P. 1834 IX, Report from Select Committee on the State of Education, p. 167).

[19]Wilderspin Papers, Lord Calthorpe to Wilderspin, 13 Oct. 1824; *Early Discipline* (1832) pp. 10-12.

[20]Young Papers, T.U. Young, "Memoir of the Late Mrs. Young" (Ms. II); *Infant Poor* (1823), p. 168.

[21]*Dawn of Light and Theological Inspector,* No. 1, Jan. 1825, p. 32; *Early Discipline* (1832), p. 26.

[22]*Early Discipline* (1832), pp. 22-5.

Christmas-time by the death of his five-month old son Samuel,[23] brought about a physical breakdown in Wilderspin's health. On his recovery, early in 1825, he decided to leave Spitalfields, despite his attachment to the people and the neighbourhood,[24] and to take up full-time work as the Society's agent, with the position of master of the projected model school in prospect.

The Society's committee, at its first meeting on 1 July 1824, had appointed Quaker Street Infant School as "the temporary place for the instruction of Masters and Mistresses for other schools", pending the building of a model school, and invited the public to apply for information to Mr. J.P. Greaves at the same address.[25] That Quaker Street should be preferred to Vincent Square was not only a tribute to Wilderspin's systematic methods but also perhaps symptomatic of the prejudice against Buchanan, which had been noticeable among many members of the Westminster Infant School Committee. The word "temporary", however, seemed to be capable of a wide meaning. The Society's first annual report of 4 June 1825 (which, according to Wilderspin, had been drafted by the young Thomas Babington Macaulay)[26] admitted failure to make even a beginning with the proposed central model school; a suitable piece of ground had not been found, despite "public advertisement and...personal search", each of the various sites examined having had some "capital defect" which deterred the committee from securing it. During the year, however, William Wilson's school at Walthamstow was also brought into use for teaching "the mechanical parts of the system" to such masters and mistresses who might be sent there for instruction.[27]

More importantly, the report revealed that Wilderspin had been selected as master of the projected central model school. "I blest my stars", said Wilderspin to himself, "that an opportunity was likely to be afforded of concentrating my views, and practically shewing and working out by degrees, a System fit for general adoption".[28] As the institution was, however, still in the planning stage, the Committee had decided, as previously announced, to divert a part of the money subscribed for its construction "to a somewhat different purpose" by employing it in sending Wilderspin to give teachers in the provinces "the information which he would have communicated to them in London had that school been erected".[29]

Wilderspin's travels on behalf of the Society were viewed as a temporary measure, a substitute, in fact, for his role as master of a model training

---

[23]The child was buried on 27 December 1824 (Burial Registers, Christ Church, Spitalfields, 1820-25).

[24]*Early Discipline* (1832), pp. 25-6.

[25]*Morning Chronicle,* 5 July 1824.

[26]Ms. Revisions, *Early Discipline* (1840), v.

[27]Infant School Society. Annual Report 1825, p. 1.

[28]*Educational Magazine,* Vol. 1, June 1835, p. 413.

[29]Infant School Society. Annual Report 1825, p. 2.

establishment, and as the years passed without a sign of a beginning being made on the school, he began to realise that his future was in question. "I was superintendent of a castle in the air", was his rueful comment.[30] The castle remained unbuilt. In the 1827 Report of the Society apologies again were made for the failure of the Committee to find a suitable site for the building which would not involve the Society in expenses it could not meet. It was small consolation to Wilderspin to learn that his position as "travelling agent" had been regularised; a move which the Report somewhat unnecessarily characterised as "a new feature of the proceedings which was not contemplated at the first formation of the Society".[31] As a sop to the subscribers, the same Report announced the establishment of two additional *ad hoc* model schools. One was at Baldwin's Gardens, Grays Inn Lane, which was apparently organised by Wilderspin;[32] the other was Buchanan's school at Westminster which was to be adapted at "considerable expense" but, as we shall see, without Buchanan.[33]

Despite the talk of "considerable expense", the utilisation of the schools at Quaker Street, Vincent Square, Walthamstow and Baldwin's Gardens as temporary model schools was an expedient, and involved a smaller outlay than the purchase of land and the erection of a new building. Wilderspin, at a later date, estimated that an institution capable of providing accommodation for thirty teachers in training would have cost £5,000 to build and £1,200 per year to run.[34] Not an impossible sum, if the bankers and merchants on the Society's committee had bestirred themselves, but one which they found the utmost difficulty in raising. The Report of 1827 revealed that in the previous two years subscriptions had amounted only to £244; added to the 1825 balance of £993, the Society's total income in its first three years of existence amounted to £1,237. When the expenditure of £1,048 was deducted, a meagre balance of £189 was left.[35]

The Society's income compared very unfavourably with that of other philanthropic bodies. In 1822 the National Society had received in subscriptions £2,500, the British and Foreign School Society £2,054 and the Sunday School Union £1,747; even organisations with aims as limited as that of Merchant Seamen's Bible Society (£649 in subscriptions) or the Irish Society of London (£403) exceeded in one year the Infant School Society's total income between 1825 and 1827, while the receipts of the great missionary bodies — the British

[30] P.P. 1835 VII, Report from the Select Committee on Education in England and Wales, p. 37.

[31] *World*, 27 June 1827.

[32] The school at Baldwin's Gardens was mentioned in the correspondence between Wilderspin and Bilby and Ridgway in the *Educational Magazine*, Vol. II, July 1835, pp. 58-9; Vol. II, Aug. 1835, p. 153.

[33] *World*, 27 June 1827.

[34] P.P. 1835 VII, Education, p. 33.

[35] *World*, 27 June 1827. Wilderspin stated that the sum of £1,048 had been spent on "paying a secretary, and the rent of an office in London, and printing, and my salary". (P.P. 1835 VII, Education, p. 37).

and Foreign Bible Society (£97,063) and the Church Missionary Society (£32,265) — were of different order entirely.[36]

* * * * *

Several factors might have discouraged the orthodox and respectable from supporting or subscribing to a society, particularly an educational society, in the 1820s: allegations of progressive or experimental principles, rumours of a "liberal" or "scientific" orientation, or, worst of all, doubts about its religious *bona fides*. The Infant School Society had the misfortune to run up against all three obstacles. At the second meeting in 1825 Lord Calthorpe mentioned "objections" raised against it, and Smith spoke of the "calumnies" it had encountered.[37] Wilderspin was characteristically more forthright and colourful. "The prejudices against this visionary scheme were great", he wrote, "it was prophesied that we were going to undermine all *existing institutions*". The new pedagogy was attacked and ridiculed:

> A gentleman from the pulpit designated the Infant System as *fashionable folly,* and wrote a pamphlet against it also; others said the schoolmaster was abroad with a vengeance — the whole thing was turned into ridicule by the wiseacres who had never studied the infant mind; and the consequence was that the *Standing Committee* could not *stand it,* and they left your humble servant to come in for his full share of *sneers.* Some persons said that any man who would assert that infants might be taught ANYTHING at eighteen months old, must be disordered in the *upper regions.* . .[38]

In Wilderspin's opinion, much of this opposition came from the clergy of the Established Church, the majority of whom, he stated in 1835, were opposed to the first infant schools.[39] It is certainly true that the great majority of the clergy, traditional guardians of the people's education, either held aloof from the infant school movement or actively opposed it; the National Society, the educational arm of the Church of England, refused to interest itself.[40] Only a handful of bishops and clergy were favourably disposed towards the new institutions.[41]

More typical, perhaps, was the response of a group of High Churchmen who set about establishing an organisation in rivalry to that of the Infant School Society. The City of London Infant School Society, founded in June 1825, was

[36]*Philanthropic Gazette,* 9 July 1823.

[37]*Evening Mail,* 4 June 1825.

[38]*Educational Magazine,* Vol. 1, June 1835, p. 413.

[39]P.P. 1835 VII, Education, p. 14.

[40]National Society, Minute Book of the General Committee, Vol. III, Minutes, 27 May 1825; 8 Mar., 5 Apr., 1826; 12 Nov. 1828.

[41]Cf. Chapter 6.

led by a tightly-knit group of opponents of non-denominational education; Robert Peel, a well known advocate of religion in education, was a Vice-Patron, the Lord Mayor of London and two bishops — Howley of London and his protegé Blomfield of Chester — were Patrons and the Rev. George Tomlinson, chaplain to the Bishop of London and tutor to Peel's family, was one of the two clergymen secretaries.[42] Howley was known for his ultra-conservatism, his virulent opposition to the "serpents" of blasphemy (which, he alleged, were aided by certain Dissenters and Evangelicals) and his belief in the National Society as the only true educational agency.[43]

The initial object of the Society was modest; to establish, in the City of London, "one or more Infant Schools for the reception of the Children of the Poor, from two to six years of age".[44] By 1828 the Society, having changed its name to the Committee of the City of London Infant Schools, felt that its aim had been accomplished by the foundation of a school in Liverpool Buildings, Bishopsgate, which also functioned as a training centre for teachers and which by 1833 claimed to have turned out fifty-three infant teachers. The institution had opened in 1826 in charge of Mrs. Hart, who was, in Wilderspin's opinion, one of "the two best teachers I ever saw".[45] Her teaching was simple and easily comprehensible, amusement was preferred to exertion and kindness to severity. But the Committee's view of the purpose of the school as an extension to the "training" of the children of the poor in habits of "order, discipline and obedience", preparatory to entering a National School; the prayers, graces, catechisms and creeds with which the curriculum was loaded; the reading of the Bible and Anglican texts; the division of the day into thirteen prescribed divisions in order to accommodate this — tended to give the school a direction and a structure very different from the Wilderspin model.[46]

Though the London Society was founded as and remained a High Church organisation, with a strong infusion of sheriffs and aldermen of the City of London, several prominent Evangelicals or their supporters were associated with it — Lord Clarendon, Henry Blanshard, John Abel Smith (all members of the original society) and Alexander Baring; Fowell Buxton and Stephen Lushington were Vice-Presidents. Moreover, Thomas Bilby, one of the leading Evangelical infant teachers and bitter opponent of Wilderspin, acknowledged the assistance of Mrs. Hart in compiling his *Course of Lessons* for infant schools, published in 1828. His encomium in the preface, of "the wise and good" among the clergy and laity who had taken up the cause of infant education

[42] *Morning Chronicle*, 6 June 1825.

[43] W. Howley, *A Charge Delivered to the Clergy of the Diocese of London...1818* (London 1818), pp. 10-11; p. 18.

[45] *Morning Chronicle*, 6 June 1825.

[45] Ms. Revisions, *Early Discipline* (1840), x.

[46] "City of London Infant Schools: First Annual Report", *Christian Remembrancer*, Apr. 1827, pp. 245-46; Third Report of the Committee of the City of London Infant Schools (London 1833), p. 5; p. 7; T. Bilby, *A Course of Lessons, Together With the Tunes, To Which They Are Usually Sung in Infant Schools...* (London 1828), *passim*.

almost certainly referred to the establishment of the London Society.[47] Apparently it acted as a focus of activity for all opponents — including some Evangelicals — of the non-denominational school of the Wilderspin type.

By the middle 1820s, these opponents, alarmed by the growth of organisations outside the paternalistic control of the Tory and High Church establishment, and by the spread of the utilitarian and scientific spirit, had become particularly vocal.[48] In 1825 the conservative *Quarterly Review* had singled out Mechanics' Institutes and infant schools as educational institutions of doubtful or even dangerous character.[49] In the same year the Rev. E.W. Grinfield, rector of Laura Chapel, Bath, and "the gentlemen from the pulpit" to whom Wilderspin had referred, attacked infant schools in the most violent and unseemly manner. The opponent of everything new or progressive, from the latest scientific advance to the Lancasterian system of education ("the readiest and shortest of methods to form Sceptics and Infidels"),[50] Grinfield chose to see the infant school movement as part of a grand design of "Mr. Brougham and his friends" to subvert the moral and religious education of the people and replace it with something "scientific and philosophical".

Basing his strictures on a single visit to Bristol Infant School,[51] Grinfield alleged that infant schools were "fashionable novelties" born of "vague and sickly philanthropy"; their custodial function was "fantastical and dangerous" and their methods "arrant humbug". He charged the proponents of the education of the people — Lancaster, Pestalozzi, Fellenberg and Robert Owen, and "all the worthies whose Christian names are so distinctly registered in Dr. Pole's pamphlet on infant schools" — with concealment of their aim, which he unflinchingly revealed; it was nothing less than the placing of the minds of the children "in a state of neutrality to all moral, religious and political opinions".[52] Everybody knew what he meant; had not the Anglican clergy (including Grinfield himself) been preaching incessantly in tract, pamphlet and sermon, that Christian education without the stiffening of the liturgy, prayerbook and catechism of the Church was "neutrality" and that neutrality led to indifferentism, indifferentism to deism and thence by short and inevitable steps

[47] *Morning Chronicle,* 30 May 1828; Bilby, *Course of Lessons,* vi.

[48] H.J. Rose, *The Tendency of Prevalent Opinions About Knowledge Considered. A Sermon Preached Before the University of Cambridge...July 2, 1826* (Cambridge 1826), *passim.* Cf. also C.J. Blomfield, *A Sermon...at the Yearly Meeting of the Children of Charity Schools* (London 1827), p. 7; p. 9.

[49] "Mechanics' Institutes and Infant Schools", *Quarterly Review,* Vol. XXXII, No. LXIV, Oct. 1825, pp. 410-28.

[50] E.W. Grinfield, *The Researches of Physiology Illustrative of the Christian Doctrine of the Resurrection* (London 1820). This pamphlet was directed against physiologists "of considerable reputation" who could "identify thought with the brain and thus reduce religion and morals to a question of mere flesh and blood" (p. 6); E.W. Grinfield, *The Crisis of Religion: A Sermon...Containing Strictures upon Mr. Lancaster's System of Popular Education* (London 1812), p. 15; p. 30.

[51] *Bath and Cheltenham Gazette,* 21 June 1825.

[52] E.W. Grinfield, *A Reply to Mr. Brougham's 'Practical Observations upon the Education of the People'* (London 1825), iv; pp. 5-6; pp. 6-7; p. 10.

to the ruin of both Church and State, as the terrifying example of France had demonstrated?

Active opposition to the infant school at the parish level had a similar quasi-political character. At Taunton, in 1828, two rival infant schools were set up, one non-denominational, the other Anglican, following bitter battles in the autumn of 1827, which divided the town into two hostile camps.[53] The Anglican opposition to the former institution, set on foot following a speech by Wilderspin, centred around the teaching of the doctrines of the Atonement and the Trinity. To ignore these fundamental principles, maintained the Rev. J.H. Stephenson, was to sanction a system of education characterised by an equal indifference to all religious creeds and directed to "the expansion of the intellect". This would have the most prejudicial effect upon the political as well as the moral and religious aspect of society; it would "keep out of sight fundamental difference", thus making children ignorant of the distinction between Protestants and Roman Catholics, and thus *"careless what preponderance* the latter acquire in the state".[54]

At Brighton a few months earlier Montague Burgoyne, a member of the committee of the Infant School Society, found himself heavily in debt when the local Anglicans opposed the liberal religious observances of the infant school he had founded. The clergy boycotted the school, refused to preach sermons in its favour or to take collections on its behalf, dissuaded people from subscribing and persuaded some to withdraw their names from the original list of subscribers.[55] In Leicester early in 1828, the proposal to found a Wilderspinian school was violently opposed by the Rev. E.T. Vaughan, a supporter of Henry Drummond's reactionary Albury conferences. Vaughan was "terrified" at the prospect of "general religion" being taught in infant schools; "I should not wonder next", he mused, "to hear that children of six years of age were to be prepared for mechanics' institutions, or the London University".[56]

* * * * *

That institutions for the teaching of children under six years of age could in any way appear to threaten the stability of the state seems ludicrous to us today. But the guardians of order of that period, with the French Revolution only three-dozen years in the past and the memory still fresh of the near-revolutionary years of 1817-1822, had a hypertrophied awareness of the dangers of deviation from the narrow norms of religious and educational orthodoxy. The Infant School Society thus found itself in a paradoxical position: its

---

[53] *Taunton Courier*, 31 Oct., 14 and 25 Nov. 1827; 15 Jan. 1828.

[54] *Taunton Courier*, 16 and 30 Jan. 1828.

[55] *Brighton Herald*, 18 Aug. 1827; 19 Jan., 9 and 23 Feb. 1828; *Commentator*, 12 Apr., 12 June 1828; M. Burgoyne, *An Address to the Governors and Directors of the Public Charity Schools* (London 1829), p. 27.

[56] *Leicester Chronicle*, 2 Feb. 1828.

viability depended on the furtherance of precisely those policies which the Tories and High Church considered as dangerous. Spirited battles were necessary if the Society were to maintain and extend the pedagogical principles set out in its Address; but in Wilderspin's words, the Committee "had not nerve enough to withstand the prejudices which assailed them. . ."[57] Instead of trying to fight back or answer the points of the opposition, the Society showed a disturbing tendency to leave charges unanswered, to conciliate the Church, and to expel or dismiss those whose views could be construed as "liberal" or "scientific". At the 1825 conference, for instance, Brougham made no attempt to answer the various charges and allegations made in Grinfield's pamphlet. He had not the time to write a reply, he declared; instead he confined his remarks to refuting Grinfield's allegation that the system was calculated to turn the child into "a little priggish animal" by pointing out the absence of restraint and the opportunities for play and amusement which the system afforded. But Brougham went on to praise, at some length, the newly-formed London Infant School Society, welcomed what he called "the conversion of the excellent bench of bishops", announced his intention of subscribing to the body, towards which he felt no jealousy, and hoped it would "outdo the efforts of the Society".[58] The reports of 1825 and 1827 also gave an uncritical welcome to the London Society, though both the Committee and Brougham must have been aware that its aims were opposed to those of the Infant School Society and ultimately inimical to the development of an independent infant system.

The 1827 meeting of the Society was a thinly-attended affair, and it is likely the Tory-Anglican offensive and the radical-millenarian reputation which the infant school movement had acquired, had had some effect on committee members. Brougham, for instance, was not present. Had he lost interest, thought it prudent to abstain from supporting an unpopular cause, or was he coming to the conclusion, as he wrote in *Practical Observations on the Education of the People,* that "the peace of the country, and the stability of the government" could be more immediately secured by the universal diffusion of "true principles. . .of population and wages",[59] rather than by the promotion of infant schools?

The chairman of the meeting was the Evangelical peer Lord Clarendon, who had not been elected to the Committee at the 1825 conference, and he admitted he had been informed of the Society's objectives but a short while before ascending the platform. Lord Calthorpe, who moved the resolution to receive the Report, arrived at the hall a few moments before Joseph Wilson concluded the reading of it, and devoted the larger part of his speech to a rebuttal of criticisms made of infant schools. Montague Burgoyne, however, made a

[57] P.P. 1835 VII, Education, p. 32.

[58] *Evening Mail,* 3-6 June 1825.

[59] H. Brougham, *Practical Observations on the Education of the People* (London 1825), p. 5. The Society for the Diffusion of Useful Knowledge was founded in 1827.

spirited contribution in favour of Greaves and the principles of Pestalozzi, and added a hope that the friends of the Society "would not lose sight of the liberal principles on which they had been founded", especially in the religious sphere. The only other speakers, both of whom made conventional speeches in support of infant schools, were a "Mr. Abouchiere" (almost certainly the Evangelical John Labouchere) and Lord Euston, who had been put up to speak because "many gentlemen, no doubt unavoidably, had been prevented from attending".[60]

A feature of the meeting was its dominance by Evangelicals, some of whom appeared to have been brought in for the occasion. It is significant that Lords Clarendon and Calthorpe, together with Labouchere, were to play a leading role in the Home and Colonial Infant School Society, an Evangelical organisation to be founded nine years later. Joseph Wilson, who seemed to have been affected by the trend towards conservatism in the Evangelical party,[61] read a report notable for its concentration on the "rescue from vice" aspect of infant schools, and its stress on their role in disseminating scriptural knowledge.[62]

In addition, as if taking to heart Grinfield's warning about the dangers of educational principles associated with the names of Pestalozzi, Owen and others, the conference began to sever its connections with individuals who subscribed to the unorthodox ideologies outlined in the previous chapter or who could be identified with support for radical or scientific trends in education. The first victim was Greaves, who in the early part of 1827 was preparing for publication a translation of a collection of Pestalozzi's letters. Greaves had originally given his services to the Society in a voluntary capacity, acting as a sort of public relations officer; it was not until the middle of 1825 that he had been appointed "Provisional Secretary", with an office at 15 Bucklersbury in the City,[63] but it was over a year before he was described as secretary to the Society.[64]

Joseph Wilson announced his dismissal at the conclusion of the Report with the words "The Committee...have thought it right to dissolve their connection with Mr. Greaves, their secretary". After giving formal thanks for his zealous and active exertions, Wilson stated that a Mr. Burbridge was the present secretary of the Society. Only Montague Burgoyne spoke up for Greaves. Burgoyne, a Broughamite of decidedly independent views and a convinced follower of Pestalozzi, praised the educational work of Greaves both in England

[60] *World,* 27 June 1827.

[61] Cf. Chapter 11.

[62] *World,* 27 June 1827. It is significant that the infant school at Baldwin's Gardens, established by a decision of this conference, was under the patronage of the Rev. Baptist Noel, a leading Evangelical (*Educational Magazine,* Vol. II, July 1835, p. 58). Lord Calthorpe, who had no formal connection with the Society, received a query about the Society's activities in November 1827. (H.R.O. Calthorpe Papers, 26M62F/C1123, Denbigh to Calthorpe, 22 Nov. 1827).

[63] Infant School Society. Annual Report, 1825, p. 1; p. 3.

[64] *Robson's London Commercial Directory...for 1826-27,* p. 170; cf. also D.G. Goyder, *The Autobiography of a Phrenologist* (London 1857), p. 186.

and in Switzerland, and compared his contribution with that of Pestalozzi himself.[65] Greaves' views, wrote Burgoyne at a later date, had been "much too liberal" for the Infant School Society, and his dismissal and subsequent ill-treatment due to his refusal to truckle to the leadership or to modify his opinions.[66]

James Buchanan also came under the Society's ban; shortly after the conference, when Westminster Infant School was being reorganised as a model school for the Society, Buchanan was relieved of his position as master. The details of the reorganisation at Vincent Square are not wholly clear, but, according to Wilderspin's retrospective account in the *Educational Magazine* in 1835, Buchanan was "discharged" from the school, "by those who professed a great deal of sanctity, and who were continually canting about piety". He went to Lea Hurst in Derbyshire, the home of Benjamin Leigh Smith's niece, Florence Nightingale, to open an infant school in the district, and Wilderspin was pressed by the Society's committee to take charge of the new model school, but refused out of loyalty to Buchanan. The responsibility was given to a teacher named Moat, who Wilderspin had to induct into infant school methods.[67] In the first week of October 1827 a public examination was held at "the model infant school at Westminster", at which "Mr. Macaulay, Mr. Smith, Mr. Wilson, M.P., Dr. Pinckard and many ladies" were present; Robert Owen was expected but did not appear.[68] At the close of the year, according to the *Buchanan Family Records,* the Society refused to relinquish the building and were "evicted with difficulty".[69] Buchanan was reinstated, after representations to the Committee had been made by Wilderspin on his behalf.[70]

Some six months after the 1827 conference there were further expulsions. Burgoyne, chairing a Society meeting at Rotherhithe at the begining of 1828, at which Greaves and Biber were speakers, declared that, though he was proud to be a member of the Infant School Society, he could not approve of some of their recent proceedings. "Several highly respectable and benevolent gentlemen of liberal and enlightened views had been removed from the Committee; Dr. Birkbeck had been actually expelled".[71] A few weeks later Biber, in a letter to the *World,* was equally critical of the Committee, "who have so ably repressed incongruous views among their members by the removal of several gentlemen whose names rank high in the list of supporters of popular education".[72]

---

[65] *World,* 27 June 1827.

[66] U.C.L. Brougham Mss., 44415, Burgoyne to Brougham, 3 Jan. 1833. Burgoyne was urging Brougham to assist Greaves, who was then living in poverty.

[67] *Educational Magazine,* Vol. II, Aug. 1835, p. 149.

[68] *World,* 10 Oct. 1827.

[69] B.I. Buchanan, *Buchanan Family Records* (Cape Town 1923), pp. 8-9.

[70] *Educational Magazine,* Vol. II, Aug. 1835, p. 149.

[71] *World,* 2 Jan. 1828.

[72] *World,* 25 Jan. 1828. Biber did not give any names.

Wilderspin escaped the censure of the Committee (in fact he was praised by Wilson at the 1827 gathering) if not the sneers of opponents. His habit of not advertising his Swedenborgian views or openly expounding Pestalozzian theory (at least until 1829, when he did so explicitly and at length both in speeches and in the fourth edition of his book) probably ensured his safety, as did his position as the sole field worker of the Society, whose services were indispensable if it were to aspire to anything more than a nominal existence.

The 1827 annual meeting was apparently the last the Society held. It was still in being, and Wilderspin was still its agent, in the spring of 1828, when he made a critical comment about its finances which can be fairly precisely dated.[73] In June of that year it was still advertisng its existence.[74] But it must have been kept alive by a mere handful of its former committee; as Wilderspin later stated "the ghost of one or two of them [i.e. of the Committee]...reappeared at a bookseller's shop in Cheapside".[75] This was a reference to the change of address of the Society, which transferred from 15 Bucklersbury to 19 Cheapside in 1828.[76] The "one or two" may have been Joseph Wilson and John Smith, M.P., to whom, together with "the noblemen and gentlemen of the London (sic) Infant School Society", Wilderspin dedicated the 1829 edition of *Infant Education,* which had been prepared in late 1828. The stationer's shop was owned by one Edward Suter, who had opened it in 1826.[77] Suter was a steward of the Spitalfields Benevolent Society, an Evangelical charitable organization of which Fowell Buxton and Samuel Hoare, members of the Committee of the Infant School Society, were officials,[78] and they may have had a hand in the move. From 1830 onwards Suter's shop housed what was termed the Infant School Society Depository,[79] which continued to be advertised in directories until the mid-1860s.

Wilderspin continued to act as the Society's agent till the end,[80] which must have come about in the very last months of 1828. "Deserted by the Society", as he put it,[81] he settled in Cheltenham, opened an Infant School Depot of his own, and began another career as a free-lance educationist.[82]

* * * * *

[73]The Committee refused to reimburse Wilderspin for expenses incurred on a journey to Scotland (Cf. Chapter 7).

[74]In W. Wilson, *Advice to Instructors of Infant Schools* (London 1828), according to D. Salmon and W. Hindshaw, *Infant Schools: Their History and Theory* (London 1904), p. 54. It has not been possible to trace a copy of Wilson's work.

[75]*Educational Magazine,* Vol. I, June 1835, p. 413.

[76]*The Post Office London Directory for 1829,* p. 221.

[77]*The Post Office London Directory for 1827,* p. 396.

[78]Twelfth Report of the Spitalfields Benevolent Society (London 1827), p. 3.

[79]*Robson's London Directory...for 1831* (Pt. I.)

[80]Ms. Revisions, *Early Discipline* (1840), xvii.

[81]*Educational Magazine,* Vol. I, June 1835, p. 413.

[82]Cf. Chapter 8.

Why did the Infant School Society fail? There is obviously more to the story of its internal politics than the few glimpses afforded by Burgoyne and Biber. It was clearly affected by the High Church campaign against "progressive" education; Biber specifically charged the supporters of National Schools with "defeating" the Society,[83] but it was a defeat which was aided from within. Robert Owen bluntly stated that on his return from America, "I discovered that its original promoters had sold it, in fact, to the Church of England party".[84] These would, of course, have been the Evangelicals who appeared to have been in charge of the Society in 1827, and who had, moreover, links with the Anglican City of London organisation. In 1828, at a public dinner given by the latter body, several members of the original Society acted as stewards — the Earl of Clarendon, Henry Blanshard, Samuel Jones Loyd, and John Abel Smith.[85]

The identification of the Infant School Society, during the first two or three years of its existence, with the *persona* of Brougham (and by extension with his educational schemes) had the unfortunate effect of attracting the vituperation of the Tory-Anglican forces, and of obscuring, to a great extent, the pedagogical value of infant schools. Brougham's robust self-confidence, his reputation as a "powerful and alarming debater" (in Hazlitt's phrase),[86] his "radical" stance and his support of utilitarian and scientific education, alarmed the orthodox and caused many to mutter about revolution.[87] His patronage was regarded by some as sufficient reason to dissociate themselves from the new schools. Lady Charlotte Lindsay's brother, asking a clergyman in 1825 why the infant school was not more generally adopted, received the answer "because it was invented by Mr. Brougham".[88]

A more confident and strongly-based society could have weathered the opposition and, in Wilderspin's view, kept its opponents "in their proper place".[89] The British and Foreign School Society, which had several members of the Infant School Society on its committees, had received equally severe criticism from Anglican orthodoxy and survived. The British Society, however, had strong bases in the localities and drew considerable strength from Dissenting sects who were gaining in numbers and self-confidence as the century progressed. It could, moreover, claim it was furthering the extension of

[83]G.E. Biber, *Christian Education, In a Course of Lectures* (London 1830), p. 174.

[84]*New Moral World,* No. 104, 22 Oct. 1836, p. 409.

[85]*Morning Chronicle,* 30 May 1828.

[86]W. Hazlitt, *The Spirit of the Age* (World's Classics Ed., 1970), p. 225.

[87]In 1835 Brougham recalled that his Select Committee on the Education of the Lower Orders had, seventeen years before, caused one class to "apprehend the utter destruction of our political system, while it filled others with alarm lest a stop should be put to the advancement of the human mind" (Parl. Deb. XXVII, 21 May 1835, 1296). The Tory *Blackwood's Magazine* felt that Brougham's *Observations* of 1825 might be construed as an attempt to educate the working class for revolution ("Brougham on the Education of the People", *Blackwood's Edinburgh Magazine,* Vol. XVII, No. C., May 1825, pp. 534-51).

[88]Lady Theresa Lewis (Ed.), *Extracts of the Journals and Correspondence of Miss Berry* (London, 3 vol., 1865), III, . p. 364.

[89]*Educational Magazine,* Vol. II, Aug. 1835, p. 150.

education for the poor in a manner sufficiently similar to that of the Church-supported National Society to pass muster as basically the same sort of enterprise. The work of the Infant School Society, on the other hand, could be construed as something quite different — an organisation based on a type of school rather than any recognised body of religious opinion. The Society's *raison d'etre* was a form of education so unlike anything previously known in the sphere of popular education as to require a peculiar pedagogical justification. In one sense this was its greatest strength; but it was also a source of weakness. Most of the active members of the Society's Committee were primarily, and increasingly, interested in the negative aspect of infant education in its role as an antidote to vice and juvenile delinquency, rather than in its educational function as perceived by Buchanan, Wilderspin, Greaves and others. When the new pedagogy aroused opposition, the Evangelical leaders of the Society were not prepared to fight for it, preferring instead to dismiss the progressives.

So the Infant School Society died. "The noble founders and their colleagues...departed this life", observed Wilderspin sardonically, "the secretary and I shed many tears at the funeral".[90] But he never ceased to mourn the fact that it was "a public calamity" which left the movement without direction and without a central establishment which could have trained a generation of teachers in its ideals, and, had it been in existence in 1833, might have received a government grant like the other societies.[91]

Nevertheless, during its short existence the Society had given an enormous impetus to the formation of infant schools. Between June 1824 and June 1825 (the date of the Society's second meeting) 60 infant schools had been founded. Wilderspin, of course, had been directly responsible for a number of them, but the existence of the Society and the publicity it generated had inspired the establishment of many more. Appendix I shows that three times as many schools (60 as against 20) were founded in the first year of its existence than in the preceding eight and a half. Of the 20 schools set up before June 1824, 10 were in the poorer quarters of London, mainly the east and south, and a further 3 were in seaports or industrial cities. More than half the schools founded in 1824-25 were in country towns, cathedral cities and semi-rural suburbs of London; infant schools apparently made a greater appeal to the middle and upper classes of the rural counties than to the industrial bourgeosie. Only 10 industrial towns or seaports appear in the whole list. Perhaps the absence of industrialists from the Society's committee had something to do with this. Certainly at this stage the Society had made few inroads into the problem presented by the wild-running children of the city streets, at least in the provinces. Nevertheless, the infant school was by 1828 a recognised educational institution which was unlikely to disappear. The demise of the Society, however, and the resulting lack of central direction, helped to pave the way for a crisis in infant education in the mid-1830s.

[90]*Educational Magazine*, Vol. I, June 1835, p. 413.

[91]*Educational Magazine*, Vol. II, Aug. 1835, p. 150; Ms. Revisions, *Early Discipline* (1840), vii.

CHAPTER 6

EDUCATIONAL MISSIONARY: NEW SCHOOLS AND OLD

Wilderspin won national recognition for his work as an infant-school missionary; yet he became the travelling agent of the Infant School Society by default. His hopes were centered on becoming the superintendent of a model infant school in London where his system could be perfected and demonstrated and whence it could subsequently be extended to other places at home and abroad. He certainly had not envisaged for himself a future of perpetual travel. "...I was reduced to the necessity of doing this", he wrote later, "because the Society fell to the ground and never erected the model school they promised me; having no building, therefore, in London where I could bring my various plans to bear, I thought it a public duty incumbent on me to go round the country and try to get buildings erected, and when they were erected, to instruct the teachers and children at the same time".[1]

This describes the essential pattern of his life from early 1825 until the late summer of 1836. The period falls conveniently into two parts: the first, from early 1825, when his travels for the Infant School Society began on a full-time basis, to the end of 1828, when the Society effectively ceased operations; the second from early 1829, when he settled in Cheltenham and continued his travels as a free-lance educationist, until August 1836, when he became a salaried employee of the Liverpool Corporation Education Committee. The story, or most of it, is told in various editions of *Early Discipline,* one of the most colourful travel books of the early nineteenth century, but also, from a chronological viewpoint, one of the most confused. The book's title was originally intended to be *The Progress of Infant Education, or Recollections of Journies Through Various Parts of the United Kingdom for Its Promotion* (a wording which aptly describes its contents) with Wilderspin as author and Charles Williams as editor.[2] Before publication, however, Wilderspin, with his aptitude for picking inappropriate titles, changed it to *Early Discipline* and dropped Williams' name from the title-page. The latter, a young Presbyterian minister from Newark[3], conceived it his editorial duty "to group in some instances the events which occurred at different visits", a reasonable procedure if adequate dating had been provided. But neither author nor editor provided a single date. This has made the task of unravelling the chronology of Wilderspin's travels extraordinarily difficult, and there are gaps in the record, sometimes at critical points. Some aspects of Wilderspin's travels remain, and probably will continue to remain, problematical. But the main lines of the story are clear enough for us to follow Wilderspin quite closely on his journeys throughout the British Isles.

[1] *Educational Magazine,* Vol. II, July 1835, p. 49.

[2] U.C.L. Brougham Mss., 10369, Wilderspin to Brougham, Nov. 1831, encl. leaflet.

[3] Williams, a former foundry worker, was born in 1796. He later became editor to the Religious Tract Society. Cf. obituary in the *Congregational Yearbook, 1867* (London 1867), pp. 326-27.

These journeys, though their beginnings coincided with the opening of the first railway, were almost all undertaken before railway travel became common and were made by coach, in the saddle, or by horse and gig. Wilderspin became an expert horseman, sufficiently skilled to ride to hounds or to undertake journeys of hundreds of miles in his gig in the worst winter weather, his books and personal belongings carried in the rear in a handsome cabinet of his own design. He was not, in the strict sense, a pioneer; Joseph Lancaster, a decade earlier, had made a similar series of journeys in order to lecture and to found schools.[4] But no other educationist in the nineteenth century approached the range of Wilderspin's journeys, displayed so much resourcefulness, kept at it continuously for so many years, or made it his profession in the way he was to do. He was the living embodiment of Brougham's phrase, "the schoolmaster is abroad in the land".

Before visiting a town to set up an infant school, Wilderspin usually obtained letters of introduction from members of the Infant School Society or from leading citizens of towns previously visited. He would also distribute circulars or insert in one or more of the local papers an advertisement announcing his arrival and purpose, offering copies of his book for sale and writing to persons interested in establishing an infant school to contact him at his lodgings. When a provisional group was assembled, he would advise them on the organisation of a public meeting, the raising of funds and the formation of a permanent committee.[5]

* * * * *

If Wilderspin's first journeys to establish infant schools had been in and around London, his trips as a full-time agent took him further afield. As he fulfilled each engagement more or less in the order in which the requests came in, he found it difficult to plan his journeys very far in advance or to organise his work on a regional basis. The generally chaotic pattern of his travels was thus established very early. During the first six months of 1825, for instance, he was shuttling between Ross-on-Wye, Hereford, Stockport, Kidderminster, Durham and Newcastle-upon-Tyne. In addition he records that among the earliest schools he opened were those at Deddington and Banbury (Oxfordshire), Sutton (Bedfordshire) and Ampton, near Bury St. Edmunds, Suffolk. All of these schools were in operation by June 1825,[6] though it is possible, as Wilderspin supplies no dates, that he had organised some of them during the previous year.

[4] *Report of J. Lancaster's Progress from the Year 1798...*(London 1811), pp. 14-15. Between 1807 and 1810 Lancaster covered 6,837 miles and founded 95 schools.

[5] *System of Education* (1840), pp. 91-4; P.P. 1835 VII, Report from the Select Committee on Education in England and Wales, p. 32; p. 36; p. 43; *Infant System* (1834), pp. 144-45.

[6] *Early Discipline* (1832), p. 30; p. 31; p. 33. For the date of the establishment of these schools, cf. Infant School Society. Annual Report 1825, pp. 1-2.

The school at Ross-on-Wye was one of the first of Wilderspin's schools to be noticed in the local press, and thus can accurately be dated. It was founded by a Quaker lady, who experienced some initial opposition in the locality to "institutions of this nature", and opened at the beginning of May 1825.[7] Shortly afterwards he was assisting a Miss Hooper of nearby Hereford. The lady was a descendant of the sixteenth-century Protestant martyr Bishop Hooper of Worcester; she was one of the women, including Lady Lubbock, Lady Olivia Sparrow, and Mrs. Ames and Mrs. Moysey of Bath, whose efforts on behalf of infant schools led the Infant School Society to vote them a special resolution of thanks at its first anniversary meeting in 1825.[8] Unable to interest her friends, Miss Hooper decided to establish an infant school on her own.

Wilderspin advised the purchase of a vacant inn, the old Commercial Hotel outside Hereford's Bye-Street Gate. Priced at £1,400, the premises included former assembly rooms adjoined by extensive gardens containing peach trees, apricots, nectarines, cherry, pear and apple trees, with a strawberry bed in the centre; these gardens, Wilderspin urged, should be preserved intact and used as a playground. When the school was in operation, each class had its own tree around which it danced, and the flowers and fruits were used not only in botany lessons but also for moral training on Wilderspinian lines; "so completely was the distinction made between *meum* and *teum* that not a single leaf was injured", Wilderspin observed. He opened the school in mid-May and conducted a public examination five weeks later. One of the local clergy wrote in the visitors' book, "Astonished and delighted! And as the best proof of my satisfaction I beg to subscribe 20 guineas".[9] The success of the school inspired two gentlemen of Coleford to purchase 20 copies of Wilderspin's book, to distribute them in the neighbourhood and set up a school there.[10]

On 16 May Wilderspin opened Stockport Infant School, housed in the large building of the famous Sunday School,[11] and then turned his attention to two schools in Worcester. One was in the city itself, opened in late May, though it is not clear to what extent Wilderspin was involved in its organisation;[12] the other was in nearby Kidderminster, and opened in the last week of June.[13] The school was patronised by Lord Lyttleton, had an active committee of twelve ladies and gentlemen and was situated in the Horse Fair in a room which Richard Watson,

---

[7] *Hereford Journal*, 26 Jan., 15 June 1825; *Early Discipline* (1832), p. 40.

[8] *Morning Chronicle*, 6 June 1825.

[9] *Hereford Journal*, 1 June 1825; *Early Discipline* (1832), p. 40ff.

[10] *Early Discipline* (1832), p. 44.

[11] *Stockport Advertiser*, 29 Apr., 24 June 1825; *Early Discipline* (1832), pp. 46-7.

[12] *Berrow's Worcester Journal*, 26 May 1825. Wilderspin stated that he "visited" the city "at an early period". (*Early Discipline* (1832), p. 30).

[13] *Berrow's Worcester Journal*, 30 June 1825.

a member of the sponsoring committee, offered rent-free for five years.[14] The master and mistress were Mr. and Mrs. Thomas Bayliss, "the best", Wilderspin wrote, "I ever had to teach".[15] Bayliss was an amateur entomologist who mounted and displayed in the schoolroom a remarkable collection of insects; the use he made of it impressed and delighted Wilderspin as a fine example of object teaching.

In the latter part of June Wilderspin was in the North East, assisting in the establishment of schools in Durham and Newcastle and distributing circulars in Sunderland and North and South Shields.[16] The Durham committee, led by the clergy of St. Oswald's and St. Giles' parishes, with token representation from Dissent, announced after their first meeting on 11 December 1824 that, while the proposed schools would be open to all denominations, the religious instruction would follow Establishment practices and that the ministers of St. Oswald's and St. Giles' would have charge of the schools. This policy led minority groups, especially Catholics, to voice their objections in the press. Dissenters, having representation on the Committee, complained less, and by February premises had been engaged and arrangements were in progress for schools in New Elvet and Claypath. The schools apparently were not opened till the early summer; Wilderspin journeyed from London with an agent and a little boy to organise them and conduct public examinations in each. He received £33.10s for his expenses, a vote of thanks signed by the Mayor and a handsome present from the committee.[17] In the latter part of June he visited the infant school in Newcastle, apparently after his work in Durham, in order to help James Urwin, the master, "in perfecting the discipline". Situated in the Orphan House in Northumberland Street, where Wesley had formerly preached, the school was widely supported and was probably the first to receive support from municipal funds; the Town Corporation made a donation of £26.5s during the first year of operation.[18]

Despite this hectic activity of the spring and early summer, Wilderspin found that requests to establish schools exceeded even his ability to cope with them, and he was forced to employ agents to assist him in carrying out the work. In *Early Discipline* he states that he employed two agents during his early missionary years, although he adds that they were hardly worth the trouble and expense. It took six weeks of training before they could go out alone, their youth and inexperience led them into indiscretions, and eventually they had to be

---

[14]Wilderspin Papers, Fourth Annual Report of the Kidderminster Infant School (Kidderminster 1829), pp. 4-5; *Early Discipline* (1832), pp. 45-6.

[15]Wilderspin's Ms. notation on the Kidderminster report.

[16]*Early Discipline* (1832), p. 45. Wilderspin noted that these had "no result".

[17]*Durham Chronicle*, 8, 15, 22 Jan., 12 Feb. 1825; *Durham County Advertiser*, 12, 19 Feb. 1825; 14 Jan. 1826; *Early Discipline* (1832), p. 45.

[18]*Newcastle Courant*, 22 Jan., 19 Feb., 5 Mar. 1825; First Report of the Infant School Society of Newcastle-upon-Tyne (Newcastle 1826), p. 6; p. 14; E. Mackenzie, *A Descriptive and Historical Account of the Town and County of Newcastle-upon-Tyne* (Newcastle-upon-Tyne, 6 vol., 1827), III, p. 456.

dismissed.[19] Wilderspin was then reduced to training his own children for the work; however, after moving to Cheltenham in 1829 he found two competent assistants who stayed with him for two or three years.

Wilderspin's first use of an agent was in April 1825, when Temple Infant School in Bristol was opened by "an intimate friend and pupil of mine, assisted by an agent".[20] The friend was James Slade, who had been a fellow member of the New Church congregation at Waterloo Road, and who became the first master of the second infant school in Bristol. The school, opened on 1 May and built to hold 200 pupils, was sponsored by John Hare, of Firfield House, a wealthy floor-cloth manufacturer of Temple Gate.[21]

Whether or not he continued to employ an agent or agents during the remainder of the year is not recorded. The latter half of 1825 appears to have been much less busy than the first. The passages in *Early Discipline* which presumably apply to this period are somewhat thin and vague. Sometime during the summer and early autumn Wilderspin must have been preparing the third edition of his book, entitled *Infant Education*, which appeared in September. Between June and September he opened infant schools at Clifton (Bristol) and Chilham, Kent.[22] He certainly was present in Manchester on and after 4 July to open an infant school for the Society of Friends in Buxton Street, and to conduct an examination therein.[23] A circular urging the establishment of a similar school in Chorlton Row, dated August 1825 and annotated "Manchester First Appeal. S.W"., suggests he stayed there for some weeks.[24] According to *Early Discipline*, he then visited Liverpool "where three schools were commenced", i.e. presumably in operation;[25] Styal in Cheshire, where he made "a beginning" on the infant school attached to Greg's cotton mill;[26] and Chester, where he apparently attended the public meeting convened by the Mayor and chaired by the Bishop, Dr. Blomfield, to consider the formation of an Infant School Society. This took place on 22 November 1825,[27] and the school was opened in the following year. It was one of several infant schools sponsored by dignitaries of the Church — bishops or archdeacons — in this period; among the others

[19] *Early Discipline* (1832), p. 28.

[20] *Ibid.*, p. 34.

[21] Cf. speech by John Hare in *Taunton Courier*, 31 Oct. 1827; *Matthew's Annual Bristol Directory; and Commercial List* (Bristol 1830), p. 13; p. 33; B.R.O. Temple Infant School. Minute Book, 1825-1868, *passim*.

[22] *Early Discipline* (1832), p. 12ff; pp. 39-40. The date of opening is deduced from lists of infant schools in *Infant Education* (1825), p. 284, and Infant School Society. Annual Report 1825, p. 2.

[23] *Manchester Guardian*, 29 June 1825; *Early Discipline* (1832), p. 55.

[24] Wilderspin Papers, circular entitled "Appeal on Behalf of Infant Schools" (1825).

[25] *Early Discipline* (1832), p. 58. According to *Gore's Liverpool Directory and its Environs* (Liverpool 1825), p. 113, there were three infant schools established in Liverpool at this date.

[26] *Early Discipline* (1832), pp. 58-9. For details, cf. P.P. 1834 XX, Factories Inquiry Commission, Supplementary Report, Pt. II, D.1, pp. 77-8; p. 302.

[27] *Chester Courant*, 25 Nov. 1825; *Early Discipline* (1832), pp. 59-60.

were Glastonbury (1824) Chelmsford (1825), Exeter (1825) and Hackney (1826).[28]

There is some evidence at this point that Wilderspin was not reconciled to his role as travelling missionary and that he felt that his restless energy could be put to other use. In the summer of 1825 he was organising the school at Chilham for J.B. Wildman, a West Indian planter, whose wife had read the first edition of the *Infant Poor*. Wildman, on his return from the West Indies the previous summer, had brought back two black boys, aged about eight and ten; on admittance to the school, they took such delight in it that Wilderspin urged Wildman to establish a similar one on his Jamaica estate. When Wildman observed that he would need a trained teacher, Wilderspin offered to go to Jamaica forthwith. "Very well", Wilderspin reported Wildman as saying, "there is a vessel lying in the river which will sail in a week or two, and you shall go by that; and at your request I will obtain the consent of the Committee by whom you are now employed". The Infant School Society, however, refused to release him and he perforce remained in England.[29].

Shortly afterwards he again displayed the impulsiveness that marked much of his early life. He suspended his travels in late 1825 and early 1826 and, in a brief romantic interlude, married again under circumstances which can only be surmised, since for some reason the marriage was never referred to in any of his books or in the family correspondence.[30] We know from the marriage record that the lady's name was Jane Mary Peacock, a spinster; that the marriage took place, by licence, on 25 February 1826 in St. Andrew Holborn; and that Joseph Mould and George Hicks were the witnesses.[31] Miss Peacock was a member of a family who were active in New Church circles in London and Manchester in the early nineteenth century. Henry Peacock, the author of a number of works on Swedenborgian doctrine, had moved from York to Birmingham in the early 1790s and had been ordained a minister of the Church on 8 February 1795 by the Rev. J. Proud. He went to Manchester in 1800 as minister of the Peter Street Society and died there a year later.[32] He was almost certainly the father of Bartholomew Peacock, bookbinder, who had been born in York. Peacock and his wife Eleanor were baptised into the St. George's Fields Society on 14 September 1817 by the Rev. Thomas Goyder. Both were aged 51.[33] David

---

[28] *Bath Journal*, 27 Sept., 11 Oct. 1824; *Chelmsford Gazette*, 27 May 1825; Fourteenth Annual Report...of the County of Essex Society for the Education of the Poor (Chelmsford 1826), p. 5; *Cottager's Monthly Visitor*, Vol. V, Nov. 1825, pp. 525-26; *Bath and Cheltenham Gazette*, 22 Nov. 1825; Minute Book of the Hackney Infant School, Bridge Street, Homerton, 1826-1880, Minutes, 14 Sept. 1826; 9 Oct. 1826.

[29] *Kentish Gazette*, 16 July 1824; *Early Discipline* (1832), pp. 12-13.

[30] It is possible, of course, that material containing references to his second marriage was deliberately destroyed.

[31] Marriage Registers, St. Andrew Holborn, 1826.

[32] J.R. Boyle, *Bibliotheca Novae Ecclesiae: A Bibliography of the Literature of Emanuel Swedenborg and of the New Church* (London 1882), Prospectus, p. 299 (facsimile page). For his location at York, cf. H.B. Peacock, *Free Remarks; Occasioned by the Letters of John Disney, D.D., F.S.A. to Vicesimus Knox* (London 1792), title page.

[33] P.R.O. R.G.4/4501, Register of Baptisms, New Jerusalem Chapel, St. George's Fields, 1816-34.

Goyder, in his *Autobiography,* remembered "this delightful family" at the Lisle Street Chapel when he, and presumably Wilderspin and his first wife, had been members in the years after 1814. Mrs. Peacock was, in Goyder's opinion, "a most charming singer" and her musical talents undoubtedly were one of the attractions of the services.[34] The Peacocks had two daughters, Rebecca Ann, a straw hat maker and Eleanor, a satin silk worker; aged 23 and 27 respectively, they were baptised on the same day as their parents.

Was Jane Peacock another daughter? She was certainly a member of the St. George's Fields' congregation. In August 1816 her name appears as one of the four teachers of the Society's Sunday School, the committee of which Wilderspin was a member,[35] and seven years later she was a subscriber to the New Jerusalem Church Free School.[36]. It is possible, however, that she was the daughter of another of H.B. Peacock's sons, Henry Peacock of Manchester, who was active in the New Church there in the 1820s.[37] Immediately after the marriage the couple went to Manchester, where they stayed for the better part of six months, the longest period in one place that Wilderspin was to spend for the next decade.

* * * * *

The sojourn in Manchester was part honeymoon, part rest period, during which Wilderspin lived on his earnings of the previous year. The move was probably made because of the location of Mrs. Wilderspin's relatives, for there was no other compelling reason for residence in that grim monument to the Industrial Revolution. The city, moreover, was in the grip of a severe economic crisis — the banks bracing themselves against the demands of depositors while idle workers were demonstrating for employment and bread.[38] When several factories were attacked, troops were called out to prevent further disorders, a mistake, Wilderspin thought, as their presence tended to prolong the general excitement. Appalled at the distress around him, he devoted several pages of *Early Discipline* to a graphic description of the bad housing conditions and social degradation of the poor, anticipating, to some extent, the classic accounts of Kay and Engels.[39]

[34]D.G. Goyder, *The Autobiography of a Phrenologist* (London 1857), p. 85; cf. also Mrs. Peacock's obituary in *New Jerusalem Magazine,* No. 2, Feb. 1829, p. 62.

[35]New Church Sunday School. Minute Book 1816, Minutes, 20 Aug. 1816.

[36]Fifth Annual Report of the Committee of the New Jerusalem Church Free School (London 1823), p. 19. The Committee of the New Jerusalem Church Free School in Account with Jervoise Bugby, Treasurer of the Said School (Ms.), entry for July 1822 - July 1823.

[37]F. Smith, *History of the Peter Street Society of the New Church, Manchester* (London 1892), pp. 76-7. *Minutes of the Fifteenth General Conference of the Ministers, and Other Members, of the New Church* (London 1822) p. 11; *Sixteenth General Conference…*(London 1823), p. 13; Report of the Committee of the Manchester and Salford New Jerusalem Church Free Day School (Manchester 1828), p. 7.

[38]W.E.A. Axon, *Annals of Manchester* (Manchester 1856), p. 172.

[39]Early Discipline (1832), pp. 49-50; *Early Discipline* (1834), pp. 50-51.

In the summer of 1826 Wilderspin conducted an examination at two Manchester infant schools: Chorlton Row on 26 June,[40] and Buxton Street (which he had opened a year earlier) on 1 September.[41] Between these dates he and his wife spent five weeks in the picturesque city of Chester, in the neighbouring county of Cheshire. At the meeting to found an infant school held the previous November, Dr. Blomfield, a rising star in the Church, had presented the case for infant schools from an Establishment point of view. Although his approach to religious instruction in the schools was, on the whole, a liberal one — free access for children of all denominations and no doctrinal teaching — Blomfield stipulated in the resolutions presented at the meeting that only members of the Church of England could be employed as masters and mistresses. As was the case in Durham, the proposal aroused vigorous protests from Dissenters. The Bishop, however, refused to back down, making the rather weak argument that, since certain Dissenters would probably not wish to have their children instructed by persons of another denomination, a teacher from the Church of England would be the least objectionable. Although a number of Dissenters withheld their support, a committee was formed on 9 December and a search begun for a suitable site for a school.[42]

The opening of the school was delayed until 31 July 1826, and the Wilderspins spent the month of August supervising it.[43] The accounts of the school in the local press are interesting because they contain the only known public references to the second Mrs. Wilderspin — comforting a delinquent child, for instance, or assisting in her husband's lessons[44] — and one of the few references, at this period, to a formal speech by Wilderspin. This was made in the presence of the Bishop, at the public examination on 30 August, and was short and inconsequential.[45]

After leaving Chester at the end of the month Wilderspin, according to the *Chester Courant,* went to Leeds to promote an infant school, which was opened on 6 November.[46] In addition, he probably went to Birmingham. The Second Report of the Birmingham Infant School Society lists a sum of £4.16s paid to him for two visits. The first infant school in the city had opened in temporary quarters on 15 March 1826 and Wilderspin's first visit would be to assist in this. It seems likely that his second trip was made in September, when the school moved into a new building in Ann Street.[47]

[40] *Manchester Courier,* 24 June 1826. The school had been in preparation a year (*Stockport Advertiser,* 26 Aug. 1825; *Manchester Guardian,* 27 Aug., 10 Oct., 24 Dec. 1825).

[41] *Manchester Guardian,* 26 Aug. 1826.

[42] *Chester Chronicle,* 25 Nov., 9 Dec., 16 Dec. 1825; *Chester Courant,* 29 Nov., 6 Dec. 1825.

[43] *Chester Chronicle,* 1 Aug. 1826; *Chester Courant,* 1 Aug. 1826.

[44] *Chester Chronicle,* 25 Aug. 1826.

[45] *Chester Courant,* 29 Aug. 1826; *Chester Chronicle,* 1 Sept. 1826.

[46] *Chester Courant,* 18 Aug. 1826; *Leeds Mercury,* 27 May, 24 June, 4 Nov. 1826.

[47] Leaflet entitled "Birmingham Infant School. The First Anniversary Meeting...Report" (n.d., but Oct. 1826); Second Annual Report of the Birmingham Infant School Society (Birmingham 1827), p. 17.

At the beginning of October he made his first trip outside England; "the opportunity I had long desired" of visiting Ireland had arrived.[48] To some extent the ground had been prepared. An Irish edition of the *Infant Poor* had been published in 1823, and this had mooted the establishment of an infant school in Dublin.[49] In 1824 he had found and trained a mistress for Lady Powerscourt's infant school in Enniskerry, the first in the country;[50] and, as we have seen, David Goyder had gone to Dublin in 1825 and lectured in the Rotunda. Arriving in Dublin in the first week of October, Wilderspin made his headquarters at Mr. Donahoe's in Townsend Street.

He was instrumental in founding a school sponsored by a number of influential Protestants in Westland Row, near Trinity College. The pupils, however, were largely Catholic and when their parents were pressed by their own Church to withdraw them, the School Committee tried to retain them by such inducements as free clothing and food. By these means the school managed to survive for over thirty years. On the back of the report for 1852 Wilderspin wrote with feeling, "This school I opened many years before. It was the first in the city of Dublin and the second in all Ireland. The first was by Lady Powerscourt in Wicklow. I have seen the blessed effects of the seed sown by it in subsequent visits. Alas! The Voluntary System does not last long".[51]

Wilderspin spent some weeks travelling in Ireland, visiting Lady Powerscourt's school and R.L. Edgeworth's famous progressive school at Edgeworthstown. He found the Irish "a people simple-minded and inquiring — delighted to receive information on all subjects except *one* — and most warmly attached to what they regard as 'the true religion'". Sometime in late November he was due to lecture at the Rotunda in Dublin but caught the typhoid fever then raging in the capital and was confined to bed for seven weeks. Returning to England in early January he was nearly drowned in a storm and then found his life further endangered on the coach drive to Manchester by a drunken coachman who, after asking him to walk up a steep hill to lighten the load, left him on a deserted moor six miles outside Bolton on a freezing winter night.[52] Such dangerous adventures were to become commonplace on later journeys throughout the British Isles.

Wilderspin had little time in which to recuperate. He spent most of January in Derby, organising an infant school for the Rev. Robert Simpson, rector of St. George's Church and taking the examination on the 28th of the month.[53] He attended a meeting on infant schools in Wandsworth at the beginning of April,

[48] *Early Discipline* (1832), p. 62.

[49] *Infant Poor* (Dublin 1823), "Prospectus of the Plan of an Infant School" (foll. vii).

[50] Wilderspin Papers, Lady Powerscourt to Wilderspin, 29 June 1824.

[51] *Dublin Evening Mail,* 11 Oct. 1826; *Early Discipline* (1832), p. 62; Wilderspin Papers, leaflet entitled "Report of the Infant Model School, Westland Row...1852".

[52] *Early Discipline* (1832), pp. 63-70.

[53] *Derby Mercury,* 20 and 24 Jan. 1827.

went to Cheltenham in May, and organised a school in Melbourne, Derbyshire, in June.[54] There were also visits to Loughborough and Leicester.[55] Some of the journeys which he undertook at this period are difficult to assign to specific dates. It is probable that during the summer of 1827 he visited the Staffordshire tape-works of Nathaniel Phillips and Co. at Tean, to open an infant school built for the children of the factory workers. The occasion was memorable for Wilderspin's first public speech to a large audience; rising above his fears, he spoke in a crowded local chapel for an hour and a half. "Since then", he stated, "I have delivered lectures and courses at various places".[56] He also records a visit to Kingstanley, near Stroud, where he opened an infant school at the Stanley Woollen Mills of Maclean, Stephens and Co.[57]

During September and October, as related in Chapter 5, he was engaged in reorganising Westminster Infant School and speaking at Taunton.[58] If we follow the sequence in *Early Discipline,* he then journeyed to Weymouth, where he tried unsuccessfully to collect an audience for a lecture before leaving for the Channel Islands to open two schools in Guernsey and to bolster a school already established in Jersey.[59] Subsequently, he states, he visited Cambridge, where infant schools had been established in late 1826.[60] At the end of the year he was in Aylesbury organising and opening a well-supported infant school, an engagement which lasted into January 1828.[61] There was also a lecture tour of the Yorkshire towns of Huddersfield, Bingley, Harden Grange, Keighley, Leeds and Bradford,[62] which probably took place shortly before his departure for Glasgow in the spring of 1828.

Whatever the exact sequence of the journeys, it is clear that the pattern of hectic dashes from one end of the country to the other was maintained throughout these years. Even when resident in Scotland in 1828, he made two long trips in September and December to lecture and open schools in the Potteries.[63] It is also evident that after the visit to Chester in the summer of 1826,

[54] *Weekly Times,* 8 Apr. 1827; *Derby Mercury,* 20 June and 4 July 1827; *Early Discipline* (1832), p. 82.

[55] *Early Discipline* (1832), pp. 74-82.

[56] *Early Discipline* (1832), p. 27; Ms. Revisions, *Early Discipline* (1840), p. 27. The date is deduced from the fact that up to and including the opening of Melbourne Infant School in June 1827, Wilderspin makes no reference to giving public lectures on his own (as distinct from making a contribution as one of several speakers), but beginning with Taunton in October 1827, he frequently spoke in public or gave pre-arranged lectures.

[57] *Early Discipline* (1832), pp. 83-4; P.P. 1833 XX, Factories Inquiry Commission, First Report, B.I., Western District, p. 35.

[58] For the speech at Taunton, cf. *Taunton Courier,* 24 Oct. 1827.

[59] *Early Discipline* (1832), pp. 99-100; *Chronique De Jersey,* 23 June 1827.

[60] *Early Discipline* (1832), p. 100; *Cambridge Chronicle,* 8 Dec. 1826; *Short Account of the Old Schools of Cambridge* (Cambridge 1842), p. 5.

[61] *Buckinghamshire, Bedfordshire and Hertfordshire Chronicle,* 15 Dec. 1827; 5 and 26 Jan. 1828.

[62] *Early Discipline* (1832), pp. 84-9.

[63] *Early Discipline* (1832), p. 90; *Staffordshire Mercury,* 27 Sept., 20 Dec. 1828; *Staffordshire Advertiser,* 20 and 27 Dec. 1828.

his second wife did not accompany him on these journeys. His account of the Irish trip makes it obvious that he went alone, and subsequent newspaper reports make no reference to Mrs. Wilderspin. In the eighth edition of the *Infant System,* published in his early sixties, he makes the revealing statement that his travels "struck at the root of domestic happiness".[64] Could the exigencies of his profession have wrecked his second marriage? It seems probable. The statement can hardly refer to his third marriage, during which he lived a much more settled life and evidently a contented one.

If his second marriage was plagued with unhappiness, it was also relatively short. He was a widower when he married Mary Dowding in 1837 and though the date of Jane Wilderspin's death is not known, it is probable that it occurred early in 1828, when he refers to "an affliction" — not an illness — that overtook him after a visit to Aylesbury to establish an infant school, and which prevented him working for several weeks.[65] He certainly went to Scotland without a wife, and apparently settled in Cheltenham in 1829 with only his daughters. Whatever the date of the second Mrs. Wilderspin's death, it was never referred to by the family. Possibly the fact that he remarried only sixteen months after his first wife's death had something to do with the veil of silence. There may have been other reasons, but, whatever they were, they are lost to history.

* * * * *

Wilderspin always attempted, within the limits imposed by the shortness of his visits, to establish schools on the model described in his early books. On the question of religious instruction, however, he generally bowed to the feeling prevailing among the founders. The size and structure were likewise out of his hands, unless he happened to be asked to advise on the design. The infant schools of the 1820s thus displayed great diversity. They might be sponsored by benevolent ladies, committees of the well-to-do middle class or groups of clergymen, both Established and Nonconformist. Their religious orientation, though generally non-denominational, sometimes exhibited doctrinal peculiarities. The buildings differed widely in design, often being adapted from existing structures, and the settings varied from the idyllically rural to the grimly urban.

One of the best-documented examples of the establishment of infant schools in the late 1820s is provided by the work of the Rev. Francis Close, assisted by Wilderspin, at Cheltenham. A pupil of the Evangelical leader the Rev. Charles Simeon, and incumbent, from November 1826, of the parish church of St. Mary's, Close had gone to Cheltenham as a young curate and rapidly established a reputation as an educator.[66] In the summer of 1824, when

---

[64] *Infant System* (1852), p. 261.

[65] *Early Discipline* (1832), p. 94.

[66] For a brief, if patchy, biography of Close, cf. G. Berwick, "Close of Cheltenham: Parish Pope", *Theology,* Vol. XXXIX, No. 231, Sept. 1939, pp. 193-201; No. 232, Oct. 1939, pp. 276-85.

curate of Holy Trinity, Close had established a Sunday School in an old farmhouse in Alstone with the aim of improving the morals of the "idle and vicious" in the community, who flocked to the fields on Sunday in a manner "most uncongenial to the spirit of the fourth commandment". A room large enough to hold a hundred children was secured in the upper storey of an old farmhouse, a master and mistress appointed, voluntary teachers obtained and sufficient subscriptions gathered to keep the school in being. Soon the number of children increased to two hundred, spreading to other rooms and even invading the staircase.[67]

A subscription was opened for a new building in the autumn of 1825;[68] about this time Wilderspin, according to his own later testimony, appeared on the scene, examining as a private individual the state of the youth in and around Cheltenham, and he advised the incumbent, the Rev. Charles Jervis, of the "necessity and expediency" of an infant school in the town. As Wilderspin put it, "the Rev. Gent declined it as visionary", though Close approved; the latter, however, was unable to act without the sanction of his superiors. A certain Dr. Coley then took up the idea and it was due to his efforts that the project got under way.[69] Coley may have been the person who the local press reported as having donated £50 to the fund.[70] Close had a different version; his last- minute benefactors were Joseph and William Wilson. There was, apparently, little prospect of success in raising the necessary funds for the new Sunday School building, although the land had been purchased, until the two brothers, visiting Cheltenham to take the waters, were approached by Close and agreed to donate £20 each, provided the new premises were used for the purpose of an infant school during the week.[71]

There is some lack of clarity as to the date of the opening of the school. The *Bath and Cheltenham Gazette* announced its commencement midway through February 1826, and two weeks later the instruction of children in "devotional duties and useful learning" was reported.[72] Close, however, in his account of the formation of the school, dated November 1827, gives the summer of 1826 as the

---

[67]F. Close, *To the Friends and Supporters of the Sunday and Infant Schools Established at Alstone in the Parish of Cheltenham* (Cheltenham 1827), p. 3.

[68]*Bath Journal,* 31 Oct. 1825, citing the *Cheltenham Chronicle.*

[69]*Cheltenham Chronicle,* 26 Oct. 1837; Wilderspin was speaking at a meeting on national education, and gave no dates, though it is clear that he must have been referring to the period when Jervis, not Close, was the incumbent at Cheltenham, i.e. before November 1826, and most probably to the autumn of 1825.

[70]*Bath Journal,* 31 Oct. 1825.

[71]Close, *Sunday and Infant Schools at Alstone,* p. 4; *Cheltenham Journal,* 10 Dec. 1849. The list of donations on pp. 8-10 of Close's pamphlet, for the period August 1826 to November 1827, shows that the Wilson brothers gave £20 each and Dr. Coley only £1, but this may not have been the first list. Two other individuals gave £20 and two others £10 each.

[72]*Bath and Cheltenham Gazette,* 14 and 28 Feb. 1826. According to J. Lee, *A New Guide to Cheltenham* (Cheltenham, n.d.? 1834), the school was opened in "the Spring of 1826" (p. 157). *The Cheltenham Annuaire for the Year 1837* (Cheltenham 1837), p. 104, states that the Alstone Infant School was opened in 1826.

date of the purchase of the land and the following winter as the time of the erection of the building.[73] Possibly the school referred to in the *Gazette* was a temporary structure or was attached to another building. The New School Room, as it became known, was, however, opened sometime during the second week of April 1827.[74] The institution, situated in what is now called Alstone Lane,[75] had from the beginning enjoyed considerable public support. The Lord of the Manor had agreed to a nominal quit-rent, fees for the transfer of the land had been waived and almost every farmer in Alstone had offered his wagons to transport building material.[76] According to Wilderspin, the poor had given shrubs and plants for the playground.[77] The building measured only 30' × 31', much smaller than that advocated by Wilderspin, but it contained a gallery and the usual forms, tables and chairs; the playground was enclosed by a wall.[78]

At the beginning of April, at Close's invitation, Wilderspin arrived from London to organize the school.[79] He instructed the master and mistress, Mr. and Mrs. Charles F. Lewis, for a fortnight, left the school in their hands for a similar space of time, and then returned for another two weeks to prepare the children for a public examination.[80] Wilderspin, in fact, conducted two examinations, one on Thursday 17 May, and another on the following day; the latter was chiefly for the parents of the children, but "fashionable company" attended on both days, including Dr. Russell, headmaster of Charterhouse, on the Friday. Wilderspin apparently was in good form, and the 95 children sang hymns and rhymes, and answered questions in a manner that was described as producing "a sensation on all who were present as we have rarely witnessed". Indeed, the school had what might now be called a multiplier effect; several of the audience were wealthy visitors to Cheltenham, who, after the exhibition, expressed their determination to set up similar schools in their own localities on their return.[81]

Under Close's energetic leadership the institution flourished, the building being used as a Sunday School for the village children and as a place of worship for the inhabitants generally.[82] Close organised another examination at the end

---

[73]Close, *Sunday and Infant Schools at Alstone,* p.4.

[74]*Cheltenham Chronicle,* 10 May 1827, stated that the school had been open "one month".

[75]We are indebted to the Rev. Alan Munden for this detail.

[76]Close, *Sunday and Infant Schools at Alstone,* p.4.

[77]*Early Discipline* (1832), p. 95.

[78]*Cheltenham Chronicle,* 21 June 1827.

[79]The "Receipts and Expenditures of Alstone Infant and Sunday Schools" for August 1826 to November 1827, in Close, *Sunday and Infant Schools at Alstone,* pp.11, list "Mr. Wilderspin's expenses from London and back"; the date is deduced from Close's account on p. 5 of the same pamphlet. For Close's invitation. cf. *Cheltenham Journal,* 10 Dec. 1849.

[80]Close, *Sunday and Infant Schools at Alstone,* p.5.

[81]*Cheltenham Chronicle,* 10, 17, and 24 May 1827.

[82]*Early Discipline* (1832), p. 95.

of July with 300 children present — presumably the Sunday School children were added to the 140 of the infant school[83] — and the gathering was attended by "many ladies of distinguished rank",[84] who were later inspired to clear the remaining debt on the school by a sale of fancy work in the Assembly rooms; this realized £160 in a single day.[85]

Close's conception of infant education did not greatly differ from that set out in the Address of the Infant School Society. An infant school, he believed, should inculcate moral discipline, habits of mutual kindness, forbearance, self-control and religious feelings. Simple, easy lessons on general and religious subjects should be given, but the particulars of the method might vary; "whether this or that technicality of the system be adopted is unimportant".[86] These views, which were similar to those of Joseph Wilson, allowed him to accept Wilderspin as organiser of the school, and Wilderspin's protegé Lewis as master.

Believing that the infant school was "the most effective engine of national improvement that has ever been brought to bear on a dissolute population",[87] Close was eager to found another in the town itself when Alstone was on a secure financial footing.[88] Accordingly, on 10 November 1828, the citizens of Cheltenham witnessed the opening of a second infant school in what proved to be temporary premises near St. James Square,[89] and on 23 February 1829 an examination of the 130 children took place; the *Chronicle,* as usual, enthusiastically praised the system, finding the "discipline, accuracy, quietude and order" of the children "truly surprising".[90]

Significantly, Close did not invite Wilderspin to open this school, preferring to bring in a person who, Wilderspin alleged, had spent only two or three weeks at one of the London schools. Wilderspin, who was probably disappointed not to be called upon (he was in the North of England at the time), dubbed the newcomer "Sir Oracle". Apparently, when the new man arrived at Cheltenham little was ready, so he went to the Alstone school, where he declared that everything was wrong. Mr. Lewis was persuaded, in Wilderspin's words, "to allow him to show off his new information, and to exert his self-prized skill". As a result, in Wilderspin's opinion, the whole system deteriorated — the parents complained, attendance fell, the master resigned and the school was nearly

---

[83] The accounts of the two schools were combined (Close, *Sunday and Infant Schools at Alstone* (p. 11)). There were 140 children in the infant school (*Cheltenham Chronicle,* 12 July 1827).

[84] *Cheltenham Chronicle,* 5 July 1827.

[85] *Cheltenham Chronicle,* 12 July, 27 Sept. and 1 Nov. 1827.

[86] Close, *Sunday and Infant Schools at Alstone,* pp. 6-7.

[87] *Ibid.,* p. 7.

[88] *Cheltenham Chronicle,* 1 Nov. 1827.

[89] *Berrow's Worcester Journal,* 13 Nov. 1828; *Cheltenham Journal,* 5 Jan. 1829; the *Cheltenham Chronicle* of Thursday, 6 Nov. 1828 had announced that the school would open on "Monday week".

[90] *Cheltenham Chronicle,* 26 Feb. 1829.

ruined. "So much", he added, "for the labours of ignorance and self-sufficiency". The original plan was subsequently reverted to, but Lewis, described by Wilderspin as "a meek, humble and respectable man", could not be persuaded to return and became one of Wilderspin's agents.[91]

"Sir Oracle" was almost certainly James Rodgers, first master of Cheltenham Infant School and author of *A Practical Treatise on Infant Education*, who had been trained at Chelsea Infant School by Thomas Bilby.[92] Both Rodgers and Bilby were prominent supporters of the Evangelical trend in the infant school movement which began in the late 1820s and which strongly opposed both the Wilderspinian system and its founder's non-denominational religious teaching.[93] Close, in favouring Rodgers as against Wilderspin, repudiated the educational position he had taken in 1827 and showed himself as a supporter of the ultra-Protestant, anti-Catholic brand of Evangelicalism which flourished in 1830s and which had a very different view of infant education from that of, for instance, the Wilsons or Thomas Babington of the previous generation. Wilderspin later said that, when he offered his teen-age daughter Sarah Anne as teacher for one of the Cheltenham schools, "the hydra-headed monster of prejudice reared its ugly face" and she was refused.[94] Wilderspin does not give the reason, but her Swedenborgian faith was obviously at the root of it. Wilderspin said nothing at the time and three years later merely remarked that he and Close differed as to what was essential but that he trusted that the latter would arrive at a different conclusion.[95] Later he was to become much more critical.

Though Close was overtly repudiating the Wilderspinian system, his views on school architecture underscored Wilderspin's strongest recommendations. The school which had opened in November 1828 was a stop-gap; Close had plans for a lavish new structure in St. James' Square itself, and he laid out £1,000 (£700 of which was mortgaged) on the land and the school house.[96] The main room was

---

[91] *Early Discipline* (1832), p. 95. Religion may have been a factor in the Rodgers-Lewis dispute. Lewis was apparently a Swedenborgian, or at least a sympathiser of the New Church. After he left Wilderspin's service he opened a school in Cheltenham and in 1838 was accused by Thomas Bowller, then master of Cheltenham Infant School, of teaching his son infidelity, being a disciple of Wilderspin and receiving the doctrines of Swedenborg. Lewis claimed to be "attached to" the Church of England, but declared he would join in any service to God. Though he denied attendance at the New Church, he did not repudiate the doctrine of Swedenborg. Cf. Wilderspin Papers, C.F. Lewis, *Letter to Mr. Thomas Bowller* (Cheltenham 1838). Wilderspin made a note on the title page that Lewis was his agent and later opened a boarding school.

[92] J. Rodgers, *A Practical Treatise on Infant Education* (London n.d.), p. 26. Rodgers described Mr. and Mrs. Bilby as "my esteemed and valued friends".

[93] Cf. Chapter 11.

[94] *Cheltenham Chronicle*, 26 Oct. 1837. Wilderspin was speaking at Cheltenham some eight years later, at the height of his quarrel with Close, and as usual gives no dates, but it is probable that he was referring to Cheltenham rather than Alstone Infant School; he had settled in Cheltenham by March 1829, and it is possible that his daughter Sarah Anne applied to be an assistant teacher. Though the girl was capable of running a school, it was doubtful if Close would have appointed an adolescent to so demanding a post as superintendent.

[95] *Early Discipline* (1832), p. 95.

[96] *Cheltenham Journal*, 15 Mar. 1830.

63' long, 30' wide and 20' high, with walls of Cotswold stone two feet thick.[97]

As far as can be ascertained, it is the oldest infant school building still in existence.[98] Now used as a printing works, it gives even today a sense of both solidity and spaciousness; along the walls at one end can be seen the marks where the gallery was fitted. As the illustration shows, it must have been an impressive sight when it opened on 26 July 1830,[99] and its situation, stated a local guidebook, was "healthy and central, near the poor and not far from the rich".[100] Wilderspin declared it was the best infant school building he had seen anywhere outside Scotland.[101] The average attendance was 250 children — grossly overcrowded by modern standards — and the running expenses were considerable, reaching over £200 per annum. It was something of a showpiece and had so many visitors that the hour of 11 a.m. to 12 noon was set aside for them.[102]

Rodgers remained as master of the school until 1834, when, according to Wilderspin, he was discharged "under rather painful circumstances"[103] and was succeeded by Thomas Bowller.[104] During the following decade, three more infant schools were built in the town,[105] but as far as is known Wilderspin was not concerned with any of them.

* * * * *

Wilderspin's work as an agent of the Infant School Society appears as an almost unbroken record of success. Where he did not succeed in establishing a school, his visits or lectures were often instrumental in arousing others to do so, and when the Society ceased operations in 1828, the infant school, largely on the Wilderspin model, had been firmly established on the educational map of Britain. It will thus be instructive at this point to attempt to assess the public reception of the new schools, the degree of support they received from different classes of society and the arguments by which they were attacked and defended.

[97] We are indebted to the Rev. Alan Munden for these measurements.

[98] The infant school rooms at New Lanark also survive, but these are part of the Institute for the Formation of Character.

[99] J. Goding, *Norman's History of Cheltenham* (London 1863), p. 548; *The Cheltenham Annuaire for the Year 1837* (Cheltenham 1837), p. 104. The sign above the entrance reads: "Cheltenham Infant School. Est. 1828"; this date refers to the opening of the temporary building.

[100] J. Lee, *A New Guide to Cheltenham* (Cheltenham, n.d.? 1834), p. 158.

[101] *Early Discipline* (1832), p. 96.

[102] F. Close, *Substance of a Lecture Delivered in the Infant's School Room at Cheltenham...*(Cheltenham 1832), pp. 14-15.

[103] Ms. Revisions, *Early Discipline* (1840), p. 114.

[104] J. Lee, *A New Guide to Cheltenham* (Cheltenham, 2nd ed., 1837.), p. 154.

[105] By 1843 Cheltenham had five infant schools. (H. Davies, *A View of Cheltenham in the Past and Present State* (Cheltenham 1843), p. 158.

Broadly speaking, infant schools were founded by the middle classes (plus some members of the aristocracy) for the benefit of the working classes; one active publicist for the new schools believed their provision was a "duty" which devolved on the middle classes.[106] But, as we have seen, Tory and High Church circles felt equally bound to oppose them, and among lay opinion there were currents of feeling critical of the schools. Throughout the 20s and 30s they were criticised on two main grounds. First, that taking children from their parents before the age of six weakened the bonds of familial affection which, as a correspondent of the *Christian Observer* remarked, "formed one of the most pleasing characteristics of the lower classes".[107] As both Wilderspin and James Simpson, his foremost Scottish supporter, pointed out in reply, the children were away from their parents for six or seven hours a day only; the separation tended to strengthen rather than weaken the mutual affection of parents and children; and, in any case, in no class of society were parents able to apply moral education as systematically and efficiently as in the infant school.[108]

The second main objection to infant schools, "frequently heard" as early as 1824,[109] and still current in the mid-30s, was that they stimulated the children at too early an age and that the teaching of subjects led to overpressure which could be detrimental to the child's physical and mental health; or as Wilderspin more colourfully phrased it, they were alleged to make children "prodigies in infancy that they might be blockheads all the rest of their lives".[110] Wilderspin and Simpson disposed of this by stressing that all the faculties of infants were attended to in turn, the feelings and the body were ministered to as well as the mind, and that no one faculty was stimulated at the expense of the others.[111]

This might be called the "technical" defence of infant schools. More frequent was the "moral" defence, advanced in letters or articles in local newspapers, reports of local infant school societies or speeches at educational gatherings; these were various in detail (though many were convinced the mere sight of an infant school would convert the doubtful), but essentially followed the "rescue from vice by creative education" line of the Address of the Infant

[106]W. Davis, letter in the *Taunton Courier*, 26 Dec. 1827. This was the sixth of seven long letters, published in the paper, which set out the case for infant schools of the Wilderspin type.

[107]*Christian Observer*, Vol. XXXIII, No. 7, July 1823, p. 426; cf. also P.P. 1835 VII, Education, p. 16. For other criticisms, cf. *Early Discipline* (1834), p. 102ff.

[108]*Infant Poor* (1824), p. 25; *Infant Education* (1825) pp. 176-78; P.P. 1835 VII, Education, p. 16; J. Simpson, *The Necessity of Popular Education* (Edinburgh 1834), pp. 151-53.

[109]According to a correspondent in the *Christian Observer*, Vol. XXXIV, No. 11, Nov. 1824, p. 688; cf. also *Bath and Cheltenham Gazette*, 31 May 1831.

[110]P.P. 1835 VII, Education, p. 16.

[111]*Ibid.*; Simpson, *Popular Education*, pp. 150-51.

School Society.[112] This could not have been seen by all who supported its argument, so it was clear that provincial individuals and groups could reach similar conclusions on the basis of visitor's reports, personal observation or the perusal of the works of Wilderspin and Pole.[113] In only a few manufacturing districts was the "industrial" argument put forward — that infant schools might provide an antidote to the rigours of child labour or provide the only education for poor children before they started work at the age of six.[114]

The attitudes of working-class parents towards infant schools have not been recorded, and we must have recourse to middle-class publications for even a hint of their views. One source is the printed dialogue issued by supporters, a form of propaganda made famous, or notorious, a generation earlier by Hannah More and her associates. If these productions are to be believed (and they would have had little point if they had been entirely fanciful), the working-class objections to infant schools were three: they were large and noisy; children did not learn to read or spell therein; and they made infants disobedient or over-inquisitive. As "a Lady" admitted in one of the dialogues, "there is a great deal of prejudice against them amongst the poor".[115] Wilderspin had noticed this during his Spitalfields days,[116] and according to J.R. Wood, the Manchester statistician, there was a general dislike of infant schools among working-class mothers in the 1830s.[117] Archibald Prentice, the Manchester philanthropist who had concerned himself with infant schools in their early days, gave a somewhat sardonic but probably basically truthful picture of the position from the vantage point of the mid-century. The efforts of Wilderspin, working almost single-handedly, he stated, had set the movement going, but infant schools were costly and even the few pence per week they charged was a good deal for a poor man to pay "for a good which they did not very well understand".

[112]Cf. *Philanthropic Gazette,* 19 Mar. 1823; J. Ketley, letter to *Christian Reformer,* Vol. X, No. CXVI, Aug. 1824; Public Address, *Newcastle Courant,* 22 Jan. 1825; *Birmingham Gazette,* 12 Sept. 1825; J.H., letter to *Brighton Herald,* 10 Dec. 1825; J. Marshall, address to Leeds Philosophical Society, *Leeds Mercury,* 11 Feb. 1826; "C", letter to *Stockport Advertiser,* 9 June 1826; report of meeting in Salford, *Manchester Guardian,* 30 Dec. 1826; report of meeting in Plymouth, *World,* 26 Sept. 1827; Second Annual Report of the Birmingham Infant School Society (Birmingham 1827); W. Davis, seven letters to *Taunton Courier,* 10 Oct., 17 Oct., 24 Oct., 7 Nov., 21 Nov., 26 Dec., 1827; 23 Jan. 1828; "A Visitor", letter to *Commentator,* 29 Mar. 1828; "Ecclesiastes", letter to *North Wales Echo,* 8 Apr. 1830.

[113]For the influence of Pole's book, cf. [H. Brougham], "Early Moral Education", *Edinburgh Review,* Vol. XXXVIII, No. LXXVI, May 1823, p. 444; for the practical effect of Wilderspin's works, cf. the examples in Chapters 3, 5 and 6.

[114]Cf. report of meeting, *Birmingham Gazette,* 26 Sept. 1825; First Report of the Infant School Society of Newcastle-upon-Tyne (Newcastle 1826); report of meeting, *Leicester Chronicle,* 2 Feb. 1828.

[115]Cf. *Dialogue on Infant Schools* (Lindfield 1827), a pamphlet probably produced by, or under the auspices of, William Allen; *A Dialogue between a Lady and a Cottager upon the Advantages of Infant Schools* (n.d.? 1828), reviewed in the *Christian Monitor,* N.S., Vol. 1, No. 1, Apr. 1828); "Infant School: Dialogue between Two Labourers", *Cottager's Monthly Visitor,* Vol. 10, Aug. 1830, pp. 352-54.

[116]P.P. 1835 VII, Education, p. 23.

[117]P.P. 1838 VII, Report from the Select Committee on the Education of the Poorer Classes in England and Wales, p. 122.

They had not felt the want and had not caught the benefit. It was a new thing proceeding from the rich without consultation with the poor, and might be, after all, only another scheme similar to the charity school, where the principal thing was how poor men's boys should pull off their caps, and poor men's girls should make their curtsey to the squire and the parson, and the squire's lady and the parson's lady. Sad perversion of thought, certainly; but those who entertained it had not enjoyed the benefit of early tuition, and the doubt was excusable.[118]

It is salutary to be reminded of the scepticism of the poor with regard to infant schools and to understand that what philanthropists might see as advantages — the fact that they were provided *for* the poor and, in most cases, embodied novel modes of education — were often seen as demerits by working people, or at least by the "mechanics", i.e. the upper strata of the workers. It was this class, according to Wilderspin, who supported and sent their children to dame schools, an alternative system of schooling for children under six.[119] The dame school, in respect of age-range and social background of the pupils, was the only institution which could directly be compared to the infant school and was, in practice, its only rival. Little has been written by educational historians about dame schools, though the protagonists of the first infant schools were well aware of their existence and united in their condemnation of them. The picture that comes down to us from eighteenth century poets — Goldsmith, Cowper, Crabbe and others — is of an apple-cheeked, white-capped widow teaching reading to a crowd of unruly infants in a cottage.[120] The dame school, however, adapted itself to industrialism and urbanisation and flourished as a form of working-class educational self-help in both the industrial districts and the countryside almost to the end of the nineteenth century.[121]

In the early part of the century William Lovett, Thomas Cooper and other artisans testified to their early grounding at a dame school.[122] Joseph Gutteridge, a Coventry weaver, remembered attending one at the time Wilderspin was teaching at Spitalfields:

> At five I was sent to a dame school kept by a Quakeress, where I soon acquired all the knowledge, educationally, that the old lady could impart. Being of a practical turn of mind, she not only taught us her limited stock of general knowledge, but instructed us — boys and girls alike — in the arts of sewing and

[118]A. Prentice, *Historical Sketches and Personal Recollections of Manchester* (London 1851), p. 340.

[119]*Infant Poor* (1823), p. 85.

[120]J.H. Higginson, The Dame Schools of Great Britain, unpublished M.A. thesis, University of Leeds 1939, *passim*; J.H. Higginson, "Dame Schools", *British Journal of Educational Studies*,, Vol. XXII, No. 2, June 1974, pp. 166-181.

[121]D.P. Leinster-Mackay, "Dame Schools: A Need for Review", *British Journal of Educational Studies*, Vol. XXIV, No. 1, Feb. 1976, pp. 33-48.

[122][W. Lovett], *Life and Struggles of William Lovett* (London 1876), p. 4; *The Life of Thomas Cooper: Written by Himself* (London 1872), p. 7.

knitting...Even now as age advances I recall her gentle, placid face and her motherly kindness in dealing with the rough untutored natures committed to her care, her repugnance of physical force and her facile and winning mode of attracting attention...At seven I had so far profited by her teaching as to be able to make out the contents of the local papers...[123]

Though conditions in dame schools varied, particularly with regard to the accomplishments of the teacher and the incidence of corporal punishment,[124] they were sufficiently similar to form a recognisable type. They were, however, comprehensively condemned by Wilderspin, Brougham, Goyder, Wilson, Close, Pole and almost all supporters of the new infant schools, usually on four grounds. First, the teachers were aged, infirm, untrained or otherwise unsuitable; second, the rooms were small, cramped, ill-lit and badly ventilated; third, the curriculum was narrow, usually limited to reading and perhaps some writing, taught by rote; lastly, the discipline was severe, with the rod and the dunce's cap ubiquitous and much in use.[125] The comparison between the light and airy infant schools, with their well-qualified teachers, wide curriculum and lack of degrading corporal punishment, and the "prisons of the most deleterious kind", as Goyder described the dame schools,[126] was always drawn. The tone was patronising, and few of the protagonists of infant schools seemed to understand the position of the poor with regard to dame schools.

As early as 1823 Pole noticed that the poor "have not readily come into the plan of paying a moderate sum for the care and tuition of their children" in infant schools, and seemed willing to pay more for "less advantageous" instruction in dame schools.[127] Brougham found "truly astonishing" the unwillingness of the poor to contribute even a penny a week to an infant school when they gave fourpence or sixpence "to the most wretched Dame schools".[128] He attributed this to "vulgar feeling" which encompassed both greed and ungratefulness;[129] but to the artisan class it was a rational position. They preferred to send their children to schools which they supported and controlled themselves, and which were, in essence, an extension of the working-class family, rather than to those provided for them by middle-class charity. Ironically, in rejecting this paternalism, the poor denied themselves the benefits of some of the most

---

[123]J. Gutteridge, *Lights and Shadows in the Life of an Artisan* (Coventry 1893), pp. 6-7.

[124]William Lovett was confined to the coal cellar for bad conduct at his dame school, c.1805 (Lovett, *Life and Struggles,* p. 3).

[125]*Infant Education* (1825), p. 80; p. 242; p. 277; *Infant System* (1852), p. 3; H. Brougham, "Early Moral Education", *loc.cit.,* p. 441; D. Goyder, *A Treatise on the Management of Infant Schools* (London 1826), pp. 37-9; W. Wilson, *The System of Infants' Schools* (London, 2nd ed., 1825), pp. 5-6; F. Close, *Substance of a Lecture...,* pp. 8-9; T. Pole, *Observations Relative to Infant Schools* (Bristol 1823), p. 9.

[126]Goyder, *Treatise,* p. 38.

[127]Pole, *Infant Schools,* p. 9.

[128]Brougham, "Early Moral Education", *loc.cit.,* p. 444.

[129]*Ibid.,* p. 445.

advanced pedagogy of the time. Infant schools thus encountered the traditions and realities of plebeian life as well as the prejudices of the middle and upper classes. Both factors hindered their development. Wilderspin, as a former artisan, was in a better position than almost anyone else to convince the upper section of the poor of the educational *bona fides* of the infant school. It is significant, however, that he found the going somewhat easier in Scotland, which had few dame schools,[130] than he had in England. It is to his work in Scotland that we must now turn.

[130]"A Dame's School", *Chambers' Edinburgh Journal,* No. 141, N.S.,12 Sept. 1846, p. 171.

CHAPTER 7

WILDERSPIN IN SCOTLAND

"I had often wished to visit Scotland", wrote Wilderspin in 1832, recalling his early days as a travelling educator, "but my friends objected, — suggested that it was unnecessary, — affirmed that many admirable plans of education were in action, — and repeated, what has often been declared with truth, — that the lower orders of people in that country are far better trained than the corresponding grades in this". Wilderspin was delighted, therefore, to receive in the spring of 1828 a letter from David Stow, a former visitor to Spitalfields, now secretary of the newly-formed Glasgow Infant School Society, inviting him to Glasgow to assist in organising the first infant school in the city.[1] The committee of the Society, anxious to establish a school on a plan that would secure general support, had already been in touch with Joseph Wilson, then acting as secretary of the Infant School Society in London; Wilson had suggested Wilderspin as the person most obviously fitted for the task.[2]

Wilderspin lost no time in getting started. For maximum freedom of travel, he obtained a spirited horse capable of carrying him the entire trip in the saddle. By starting early each morning he was able to cover fifty miles by mid-afternoon, leaving the late afternoon and evening free for calling upon influential citizens and distributing circulars in the principal towns he passed through. In eight days, Wilderspin was on the outskirts of Glasgow; there, however, he encountered an almost fatal delay. His horse, frightened by a dog, bolted from the road and plunged over the edge of a quarry. Wilderspin was thrown, landed on a heap of small stones and was unhurt; but his horse, the finest he ever owned, was "dreadfully mangled" and had to be sold.[3] His Glasgow hosts compensated him for the loss, as the unusual entry in the Society's first balance sheet shows:

> By [Mr. Wilderspin], by order of the Directors, to assist to indemnify him for loss of his Horse, when engaged in the Society's Business, £20.0.0.[4]

The Infant School Society in London, Wilderspin remarked ruefully, "gave me only their sorry regrets, because, I imagine, they were as costless as the priest's blessing".[5]

The school that Wilderspin was called upon to open was situated in the Drygate, one of the poorest parts of Glasgow, near the monument to John Knox, which was visible from all parts of the playground. On 23 April 1828[6] one

[1] *Early Discipline* (1832), p. 102.

[2] First Report of the Glasgow Infant School Society, 1829 (Glasgow 1829), p. 18.

[3] *Early Discipline* (1832), pp. 102-04.

[4] First Report G.I.S.S., p. 22.

[5] *Early Discipline* (1832), p. 104.

[6] First Report G.I.S.S., p. 22, which gives the starting date of the master's salary as 23 April 1828.

hundred and thirty children were admitted, many without shoes and stockings, Wilderspin recalled, and "exceedingly dirty in their appearance". Mr. and Mrs. David Caughie, the new master and mistress, had never seen an infant school, but were apt pupils; by barring all visitors during the training period, progress was so rapid that the school was ready for public examination in a month,[7] and Wilderspin had time to lecture in the Trades Hall on 30 April to stimulate public interest.[8] After several advertisements in the Glasgow papers, the public examination was held on 20 May in the Rev. Mr. Gunn's Gaelic Chapel on Hope Street, about a mile from the school.[9]

In a striking display of showmanship, Stow and Wilderspin had the children carried from the school to the Chapel in wagons decorated with green boughs and guarded on each side by detachments of police. Bringing up in the rear were the friends and parents of the children, augmented by a crowd of the curious which rapidly increased as the procession approached the Chapel. Singing as they entered, the children took their places in a gallery erected for the occasion and found themselves facing nearly a thousand people, including some of the most influential persons in Glasgow. The singing of the simple hymns and the responses of the children to questions from the floor delighted the audience, who contributed nearly £24 to the school's funds, enough to reimburse the Society for Wilderspin's travelling and living expenses while in Glasgow.[10]

The novelty of the exhibition in Hope Street made a deep impression upon the public mind. A correspondent in the *Glasgow Herald* was moved to point out that if infant schools had existed during the past twenty years, one-half the city's juvenile delinquency would have been prevented,[11] and Dr. David Welsh, the influential minister of St. David's Church and one of the founders of the Society, approaching Wilderspin a few days later, flattered him by saying, "Sir, you are a great man!"[12] Capitalising on the interest aroused, Wilderspin lectured on 22 May in the Andersonian Institution in John Street.[13]

The opening of the school and the success of the exhibition also redounded to the credit of the Glasgow Infant School Society and to that of David Stow, the moving spirit of the institution. He was a young Evangelical silk merchant, a protegé of Dr. Thomas Chalmers, one of the strongest advocates of the extension of education to the poor of the rapidly-growing industrial cities. Impelled by sentiments similar to those of his fellow silk merchant Joseph Wilson and his Spitalfields associates, Stow had turned to infant schools as a more effective means of combating the forces of evil than the Sunday School he

[7] *Early Discipline* (1832), p. 105; p. 107.

[8] *Glasgow Chronicle*, 28 Apr. 1928.

[9] *Glasgow Courier*, 10 and 17 May 1828; *Glasgow Herald*, 12 and 19 May 1828; *Early Discipline* (1832), p. 107.

[10] *Early Discipline* (1832), pp. 107-09; First Report G.I.S.S., p. 22.

[11] *Glasgow Herald*, 26 May 1828.

[12] *Early Discipline* (1832), p. 110.

[13] *Glasgow Herald*, 19 May 1828.

had opened in 1816.[14] The Glasgow Infant School Society had been set on foot in the autumn of 1827.[15] Its Directors were a group of business and professional men, plus a number of ministers from the various denominations, nearly all strongly Evangelical in principles or sympathies.[16]

The early reports of the Society, were not, however, heavily weighted with the trappings of vital religion. A few phrases revealed to the observant the basic orientation: "the fallen condition of our race", the importance of "scriptural education" and the necessity of employing a teacher "living and acting under the influence of evangelical truth". For the rest, the main emphasis was on the merits of a Wilderspin-type theory and practice and the deficiencies of traditional Scottish schooling, with its verbalism, rote learning and harsh punishment; the second report was largely devoted to a searching analysis of the role of education in industrial society in a manner redolent of that of Adam Smith in *The Wealth of Nations*.[17] Under the guidance of David Stow, the Society and its successor, the Glasgow Educational Society, continued to work in the same spirit. During the 1830s, however, Stow refashioned many of Wilderspin's methods into a system bearing his own name; this ultimately led to friction between the two educators.

* * * * *

On 26 May 1828 the Society had announced that Mr. Wilderspin had consented, with the permission of his London employers, "to remain in Scotland for some time to devote his attention to the organisation of Infant Schools and delivering lectures explanatory of the system in such of the towns and villages of Scotland as may request his services".[18] Requests soon came in and Wilderspin spent the summer fulfilling engagements, mainly in the West of Scotland. The exact sequence cannot be fixed with certainty, but he apparently spent most or all of June in Paisley, opening a school there on 7 July. His increasing confidence as a public speaker was evident in a preliminary lecture, given to over a thousand people, which lasted two and a half hours. To increase the flow of subscriptions, Wilderspin had Caughie bring two coachloads of children from Glasgow for a public demonstration in Paisley High Church. A young weaver named William Wright was taken from the loom in one of the local factories and trained as master, with his wife as mistress.[19]

[14] W. Fraser, *Memoir of the Life of David Stow* (London 1868), pp. 1-57, *passim;* G.P. Insh, *The Life and Work of David Stow* (Edinburgh 1938), pp. 1-10, *passim.*

[15] R.R. Rusk, *The Training of Teachers in Scotland* (Edinburgh 1928), p. 35.

[16] Fraser, *Memoir of Stow,* p. 81; Insh, *Life of Stow,* p. 11.

[17] First Report, G.I.S.S., *passim;* Second Annual Report of the Glasgow Infant School Society, 1830 (Glasgow 1830), *passim.*

[18] *Glasgow Herald,* 26 May 1828.

[19] *Early Discipline* (1832), pp. 115-16; First Report G.I.S.S., App. III, p. 26.

Engagements to open schools followed in Greenock (in September and October) and in Rothesay, the scenic watering-place on the Isle of Bute. On each occasion, children from the Glasgow school were taken by steamer to give demonstrations of the system, charming and amazing both the passengers (for whom impromptu demonstrations were given) and the audiences at the schools.[20] Some of Wilderspin's other activities during his first six months in Scotland are more difficult to trace. In *Early Discipline* he mentions visits to Dumbarton, Falkirk and Kilmarnock, in each of which he gave lectures without arousing much response. He also records a visit to Perth for two examinations of a school established by Lady Ruthven; these took place at the end of November, and may well have been his last assignment before moving to Edinburgh.[21]

In addition to his educational duties, Wilderspin found time to indulge his hobby of observing "human nature in all its forms". The Scottish chapters of *Early Discipline* are filled with anecdotes, observations of people and places and vivid accounts of Scottish customs. These are more than colourful backdrops to the narrative; he clearly felt that the Scots were outstanding in hospitality, cultural richness and love of learning, and this belief not only strongly influenced his views on the potentialities of education but also provided a standard by which he judged — and found wanting — the educational and cultural aspirations of the Irish, Welsh and English. At Paisley, for instance, Wilderspin was impressed by the grace and beauty of the young factory girls as they returned barefoot from work, wearing plaid cloaks with a hood under the chin with a green ribbon. At Greenock he was fascinated by the various "charms and spells" by which the Scottish peasants propitiated the goblins, elves and other spirits of Halloween. On another occasion, while strolling in the countryside, he observed two peasant women washing their linen by gaily treading the clothes, churning the water in the tub to a froth. Asking for some milk, he was served instead with whiskey and water, each to be taken separately. From the older woman he learned that her one wish was to give her seven children the "one thing needful"— namely, a religious education. On his visits to Scottish schools he was impressed with their high standards and degree of specialisation.[22]

During a summer holiday at Loch Lomond, he explored the countryside with a white-haired guide of over seventy, who took him by boat up wooded creeks and solitary streams. "Birds all around were sending forth their carols", he recalled; "the trout were gaily leaping after the insects designed to be their food; butterflies of various and richest colours were sporting in the sunbeams; wild bees were eagerly drinking their nectar; and now and then the gorgeous dragonfly whizzed through the air". To Wilderspin these were the works of the

[20] *Early Discipline* (1832), pp. 125-28; pp. 131-34. Wilderspin arrived in Greenock on 28 September and was still there at the end of October (*Scotsman,* 1 Oct., 8 Nov. 1828). Rothesay follows Greenock in the sequence in *Early Discipline.*

[21] *Early Discipline* (1832), pp. 142-43; pp. 198-200; *Perthshire Courier,* 13 Nov., 4 Dec. 1828.

[22] *Early Discipline* (1832), pp. 118-29, *passim.*

Deity; his guide seemed insensible to them but he spoke of the Scottish Church and John Knox with heart-stirring enthusiasm. "Ye're no' to be offended, mind, at what I'm saying", he warned, "but I think that in ye're country ye hae owre muckle shew! We had it once; but John Knox stripped off those trappings, and left religion what it should be. And did he not urge it, joost as it ought to be, on royalty itself?" Wilderspin confessed that he had to admit to the force and truth of his guide's remarks. After a sojourn in a Highland cottage on a bed of straw, and the pleasures of a diet of oat-cake, eggs, whiskey and milk, Wilderspin's constitution was fully restored and his favourable impression of Scotland and the Scots strengthened.[23]

* * * * *

Wilderspin had left Scotland in the early autumn of 1828 for a flying visit to Hanley, in the Potteries, where he lectured on 22 September.[24] On the return journey to Greenock on the Liverpool steam pacquet he met George Combe, the famous Scottish phrenologist, who invited him to visit Edinburgh.[25] Wilderspin assented, but was unable to fulfil his promise until his outstanding engagements were completed, and his arrival was delayed until the end of November. In Edinburgh he found an atmosphere very different from the parochialism of the smaller Scottish towns and the rather dour and narrow churchmanship of the Glasgow Infant School supporters. The capital city, basking in the afterglow of the Scottish Enlightenment, still prided itself on its reputation as the Modern Athens.[26]

Wilderspin was taken up by the liberal wing of the phrenologists, then at the height of their influence under the leadership of George Combe. An Edinburgh lawyer, born in 1788, Combe had been converted as a young man to the phrenological doctrines of Gall and Spurzheim, and when he met Wilderspin he had recently published *The Constitution of Man,* a treatise on phrenology so popular that it sold a thousand copies in a single week and made his reputation as one of the leading philosophers of the age.[27] In Edinburgh he had a number of influential followers among the intelligentsia of the city — his younger brother Andrew, a celebrated physician, his nephew Robert Cox, writer and journalist, Charles MacLaren, editor of the *Scotsman,* James L'Amy and James Simpson, advocates, James Bridges, and William Ritchie, also of the *Scotsman.*[28]

[23] *Early Discipline* (1832), pp. 134-41.

[24] Cf. Chapter 6.

[25] N.L.S. Add. Mss., 7384, ff. 172-75, Combe to Rev. D. Welsh, 9 Dec. 1828.

[26] Cf. *Scotsman,* 28 Apr. 1830.

[27] D. de Giustino, *Conquest of Mind: Phrenology and Victorian Social Thought* (London 1975), pp. 1-30, *passim.*

[28] C. Gibbon, *The Life of George Combe* (London, 2 vol., 1878), I, pp. 261-64; De Giustino, *Conquest of Mind, passim.*

Phrenology, a semi-scientific theory of the functions of the brain, claimed to have discovered thirty-seven faculties of the mind whose location could be ascertained by the configuration of the skull. Its main adherents also embraced, however, an advanced and progressive educational theory which echoed many of the finest sentiments of the European Enlightenment. Combe, for instance, saw education in a two-fold aspect, as the training of the faculties and as the acquisition of knowledge, both positive and instrumental, for the tasks of life. His proposed curriculum was encyclopaedic, embracing most of human learning, but favouring the physical and moral sciences at the expense of classical languages and traditional religious instruction. James Simpson's central concern was the structure of the educational system, and in his evidence to the Select Committee on Education in Ireland in 1836 he put forward the first detailed plan for a comprehensive system of education; this was to be compulsory, free and state-aided, commencing in the infant school and continuing to the age of fourteen.[29]

Phrenologists welcomed infant schools because they recognised that educational growth proceeded in stages from infancy onwards and that there were studies appropriate to each of the faculties as they developed.[30] They were thus prepared to back Wilderspin's efforts when he came to Edinburgh. George Combe had promised him "the aid of the *Scotsman* Newspaper and of some active individuals",[31] and the way was prepared with articles on infant education in the *Scotsman*, Wilderspin's introduction to MacLaren and Bridges, and Combe's personal invitation to "persons of substance and activity" to attend Wilderspin's first lecture.[32] This was to be given at the Clyde Street Hall (the usual meeting place of the Edinburgh phrenologists) on Thursday 27 November, at three o'clock in the afternoon.[33]

"Those who expected *a lecture*", reported the *Scotsman*, "or a discussion of philosophical principles, would be disappointed; but they, on the other hand, who desired a clear and practical illustration of a method of dealing with the infant mind, would be highly gratified. . ."[34] This was a diplomatic way of stating that Wilderspin had given a very plain and factual description of his model of the infant school. A second meeting was, however, held on 1 December, at which it was decided to take immediate steps to establish an infant school, Wilderspin having previously declared his willingness to organise it.[35] Combe and Bridges drew up a list of committee members, but at the first meeting of the committee

[29] For Combe, Simpson, phrenology and education, cf. W.A.C. Stewart and W.P. McCann, *The Educational Innovators 1750-1880* (London 1967), pp. 280-86.

[30] De Giustino, *Conquest of Mind*, p. 174. Cf. also Chapter 9.

[31] N.L.S. Add. Mss., 7384, ff. 172-75, Combe to Rev. D. Welsh, 9 Dec. 1828.

[32] Combe to Welsh, 9 Dec. 1828; cf. *Scotsman*, 1 Oct., 22 Nov. 1828.

[33] *Scotsman*, 26 Nov. 1828.

[34] *Scotsman*, 29 Nov. 1828.

[35] *Scotsman*, 29 Nov., 3 Dec. 1828.

the plan ran into difficulties. Some Evangelical members argued that the inclusion of Combe, the author of an "infidel book" (*The Constitution of Man*), would "shipwreck the measure", and that if he didn't withdraw, they would. To avoid controversy Combe offered to withdraw; Simpson, Ritchie and L'Amy, however, insisted on his remaining. At the next committee meeting L'Amy proposed that the committee be broadened by including representatives of all the denominations, but still including Combe. This was put to the vote and the Evangelicals defeated. The committee then planned a public meeting which would include men of all parties.[36] They succeeded in drawing together a number of distinguished academics, clergy (both Established and Dissenting), and public men, including the Lord Justice-Clerk and the Lord Provost, together with representatives of the medical, mercantile and trading sections of the community.[37]

The meeting, postponed until 6 January 1829, was preceded by a fanfare of publicity. MacLaren printed a laudatory article on infant schools in the *Scotsman,* the scientist Sir John Sinclair issued an address to the citizens of Edinburgh on infant schools, and on 3 January the *Scotsman* splashed a review of the fourth edition of Wilderspin's book (now titled *Infant Education)* across its front page.[38] The speeches, particularly those of the public officials, tended to dwell on the contribution infant education might make to the diminution of juvenile delinquency, and Ritchie and Simpson did not parade their phrenological principles.[39] A committee of forty-three was elected to run the Infant School Society; Combe, L'Amy and Simpson were the only notable phrenologists among the office bearers, though Simpson held the key post of convener of the Ordinary Directors; most of the members, including the Duke of Buccleuch (an Evangelical sympathiser) and Francis Jeffery, the Lord Advocate, were opposed to or uninterested in phrenology.[40] Nevertheless, as Combe observed, "through all the town the cry is raised that the infant school is an infidel and phrenological job".[41]

A site for the proposed school was chosen in the Vennel and in April 1829 Wilderspin, by now an independent educationist, was brought from Cheltenham to plan the buildings and lay out the playground.[42] Progress was somewhat delayed by negotiations with the civil authorities for permission to abut the

[36]N.L.S. Add. Mss., 7384, f. 191, Combe to Spurzheim, 20 Jan. 1829.

[37]*Scotsman,* 6 Jan. 1829.

[38]*Scotsman,* 13 Dec. 1828; 3 Jan. 1829.

[39]*Scotsman,* 7 Jan. 1829.

[40]Report of the Edinburgh Infant School Society (Edinburgh 1832), p. 6; p. 15. Dr. David Welsh, an Extraordinary Director and a supporter of phrenology, turned against phrenology in 1831 (Gibbon, *Life of Combe,* I, p. 241).

[41]Combe to Spurzheim, 20 Jan. 1829.

[42]Report E.I.S.S., p. 3; *Scotsman,* 18 Apr. 1829.

building against the city wall,[43] and also by a shortage of subscriptions. The latter was partly due to crude propaganda against infant schools by sections of the Tory press, including the *New Scots Magazine* and *Blackwood's,* the March issue of which labelled infant schools as "education driven to absurdity" and prophesied that the attempt "will soon fall out of the hands of weak enthusiasts and expire!"[44]

To restore the prospects of the Infant School Society, Wilderspin agreed to give a series of lectures, the success of which soon falsified the prediction of *Blackwood's.* The lectures, held on three successive days, commencing on 22 April, were a great success, not a little of which was due to the presence of Caughie and twelve children from the Glasgow school, brought by coach to Edinburgh. The children, poorly clad but eager, made a dramatic late entrance, gave an animated display of mental arithmetic, reading, spelling, movement and singing, and sent the audience and the local press into raptures.[45] This "astonishing exhibition of intellectual progress" had the desired effect and, according to Wilderspin, £500 was collected in a fortnight towards the cost of the school.[46]

Some six months later the foundation stone was laid by the Lord Provost in an impressive ceremony, and the building was completed by the following spring. Designed by William Hamilton, architect of the Edinburgh High School (who gave his services free as a contribution to the school) and "completely approved by Mr. Wilderspin, almost to the driving of the last nail", it was, in Simpson's estimation, "a school on the first scale in every respect. . .a model to the whole country", with all the latest equipment and apparatus. Wilderspin declared it the best he had ever seen.[47] The total expenditure on the school amounted to £1,050, making it probably the most expensive school for the poor in Britain.[48]

Opened in April 1830 for the reception of pupils, the school was superintended by the former Paisley teachers William Wright and his wife; people as fitted for their task as any he had ever met, declared Wilderspin.[49] The latter came down from Montrose to lecture and to hold the first public examination, (repeated a week later) in the Waterloo Rooms. The ceremonies

[43] Warrants of the Lord Dean of Guild and the Council, Edinburgh. Petition, 29 Apr. 1829; Minute, 20 May 1829; Act of Council, 20 May 1829; Minute 26 May 1829; Act of Council, 1 July 1829; Petition, 9 July 1829.

[44] "Noctes Ambrosianae", No. XLI, *Blackwood's Edinburgh Magazine,* Vol. XXV, No. XLI, Mar. 1829, p. 393; *New Scots Magazine,* Vol. I, Jan. 1829, pp. 68-9; *Scotsman,* 18 and 22 Apr. 1829.

[45] *Early Discipline* (1832), pp. 155-56; Simpson to Stow, 23 Apr. 1829, requesting the children stay an extra day in Edinburgh (First Report G.I.S.S., p. 20); *Early Discipline* (1832), p. 156; *Scotsman,* 25 Apr. 1829.

[46] *Caledonian Mercury,* 27 Apr. 1829; *Bath and Cheltenham Gazette,* 24 May 1831, reporting a speech by Wilderspin in Bath.

[47] *Scotsman,* 29 Apr., 5 and 12 May, 17 Oct. 1829; Report E.I.S.S., p. 3.

[48] Simpson's estimate, in *Scotsman,* 5 May 1830. The highest cost of a National School built in England between 1812 and 1835 was £718. (M. Seaborne, *The English School* (London 1971), pp. 140-41).

[49] Report E.I.S.S., p. 3; *Edinburgh Evening Courant,* 3 May 1830.

were conducted with the usual public pomp, the children marching to and from the hall, crammed for the occasion with members of the higher classes.[50]

Wilderspin's experiences in Edinburgh were a high water mark in his career. For the first time his system was taken seriously by an influential group of intellectuals, meticulously put into practice and publicised on a hitherto unprecedented scale. The Edinburgh Infant School Society thanked him lavishly in its First Report and laid it down as its first rule that the school should operate on the mode of instruction set out in the fourth edition of his *Infant Education*.[51] Wilderspin also gained many influential supporters: Charles MacLaren, editor of the *Scotsman;* the brothers Robert and William Chambers, phrenologists and publishers, who popularised Wilderspin's work in their book on infant education;[52] Sir John Sinclair, who, declining Dr. Andrew Bell's request to run the infant school on monitorial lines, was converted by Wilderspin's exhibitions and arranged for him to address the General Assembly of the Church of Scotland in furtherance of a scheme to join infant schools to the parochial system;[53] above all, James Simpson became a lifelong friend and supporter. He kept Brougham informed of the progress of the Edinburgh school and in his widely-read *Philosophy of Education* he praised Wilderspin's system and drew attention to his tireless efforts on behalf of infant education.[54] Several years later he was briefly to join Wilderspin in a nation-wide campaign for national education. Simpson also was the first to analyse Wilderspin's system on phrenological lines and to demonstrate that it was in perfect accord with phrenological principles.[55]

Close association with the Edinburgh phrenologists also affected Wilderspin's views. He had arrived in Scotland with no knowledge of phrenology and a sceptical attitude towards it. He was, however, persuaded to hear Spurzheim lecture in Glasgow, and later met him in Edinburgh. After consideration, he informed Simpson that phrenology gave support to his own views on education and, if he had known about it earlier, it would have "incalculably abridged his labours and shortened his road to his present

[50]*Scotsman,* 21 and 28 Apr., 5, 8 and 12 May 1830; *Edinburgh Weekly Journal,* 5 May 1830; *Edinburgh Evening Courant,* 6 May 1830.

[51]Report E.I.S.S., p. 13; p. 17.

[52]W. and R. Chambers, *Infant Education* (Edinburgh 1836), p. 3 ff.

[53]A. Bell, *Letters to the Rt. Hon. Sir John Sinclair, Bart. on the Infant School Society of Edinburgh* (London 1829), *passim; Scotsman,* 12 May 1830; *Early Discipline* (1832), pp. 202-03. Wilderspin assigns no date to these lectures, but they were most probably given in 1830 or 1832; in the spring of both these years he was in Scotland.

[54]U.C.L. Brougham Mss., 44687, Simpson to Brougham, 16 Apr. 1833; 23612, Simpson to Brougham, 20 June 1835; J. Simpson, *The Philosophy of Education* (Edinburgh, 2nd ed., 1836), pp. 108-09.

[55][J. Simpson], "Phrenological Analysis of Infant Education in Mr. Wilderspin's System", *Phrenological Journal,* Vol. VI, No. XXXV, 1830, pp. 418-33. For Simpson's authorship of this article, cf. W. Jolly, *Education: Its Principles and Practice as Developed by George Combe* (London 1879), p. 322 n; N.L.S. Add. Mss., 7229, ff. 19-20, Mackenzie to Combe, 25 Apr. 1832.

position".[56] Some years later, in Dublin, he admitted to Archbishop Whately, himself an adherent of phrenology, that he professed himself a "semi-convert" to the doctrines.[57] The results of his interest in phrenology were apparent in his books and lectures during the 1830s.

* * * * *

The model infant school in Edinburgh encouraged the establishment of others in cities and towns along the east coast of Scotland. Two of the most interesting developments were in Aberdeen and Dundee, and Wilderspin helped to lay the foundation of infant education in each city. A few days after the lectures and exhibitions at Edinburgh in April 1829 he travelled northwards to Aberdeen, where he gave two lectures at Machray's Hotel on 28 and 29 April.[58] His visit stimulated sufficient interest for a meeting to be called on 25 June to establish an Infant School Society. The committee, as was not unusual in Scotland, was heavily weighted with the local landed gentry and contained only one clergyman. The speeches, outlining the reasons for the establishment of the Society, differed somewhat from those commonly heard in England. Though it was argued that infant schools would reduce crime and vice among the children of the poor, the main emphasis was on the schools' role in imparting elements of knowledge, advancing character, promoting happiness and generally benefiting the community — for which reasons, incidentally, the proposed school was to be non-denominational. Several speakers suggested that infant schools could play a role in industrial society that parish schools had played in raising "the moral condition of the peasantry of Scotland so far above that of any other nation in Europe".[59]

The opening of the school was delayed by shortage of funds,[60] and it was some two and a half years after the first meeting that Wilderspin was recalled to open the school. He travelled up from England in October 1831 with his daughter Sarah Anne, then aged seventeen; he had been summoned by a letter from Stephen Pellatt, writing on behalf of the local Infant School Society.[61] After Wilderspin had given a preparatory course of four lectures on 7, 8, 10 and 11 November, he staged a public examination that drew six hundred people to the Assembly Rooms on the 17th; it was repeated before a similarly numerous audience on the 21st, in spite of high winds and rain. At both exhibitions the

[56]Simpson, *loc.cit.,* p. 419. For Wilderspin's meeting with Spurzheim, cf. *New Moral World,* Vol. 1, 3rd Sers., No. 19, 7 Nov. 1840, p. 291.

[57]N.L.S. Add. Mss., 7248, f. 168, Whately to Combe, 16 Mar. 1838.

[58]*Aberdeen Journal,* 29 Apr., 6 May 1929.

[59]*Aberdeen Journal,* 1 July 1829.

[60]*Aberdeen Journal,* 6 May 1830.

[61]Wilderspin Papers, Letter Book 1831-1832, entry 22 Aug. 1831; *Aberdeen Journal,* 28 September 1831.

children, carrying flowers, marched into the hall in military order to the tune of "There's nae luck about the house"; when seated, all the children gave up their flowers without a murmur, which the *Aberdeen Observer* thought was "a fine moral lesson". Wilderspin then went through the routine of questions, commands, movements and music with such theatrical flair that the local *Journal* compared his handling of children to Paganini's skill on the violin.[62] Three days after the second exhibition Wilderspin concluded his work in Aberdeen with a further course of four lectures at Machray's Hall.[63]

Aberdeen had been slow but sure in establishing its infant school. Dundee also moved with some deliberation, but the outcome was three schools rather than one. Wilderspin's first visit to Dundee was in early May 1829, immediately after his trip to Aberdeen. Some individuals already had taken preparatory steps towards establishing an infant school, so his lectures, on 2 and 4 May, attracted favourable attention. His ability as a speaker appeared to have greatly improved since his first lecture at Edinburgh only five months before; he had "an air of benevolence", reported a local paper, "much fluency and propriety of expression" and "a degree of humour that excited general laughter".[64] His efforts stimulated the formation of a committee of ladies, under the presidency of the redoubtable Mrs. Riddock, which opened a school at Hawkhill on 29 October 1829.[65] There was no mention of Wilderspin's presence at the ceremony. The first teacher was George Scott, a well-educated man who, however, left teaching after a few years to become a clerk in the city. He also acted as Wilderspin's agent in Scotland, supplying apparatus to schools in the eastern part of the country.[66]

Wilderspin returned to Dundee from South Wales at the end of February 1830, at the request of Mrs. Riddock's committee.[67] He announced that he would remain there a month, before undertaking a lecture tour for the purpose of a more general extension of his system in Scotland.[68] In Dundee he gave three lectures at the Thistle Hall on 1, 8 and 11 March and began to prepare the children of Hawkhill school for an exhibition, which was held on the 24th.[69] Inspired by the success of Hawkhill, two other infant schools were in course of preparation[70] — Wallace Craigie (later known as Wallace Feus) under the

[62]*Aberdeen Chronicle,* 5 and 12 Nov. 1831; *Aberdeen Journal,* 9 and 12 Nov. 1831; *Aberdeen Observer,* 18 Nov. 1831.

[63]*Aberdeen Journal,* 23 Nov. 1831.

[64]*Dundee, Perth and Cupar Advertiser,* 30 Apr., 7 May, 6 Aug. 1829.

[65]*Dundee, Perth and Cupar Advertiser,* 5 Nov. 1829.

[66]Brechin Infant School Society Correspondence Book; No. 3, Hunter to J. Barclay, 29 Aug. 1835. Apparently the East Coast was supplied by Dundee, the West by Glasgow. (Brechin Infant School Society Correspondence Book; No. 3, A. Hamilton to W. Shiress, 7 Apr. 1837).

[67]*Early Discipline* (1832), pp. 184-85.

[68]*Dundee, Perth and Cupar Advertiser,* 4 Mar. 1830.

[69]*Dundee, Perth and Cupar Advertiser,* 25 Feb., 4, 18 and 25 Mar. 1830.

[70]*Montrose, Arbroath and Brechin Review,* 12 Mar. 1830.

sponsorship of Mrs. Riddock's ladies, and Maxwelltown, established by an all-male committee under the presidency of the Rev. John Jaffray.[71]

Wilderspin gave two lectures in the neighbouring town of Montrose on 29 and 31 March,[72] which led to the establishment of an infant school in the autumn of 1834, conducted "very nearly upon Mr. Wilderspin's system but without adhering closely to it".[73] He then proceeded to Edinburgh for the exhibitions already described; during his stay there, with seemingly inexhaustible energy, he made two short visits to nearby Leith to deliver lectures, "under the patronage of the magistrates", on 7, 10 and 13 May.[74]

He then returned to Dundee, where the three infant schools were now in full operation, a circumstance which a local paper did not fail favourably to contrast with the situation in the capital.[75] When Wilderspin planned a joint exhibition of the two new schools, Hawkhill asked that it also be included, bringing the total number of children to be examined in the local church to nearly five hundred. Doubting his ability to manage so many children at one time, Wilderspin brought an agent, probably Robert Warner, up from Sheffield to assist him. With so many of the townspeople's children involved, the examination took on the character of a popular festival. The infants, headed by their teachers, marched from their schools to the church. The police kept order along the line of procession, many shops were closed, and spectators lined the curbs and leaned from windows to cheer the children as they passed in their holiday attire. On their arrival at the church, each school was stationed in a different part of the churchyard, and a half-hour was required to sort the children out and arrange them in the large baize-covered gallery erected for the occasion, the Hawkhill School occupying the centre, flanked by Maxwelltown on the right and Wallace Craigie on the left.[76] "They looked like a bed of roses, fanned by a western breeze", rhapsodised the *Dundee Advertiser,* "they were at once so pretty, so quiet, and so fluttering".[77]

Wilderspin managed to hold the attention of the children "with some difficulty" for two hours; in his view the spectacle had, perhaps, never been surpassed for interest and impressiveness. At the conclusion buns and milk were dispensed

[71]Report of the Committee of the Dundee Infant Schools, for 1831; Report of Committee of Maxwelltown Infant School, Dundee, 1832.

[72]*Montrose, Arbroath and Brechin Review,* 26 Mar. 1830.

[73]Brechin Infant School Society Correspondence Book; No. 2, W. Shiress to Rev. Foote, 31 July 1835.

[74]*Scotsman,* 12 May 1830; *Caledonian Mercury,* 13 May 1830.

[75]*Montrose, Arbroath and Brechin Review,* 26 Mar. 1830.

[76]*Dundee, Perth and Cupar Advertiser,* 8 and 15 July 1830; *Early Discipline* (1832), pp. 191-92.

[77]*Dundee, Perth and Cupar Advertiser,* 29 July 1830.

[78]*Early Discipline* (1832), p. 193.

amid a strange confusion of sounds and stretching forth of hands; the children exclaiming, "Maister, I hae no got ane"; "Me ye ken"; "I want ane"; the teachers replying, in soothing tones, "Stop a little, my dear", "I'll come to you, my love"; and occasionally the voice of some anxious parent joined in with (though only to be called to order), "My callant has nae gat ane; that's he with the braw red face".[78]

* * * * *

Wilderspin's most important work in Scotland covered a more or less continuous period of two and a half years, from the initial visit to Glasgow in April 1828 to an engagement in the same city in October 1830. The two main breaks were in the first three months of 1829, when he was establishing a residence and depot in Cheltenham, and in the winter of 1829-30. Again he spent part of this time in Cheltenham, where he gave three lectures at the beginning of September,[79] but the length of his stay is not known. He appears to have returned to Scotland, probably at the beginning of the new year, to give a lecture in the Town Hall at St. Andrews. After the lecture he not uncharacteristically decided, despite the wintry weather, to make a journey by gig to South Wales. He then went back to Scotland for his second visit to Dundee.[80]

Many of his most fruitful (and well-publicised) efforts, particularly in Glasgow, Edinburgh, Aberdeen and Dundee have been covered; but a few others, not always assignable to definite dates, remain to be noticed. Immediately following his first lectures in Dundee in May 1829, for instance, he recounts that he visited Forfar and Arbroath.[81] The lectures he gave in both places were ultimately productive. Arbroath Infant School was opened in the summer of 1831, "constituted on the principles of Wilderspin, or on a modification of those principles".[82] The school at Forfar, supported by James L'Amy, the Sheriff of the county, opened two years later; it was organised by George Scott, equipped with £16 worth of Wilderspin's apparatus and boasted one of the finest playgrounds in Scotland, landscaped and planted at a cost of £18.[83]

Wilderspin's movements during August 1830 have not been ascertained; this may have been the time when he visited the small towns of Musselburgh, Dalkeith and Haddington, lying in a line east of Edinburgh; he recorded indifferent results in each. During this summer he may also have visited

[79] *Cheltenham Chronicle*, 3 Sept. 1829.

[80] *Early Discipline* (1832), pp. 184-85.

[81] *Ibid.*, p. 169.

[82] Brechin Infant School Society Correspondence Book; No. 105, "Rules and Regulations", Arbroath Infant School Society (Ms.).

[83] Brechin Infant School Society Correspondence Book; No. 100, First Annual Report of the Directors of the Infant School at Forfar (1834); No. 96, Second Annual Report. . .(1835).

Portobello where, as a result of his lectures, a school for the higher classes was opened. He recounts the fact that just after his visit there he was stung by a jellyfish while swimming in the Firth of Forth and was seriously ill for a fortnight.[84]

In the first three weeks of September 1830 he made the short trip south of the border to lecture in Cumberland.[85] He was booked to lecture in Glasgow at the beginning of October and on the return journey north he stopped to lecture at Dumfries and Ayr, again failing to stimulate the formation of schools. Wilderspin was apparently an ardent admirer of the poet Burns, and his Ayrshire journeys re-kindled his interest, for he wrote with fine feeling of the poetic talents and personal tragedies of the Scottish bard, devoting three pages to the subject in *Early Discipline*. At Dumfries he visited Burns' tomb, at which he found the aged woman who acted as gatekeeper "so much under the influence of whiskey as to render her remarks unintelligible"; he then called on Burns' widow — a brief visit as she was reluctant to engage in conversation. He also attended a Scottish church service, where he was struck by the "propriety, decorum and solemnity" of the large congregation.[86] The lectures at Glasgow in the Assembly Rooms on 5 and 7 October were designed to show the applicability of his system to children of the higher classes and attracted "a very genteel audience, consisting mostly of ladies". His talents as a lecturer attracted overflow audiences and he was persuaded to remain and give two additional lectures on 14 and 15 October before returning south of the border to Westmoreland.[87]

The last phase of Wilderspin's missionary work in Scotland was a series of flying visits to the Highlands and the North during his resumed tours of England in 1831 and 1832. Following the successful opening of Aberdeen Infant School in November 1831, Wilderspin spent the next three months — December 1831, January and February 1832 — shuttling between Elgin, Dingwall, Inverness and Banff, in the Highlands and on the coastline around the Moray Firth, but finding time also to investigate the peasants' houses and to attend a highland wedding.[88] The educational results may quickly be summarised. In Elgin, following a lecture in a crowded chapel, a committee was formed and a school opened about a year later.[89] Dingwall was visited twice in December, where a school planned by the phrenologist and scientist Sir George Mackenzie "excited

---

[84] *Early Discipline* (1832), pp. 196-97; p. 201.

[85] Cf. Chapter 8.

[86] *Early Discipline*, pp. 145-46; p. 149. The date of Wilderspin's visit to Dumfries is deduced from his statement in *Early Discipline*, p. 149, that he was there when Caughie took some children from the Glasgow School to Stranraer; Caughie visited Stranraer between 25 and 28 September 1830 (*Glasgow Herald*, 8 Oct. 1830).

[87] *Glasgow Herald*, 1 and 8 Oct. 1830; *Glasgow Chronicle*, 6 Oct. 1830; *Scotsman*, 6 Oct. 1830.

[88] *Early Discipline* (1832), pp. 234-36.

[89] *Ibid.*, pp. 228-29; *Aberdeen Journal*, 18 Jan. 1832.

the people in an extraordinary manner".[90] A foray in January to Banff, on the picturesque coast between Buckie and Fraserburgh, resulted in the establishment of an Infant School Society.[91] At Inverness a school was expeditiously established in an old thread mill and a public procession staged for the ceremonial opening; the institution eventually became a model school for the North of Scotland and a depot for Wilderspin's lessons and apparatus.[92]

It is probable that Wilderspin was in Scotland in April 1832, for he stated in *Early Discipline* that he opened the fourth and fifth schools of the Glasgow Infant School Society, the so-called New Model Infant School in Saltmarket and St. David's Parish School in High John Street; the first half-yearly examination of the former was held on 26 October, so it is likely that it was opened in April. The first public examination of the latter was held on 13 November 1832.[93]

A final task remained — to organise Mackenzie's school in Dingwall. "Wilderspin is with me just now", wrote Mackenzie to Brougham on 9 September 1832, ". . .and such is the interest taken in infant education that there are upwards of 120 children already in the school which will hold about 200".[94] A planned journey from Dingwall to John O'Groats had to be abandoned because of an outbreak of cholera,[95] and Wilderspin returned south, his work in Scotland over.

* * * * *

Though Wilderspin's work in Scotland was an almost unqualified success, there were certain initial obstacles that had to be overcome. Apart from familiar objections to infant schools *per se* — that they undermined parental affection, overloaded children's minds, injured their health, and so on[96] — there were difficulties peculiar to the country itself. "The physical hardships of weather and terrain, and the frugality of parents", Marjorie Cruickshank notes, had

[90]*Scotsman,* 7 Jan. 1832; *Early Discipline* (1832), pp. 232-33; N.L.S. Add. Mss., 7227, f. 156, Mackenzie to Combe, 31 Dec. 1831. Cf. also Add. Mss. 7229, ff. 19-20, Mackenzie to Combe, 25 Apr. 1832.

[91]*Aberdeen Journal,* 18 Jan. 1832; *Early Discipline* (1832), p. 233.

[92]*Early Discipline* (1832), pp. 229-30; *Early Discipline* (1834), pp. 268-73; Wilderspin Papers, Letter Book 1831-32, entries 12 and 24 Dec. 1831.

[93]According to an article by David Stow in J. Cleland, *Enumeration of the Inhabitants of the City of Glasgow* (Glasgow, 2nd ed., 1832) these schools were to be opened in 1832. Wilderspin's statement is in the first edition of *Early Discipline,* which went to the press after April 1832, to judge by the date of the preface. For the names and locations of the schools, cf. [D. Stow], *Infant Training* (Glasgow, n.d.? 1833), App., p. 125. For the dates of examinations, cf. *Glasgow Herald,* 29 Oct. and 19 Nov. 1832.

[94]U.C.L. Brougham MSS., 42897, Sir George Mackenzie to Brougham, 9 Sept. 1832.

[95]*Early Discipline* (1834), pp. 276-78; Wilderspin Papers, Mackenzie to Wilderspin (n.d.? Oct. 1832).

[96]According to Stow, in Cleland, *Inhabitants of Glasgow,* p. 40.

combined to make it customary to postpone schooling till the age of seven.[97] In addition, the Scottish newspaper and periodical press in the early 1820s was active in drawing attention to the supposedly irreligious tendencies of infant schools[98], possibly with the example of Owen and New Lanark in mind. Wilderspin's association with the Evangelicals, a growing force in the Church of Scotland, probably made his first venture more palatable to public opinion. In any case, certain other aspects of Scottish life asserted themselves in his favour — the widespread provision of public education and the respect for learning that had its origins in the Reformation period, the high status of the teacher and, in comparison with the situation in England, the virtual absence of the intrusion of religious politics in the educational scene. In addition, he found that the Evangelicals and the phrenologists, for their own separate reasons, were more than willing to give him the kind of acclaim that he had seldom found in England. If Wilderspin entered Scotland in 1828 as an experienced but obscure educational missionary, he left it in 1832 as an individual whose name was sufficiently known to be quoted in the press without qualification as to profession.[99]

Wilderspin's blend of instruction and encouragement, amusement and movement appealed to enlightened Scottish educationists because it was in sharp contrast to the authoritarian strain in Scottish education as exemplified in the methods of the traditional dominie, whose rigorous regime was enforced by biting sarcasm and the liberal use of the tawse.[100] Paradoxically, it was the status of the Scottish teacher — achieved in part by these methods — which also helped to advance the cause of infant education and, incidentally, the position of Wilderspin himself. In Scotland, he observed, (stressing the male gender with satisfaction)

> "the *schoolmaster"* is, literally "abroad". There he is treated with great respect, received into the best society, appears to be next in rank to "the minister", and, though only the tutor of a parochial school, has generally a vacation of two months, and may be met with at watering places, seeking that health and strength which are so necessary in the discharge of his important and responsible duties. The contrast between his circumstances and those of many bearing the same name in England is humiliating and distressing.[101]

Infant school teachers inherited this tradition and, with respect to learning and accomplishments, carried it forward. George Scott of Dundee Infant School, Hamilton, first master of Brechin Infant School, and Wright of Paisley and Edinburgh, (who made himself master of geography, mathematics and

[97]Marjorie Cruickshank, *History of the Training of Teachers in Scotland* (Edinburgh 1970), p. 34.

[98]Rusk, *Training of Teachers in Scotland,* p. 27.

[99]*Glasgow Herald,* 16 July 1832, relating an anecdote of "Mr. Wilderspin's" teaching experience.

[100]Cf. *Dundee, Perth and Cupar Advertiser,* 25 Mar. 1830.

[101]*Early Discipline* (1832), pp. 117-18.

natural philosophy) were typical examples.[102] James Milne, Wright's successor at Edinburgh, published a book on national education and was canvassed by Simpson in 1839 as superintendent of the infant department of the projected British Normal School.[103] Milne based his teaching on short and varied lessons — spelling, object lessons, singing, question-and-answer on Scripture pictures, work with the arithmeticon and gonigraph, reading lessons, the singing of pence tables, anecdotes "told elliptically", lessons in natural history, geography and history, and "scientific hymns", the whole interspersed with manual exercises and periods in the playground.[104] In addition, nearly all infant schools in Scotland followed Wilderspin's ideal of non-denominational religious teaching and there is little evidence that, during his stay in Scotland, infant schools were being used to promote sectarian doctrines. The exception was the Duchess of Gordon's school at Fochabers in the Highlands, much admired by Thomas Bilby and R.B. Ridgway, the leading Evangelicals in the English infant school movement.[105] The Drygate School remained non-denominational until 1832, when the local Catholic clergy, discovering one of the Glasgow Society's handbills, ordered the parents of the sixty Catholic pupils to withdraw their children from the school. After this, according to Simpson, "the doctrines of *one* sect [were] authoritatively instilled".[106] Stow's genuine interest in educational theory and his desire to patent a system of his own ensured, however, that the original pedagogical practices remained largely intact, despite the insistence on "Bible Training".[107]

Stow admitted that his own "system" owed much to Wilderspin; not surprisingly, his main criticism was of Wilderspin's religious instruction, which he found "very incomplete".[108] Reading Stow's dialogue on infant training, popularly known as "Granny and Leazy",[109] one is struck by the similarity of the daily routine to that of Spitalfields (which Stow had, of course, visited). Even those aspects which Stow claimed as peculiarly his own — "training", "the sympathy of numbers" and "picturing out" — were basically Wilderspinian

---

[102]For an example of Hamilton's literary style, cf. Brechin Infant School Society. Minute Book 1835-1873, Minutes, 6 Mar. 1837; for Wright's accomplishments, cf. *Early Discipline* (1832), pp. 116-17.

[103]Cf. J. Milne, *National Education* (Edinburgh 1839); U.C.L. Brougham Mss., 15913, Simpson to Brougham, 9 May 1837.

[104]Chambers, *Infant Education*, pp. 42-7.

[105]For the Duchess of Gordon's school, cf. *Manchester Times*, 7 Mar. 1829, citing *Elgin Courier*, 27 Feb. 1829; Rev. A.M. Stuart, *Life and Letters of Elizabeth, Last Duchess of Gordon* (London, 3rd. ed., 1865) pp. 121-26; p. 130 ff; N.P. Willis, *Pencillings By the Way* (London, 3 vol., 1835), III, pp. 209-10; T. Bilby and R.B. Ridgway, *The Infant Teacher's Assistant* (London, 3rd ed., 1833), iii.

[106]Simpson, *Philosophy of Education*, pp. 195-96.

[107]For evidence of this, cf. D. Stow, *Moral Training, Infant and Juvenile* (Glasgow, 2nd ed., 1834), p. 75 ff.

[108]D. Stow, *The Training System* (Glasgow 1836), pp. 4-5.

[109][D. Stow], *Infant Training. A Dialogue Explanatory of the System Adopted in the Model Infant School, Glasgow* (Glasgow n.d. ? 1833), *passim*.

ideas in a somewhat different form. "Training", which Stow felt should replace "instruction", was closely akin to Wilderspin's principle that the heart should be appealed to rather than the head when improving a child's moral nature. "Sympathy of numbers" might be described as the moral effect of the community, which in the streets worked for evil but in the atmosphere of the infant school could be a force for good; the concept was perhaps less developed by Wilderspin than some others, but present in his belief in the power of social relationships among large numbers of children. "Picturing out" was Stow's amalgamation of Wilderspin's interrogatory and elliptical methods; the master would omit a word in a statment or question and allow the children to supply it themselves.[110] Wilderspin was often over-sensitive about other people copying his ideas — and sometimes downright inaccurate — but when he challenged Stow in 1840 to show that there was not a single idea in "what he chooses to call his training system" that he did not exhibit himself in his visits to Glasgow, he was on safe ground.[111]

Scottish infant schools escaped the crisis that afflicted their English counterparts in the mid-30s. Unlike many of the latter they were carefully planned, often over a period of several years; subscriptions were garnered slowly but carefully; and in many cases the governers had strong roots in the county and the municipality — scarcely a school lacked a Sheriff, Lord Provost or Magistrate as a committee member. The teachers, it hardly needs repeating, were of good calibre and often well trained at Stow's Normal School in Glasgow.[112] Wilderspin had no hesitation in stating to the Select Committee on Education in 1835, that of all the four countries in the British Isles the potential for infant school development was greatest in Scotland.[113]

Yet the system did not continue to flourish there as might have been expected from this confident and apparently well-founded statement. In 1841, for instance, Wilderspin was informed by a friend in Inverness that "the beautiful little building close to the Castle Hill which was organised as an infant school by you has been neglected and the Infant System has vanished".[114] Six years later the Edinburgh School was closed.[115] By 1861 only 2% of children under five were at school in Scotland, compared to 16% in England and Wales.[116] Part of the reason for the slowing down of the spread of infant schools,

[110]This paragraph relies largely on A.I. Short, The Development of Infant Education in England from 1818 to 1870 with particular reference to the work of Samuel Wilderspin, unpublished M.Ed. thesis, University of Newcastle-upon-Tyne 1972, pp. 147-57.

[111]*System of Education* (1840), p. 94. Wilderspin later modified his criticism of Stow and paid tribute to his work for Scottish education (*Infant System* (1852), p. 11).

[112]Cf. e.g., Third Report of the Glasgow Educational Society's Normal Seminary (Glasgow 1836), *passim.*

[113]P.P. 1835 VII, Report from the Select Committee on Education in England and Wales, p. 15.

[114]Wilderspin Papers, J. Buchanan to Wilderspin, 5 Sept. 1841.

[115]Wilderspin Papers, J. Simpson to Wilderspin, 14 Aug. 1847.

[116]A.F.B. Roberts, "Scotland and Infant Education in the Nineteenth Century", *Scottish Educational Studies,* Vol. 4, No. 1, May 1972, p. 41.

a Scottish observer noted as early as 1835, was that the Scottish people valued education largely for its instrumental value in providing literacy, and were suspicious of or uninterested in the more sophisticated methods and curricula of infant schools.[117] It was certainly true that the movement in Scotland in the late 1820s and early 1830s was entirely supported by the middle-class intelligentsia and public men of the cities, the clergy and the county gentry. Though they might have a somewhat higher level of culture and a greater sense of concern for community welfare than their English counterparts, nevertheless, as in England, they provided infant schools for the people. The latter's role was largely that of consumers and ultimately, it would seem, the offering was somewhat too exotic for their taste.

As for Wilderspin, he certainly founded his reputation as an educational entrepreneur in Scotland. His partial adoption of the "scientific" and "progressive" doctrine of phrenology widened the scope of his educational theory. He gained greatly in confidence as a public speaker. He perfected the public presentation of his system — the procession of infants through the streets, their dramatic entry onto the platform in a hall or church, the "exhibition" of their achievements under his system. Wilderspin had an explanation for his widespread use of the exhibition in Scotland: the Scots, he maintained, would take nothing on trust; they would listen to his lectures, but he always had to prove his words with the children themselves.[118] Be that as it may, the exhibition, in the long run, did as much harm as good to his reputation.[119] One other aspect of his Scottish experiences was to have some effect on his future. He became convinced that education had given the Scots habits of industry, "elevated and expanded" minds, a high level of knowledge and a low crime rate; the Irish on the other hand, for want of education, suffered from "idle and aimless habits", "uncultivated faculties", ignorance, and a high level of crime.[120] It was an attitude which was to redound to his disadvantage when he took up employment in Ireland in 1837.

[117]J. McK., "Remarks on Infant Tuition", *Glasgow Infant School Instructor,* No. II, Feb. 1835, pp. 38-41.

[118]*Infant System* (1852), p. 11.

[119]Cf. Chapter 12.

[120]*Early Discipline* (1834), p. 105.

CHAPTER 8

A NATIONAL AND INTERNATIONAL REPUTATION

The demise of the Infant School Society at the end of 1828 left Wilderspin facing an uncertain future. His response, however, was swift and positive; his recent successes in Glasgow and Edinburgh, and his growing reputation at home and abroad, convinced him that there might be a promising future for a practical exponent of the infant school concept working on his own. Something like a boom in infant schools was under way in Britain, Europe and America; it is probable that the international fame of New Lanark a decade earlier had paved the way, but Wilderspin could take satisfaction from the fact that nearly all the new schools, from Paris to Vienna, from Budapest to New York, had been inspired by the model he had pioneered. Historians of education have made us aware of the migration overseas of the monitorial systems of Bell and Lancaster, but nothing has been published on the rather similar spread of the Wilderspin system in the 1820s and 1830s; a beginning is made in the second half of this chapter.

Faced with a rising market for his product, as it were, Wilderspin took the plunge and set himself up as an independent missionary for infant education, ready at moment's notice to travel to the four corners of the British Isles to found an infant school. For this he needed a base from which to work, and he chose Cheltenham, a town with which he was familiar and in which he had already established a reputation as the organiser of Alstone Infant School. Described as a community "fast rising into importance and rapidly increasing its fame. . .as a fashionable rendezvous",[1] Cheltenham was more centrally situated than London, both as a starting-point for journeys and for the location of a depot for infant school apparatus he intended to set up.[2]

He found a suitable residence, spacious enough for his family of three daughters — Sarah Anne, Rebecca and Emily — and for the office and supply depot, in the Bayshill district of Cheltenham, where he rented Dr. Thomas Jenner's former home, locally known as "the Pest House" from its association with Jenner's vaccination campaigns.[3] A water colour sketch done at the time shows a commodious two and a half storey stuccoed building with eleven front windows, covered entrance and spacious grounds bordered with flowers and

[1]*Cheltenham Chronicle,* 6 Sept. 1827.

[2]*Cheltenham Chronicle,* 19 Mar. 1829.

[3]We are indebted to Mr. S.J.D. Gegg. of Spirax Sarco Ltd., the present occupants of the premises, for information re Wilderspin's renting of the house.

trees.[4] Wilderspin renamed it Alpha House and to help in meeting his costs offered to take in as temporary boarders persons interested in being trained in the two Cheltenham Infant Schools, both of which, he said, were operated on his plan and were within a five-minute walk.[5]

Alpha House, in which he had settled by March 1829,[6] was an ideal headquarters for the increased volume of work he had to undertake in the early 1830s. His staff included three persons: his office manager, C.F. Lewis, the former master of the Alstone Infant School; his daughter Sarah Anne, now fully competent to open small country infant schools by herself; and an experienced agent, Robert Warner, who worked in the larger cities or preceded Wilderspin on his lecture tours to make advance arrangements. Wilderspin paid his agents £100 per year.[7] His income was based on a standard fee of £10 or £15 for a course of lectures, depending on the number, plus travelling expenses.[8] In a good year he might earn £400 or more, though most years probably brought in somewhat less. On occasion his travelling expenses were not always fully reimbursed (he once lamented that he had been offered three sovereigns to cover the expenses of a journey from the east of Scotland to South Wales)[9], and the Letter Book that Lewis kept during 1831-32 shows that even at the best of times clients defaulted in settling their accounts, and that suppliers of apparatus pressed for payment. The sale of clock faces, brass letters, prints, swings and other paraphernalia was, however, an additional source of income; sets for small schools were priced at £10 and those for larger schools up to £15.[10]

On the whole he had a comfortable living, with an income at least three times that which he had earned at Spitalfields, and the move to Cheltenham represented a commensurate step up the social scale. Like many others who rise from humble backgrounds by their own skill and enterprise, he wished to attain acceptance and social respectability. At the same time, as a prospective entrepreneur, he needed a cachet of his own. In an age of systems — those of Bell, Lancaster, Black and Jacotot spring to mind — it was necessary to have something different or original to offer. He had already described himself — or allowed himself to be described — as the "Founder of Infant Schools";[11] to sustain this role he felt it desirable to demote New Lanark and Westminster from their position as the first infant schools and to conceal the previously-acknowledged assistance of Owen and Buchanan. In the first three editions of his book, Wilderspin had described Owen as "the first person with whom had

[4] Wilderspin Papers, sketch of Alpha House (n.d.), probably by T.U. Young.

[5] *Cheltenham Chronicle*, 19 Mar. 1829.

[6] The first advertisement for the new headquarters appeared in this month. (*Cheltenham Chronicle*, 19 Mar. 1829).

[7] *Manchester Guardian*, 9 Sept. 1846. The reference is to the 1830s.

[8] Wilderspin Papers, Letter Book 1831-32, entries for 25 Jan., 3 Apr. and 5 June 1831.

[9] *Early Discipline* (1832), pp. 217-18.

[10] *Cheltenham Chronicle*, 27 Aug. 1829.

[11] Cf. *Staffordshire Mercury*, 13 Sept. 1828.

originated the idea of educating infant children on an extensive scale", and his institution at New Lanark as a "school"; Westminster was characterised as the first infant school in England. In *Infant Education,* published at the beginning of 1829, New Lanark Infant School was transformed into an "asylum", and the thanks to Owen for assistance, which had appeared in the first three editions, were omitted.[12] In *Early Discipline,* published in 1832, Westminster Infant School became an asylum in its turn.[13]

No doubt the elimination of the tribute to Owen, now returned from the U.S.A. and beginning to interest himself in the British labour movement, was designed to ensure respectability. Like many essays in opportunism, however, it did not wholly succeed, at least in Cheltenham. In his first public lectures in the town, delivered in the Assembly Rooms in March 1829, he was moved to complain of the prejudice he had encountered. *The Chronicle* reported that at the close of his lectures "he adverted with some feeling to the unkind and unhandsome reports which had been circulated relative to the nature of his religious opinions and took occasion to deny in the strongest and most unequivocal terms the imputation of holding Socinian views".[14] Whatever position he took, however, he was fated to be considered something of an outsider in a town increasingly dominated by the Rev. Francis Close; moving, like his fellow-Evangelicals, to a more conservative and militantly Protestant position, Close was finding correspondingly less appeal in the Wilderspin-type pedagogy, divested though it might be of Owenite connections.[15] Wilderspin, for his part, was to object strongly to the growing Evangelical influence in the infant school movement. The antagonism smouldered during the early 1830s, to burst into furious flame during the national education controversy in 1837.

* * * * *

For the most part Wilderspin's travels from 1829 to 1836 are well-documented. For some years it is possible to chart his progress on a week-by-week basis. In others there are gaps — for instance, from November 1829 to March 1830, from April to November 1832, from February to July 1834, and in the last four months of 1835. Short of a search through the whole of the provincial press or serendipity on the part of a local researcher, it will not be possible to confirm this apparent lack of activity. The three editions of *Early Discipline* are of little help. Nearly all the visits recorded there have been verified in the local press and the book provides no explanation for the missing months.

[12]*Infant Poor* (1823), pp. 103-07; p. 104n; *Infant Poor* (1824), pp. 178-82; *Infant Education* (1825), pp. 232-34; *Infant Education* (1829), p. 51; p. 67; p. 69.

[13]*Early Discipline* (1832), p. 2.

[14]*Cheltenham Chronicle,* 2 Apr. 1829.

[15]Cf. Chapter 6.

It is possible, indeed likely, that Wilderspin had no offers of work during these periods. He may, on the other hand, have taken time off to write the books which appeared at frequent intervals between 1829 and 1840, though none of the fallow periods immediately precede the date at which the writing of the volume was completed.

After securing his base in Cheltenham, however, Wilderspin returned to Scotland in April 1829, remaining there, as we have seen, for the better part of two years; his main activity in England during this period was a detour to the Fells and the Lake District at the end of 1830 to lecture and open schools.[16] Returning to England, he began the busiest year of his career; in scarcely a week of 1831 was he not employed in travelling, lecturing and organising. Most of this activity was spontaneous and unplanned, in the sense that he fulfilled engagements one by one, from whichever part of the country they emanated. He must have been an oft-seen figure on the highways of Britain, hastening from place to place in his gig, his spirited horse setting a fast pace in front, his travelling bookcase mounted in the rear, and his faithful white terrier following behind or sharing the driver's seat with his master.

The first journey of 1831 began as the New Year festivities were ending and by 10 January Wilderspin was in Llandovery, Carmarthenshire;[17] his activities there will be noticed in the section on Wales later in the chapter. From Llandovery he travelled east to lecture in Lincoln, delighting the local public with his arguments in favour of universal education.[18] By the beginning of February he was in the north of England, though there is no record of the places he visited.[19] He then began a tour of the Midlands and south Yorkshire which was one of the most arduous of his career. In seven weeks he gave nineteen lectures in eight places: two in Evesham, four in Worcester, one in Kidderminster, three in Coventry, three in Sheffield, three in Chesterfield, one in Mansfield and two in Reading.[20] For some of the time, at least, he appears to have had the assistance of his agent Warner, who had been active in the organisation of an infant school at Droitwich in January.[21]

The engagement at Coventry provided the most interest. "We had established in Coventry two infant schools on the Wilderspin system", recalled Charles Bray, the phrenologist, in his autobiography.[22] As had happened at Taunton four years earlier, one school was supported by the Church, under the leadership of the Rev. W.F. Hook, vicar of Holy Trinity — "active in good

---

[16] *Cumberland Pacquet,* 31 Aug., 4, 7, 14 and 21 Sept. 1830; *Carlisle Journal,* 4 Sept. 1830; *Westmoreland Gazette,* 13 Nov. 1830; *Westmoreland Advertiser and Kendal Chronicle,* 20 Nov. 1830.

[17] Wilderspin Papers, Letter Book 1831-32, entry for 10 Jan. 1831.

[18] *Lincoln and Newark Times,* 22 Jan. 1831.

[19] Wilderspin Papers, Letter Book 1831-32, entry for 4 Feb. 1831.

[20] For details and references, cf. App. II.

[21] Wilderspin Papers, Letter Book 1831-32, entries for 7, 10 and 24 Jan., 14 and 16 Feb. 1831.

[22] C. Bray, *Phases of Opinion and Experience During a Long Life; an Autobiography* (London n.d.), p. 20.

works, but a bigoted Churchman", according to Bray — and the other mainly by Dissenters. Advertisements for the initial meetings of both committees appeared in the same column of the *Coventry Herald* on 14 January; though the "Church" school claimed that it was open to all children without exception, Dissenters alleged that the Church Catechism would be taught and that the teacher would have to be a member of the Church of England.[23] Wilderspin, in conformity with his usual policy, avoided taking sides in the dispute. The *Coventry Herald* assured its readers that "Mr. Wilderspin does not interfere in the smallest degree, with the religion to be taught in the schools; that, he says, should be left wholly to the decisions of the respective committees, so that both Churchmen and Dissenters can attend these lectures without fear of offence.[24] The wisdom of this policy, especially in the charged atmosphere of Coventry, was demonstrated when Wilderspin's three lectures in St. Mary's Hall on 9, 10 and 11 March drew good audiences, including a sprinkling of local charity-school teachers he admitted free.[25] As a result of the conflict, wrote Charles Bray, "we had two good schools instead of one".[26]

During the spring of 1831 Wilderspin's range of travel was somewhat lessened, though he was kept equally busy, mainly at Cheltenham and nearby Bath, where he gave two sets of lectures in April and May.[27] The latter series was one of the high points of his career and added greatly to his reputation. He came to the city, the *Bath Journal* noted, having "not merely the hopes of posthumous fame, but. . .gaining already the reward of a considerable share of popularity".[28] He commenced by giving three lectures at the Avon Street Infant School on 9, 11 and 12 May.[29] At the request of Mrs. Ames, the founder of the school and one of the earliest patrons of infant education, he gave an exhibition of the children's accomplishments, pointing out "the advantages connected with his plan of instruction".[30] The lectures were so well received that he repeated them twice in the Kingston Institute, once on the afternoons of 18 and 20 May for a "select" audience at 5 shillings for the course, and again in the evenings of the 17th, 19th and 21st for a more popular assemblage at half the price.[31] Describing Wilderspin variously as "unrivalled as a lecturer", a "philosophical instructor", a man whose "comic recitals. . .restore the spirits of many a drooping

---

[23] *Coventry Herald,* 14 and 28 Jan. 1831.

[24] *Coventry Herald,* 4 Mar. 1831.

[25] *Coventry Mercury,* 6 and 13 Mar. 1831.

[26] Bray, *Autobiography,* p. 21.

[27] Cf. Appendix II.

[28] *Bath Journal,* 30 May 1831.

[29] *Bath and Cheltenham Gazette,* 3 May 1831; *Bath Journal,* 16 May 1831.

[30] *Bath and Cheltenham Gazette,* 17 May 1831.

[31] *Bath Herald,* 14 May 1831.

hypochondriac" and a "blessing to his country and his age", the local press gave him extensive and complimentary coverage.[32]

The content of his lectures, obviously given *extempore,* was a rather jumbled summary of the main points of his published works: the importance of early childhood; the curiosity and restlessness of children under seven; the need to communicate via the five senses a knowledge of things, followed by the appropriate words; an account of his own first steps, followed by an elaboration of his mature methods; the importance of the cultivation of the feelings and the moral sense, particularly in the playground; and the need for sympathetic teachers with an understanding of human nature. The general tenor of the lectures was a belief in the educability of children under six and their receptivity to lively, amusing, practical and sympathetic teaching.[33] It was also obvious that Wilderspin had developed a popular platform manner, with a colloquial turn of phrase and the use of amusing anecdotes. The interest aroused by his description of teaching methods, the *Gazette* pointed out, "depended solely on Mr. W's manner of relating them".[34] It is clear from these reports that his secret was to wrap a serious message in entertainment; his down-to-earth, rather simplistic style may not have served him so well in his books, but it worked to great advantage in his lectures, enabling him to establish complete *rapport* with his audience. Proof of this was evident in Wilderspin's final exhibition at Bath, when he put five hundred infants through their paces before an audience of 2,000 people.[35]

After a short break in Cheltenham, where he gave another course of three lectures in the second week of June,[36] Wilderspin set out on an extensive tour of the East Midlands and the Eastern counties. Though this tour covered a relatively small area, it was, like most of his trips, largely unplanned; many of the visits were requested following reports of a lecture in another town. A large part of the interest was generated by the *Lincoln, Rutland and Stamford Mercury,* one of Wilderspin's most enthusiastic and consistent supporters; on one occasion it ventured to advise its readers to peruse James Simpson's analysis of Wilderspin's system in the *Phrenological Journal,* "a work which notwithstanding the forbidding title", the paper explained, "seems to contain matter of varied and miscellaneous interest".[37] The tour took in Lincoln,

[32] *Bath Journal,* 16 May 1831; *Bath Herald,* 21 May 1831.

[33] The three lectures were reproduced *verbatim* in the *Bath and Cheltenham Gazette,* 24 and 31 May, 7 June 1831.

[34] *Bath and Cheltenham Gazette,* 7 June 1831.

[35] *Bath Journal,* 23 May 1831.

[36] *Cheltenham Chronicle,* 2 June 1831.

[37] *Lincoln, Rutland and Stamford Mercury,* 1 July 1831.

Newark, Boston, Louth, Stamford, Cambridge and Nottingham.[38] Wilderspin stayed in Newark during August, September and early October, and it was here that he met Charles Williams, a young Presbyterian clergyman, who assisted him in the compilation of *Early Discipline,* published in the summer of the following year.[39] From Newark Wilderspin went to the north of Scotland, where he spent the remainder of the year fulfilling the engagement in Aberdeen described in Chapter 7.

* * * * *

Wilderspin's experiences in Ireland and in Wales formed a striking contrast. Despite the fact that the Catholic priesthood was opposed to infant schools — Wilderspin stated in 1835 that all the assistance he had received in Ireland had been from Protestants[40] — no fewer than nineteen infant schools had been founded as early as 1831.[41] He was confident he could increase the number. "I am certain", he wrote to Brougham in November 1831, in a bid for his support, "much good could be done in Ireland by extending the system. I am anxious to spend some years there to try the experiment".[42] In the event, he managed only a few journeys, but his lectures were well received and several schools established. Wales, however, was a different proposition. Few invitations materialised and his activities there were relatively unproductive. Possibly his attitude to the Welsh affected his enthusiasm somewhat; he found them socially and economically behind the rest of the country and he was appalled at the prevalence of superstition, which he felt "almost defies belief".[43] His most productive work in Wales was, significantly, done in the industrial areas of the South.

Wilderspin's journey to Ireland in the spring and summer of 1833 began with lectures in Belfast at the end of April, followed by an examination of the infant schools of the city a month later.[44] The interest aroused was sufficient for him to receive urgent requests from half-a-dozen other places.[45] Pausing only to return to England to recover from an attack of influenza, he lectured in Newry,

[38]Cf. Appendix II. Wilderspin returned to Lincoln in February 1832 from Scotland to open a school. (*Boston Gazette,* 28 Feb. 1832; *Lincoln, Rutland and Stamford Mercury,* 23 Mar. 1832; *Early Discipline* (1832), pp. 239-40). For Wilderspin's activities in Lincolnshire, cf. R. Russell's unpublished Ms., "The Lindsey Infant Schools and Samuel Wilderspin" (n.d.).

[39]Wilderspin Papers, Letter Book 1831-32, entries for 5 and 30 Aug. 1831; *Lincoln, Rutland and Stamford Mercury,* 23 and 30 Sept. 1831; *Drakard's Stamford News,* 7 Oct. 1831; *Early Discipline* (1832), p. 225.

[40]P.P. 1835 VII, Report from the Select Committee on Education in England and Wales, p. 25.

[41]According to Wilderspin in a speech at Bath (*Bath and Cheltenham Gazette,* 24 May 1831).

[42]U.C.L. Brougham Mss., 10369, Wilderspin to Brougham, Nov. 1831.

[43]*Early Discipline* (1832), pp. 174-81, *passim.*

[44]*Belfast Newsletter,* 9 and 23 Apr., 14 and 21 May 1833; *Belfast Commercial Chronicle,* 17 and 24 Apr. 1833.

[45]*Belfast Newsletter,* 10 May 1833.

Dungannon, Monaghan, Dublin, Booterstown, Kingstown and Londonderry.[46] Returning to Ireland the following year, he gave five lectures in Waterford, following which an infant school was formed. The examination of the children drew 600 spectators — a sight, wrote the local *Mirror,* as was never before seen in Waterford.[47] Wilderspin then moved to Cork, where he gave four lectures in late September and early October 1834.[48]

If the Irish press was generally ecstatic in praise of Wilderspin's system — "of more intrinsic value", maintained the *Waterford Mirror,* "than any...of the important discoveries, either in the Arts or Sciences"[49] — the Welsh newspapers were singularly silent, and middle-class philanthropists somewhat lacking in zeal. Though Wilderspin, as shown in Chapter 7, travelled 700 miles over icy roads early in 1830 to carry his message to South Wales, little came of the expedition. Pembroke, Haverfordwest, and other isolated fishing towns of Pembrokeshire were unresponsive to the idea of infant schools, and his one success came about by accident. Hearing of a hunt in the neighbourhood, he rode over to watch, and not wishing to appear an outsider, he joined the field. Unwilling to restrain his horse, now rested and in high spirits, he decided to go, if possible, all the way. In a wild scramble down a bank in pursuit of the fox, his mount leaped a fallen horse and rider, kept its feet and came in at the finish. Among the huntsmen was a nobleman to whom he explained the purpose of his journey; later the Earl's wife opened, Wilderspin does not say where, one of the few infant schools in Wales.[50]

A year later Wilderspin was again in the Principality; a correspondent in Llandovery had been importuning him for nearly a year to visit the town. On his arrival there on 10 January he was astonished to find he had been "billeted" in an inn on a contract for fifteen shillings a week. Asking for a glass of ale, he was told that nothing but water could be provided. Nevertheless, Wilderspin stayed on at considerable personal expense, opened a school and gave a course of free lectures. The rapid progress of the children impressed the local gentry, who partially covered his costs by subscribing to a second course of lectures, with tickets at half-a-crown.[51] Four months later he journeyed from Reading to Swansea, where he gave three lectures; these resulted in the establishment of a large and well-provided infant school under the patronage of the Duchess of Beaufort, the Duke providing the land rent free on a lease for sixty years.[52] Following the Swansea lectures he went to Neath, where the copper miners and

[46]Cf. Appendix II.

[47]*Waterford Mirror,* 26 and 30 July, 2 Aug. and 13 Sept. 1834.

[48]*Cork Evening Herald,* 26 Sept. and 6 Oct. 1834.

[49]*Waterford Mirror,* 2 Aug. 1834.

[50]*Early Discipline* (1832), pp. 182-83.

[51]Wilderspin Papers, Letter Book 1831-32, entry for 10 Jan. 1831; *Early Discipline* (1832), pp. 217-18; *Carmarthen Journal,* 14 Jan. 1831.

[52]*Cambrian,* 9, 16 and 30 Apr. 1831; P.P. 1847 XXVII 1, Reports of the Commissioners of Inquiry into the State of Education in Wales, pp. 376-79.

their employers jointly opened an infant school.[53] In 1836, probably during the summer, Wilderspin returned to Wales to advise the proprietors of the collieries and ironworks at Pontypool on the best location for infant schools and to provide plans for their construction.[54]

* * * * *

Five years after he had settled in Cheltenham, Wilderspin decided to add to his income — and possibly also to add to his prestige — by establishing a school at Alpha House. Designated for "the Education of the Children of the Higher Classes, from One to Ten years of Age", the school was under the superintendence of Sarah Anne Wilderspin and a widow, Mrs. Charles Cuff. Opened on 30 July 1834, it offered "Reading, Writing, Arithmetic, the elements of Music, Geography, Geometry, Natural History, French, Latin, etc". Terms were 40 guineas per annum for yearly boarders, 35 guineas for weekly boarders and 20 guineas for day boarders; drawing, dancing, and special instruction in music were extra. The school's location was described as "pleasant and airy, within a few minutes walk of the Spas". Patrons were assured that "a delightful playground and garden are attached to the premises. where the children, even in the hours set aside for recreation, will receive useful instruction, found in the surrounding natural objects — it being an essential part of the plan to exercise conjointly the physical and mental faculties on all suitable occasions". As a concession to the dominant faith of the privileged classes of the town, religious instruction would be given "in accordance with the principles of the Established Church, unless objected to by the parents".[55] Highly praised by the local press,[56] the school remained at Alpha House until Sarah Anne Wilderspin married T.U. Young in 1837, whence it was continued in another location by the latter's sisters.[57]

Though the school was advertised as enjoying "the advantage of Mr. Wilderspin's superintendence, when at home",[58] there is no evidence that he spent a great deal of time there. His energies and interests were concentrated on travel and he continued to visit all parts of the British Isles throughout the first half of the 1830s.[59] His English journeys included a tour of the Yorkshire towns of Wakefield, Huddersfield Halifax and Doncaster in the winter of 1831-32;

---

[53] *Early Discipline* (1832), p. 220.

[54] *Early Discipline* (1840), p. 323.

[55] Wilderspin Papers, Prospectus of Alpha House School, Alstone near Cheltenham (1834); *Cheltenham Chronicle,* 19 June 1834; *Cheltenham Journal,* 28 July 1834.

[56] *Cheltenham Looker-On,* 24 Sept. 1836.

[57] Young Papers, T.U. Young, "Memoir of My Father's Family" (Ms.).

[58] Pamphlet entitled *Extracts on Infant Schools* (Bury 1835), p. 8.

[59] Cf. Appendix II.

visits to Bury, Wigan, Bromsgrove and Chorley in the spring and summer of 1835, with a break in June to give evidence in London at the Select Committee on Education;[60] and an extended tour of the Eastern counties, with stops at Swaffham, Wells, Yarmouth and Norwich, early in 1836. At Bury he was saved from disaster by mere chance. While conducting an exhibition of infants at the National School, the hastily-erected gallery collapsed. He described the incident in a letter to Simpson:

> In our exhibition the gallery was high up so that the children might be seen. Well...the whole came down with a *crash* and the infants found the nearest way to the floor. Ladies fainted, &c, &c. We got the children out, in amongst the broken timbers, and strange to say none of them were hurt. We reassembled them in another room, got them in order and finished the examination, to my own astonishment, as well as to the satisfaction of the wondering auditory.[61]

At Norwich, in March 1836, he conducted the largest exhibition of his career, with 700 children on the platform and 1,700 people in the audience.[62] Four months later he lectured at Windsor, where he opened an infant school with the encouragement of the royal family, Queen Adelaide contributing to the expense and King William IV presenting a set of gymnastic apparatus originally made for the Prince of Cumberland.[63] On the strength of these royal favours, and Queen Adelaide's permission to dedicate to her the sixth edition of the *Infant System,* Wilderspin was able to present himself to the public as receiving "the Patronage of Her Most Gracious Majesty the Queen", or "the Patronage of their Majesties, the King and Queen". Engagements to lecture followed at Hereford and Kingston in August, with a public examination of the children at the former school, which he had opened eleven years earlier, on the 18th of the month.[64]

This was to be his last examination as an itinerant educator for over four years. In the early part of the summer he had received, almost simultaneously, two offers of work of a different kind, one from the U.S.A., the other from Liverpool. On 21 May 1836 George Combe had written from Edinburgh, conveying an invitation from Charles Dunkin, Principal of the Paul Street Academy in Albany, New York, to come to America to re-organise the Academy's Infant Department as a Model School.[65] Wilderspin, in reply,

[60]His appearance at the Committee was due to the good offices of Lord Sandon, M.P. for Liverpool (*Early Discipline* (1840), p. 322).

[61]Archives of W. and R. Chambers, Wilderspin to J. Simpson, 25 June 1835.

[62]*Norwich Chronicle,* 26 Mar. 1836.

[63]*Windsor and Eton Express,* 25 June 1836; *Early Discipline* (1840), p. 315.

[64]Wilderspin Papers, leaflet entitled "A Course of Four Lectures, at the Infant School, Hereford" (Aug. 1836); *Hereford Times,* 6 and 13 Aug. 1836; Wilderspin Papers, leaflet entitled "A Public Examination...at the Infant School, Hereford" (15 Aug. 1836).

[65]N.L.S. Add. Mss., 7387, f.9, G. Combe to Wilderspin, 21 May 1836.

intimated that six weeks would be ample time in which to organise a model school, provided that certain conditions were met, and that the remuneration could be fixed by either Combe or Dunkin. "I. . .have no wish at present, finally, to settle in the United States", he concluded, "However, wherever I saw my doings were most appreciated and the means for doing most good, there would I pitch my tent".[66]

That Wilderspin finally pitched his tent in Liverpool rather than in Albany was probably due to the tergiversations of George Combe, who gave Wilderspin a reference that would have deterred almost any employer from engaging him. Aware of his duplicity, Combe addressed the letter to his own brother and instructed Dunkin and his committee to keep it "strictly private and confidential". Wilderspin, asserted Combe, was the best man alive for starting an infant school and teaching his method, "but he is not the man to be appointed its permanent teacher". Combe then listed the reasons for this statement: Wilderspin was "not an educated person, but a man of strong practical instincts"; "he is consumed by vanity and the love of money"; "after he has made the *grand éclat,* and after he has received his payment he retreats(?) and disappoints his employers"; "he is. . .full of great promises which are never fulfilled. .".., and so on at considerable length.[67]

Combe's observations were something of a caricature of Wilderspin's attitudes and *modus operandi.* Though Wilderspin had not remained in one place for more than a few months during the whole of the preceding twelve years, this was largely due to the exigencies of his calling as an educational missionary, and though he liked his share of fame and money, these wordly concerns were subordinate to what he conceived to be his mission. As his engagements in Liverpool and Dublin during the following three years were to show, he did not lack the capacity for sustained work when the opportunity offered. In July 1836, having heard no more of the American offer, he was able to arrange a contract with the Liverpool Corporation to organise their schools; after a year in this post he went to Dublin to work for the Irish National Board of Education, an engagement which lasted until the summer of 1839.[68]

* * * * *

The offer of employment in the United States was an indication of the spread of Wilderspin's reputation abroad, a situation of which both he and his contemporaries were aware. In 1839, in a speech at Warrington, he had pointed out (perhaps with some exaggeration) that his system had progressed in Scotland, Ireland, America, the East and West Indies, and the Cape of Good

[66]N.L.S. Add. Mss., 7241, f. 184, Wilderspin to G. Combe, 23 May 1836.

[67]N.L.S. Add. Mss., 7387, f.15, G. Combe to C. Dunkin, 28 May 1836.

[68]Cf. Chapters 12 and 14.

Hope more steadily and with better effect than in England.[69] During his retirement he was introduced at a meeting as bearing a name "not only of English, but of European reputation"; other hemispheres, the speaker added, had no doubt also recognized his "great and valuable labours".[70] His reputation abroad was being made more or less at the same time that he was becoming known as an independent educator in Britain — the late 1820s and early 1830s. As the English infant school multiplied rapidly in Britain, particularly after the formation of the Infant School Society in 1824, so its reputation spread over the Channel and across the Atlantic. Visitors from abroad came to inspect Spitalfields and other London schools, educators and philanthropists wrote to Wilderspin for advice and literature, and his books, together with those of Goyder and Wilson, were circulated, quoted from, translated and published on a wide scale. Wilderspin himself did little positive to encourage these developments, though he responded as best he could during intervals between his travels.

A detailed account of the rise of infant schools on the Continent and in North America is a subject for future research; only some of the more important aspects that relate to Wilderspin can be touched upon here.[71] It is clear that in the period under review, there was an informal network of infant school enthusiasts in Europe, prominent among whom was Joseph Wertheimer, Viennese banker and philanthropist, who in 1826 translated into German the third edition of Wilderspin's book, *Infant Education*. European interest in the early years of childhood had, however, begun some time before this and, as shown in Chapter 3, may have influenced, or strengthened, Robert Owen's ideas on the subject. The first infant school of modern times is usually credited to Frédéric Oberlin, who became pastor of Ban de la Roche in Alsace in 1767. Oberlin was, significantly, an admirer of the theology of Swedenborg,[72] and carried out an enlightened programme of agricultural and social improvement in his parish. With the aid of assistants, he ran schools for children from one to thirteen years of age, in which pictures and natural objects were used in teaching, and in which exercise, games and amusements formed a large part of the curriculum. Whether the classes for children under six could be called an infant school in the sense

---

[69] *Manchester Guardian,* 5 Oct. 1839. The East and West Indian infant schools were staffed with teachers trained by the Home and Colonial Infant School Society (*Record,* 31 May 1841) so could not be considered as strictly falling within Wilderspin's system; the school at the Cape of Good Hope had, of course, been founded by his former mentor James Buchanan.

[70] *Wakefield Journal,* 13 Dec. 1850.

[71] This section relies heavily upon: F.A. Young, The Life and Work of Samuel Wilderspin, unpublished Ed.D. thesis, Harvard University 1949, Chapter VI, pp. 213-31; O. Vag, "The Spread of a New Type of Educational Institution: Public Pre-School Education", paper presented to the Second International Conference on the History of Education, Warsaw, 1980.

[72] Cf. J.H. Smithson, "Visit to the Celebrated Oberlin...", *Intellectual Repository and New Jerusalem Magazine,* Vol. I, N.S., 1840, pp. 151-62.

understood by Owen and Wilderspin may be a matter of debate, but it is clear that Oberlin did anticipate several of the features of their schools.[73]

In the first year of the new century, Mme. de Pastoret opened an *asile* or day-care centre for children of working mothers in Paris, the school described by Maria Edgeworth in *Madame de Fleury*. A similar school was set up by Princess Pauline of Lippe in Westphalia a few years later. A link between these institutions was provided by Baron de Gérando, philosopher and social reformer and friend of both Oberlin and Mme. de Pastoret. Gérando also provided the inspiration for further developments in infant education in France in the 1820s. Having campaigned for the cause of elementary education for many years without success[74] (though Owen's schools were known in France)[75] Gérando visited England in 1825 and brought back favourable reports of Westminster and other infant schools. Shortly afterwards, in March 1826, a committee of four women met at the house of Mme. de Pastoret, published a prospectus and opened a *salle d'asile* for infants from two to six years of age; this was supervised by two sisters of the Order of Providence, who attempted to organise the school on lines advocated by Wilderspin and Goyder, whose works had been translated (but apparently not published) at the beginning of 1826. Wilderspin's book — probably *Infant Education* of 1825 — formed the basis for subsequent French manuals on early childhood.[76]

The committee felt, however, that a closer examination of English infant schools was necessary if the school were to be properly run. In May 1827 the committee came into contact with Jean-Denis Cochin, a young lawyer and mayor of the twelfth district of Paris, who had already opened an *asile* of his own in the Rue des Gobelins.[77] Cochin undertook to find an envoy who would make the journey to England, and found the right person in the wife of Frédéric Millet, the noted miniaturist, who was engaged in painting his portrait. Eugénie Millet, Cochin discovered, had a passionate interest in the welfare of young children and eagerly offered to go to England. "Mais vous ne savez pas l'anglais", exclaimed Cochin. "Tant mieux", she replied, "au moins je ne serai pas distraite par les mots, et je n'en saisirai que mieux l'esprit de la chose".[78]

The language problem was solved by J.P. Greaves, who acted as her

---

[73] D. Deasey. *Education under Six* (London 1978), pp. 17-20. According to one biographer, Oberlin taught singing, natural history, simple botany, drawing and colouring, religion, morals, speech training, knitting, sewing and spinning. Not all of these subjects would be taught to the infants (H. Holman, *Oberlin and His Educational Work* (London, n.d. ? 1904), p. 72; p. 81).

[74] Deasey, *Education Under Six*, p. 21; in July 1824 the *Journal d'Education*, carrying an account of the inaugural meeting of the Infant School Society from its London correspondent, concluded that the time was not yet ripe for a similar organisation in France. (*Journal d'Education*, Tome Seizième, No. X, Juillet 1824, p. 210).

[75] Marie Matrat et Pauline Kergomard, *Les Ecoles Maternelles* (Paris 1889), I, p. 10.

[76] *Ibid.*, I, p. 16.

[77] J.D. Cochin, *Manuel Des Salles D'Asile* (Paris 1845), Appendice, pp. 196-98.

[78] E. Gossot, *Les Salles D'Asile en France* (Paris 1884), p. 62.

interpreter during a sojourn of two months in the autumn of 1827. She visited several schools, but paid special attention to Spitalfields, which seemed to her to be greatly superior to the others. It was then under the superintendence of Wilderspin's brother-in-law James Brown, whom she described as "un homme jeune encore, de bonne et douce figure", and she was impressed by his spontaneous but fatherly manner with the children, the music, movement, play and amusement in combination with lessons on objects, scripture and geography *à la* Wilderspin.[79] On her return to Paris she put into practice in the *salle d'asile* the lessons she had learned in London, and later opened another school. Cochin, who had also visited England, organized a model *salle d'asile* which the Scottish educationist Prof. Pillans, after a visit there, declared to be "as well conducted as any I have seen in Britain".[80] Cochin later wrote a manual for *salles d'asile* which went through several editions. By 1836, there were 102 institutions for the teaching of infants in France; officially recognised and supported the following year, they became the foundation of a system of pre-primary education.[81]

The work of Wertheimer in Vienna was quite separate from developments in France. His interest in English education stemmed from the fact that his sister was married to an Englishman,[82] and because of this "personal relationship", he wrote, he was able to watch the "blossoming" of Spitalfields Infant School.[83] Presenting Wilderspin with a copy of the translation of *Infant Education* (1825), Wertheimer informed him that he had "made bold to subjoin to your valuable work such limited views as personal experience, reflection and reading have enabled me to take of this important matter. . ."[84] In a second edition, published in 1828, Wertheimer added further material from the works of Wilson, Brown, Mayo and others,[85] and in 1832 he published *Therese,* a practical handbook for infant education, based on Wilderspin's work.[86]

Wertheimer's efforts popularized the English infant school throughout the Austro-Hungarian Empire (which then included most of Italy). The keenest interest was taken by a Hungarian aristocrat, Theresa Countess of Brunswick. Born in 1775, with a father who was an enthusiast for the independence of America, she grew up with the ideas of Washington and Benjamin Franklin.[87] A

[79] Mme. E. Millet, *Observations sur Le Système Des Ecoles D'Angleterre Pour La Première Enfance* (Paris 1828), *passim.*

[80] Cochin, *Manuel,* p. 198; P.P. 1834 IX, Report from Select Committee on the State of Education, p. 51.

[81] Deasey, *Education Under Six,* p. 22ff.

[82] We owe this detail to Dr. Otto Vag.

[83] J. Wertheimer, *Ueber die Fruhzeitige Erziehung der Kinder und die Englischen Klein-Kinder-Schulen* (Vien 1826), iv.

[84] Wilderspin Papers, J. Wertheimer to Wilderspin, 1 May 1826.

[85] Vag, "Pre-School Education", p. 7.

[86] J. Wertheimer, *Therese, ein Practisches Handbuch fur die Erziehung des Ersten Kindesalters* (Vien 1832)

[87] P. Nettl, *Beethoven Encyclopaedia* (London 1957), p. 20.

friend of Beethoven, she achieved fame as his "Immortal Beloved"; her later life, however, was devoted to good works. She went to see Pestalozzi at Yverdon and, according to Buisson, also visited "les salles d'asile de Wilderspin" in England, though it is not clear whether she actually met Wilderspin himself. She founded the first infant school in Hungary on the Wilderspin model in Buda in 1828, giving it the name "Garden of Angels".[88]

Directly and indirectly, Wilderspin thus had an influence in the growth of the Hungarian infant school movement. A translation of his *Infant Education* was actually made by Lajos Kossuth, but was never published. An infant school society was also set up and other schools founded, and by 1840 twenty-five schools on Wilderspin's system were in operation in Hungary.[89] The Countess of Brunswick corresponded with Wertheimer, who visited Buda before the establishment, with the personal assistance of the Countess, of the first infant school in Vienna in 1830.[90] The Countess also made contact with the infant school movement in France and encouraged the formation of schools in Germany.[91] By 1834 there were four infant schools in Berlin.[92] Four years later, a Dr. Hirschfeld of Bremen informed George Combe that a translation of one of Wilderspin's books was in the process of being printed.[93]

Italy had been among the first countries to show an interest in Wilderspin's work. As early as March 1824, a gentleman named Crane from Milan had called on Brougham, who directed him to Wilderspin at Quaker Street.[94] Crane was one of the pioneers in the formation of infant schools and an infant school society in his native city.[95] Perhaps the most important Italian educationist to take an interest in infant education was, however, Ferrante Aporti, who had met Wertheimer during studies in Vienna in 1815-18. Eight years later Wertheimer sent Aporti a copy of the translation of Wilderspin's book and the Italian opened an infant school at Cremona in 1827 on an experimental basis, establishing it officially as a fee-paying school two years later. A free infant school for the poor was opened in 1831, and other schools followed. Aporti had, however, to keep secret the fact that his schools were inspired by Wilderspin, fearing that reactionaries might see them as an inspiration in the struggle for liberty, and

[88]F.E. Buisson, *Dictionnaire de Pédagogie et D'Instruction Primaire,* 1er Partie, Tome Premier (Paris 1882), p. 288.

[89]Vag, "Pre-School Education", p. 4; pamphlet entitled *Extracts on the Advantage of Mr. Wilderspin's Training System* (London 1840), p. 1n.

[90]Vag, "Pre-School Education", p. 4; Miriam Tenger, *Recollections of Countess Teresa Brunswick* (London 1893), p. 37.

[91]Vag, "Pre-School Education", p. 4.

[92]According to the German educationist Dr. N.H. Julius (P.P. 1834 IX, Education, p. 131)

[93]N.S.L. Add. Mss., 7247, ff. 62-3, Dr. Hirschfeld to G. Combe, 5 Jan. 1838. It is not clear whether this was a re-printing of Wertheimer's translation or a new translation of another work.

[94]Wilderspin Papers, Brougham to Wilderspin, 4 Mar. 1824. Brougham mis-spelled the name as "Crain".

[95]We owe this information to Dr. Simonetta Soldani.

Italian nationalists as the slavish copy of foreign models.[96]

Educators in at least two other European countries, Switzerland and Sweden, were inspired by Wilderspin's work. Switzerland was one of the earliest European countries to establish infant schools, stimulated by Edouard Diodati's *Quelques Réflexions sur les Ecoles d'Enfants,* published in Geneva in 1827. The organisers of the first school, founded in Geneva in the same year, had corresponded with English educators, and the superintendent, J.M. Monod, had read Wilderspin's works and incorporated many of his practices in the daily routine of the school.[97] Some years later, in December 1832, Wilderspin received a letter from Mrs. von Koch of Stockholm, Sweden, requesting material for an infant school to be set up by "some benevolently-minded ladies" of that nation. Mrs. von Koch had visited London in early 1832 and had spoken to him at the end of one of his lectures, returning home with a copy of each of his books.[98]

Further investigation might reveal more evidence of Wilderspin's influence in Europe, for in addition to the schools established in France, Germany, Italy, Hungary, Switzerland and Sweden, others were founded in Holland, Belgium, Norway, Denmark, Russia, Poland, Spain and Portugal,[99] though the present state of research does not reveal to what extent, if any, the infant schools in the latter group of countries owed their inspiration to Wilderspin. Sufficient has been done, however, to show that during the period of his greatest influence in Britain, a European movement largely inspired by his work was also under way. The evidence suggests that in most cases the schools were sponsored by much the same social stratum as in Britain — the liberal intelligentsia, aided here and there by socially-conscious members of the aristocracy.

* * * * *

The United States of America had not lagged behind, and there also Wilderspin played an influential role. By the middle 1820s, copies of his works were to be found in New England libraries,[100] and the *American Journal of Education,* founded in 1826, included in its first three volumes extensive extracts from his works, together with those of William Wilson and David Goyder.[101] In 1826 Wilderspin received a letter from the prominent Boston educationist J.W. Ingraham, enclosing some of his own pamphlets and asking Wilderspin for

[96] Avril Wilson, "Ferrante Aporti—Apostle of Infancy", *British Journal of Educational Studies,* Vol. XXVII, No. 3, Oct. 1979, pp. 221-31.

[97] Vag, "Pre-School Education", pp. 2-3; *American Annals of Education and Instruction,* Vol. 1, Nos. 5-9, May-Sept. 1831, for a detailed description of the school.

[98] Wilderspin Papers, E. von Koch to Wilderspin, 13 Dec. 1832.

[99] Young, Samuel Wilderspin, pp. 213-20; Vag, "Pre-School Education", *passim.*

[100] Young, Samuel Wilderspin, p. 223.

[101] *American Journal of Education,* Vols. I-III, 1826-28, *passim.*

copies of his books and other literature on the infant school movement. Ingraham ran a Sunday School on principles largely derived from those of Wilderspin, and this had attracted favourable attention. "The report of your labours in the cause", he wrote from Boston, "is not unknown here among the friends of education".[102]

As in England, Swedenborgians were prominent in the early years of the American movement. One of the pioneers was Maskell M. Carll, a Swedenborgian clergyman from Philadelphia and a friend of Bronson Alcott, Transcendentalist and infant school educator, who was also influenced by Swedenborgian ideas.[103] Carll toured England in 1824; he arrived in London in February, stayed with Thomas Goyder and visited Spitalfields Infant School.[104] Returning home, Carll joined with Matthew Carey, a Catholic publisher and prolific writer on social questions, in publicising infant schools. The first school in Philadelphia was opened in October 1827 under the superintendence of E. Bacon, who added a supplement to the American edition of James Brown's *Essay on Infant Cultivation* (1828) and later published a manual of his own.[105]

In New York, infant schools began under the inspiration of De Witt Clinton, Governor of the State. Clinton, in January 1825, had received a letter from an (un-named) friend in England, giving a description of the infant schools of London. He at once wrote to Mrs. Joanna Bethune, a philanthropic lady who regarded education "as a science as well as a charity", urging their establishment in New York City.[106] Mrs. Bethune was in communication with John Hare of Bristol (his Temple Infant School, it will be remembered, had been organised by an agent of Wilderspin and superintended by his friend James Slade), who sent her a number of papers and books.[107] These certainly included some of Wilderspin's, for her biographer remarked (not quite accurately) that "the infant school system, as organised by Wilderspin, on the basis of Pestalozzi's plan of development...deeply interested her". She helped to found the New York Infant School Society in May 1827, with De Witt Clinton as patron, and opened her first infant school two months later; nine infant schools were eventually established in the city.[108] Mrs. Bethune, under the title of "A Friend of the Poor", also edited and adapted for American consumption Wilderspin's *Infant*

---

[102]Wilderspin Papers, J.W. Ingraham to Wilderspin, 13 May 1826.

[103]"Like Emerson, he was fascinated but never quite converted by the writings of Swedenborg" (O. Shepard (Ed.), *The Journals of Bronson Alcott* (Boston 1938), xxiii.)

[104]"Visit to England of the Rev. Mr. Carll", *Intellectual Repository,* Vol. I, N.S., 1824, pp. 162-63; Young, Samuel Wilderspin, p. 224.

[105]Young, Samuel Wilderspin, pp. 224-25.

[106]E.A. Fitzpatrick, *The Educational Views and Influence of De Witt Clinton* (New York 1911), pp. 106-07; G.W. Bethune, *Memoirs of Mrs. Joanna Bethune* (New York 1864), p. 122.

[107]*Taunton Courier,* 31 Oct. 1827. The *Courier* asserted that infant schools in both New York and Philadelphia owed their rise "to the instrumentality of...Mr. John Hare". (*Taunton Courier,* 25 Nov. 1827).

Education (1825), to which she added extracts from the works of David Goyder and others.[109] Another edition was published in Portland, Maine, a year later.[110]

Perhaps the most important American educator to be influenced by the English infant school movement was Bronson Alcott, later to give his name to the school at Ham Common in Surrey at which Wilderspin's daughter Emma taught for a while.[111] Alcott's growing interest in education was stimulated by the formation of an Infant School Society in Boston in April 1828. Brought into activity by Abba May, who later became his wife, he was invited to take charge of the first Boston infant school for three months. To prepare himself for the task he visited the schools in New York and Philadelphia (which he felt were, respectively, mechanical and orthodox), and read the American editions of Wilderspin's *Infant Education* and Higgins' *Exposition of the Principles of Infant Education.*[112]

It is clear from Alcott's own book, *Infant Instruction,* that his conception of infant education was close to that of the English model; he advocated the use of visual and tangible apparatus, music, singing, movement and play, but put less stress on the more mechanical features — no monitors were used — and more on the child's presumed inner urge to educational development.[113] Some years later Alcott was to be converted by J.P. Greaves to the view that birth, not education, was primary in moral reform.[114]

The American infant schools clearly owed much to British models and to British treatises. As late as 1841 Wilderspin was sending his books to Charles Barnard in Boston via his friend Ezra Weston.[115] Apparently George Combe was also recommending literature, for he received a stinging letter from Simpson on 20 March. "Why did you refer the Americans to the books of Wilderspin and Stow *alone* for Infant School information?" *We* [i.e. the phrenologists] have put it on a foundation of principle — on the human faculties. Stow is empyrical (sic) and often wrong and is one of our religious opponents".[116] Despite Simpson's

---

[108]Bethune, *Memoirs,* pp. 122-23; p. 163; Fitzpatrick, *De Witt Clinton,* pp. 107-08.

[109]*Infant Education; or Remarks on the Importance of Educating the Infant Poor…With an Account of Some of the Infant Schools in England, and the System of Education There Adopted. Selected and Abridged from the Works of Wilderspin, Goyder and Others* (New York 1827).

[110]Young, *Samuel Wilderspin,* p. 233 n.

[111]Cf. Chapter 15.

[112]Dorothy McCuskey, *Bronson Alcott, Teacher* (New York 1940), pp. 40-45. For the circulation of infant school literature, including British works, in the U.S.A., cf. J.J. McCadden, *Education in Pennsylvania 1801-1835* (Philadelphia 1937), pp. 57-8.

[113]A.B. Alcott, *Observations on the Principles and Methods of Infant Instruction* (Boston 1830), *passim.*

[114]McCuskey, *Alcott,* pp. 118-25.

[115]Wilderspin Papers, C.F. Barnard to Wilderspin, 1 Mar. 1841.

[116]N.L.S. Add. Mss., 7262, ff. 21-3, J. Simpson to G. Combe, 20 Mar. 1841.

concern, however, there is no evidence that Stow's principles were influential in the United States. Indeed, by the 1840s, independent infant schools were on the wane. Apart from a dozen or so cities on the Eastern seaboard, America was not to witness the growth of a movement on British lines; most of the new institutions were incorporated in the expanding public primary school system, facilitated by the fact that the infant schools took children at a later age than those in Europe. In addition, Americans had a democratic distaste for the aura of charity and class distinction which, in their eyes, clung to the English infant school.[117]

[117]Young, Samuel Wilderspin, pp. 221-22.

SAMUEL WILDERSPIN

JAMES BUCHANAN

DAVID GOYDER

J.P. GREAVES

THE INTERIOR OF BRISTOL INFANT SCHOOL, MEADOW STREET

THE INTERIOR OF WALTHAMSTOW INFANT SCHOOL

DRYGATE INFANT SCHOOL, GLASGOW

CHELTENHAM INFANT SCHOOL, ST. JAMES' SQUARE

DUBLIN MODEL INFANT SCHOOL

THOMAS URRY YOUNG

SARAH ANNE YOUNG

"BABY-LONIAN UNIVERSITY", BY GEORGE CRUIKSHANK

CHAPTER 9

THEORY AND PRACTICE

Wilderspin wrote his first three books — published between 1823 and 1825 — at a time when general principles of education were of limited public interest and when the view that viable classroom practice needed to be guided by a coherent theory had hardly been established. He had, moreover, set himself the task, in these volumes, of acquainting the world with the actual working of a new system of education more or less as he was devising it. He was well aware of the situation. He felt that his books would be more readily acceptable if he played down the theoretical side of his work; "dry philosophical detail", he believed, "would neither be received nor read". But, he added, this did not mean that "I was unacquainted with the philosophy of my own plans, merely because I preferred the doing of the thing to the writing about it".[1]

His "philosophy", of course, had its roots in the educational ideas of Emanuel Swedenborg, about which he found it expedient to remain silent during his periods of employment with Joseph Wilson and the Infant School Society. During the 1830s, however, after his acquaintanceship with philosophically-inclined educationists — Greaves, Combe, Simpson and others — who introduced him to the ideas of Pestalozzi and the phrenologists, he wove these several strands of thought into a developmental theory of early childhood education which anticipated many twentieth-century ideas.

A reader of Wilderspin's early works could hardly have anticipated this outcome. The stress was on the practical which, he maintained, "surpasses all theoretical views",[2] and such statements of general principle that may be found were very much in the empirical tradition of John Locke. This was partly due to Locke's pervasive influence, even as late as the third decade of the nineteenth century. It also owed something to the special regard which Swedenborgians had for this "sincere seeker of the truth", whose name was "particularly dear to every Englishman";[3] Swedenborg himself had been acquainted with and was to some extent influenced by Locke's psychological theories.[4] Thus we find Wilderspin, in the first edition of the *Infant Poor,* adopting Locke's position on the rejection of innate ideas, and in the second edition quoting his well-known concept of the

---

[1]*Infant System* (1840), p. 143; p. 145.

[2]*Infant Education* (1825), pp. 1-2.

[3]Cf. the anonymous preface to E. Swedenborg, *The Doctrine of Life for the New Jerusalem* (London, 4th ed., 1791), iii. The author probably had in mind Locke's *The Reasonableness of Christianity as Delivered in the Scriptures* (London 1695), esp. 1-25, in which Locke criticises, as did Swedenborg, the doctrine "that would have all Adam's posterity doomed to eternal infinite punishment for the transgression of Adam" (1). Swedenborgians also believed that Locke held similar views to themselves on the life of the soul in a substantial body after death ("Important Sentiments of the New Church Advocated by Dr. Watts and Mr. Locke", *Intellectual Repository,* N.S., No. 11, Apr. 1824, pp. 127-32).

[4]Inge Jonsson, *Emanuel Swedenborg* (New York 1971), pp. 78-80. Jonsson takes the view that Swedenborg's ideas were a compromise between the rationalistic belief in innate ideas and the empirical belief that consciousness is entirely formed by sensory experiences.

mind as a blank sheet.[5] Wilderspin also upheld one of the central tenets of Locke's *Essay Concerning Human Understanding* in believing that children were creatures of sense and that all learning took place by means of the senses, pointing out, for instance, that the first thing that attracted the child's attention was light, and that the second was colour.[6] The practical application of this was the use of coloured pictures in Scripture teaching and the invention of the arithmeticon — initially a series of coloured balls strung on wires — for instruction in arithmetic. Children, Wilderspin pointed out, were constantly acquiring "habits of perception" by using their eyes and their hands and finding something novel in everything they discovered.[7] Whether he was fully aware of it or not, his pedagogical scheme took into account activities which fostered the development of perception, which is a major factor in cognitive growth.

The three main natural characteristics of children, he held, were imitativeness, curiosity (the "inquisitive spirit") and liveliness — and each ought to receive expression in the learning process.[8] The last two were given some prominence by Locke, and another of Locke's propositions — the need for diversion and recreation when children's restlessness with learning manifested itself — was elaborated by Wilderspin to fit the classroom situation. Children's minds, he held, were formed for "endless variety", and children were constantly searching for new objects of interest.[9] This led him, as we have seen, to give short lessons on different subjects, to move children from one room to another, to intersperse instruction with gymnastic exercises, marching and running about in the playground. This recognition of children's need for variety and change of scene is characterized by Alice Paterson, in her thesis on Wilderspin, as a "genuine pedagogical principle", and one cannot but agree with her.[10] On the other hand, if he had fully considered the implications of his statements concerning children's sense of curiosity and their ability to learn through the senses, he would hardly have given them so much abstract and inert matter to learn by heart. The third edition of his book — *Infant Education*, published in 1825 — contained many pages devoted to specimen question and answer lessons (in which a great deal of inert knowledge was enshrined), arithmetical and other

[5]*Infant Poor* (1823), p. 45; *Infant Education* (1824), p. 196. Locke's actual words were "...white paper, void of all characters, without any ideas". (P.H. Nidditch (Ed.), J. Locke, *An Essay Concerning Human Understanding* (Oxford 1975), Bk. II, Ch. 1, 2).

[6]*Infant Poor* (1823), p. 42; p. 46. Cf. Locke, *Essay*, Bk. II, Ch. 1, 6, "Light, and colours, are busy at hand everywhere, when the eye is but open".

[7]*Scotsman*, 29 Nov. 1828; *Infant System* (1834), p. 74.

[8]*Infant Poor* (1823), p. 21; p. 42; p. 123; *Infant Poor* (1824), p. 40; *Infant Education* (1825), p. 187; *Infant Education* (1829), p. 149; p. 277.

[9]*Infant Poor* (1823), p. 20; p. 50; J.L. Axtell (Ed.), *The Educational Writings of John Locke* (Cambridge 1968), *Some Thoughts Concerning Education*, 46; 63; 108; 118.

[10]Alice Paterson, Samuel Wilderspin and the Infant System, Ph.D. thesis, Jena 1906, p. 100. The insights and observations in this thesis have been of particular value in this chapter.

tables, collections of "improving" verse, and specimens of the "elliptical" method, in which children supplied a missing word in a sentence in order to complete the meaning. This last method was suggested by Dr. Borthwick Gilchrist, the orientalist and supporter of Mechanics' Institutes, who visited Spitalfields in 1825.[11]

Wilderspin's early writings thus lean towards the empirical, and also display a tendency to make the infusion of useful knowledge a part of infant instruction. As an intelligent and upwardly-mobile artisan living in the age of "the march of the intellect", and an admirer of Brougham to boot, Wilderspin never lost this reverence for knowledge; but its introduction into the infant curriculum in its raw state, as it were, was to conflict with his later attempts to devise methods of teaching appropriate to a relatively sophisticated learning theory.

Robert Owen, on the other hand, influenced by the ideas of Rousseau and Helvétius, was more consistently theoretical in his approach; he was largely free of didacticism, and inconsistencies in his practice were usually a result of his bowing to necessity. Like many who were influenced by Enlightenment ideas, he had unbounded faith in the possibilities of education, believing that it could help to attain "every object of human society". But Owen's educational edifice was reared on a somewhat paternalistic conception of the malleability of child nature. To Owen, children were "passive and wonderfully contrived compounds", creatures of circumstances whose "natural powers and faculties" were entirely subject to the control of adults.[12] James Mill, the other educational theorist of stature of this period, again drawing on Enlightenment ideas, held similar views of the ductility of the young and of the power of education; by means of education, asserted Mill, the whole human race could reach "the greatest attainable heights of wisdom and virtue". In his essay entitled "Education", written in 1818, he had extended the theory of ideas of Locke, Condillac and others to the educational field, attempting to place "the knowledge which we possess respecting the human mind, into that order and form, which is most advantageous for drawing from it the practical rules of education". The result was, paradoxically, a theoretical underpinning of the mechanical and repetitive methods of the monitorial system. The task of the teacher who followed Mill's prescription was the arrangement and ordering of "successions" of discrete particles of meaning in the minds of his pupils into useful associations and sequences of ideas.[13] Progress in learning was thus a matter of addition and arrangement rather than of organic growth involving

---

[11] *Infant Education* (1825), vii-ix. A similar method, known as Teach Yourself English, was employed in British secondary schools in the mid-twentieth century.

[12] *New View of Society,* Second Essay, Owen, *Life,* 1, p. 272; "Report to the County of Lanark", Owen, *Life,* 1A, p. 294.

[13] J. Mill, "Education", in W.H. Burston, *James Mill on Education* (Cambridge 1969), p. 45; p. 52 ff; T.W. Moore, *Educational Theory: An Introduction* (London 1974), pp. 37-42.

qualitative changes in the child's cognitive processes.

Optimistic views of education tended to give greater importance to the intention of the teacher than to the interests and aspirations of the child. Wilderspin saw the child more in the manner of Locke — active, inquisitive, but of changeable disposition and temper, and the educational process as an interaction between teacher and pupil which might have variable results.[14] Had Wilderspin's thinking remained within the bounds of Lockean empiricism, however, his growth as an educational theorist might well have been retarded, for it is doubtful if a developmental theory of infant education could have been constructed within the confines of Locke's psychological categories and educational precepts; the *Educational Magazine,* in 1835, pointed out that Locke's philosophy "reject[ed] the notion of anything to be developed".[15] Wilderspin, however, began to interest himself in the new philosophies which, originating on the Continent, were becoming known in Britain; in 1827 Pestalozzi's *Letters on Early Education* had been published, followed a year later by Combe's *Constitution of Man.* After 1829, free from association with patrons or employers, and self-confidently beginning a career as a free-lance educationist, Wilderspin began to develop the theoretical side of his system, bringing into focus the educational principles of Swedenborg.

* * * * *

What was the extent of Wilderspin's commitment to Swedenborgian ideas? His life-long policy of public silence with regard to Swedenborg and his theology makes it difficult to give a precise answer. There are, however, some indications that after relinquishing his active role in the New Church in 1825 he remained a Swedenborgian at heart during the remainder of his professional life. On his travels he made contact with provincial New Churchmen,[16] and lecture notes and correspondence preserved among his papers show him expounding the important Swedenborgian concept of the connection between the will and the understanding.[17] More importantly, a close study of his writings indicates that he was familiar with the main principles of Swedenborgian educational theory.

These were set out in an authoritative article entitled "On Education" which appeared in two parts under the initials W.M. in the *Intellectual Repository* in

---

[14]Locke, *Thoughts Concerning Education,* 73ff; 95-117.

[15]"Education in England, No. 1. The Infant System", *Educational Magazine,* Vol. I, Feb. 1835, p. 67.

[16]Wilderspin was invited to establish an infant school in Louth in 1831 by John Bogg, a local Swedenborgian, who later corresponded with him (*Intellectual Repository,* Vol. XIII, No. 150, June 1866; Wilderspin Papers, J. Bogg to Wilderspin, 27 Mar. 1846.) On a visit to Birmingham in the early 1830s he entertained J.H. Madeley, a prominent member of the New Church and apparently influenced the latter's decision to establish Swedenborgian day schools in Birmingham (C. Higham, "Samuel Wilderspin", *New Church Magazine,* Vol. XXXIV, No. 399, Mar. 1915, pp. 106-12; No. 400, Apr. 1915, p. 170n).

[17]Wilderspin Papers, "Two Lectures on the Principles of Education by S. Wilderspin Esq". (n.d.); "Syllabus: Heads of Lectures S.W". (n.d.); Wilderspin to Sir Francis Mackenzie (n.d.? 1839).

1817.[18] A classic summary and exposition of the educational ideas scattered throughout Swedenborg's voluminous works, particularly *Arcana Coelestia,* it equipped New Churchmen with a developmental theory of education capable of being applied to the infant domain. The article began with a description of Swedenborg's analysis of the mind; the two major faculties were the will, the seat of the affections, and the understanding, in which was located the intellect. (Locke had also used these terms, describing the faculties of the will and understanding as "the two great and principal actions of the mind".)[19] Swedenborgian education had a two-fold nature: the education of the intellect, where the aim was to form "right conceptions" in the understanding by means of the cultivation of the mind; and the education of the affections or feelings, the purpose of which was to form good dispositions by submitting the will to "proper discipline". Wilderspin made a similar statement in 1825; the promoters of infant schools, he wrote, wished "to operate on the will and its affections as well as the understanding and its thoughts; they want to make good men rather than learned men — men of *wisdom,* rather than men of *knowledge*".[20] This foreshadows the modern emphasis on the affective and cognitive domains.

Swedenborg, again in keeping with Locke, rejected the concept of innate ideas and located the roots of intellectual development in the material world. Without "things of science" (i.e. tangible natural objects), explained W.M., man was incapable of forming a single idea or thought; "the ideas of thought are grounded upon those things which are impressed on the memory by the objects of sense". Furthermore, "man has not. . .any innate science (i.e. in this context, knowledge), but he is formed to begin from the lowest degree of science, and gradually to ascend higher and higher without ever reaching the summit". Wilderspin, as we have seen, endorsed these views and indeed paraphrased the latter in his first book; "so wonderfully is man formed by his adoring Creator, that he is capable of increasing in knowledge and advancing towards perfection to all eternity, without ever being able to arrive at it".[21]

The possibility of this development lay in the special characteristics of infants, who were endowed with both curiosity and the love of knowledge ("the affection of knowing"); children were continually making inquiries concerning "the various objects which strike their senses", and the role of the teacher was to foster this curiosity and encourage a child to think for himself. As it was "wisely ordered, that the activity of every affection should be attended with a corresponding delight", wrote W.M., the teacher should endeavour to make knowledge agreeable to young people and increase their delight in discovery; to

---

[18]W.M., "On Education", *Intellectual Repository,* Vol. III, No. XXI, Jan.-Mar. 1817, pp. 283-91; Vol. III, No. XXII, Apr.-June 1817, pp. 354-61. The following paragraphs are based on this article.

[19]Locke, *Essay,* Bk II, Ch. VI, 2.

[20]*Infant Education* (1825), pp. 53-4.

[21]*Infant Poor* (1823), pp. 45-6.

the degree that study was interesting so was it "permanently impressed on our memories". Wilderspin was later to inform the Select Committee of 1835 that children "delighted in acquiring knowledge" and that "we endeavour to make it agreeable, by giving it in a pleasing manner".[22]

The major part of the article was concerned with the moral and intellectual development of a human being from infancy to maturity, as Swedenborg conceived it. The first stage roughly corresponded to the period of infancy, i.e. the first half-dozen years of life, which, as the foundation period, was regarded as the most important of all. Intellectual education should be based upon things which young children can apprehend and understand, namely things of sense ("sensuals"), for whatever was not understood abided in "a dead state" in "the outer court of memory". Children should be guided to make deductions for themselves, for knowledge thus acquired was more durable than that learned by rote. "Celestial affection" attracted children to "the historicals of the Word" (i.e. Biblical facts and narratives), provided the teacher made them interesting, pointed a moral and eschewed the repetition of "the sacred names of God and religion" and the overloading of children's minds with "hymns, prayers and long catechisms". This prescription, as we have seen, was faithfully followed by Wilderspin throughout his professional career; his close paraphrases of these (and other) sentiments lend further strength to the assumption that he was familiar with the *Repository* article.

The stage of infancy was seen by Swedenborg as also crucial to moral development. Parents and teachers had to safeguard the innocence of childhood by a consistent and judicious policy of bringing the selfish passions under control; corporal punishment was allowed, but only as a last resort. Wilderspin, on this point, obviously followed Swedenborg rather than Owen.[23]

The laying of intellectual foundations and formation of good dispositions in infancy prepared the way for, and was vital to the success of, the second stage of life and education, which corresponded to the period of childhood and youth. Teaching was now largely concerned with "exterior scientifics": knowledge of language; the history of nature; the productions of art; the inventions of man; civil institutions and states of society in different countries and periods; the knowledge and effects of moral actions. Taken together, these constituted "a good education"; to them the author of the article added writing, arithmetic, grammar and geography. Exterior scientifics, Swedenborg stressed, were "spiritual riches", whereby a man did service to himself, his neighbours and his country.

These aspects of natural knowledge prepared the way for the third stage, in which "interior spiritual instruction" was revealed from the truth of the Holy

---

[22]P.P. 1835 VII, Report of the Select Committee on Education in England and Wales, p. 21.

[23]Cf. *Infant System* (1834), p. 147, in which Wilderspin wrote that corporal punishment should be administered with great prudence and never employed but as "a last resource".

Word or, as Wilderspin paraphrased it: "Having thus made [the child] slightly acquainted with the A.B.C. of nature's book, you prepare his inquiring mind for the A.B.C. of God's revealed will...in the Holy Scriptures".[24] This was in accordance with Swedenborg's theory of correspondence; "things natural", knowledge of which was obtained from observation and education, corresponded with "things spiritual", obtained from the Writings when the mind, by regeneration, had entered the spiritual state.

* * * * *

It is always difficult to trace the geneaology of ideas or to demonstrate the precise degree of influence of one thinker upon another, but Wilderspin's debt to the educational principles of Swedenborg hardly needs further emphasis. The whole of Swedenborg's educational theory was, of course, shot through with spiritual and idealist conceptions; but it was possible for the practising educator to separate out appropriate aspects and utilise them as a guide to his work. Wilderspin made four fundamental propositions — the conception of education as a series of stages consistent with the developing nature of the child; the importance of early childhood to future development; belief in the innocence of infancy, and the important role given to the senses and the affections in the educational process — the groundwork of his pedagogical scheme.

The ideas and principles of Pestalozzi which he embraced were largely derived from *Letters on Early Education Addressed to J.P. Greaves, Esq. by Pestalozzi,* published in translation in September 1827.[25] Though concerned with the child's psychological development during the period of infancy spent with his mother, the work contained a number of concepts and insights which could be adapted to the infant schoolroom. Some, it is evident, had already been formulated by Wilderspin himself. The most important propositions of the *Letters* were: that the great object of early childhood education was the development of the infant mind; that all the human faculties needed to be developed, with particular exercises for each; that imitation was among the first manifestations of the faculties; that the education of children was advanced by bringing objects before their senses, or pictures if objects were not available; that the names of objects should then be given, followed by a description of their nature; that the memory alone should not be exercised; that all ideas should be conveyed by the media of number (taught by means of objects), form (taught by

[24]*System of Education* (1840), p. 229.

[25]They were written between Ocotber 1818 and May 1819 and were passed to Greaves (who did not speak German) during his residence at Yverdon. Greaves was probably "the friend" who assisted Wilderspin in the composition of *Infant Education* published in 1829 (*Infant Education* (1829), vii), which was the first of Wilderspin's works to incorporate Pestalozzian principles on any scale, particularly the inclusion of the categories of language, form and number.

the analytical method) and language; that the "curriculum" should include drawing, modelling, geometry, geography, music (as a moral agent) and physical exercises.[26]

Wilderspin's debt to phrenology is less easy to particularise, but can be seen in his frequent use of the term "faculties" after 1829 — "infant faculties", "intellectual faculties", "the faculty of perception", etc., the specific division of education into moral, mental and physical branches,[27] and the greater prominence he gave to the way in which lessons on objects in nature could be made the vehicle of allusions to and illustrations of the power of the Creator — a view similar to the natural theology which Simpson believed was inherent in every lesson.[28]

Wilderspin characteristically avoided all mention of the phrenologists in his works, despite his private admission that he was a "semi-convert" to the doctrine,[29] but they, on their part, were quick to claim him as their own. James Simpson, in the article referred to in Chapter 7, argued that both Wilderspin and phrenology had arrived at the truth, as their views as to man's animal (i.e. physical), moral and intellectual nature were entirely coincident. Both promoted health and the physical powers of children, both stressed the development of individual cognition by means of the observation of tangible objects and an analysis of their nature and both exemplified the moral laws of nature by the encouragement of group and community activity, the benevolent actions of the teacher and the inculcation of "a sound natural religion".[30] Phrenological theory postulated the existence of a number of faculties of the human mind which were localised in different parts of the brain; variations in these faculties had a corresponding effect on the exterior formation of the skull, so that it was seen as a relatively simple matter to diagnose a person's psychological and intellectual make-up.[31] Spurzheim, one of the founders of phrenology, had argued that the human faculties developed in a certain order, which presupposed stages of

[26]*Letters on Early Education, Addressed to J.P. Greaves, Esq. by Pestalozzi* (London 1827), *passim.* Cf. also Paterson, Samuel Wilderspin, pp. 72-3. Wilderspin was loth to acknowledge his debt to Pestalozzi. He stated that he had not read any of his works when he published the *Infant Poor* in 1823. This was probably true, but his assertion that he had not known of his existence for some years afterwards, made in 1829 and 1834 (*Infant Education* (1829), viii; *Infant System* (1834), pp. 258-59) gave an incorrect impression of the extent of his knowledge of Pestalozzi's theories. In 1852 he declared that "I am not aware that any one individual, not even Pestalozzi, has run a similar course" (*Infant System,* (1852) p. 119).

[27]A division also used by Pestalozzi.

[28]*Infant Education* (1829), *passim; Infant System* (1834), *passim;* P.P. 1835 VII, Education, pp. 13-37, *passim.* For Simpson's views, Cf. P.P. 1836 XIII, Report from the Select Committee on Education in Ireland, Pt. I, p. 240; p. 261; pp. 268-69.

[29]Cf. Chapter 7.

[30][J. Simpson], "Phrenological Analysis of Infant Education in Mr. Wilderspin's System", *Phrenological Journal,* Vol. VI, No. XXLV, 1830, pp. 418-33.

[31]Cf. G. Combe, *Essays on Phrenology* (Edinburgh 1819), pp. 1-28; G. Combe, *A System of Phrenology* (Edinburgh 1825), pp. 25-35; J.D. Davies, *Phrenology: Fad and Science* (New Haven 1955), *passim;* D. de Giustino *Conquest of Mind: Phrenology and Victorian Social Thought* (London 1975), pp. 12-30.

intellectual growth, with an education appropriate to each. Infant schools thus fulfilled the function of developing those faculties which appeared earliest; these included almost all the sentiments (which pointed to the need for moral education) the faculties of Individuality, Form, Comparison and Language, followed by those of Size, Colour, Locality, Tune, Number, and Order.[32]

From these elements, could Wilderspin be said to have forged an educational theory, in the sense of "an organised body of principles and recommendations directed towards those concerned with educational practice?"[33] Modern philosophers of education have suggested that a valid theory should comprehend a fairly long-term aim with regard to the type of individual and the kind of society that education might hope to produce; an understanding of the nature of the child and an outline of the stages of its development; an analysis of the nature of knowledge and of the methods appropriate to teach it; finally, an attempt to relate these methods of teaching to the appropriate stage of development of the child.[34] Wilderspin, of course, must be judged in relation to his contemporaries, not by the standards of late twentieth-century philosophical thought. The above criteria can, however, serve as organising principles for his somewhat haphazardly-presented ideas, as well as means of indicating, as a matter of interest, the extent to which he anticipated modern conceptions.

Swedenborgians had reasonably clear-cut aims with regard to education. W.M., the author of the article cited earlier, had pointed out that members of the New Church gave central importance to "educating the rising generation in the Church in such a manner as to fit them to become...pillars of strength and beauty in the sacred temple, and, at the same time, good and useful members of society at large".[35] Something of this dual aim can be discerned in Wilderspin's works. On occasion he could state that infant education would raise a generation superior to the last in "religious and intellectual requirements", which would result in "a glorious change in the moral world", even the creation of "a paradise".[36] At other times he believed improved education would eliminate "reckless mischief, hard-heartedness and cruelty, vices which render the lower orders dangerous and formidable", and help to form a race of workers with "improved taste", "an expanded heart" and "a contented mind", who would be able to lead "a goodly and righteous life" — in short, people with "a solid, useful and virtuous character".[37] Such were the objectives; but a consistent theory implies a certain harmony between the stated aim and the type of education

[32]"Spurzheim on Education", *Phrenological Journal,* Vol. I, No. II, 1824, p. 387.

[33]Moore, *Educational Theory,* p. 9.

[34]This largely follows Moore, *Educational Theory,* p. 17ff.

[35]W.M., "On Education", *loc.cit.,* pp. 358-59.

[36]*Infant System* (1840), p. 153; p. 158; *Infant System* (1852), p. 12.

[37]P.P. 1835 VII, Education, p. 18; *Infant System* (1840), p. 168; *System of Education* (1840), p. 6; *Infant System* (1834), p. 69.

proposed; the methods pursued and the theory of learning animating them should exhibit a reasonable likelihood of producing the intended result. Was Wilderspin's learning theory likely to foster the development of the kind of human being he had in mind?

Wilderspin did not subscribe to the "free development" ideal of the nature educationists.[38] In fact he warned against the conclusion of "a most ingenious writer" (i.e. Rousseau) that allowing children to develop naturally implied a preference for the savage rather than the social life. On the contrary, he argued, the intention of nature, by equipping the child with "the natural principles of imitation and belief", was that education should assist in forming the man. But the role of the teacher was of crucial importance — "[his] superior judgement is required to ascertain when to teach and what is to be taught".[39] Children should not be allowed to develop by and for themselves; this would lead to comparative ignorance and an unformed and uncultivated mind. On the other hand, they should not be subjected to the "past system" of giving "dogmas instead of problems", or storing the immature mind with "a useless heap of notions"; the result would be an ignorant and narrow understanding. They must be allowed to think for themselves, as Swedenborg had suggested, but the teacher should be at hand so that if they arrived at erroneous conclusions they might be assisted to attain the truth, though care should be taken that they arrived at it by their own exertions. Little good was done by the teacher telling the child an answer was right or wrong "unless you enable it to see the error of the one and the truth of the other". The child, after all, was a rational being and its intellectual faculties could develop in no other way. But the key to the whole process was to give the child nothing he was not competent to understand.

This was exemplified in Wilderspin's approach to reading. Instead of making the child repeat meaningless letters and syllables, he advocated approaching the subject somewhat in the modern way by preparing the senses of the child in advance. Learning to read, he declared, was secondary to discovering "the natures and properties of things, of which words are the signs"; if this were done, the child would naturally be led to inquire their names. The teacher's first endeavour was to excite the spirit of inquiry and to keep it alive by never quite satiating it with repetition. It should then be directed to the proper objects, specifically things which could be apprehended by the senses; forms, sizes, weights, colours, properties, sounds were all "objects of delightful contemplation".[40] The child's "ideas" of each object should then be elicited by judicious comparison of the opinion of both the child and the teacher. Essentially this was a developmental process, in which the child was led, step by

---

[38]The following paragraphs are based on *Infant Education* (1829), pp. 143-50, and *Infant System* (1834), pp. 69-80.

[39]*System of Education* (1840), p. 45.

[40]*Ibid.*, p. 28.

step along the path "nature had marked out", one thing being mastered before another was attempted. "We deprecate the unnatural system", he declared, "which gives children tasks beyond their powers, and for which their infantine faculties are not qualified". The correct course was to induce children "to examine, compare and judge, in reference to those matters which their dawning intellects are capable of mastering".[41] Given correct guidance, children could form elaborate concepts at an early age:

> The complex operation of connecting things by their points of resemblance, and at the same time of distinguishing them individually by their points of dissimilarity, is one of the highest exercises of our reason; yet it may be carried on in children at a much earlier period than is generally imagined...[42]

It is clear that Wilderspin had grasped some important aspects of perception — the role of classification, and the use of language in fixing an idea in the mind. But he also relied on the Lockean concept of reflection:

> ...it is our wish and endeavour to cultivate the higher intellectual faculties primarily; to call forth into activity the understanding, and to exercise the *judgement,* rather than to burden the *memory.* We wish to make them *think,* to *reflect,* and decide *themselves* on things...it is reflection which converts the crude mass into the nutritious principle of wisdom. For the purpose of encouraging reflection, the judicious teacher enters into conversations with the children, which are likely to induce reflection...[43]

All educators must generalise about the learning process, and Wilderspin was no exception. But he added two important provisions which were warning lights to teachers. First, that children had different ways of learning and that a child's demeanour was no sure guide to the operation of its mental powers; children's apparent lack of concern in the classroom, for instance, did not necessarily betoken idleness or stupidity, but might be "*their method* of receiving instruction".[44] Second, (in line with Swedenborg), that children had dissimilar interests and different learning rates, which led some to excel at arithmetic while others lagged, some to pick up spelling more quickly than others, and so on. "We find it impossible", he asserted, "to regulate the infant mind by the clock".[45]

Though he had blended some of the leading ideas of Locke, Swedenborg, Pestalozzi and the phrenologists into a creative and developmental theory, Wilderspin was no mere syncretist; his theory had a strong admixture of the wisdom he had gained from the observation and teaching of over 17,000

[41] *Bolton Chronicle, 2 May 1835.*

[42] *System of Education* (1840), p. 196.

[43] *Ibid.,* p. 33.

[44] *Early Discipline* (1834), p. 285.

[45] P.P. 1835 VII, Education, p. 27; *System of Education* (1840), p. 25. Swedenborg believed that infants had different geniuses and inclinations, inherited from their parents and should therefore be educated in accordance with these differences (*Arcana Coelestia,* 2300-301).

children.[46] In comparison with his Continental contemporaries Pestalozzi and Froebel his work is very much in the "common sense" tradition, free from metaphysical overtones. There are no grounds, however, for describing the philosophical basis of his system as "crude and vague", as was done in the historical section of the Board of Education Report on Infant and Nursery Schools of 1933.[47]

* * * * *

To what extent did Wilderspin succeed in devising educational situations which would ensure the best practical expression of his theoretical programme? After 1829 he usually divided education into intellectual, physical and moral elements, with methods and practices appropriate to each; it will be convenient, therefore, to examine these in turn. The basis of Wilderspin's intellectual education was a wide curriculum. In 1835 he informed the Select Committee on Education that by the time a child left an infant school he ought to know addition, subtraction, multiplication, and division, much of it taught by practical methods; the ability to read "simple language"; the elements of geography, taught partly by activity methods but also by maps and pictures; a "tolerable knowledge" of the things of everyday life; a "slight" knowledge of natural history, from pictures; a knowledge of form — i.e. how to distinguish triangles from squares and hexagons from octagons; and "a tolerable knowledge of the leading facts of the New Testament", from pictures.[48] This curriculum has led critics of Wilderspin to charge him with premature development of the intellectual powers of infants. But the amount of material is no more than a child of six or seven would be expected to know today, and modern educationists recognise that the widest variety of activity and experience has a beneficial effect on the child's powers of perception and cognition.

Wilderspin's theoretical prescription for teaching reading was, as we have seen, well-conceived and surprisingly modern. He rejected Owen's advice that it was time enough to begin teaching reading at seven years of age and consciously or unconsciously followed Locke in believing that a child could start to learn letters as soon as he could talk.[49] The alphabetic and syllabic repetition he had advocated in his early works, redolent of the methods used in dame and monitorial schools, might well, however, have been abandoned after formulation of the theory. On occasion he taught whole words by accompanying them with appropriate actions,[50] and instruction in grammar utilised objects of

---

[46]P.P. 1835 VII, Education, p. 18. Wilderspin stated "I have had more than 17,000 babes through my hands".

[47]Board of Education. Report of the Consultative Committee on Infant and Nursery Schools, 1933, p. 7.

[48]P.P. 1835 VII, Education, pp. 20-21.

[49]Ibid., p. 16; Locke, Thoughts Concerning Education, 148.

[50]Early Discipline (1832), p. 5.

the classroom to give children a grasp of concepts before technical terms were learned.[51] Both these methods, it could be argued, fell within the bounds of the theory. Other practices were more dubious. In the 1830s he devised cards on which were printed a letter of the alphabet and a picture of an object in nature, apparently with the intention of associating object and sign in the child's mind, but it was hardly an adequate way of teaching the letter sounds needed for reading skills; the pronunciation of "A" in "Apple" bore no resemblance to the sound which identified it as the first letter of the alphabet, and the picture of an apple had no intrinsic connection with the letter "A". Nor was his goal of language learning furthered by a refinement of this method which he called "developing lessons", in which questions and answers on the properties of the objects were added, aided by a short text printed below. The letter "X", for instance, was illustrated by a portrait of Xenophon and gave rise to a catechetical exchange on that worthy's character.[52]

The deficiencies of this method were undoubtedly due to a somewhat loose application of theory. Attempts at object lessons using the gallery and monitors also had serious shortcomings; in these cases, however, they were largely due to a refusal to acknowledge that attempts to instruct infants of varying ages in large numbers contradicted a theory that called for teaching methods adapted to individual differences and discrete age-groups. Wilderspin was inordinately proud of his gallery methods and devoted a whole chapter to them in the 1840 edition of the *Infant System*. Placing an object before the assembled pupils, he tried to accomplish three things: first, to get every idea from the children relative to the object before them, which was acting "according to nature's law"; second, to give the children as much information about the object "as they will likely be able to digest properly"; third, to get this information back from them by question and answer "in order to impress it more firmly on their understandings".[53] But could this be done with children of all ages from two to six, often a hundred or a hundred and fifty strong? Even a resourceful and energetic teacher like Wilderspin himself, when faced with "the inclined plane of unfortunate infants" so mercilessly satirised by Charles Dickens in *Our Mutual Friend*,[54] could do little more than undertake a "free lecture", and his hoped-for objectives could, at best, be achieved by only a minority. Realising that all could not benefit equally, he argued that the youngest children learnt "through sympathy and communion" with their older brethren, a proposition very

[51] *Infant System* (1834), pp. 188-90; *Infant System* (1852), p. 331.

[52] *Infant Education* (1829), p. 170ff; *Infant System* (1834), p. 165; pp. 183-84.

[53] *Infant System* (1840), pp. 145-48.

[54] Charles Dickens, *Our Mutual Friend* (Penguin English Library Ed., 1971) pp. 264-65. Dickens described "yawning infants, restless infants, whimpering infants...repeating the word Sepulchre (commonly used among infants) five hundred times, and never once hinting what it meant; the whole hot-bed of flushed and exhausted infants exchanging measles, rashes, whooping-cough, fever, and stomach disorders, as if they were assembled in High Market for the purpose".

difficult to prove.[55] As with all question and answer techniques, the method tended to favour children with good memories, verbal facility and lack of shyness in public.

The large number of pupils — up to 200 — which Wilderspin believed a teacher and an assistant could handle,[56] made the use of monitors almost inevitable. Admittedly he confined their use almost entirely to the instruction of children at lesson posts "in that part which is purely mechanical and in that only",[57] but it could be argued that his theory did not presuppose that any part of the learning process was mechanical. The introduction of objects on lesson posts — a description of which had to be repeated by each group in turn to a monitor — failed to stimulate all the senses or give each child "variety", as Wilderspin believed it would.[58] All these methods were broadly concerned with reading or reading readiness, though it is clear that Wilderspin could rarely resist an opportunity to impart useful knowledge, whatever the method in use. With regard to writing he followed Locke in leaving instruction in that art until a child had mastered reading.[59] The initial steps in writing were, as we have seen, the tracing of letters on slates and this, apparently, was as far as it was taken.

He felt that arithmetic, that most difficult of subjects to teach, should be approached by getting the children to observe objects, to associate them with the signs of number and then to proceed to the abstract consideration of number, progressing in each case from the simple to the more complex. These methods, he correctly pointed out, reversed the usual procedure of arithmetic teaching in monitorial and other schools, which began with the abstract in the form of table and rule and then proceeded to exercises involving concrete operations.[60] The manuals used in the Bell and Lancaster monitorial schools rigidly graded the arithmetical exercises, which began with the verbal repetition of tables, rules and computations.[61]

Wilderspin's use of wooden cubes in calculation and the use of a machine called the arithmeticon — an arrangement of wires, each containing moveable balls, in a rectangular frame — exemplified his theory. Below the frame of the arithmeticon was a board in which brass numerals could be placed in horizontal slots; the numerals corresponding to the number of balls the teacher moved could thus immediately be demonstrated. He used this apparatus for the

[55] P.P. 1835 VII, Education, p. 27; *Infant System* (1852), p. 15.

[56] P.P. 1835 VII, Education, p. 14.

[57] *Infant Education* (1825), p. 275.

[58] *Infant System* (1840), p. 112-22.

[59] Locke, *Thoughts Concerning Education*, 160.

[60] *Infant Education* (1829), p. 187.

[61] Cf. *The Manual of the System of Teaching Reading, Writing, Arithmetic and Needlework, in the Elementary Schools of the British and Foreign School Society* (London 1816), pp. 23-24; *The Practical Manual of the Madras or National System of Education* (London 1833), pp. 10-19.

teaching of addition, subtraction and multiplication, while the children verbalised the operations, though he unfortunately went beyond their comprehension by attempting to teach numbers running into millions.[62] More seriously, he never gave up the practice of having children chant arithmetical tables, rhymes embodying rules, and some complex doggerel he had composed himself — "in thirty-four are four times eight and one fourth of eight", and so on.[63]

Form was a peculiar feature of Wilderspin's pedagogy. Turning his back on Pestalozzi's conception that form was a necessary component of the child's attempts to bring order out of confused sense impressions, Wilderspin followed Swedenborg and confined his use of form to that of geometry. Swedenborg, to whom geometry was the most fascinating of sciences, propounded a doctrine of forms, "the knowledge of which we have procured to ourselves from objects which affect the sight of the eye". These forms ranged from the lowest or the angular — "the proper object of our geometry" — via the spherical, spiral and vortical to the celestial, or highest, form.[64] Wilderspin utilised a jointed stick called a gonigraph, by means of which various figures could be simulated for identification, but reduced the method almost to absurdity by asking them to name and describe equilateral and scalene triangles, heptagons and similar abstruse and useless figures. He was, however, proud of his pupils' ability to identify the forms of common objects, judging by the number of anecdotes he told about amazed parents listening to children describing an "elliptical frying pan", a "circular plate", a "perpendicular lamp-post" and so on.[65]

The verdict on Wilderspin's teaching of the 3Rs must be a guarded one; in several cases his methods followed logically from his theory, and he strove to use apparatus and concrete manipulative materials wherever possible; almost as often, however, practices were arbitrarily imposed in flagrant contradiction to the principles he advocated. To some extent this applied to the teaching of other subjects in the curriculum. He included, for instance, a large amount of encyclopaedia-type knowledge under "things of everyday life", particularly some racial and social stereotypes under the title "The Different Races of Man".[66] On the other hand he taught geography by sketching a map of England on the floor of the school and letting the children make journeys from one county to another by walking across the map; a variation of this — "not only a useful but a really amusing study" — was to place on each county a commodity

[62]*Infant Education* (1829), p. 188ff; *Infant System* (1834), pp. 195-96.

[63]*Infant System* (1834), p. 180ff. Wilderspin believed, however, that verbal repetition was merely one way of learning mathematics and that the rote-learning of tables left children no wiser than before (*Ibid.*, p. 221).

[64]E. Swedenborg, *On the Worship and Love of God* (London 1801), 5n.

[65]*Infant Education* (1829), pp. 202-08; *Infant System* (1834), p. 211; *Bath and Cheltenham Gazette,* 31 May 1831; *Early Discipline* (1832), p. 109; *Infant System* (1840), p. 254.

[66]*Infant System* (1840), p. 114ff.

for which it was known — a cheese in Cheshire, a piece of cloth in Gloucestershire, a knife in Sheffield — and ask the children to explain its origin and mode of manufacture on arrival at the location.[67]

In the 1830s he consistently advocated the teaching of natural history to children. One of the distinguishing features of the doctrines of the New Church, its adherents believed, was that they "illustrate and elevate all subjects of natural science",[68] and Wilderspin gave the study of nature a prominent place in the curriculum. Characteristics of animals and plants could be taught in the classroom by means of pictures, but the world of nature ideally should be studied outside the classroom. A small garden plot would make an admirable adjunct to a school; cereals could be grown there and the grains examined under a microscope. Lessons should, in fact, be held "in the garden, in the lanes and in the fields", where children could examine all types of flora, and museums should be attached to every school. A few live animals should be kept among the children, and "kindness to them should be encouraged, and unkindness to them repressed".[69]

Painting, poetry and music he considered as "efficient auxiliaries" in the infant school; they improved "the power of observation and [cultivated] the ear, the voice and the general taste".[70] Music was used by Wilderspin for two purposes: as a teaching aid and as a means of psychological stimulation. The alphabet was set to music, sung by the master, and imitated by the children; the distinction between vowels and consonants was embodied in a tune, with monitors pointing out appropriate letters as the children sang; arithmetical tables were learnt in song, with hand movements added for emphasis.[71] He also used music to "soften the feelings, curb the passions and improve the temper", and felt it was strange that it had not been employed in education before the advent of the infant school, to which it was "absolutely indispensable". A "simple and touching air" could soften aggressive feelings and on dull days timely music could stimulate lethargic children to a state of pleasing activity.[72] A piano was an essential item of school equipment and a good infant master should possess a tenor voice and be able to play the violin, flute or clarinet.[73]

Moral education had an important place in the Wilderspinian infant school, as it had in all schools for the poor in the early nineteenth century. In the

[67]P.P. 1835 VII, Education, p. 27; *North Cheshire Reformer,* 27 Sept. 1939.

[68]W.M., "On Education", *loc.cit.,* pp. 356-57.

[69]*Infant System* (1834), p. 242; *Infant System* (1852), p. 77; *Infant System* (1840), p. 288; *System of Education* (1840), p. 45.

[70]*Londonderry Sentinel,* 28 Sept. 1833.

[71]*Infant System* (1834), pp. 269-70.

[72]*Infant System* (1834), pp. 282-83; P.P. 1835 VII, Education, p. 17.

[73]*System of Education* (1840), xv; *Infant System* (1834), p. 282.

voluntary schools it was taught by precept, mainly in the form of learning by heart passages from the Bible, catechisms, and other formularies.[74] Wilderspin derived most of the content of his moral teaching from the Scriptures,[75] but placed the greatest emphasis on love and charity; one of his main aims was the elimination of selfishness which, following Swedenborg, he considered to be "the great defect" in human character.[76] Unlike most moralists of the time, however, Wilderspin favoured example rather than precept; "the magnetic power" of example, he argued, "acts as a talisman on the inmost feelings of the soul, and excites them to activity".[77] In addition, following Owen and anticipating modern practice, he felt that the security provided by co-operation and mutual respect among children was essential to both their moral and intellectual development. "Many of the infant faculties", he stated, "cannot be brought into play by any other means than by unison with its fellows".[78] For this reason he abandoned place-taking and competition, as leading to "injustice and strife"; "children may very soon perceive", he concluded, "that each has some excellent parts about him that he may be admired for and on that account there is no need of having any distinctions".[79]

The most original aspect of Wilderspin's efforts to inculcate morality was his use of the playground. At Spitalfields the moral function had been largely concerned with self-denial, but he came to view the playground as a place where the child's conduct, free from the restraints of the classroom, would manifest itself spontaneously, enabling the teacher to observe and, if necessary, amend it; thus the playground could have a greater effect on the formation of character than the school itself. Children could, for instance, learn to practise carefulness and to become less selfish when playing on the swings. But "the soul of the system" lay in the teacher continually observing the infants during their spontaneous interactions and allowing no incident to pass without investigation and adjustment, usually by the employment of a child jury.[80]

The playground, however, was primarily a place for exercise and play. An "instinctive impulse to activity" existed in every young child, Wilderspin

---

[74] For a closer examination of this practice, cf. P. McCann, "Popular Education, Socialization and Social Control: Spitalfields 1812-1824", in P. McCann (Ed.), *Popular Education and Socialization in the Nineteenth Century* (London 1977), pp. 24-5.

[75] "When morality is adverted to in this chapter", he wrote in the *Infant System* (1834, p. 90) "let it not be forgotten by it is meant the morality of the Scriptures".

[76] E. Swedenborg, *The Heavenly Doctrine of the New Jerusalem* (London 1790), 59; 65; 76; 84; 99-104; *Infant System* (1834), p. 83.

[77] *Infant System* (1834), p. 83; cf. also *Cheltenham Looker-On,* 4 Oct. 1837.

[78] *System of Education* (1840), p. 53; cf. also *Infant System* (1840), p. 162.

[79] *System of Education* (1840), p. 40; *Infant System* (1834), pp. 81-2; P.P. 1835 VII, Education, pp. 27-8; *North Cheshire Reformer,* 27 Sept. 1839.

[80] P.P. 1835 VII, Education, p. 23; *System of Education* (1840), p. 30; p. 32; *Infant System* (1852), p. 106; *Glasgow Herald,* 26 May 1828; *Bath and Cheltenham Gazette,* 31 May 1831.

believed, but the "old plan" of education (presumably in dame schools) made children dull and soporific by keeping them "rivetted to their seats". Swings, skipping ropes and other apparatus should be in every playground in order to provide opportunities for healthful exercise, of which the poor, in Wilderspin's view, had too long been deprived; more attention was paid to the exercising of gentlemen's horses and dogs, he pointed out, than to the physical education of the poor. The playground exercise was not mere movement, however; the infant system was so agreeable "that the child, while literally at play, is acquiring a large amount of valuable knowledge", a concept which is strongly advocated today. Sometimes games might be organised — drill, for instance, could be used to teach geometrical form. But generally, Wilderspin felt, the infants should not be supervised, for if they "play at what they choose", he argued, "they are free beings, and manifest their characters; but if they are forced to play at what they do not wish, they do not manifest their characters, but are cramped and are slaves, and hence their faculties are not developed".[81]

* * * * *

If Wilderspin did not produce a theory in the twentieth-century sense of the term, he certainly provided enough general guidance for teachers to enable them to push the frontiers of infant education beyond anything previously seen in schools for the poor; the best chapters of the 1834 edition of the *Infant System* might be read with profit even today. His weakness lay in a failure to translate his theory into a coherent and appropriate practice. In 1831 he had confidently asserted that "everything will appear easy to the comprehension of the child, if we can discover an easy method of teaching it";[82] unfortunately he was only partly successful in this endeavour. There were two main reasons for this.

One was a general lack of theoretical expertise. Like many Englishmen he lacked familiarity with philosophical principles and theoretical concepts, a familiarity which gave unity and vitality (but sometimes also obscurity) to the writings of his contemporaries Pestalozzi and Froebel.[83] This led him into several errors. He was prone to think that if "ideas" were annexed to "words" then understanding took place, even if the words were sung or chanted and the ideas were masses of useful knowledge supplied by the teacher.[84] Similarly, he could convince himself that children were learning how to do mental arithmetic,

---

[81] *Infant Education* (1825), pp. 181-83; *Infant System* (1834), p. 71; *Infant System* (1840), p. 123; p. 143; *System of Education* (1840), xi; *Infant System* (1852), p. 314.

[82] *Bath and Cheltenham Gazette,* 31 May 1831.

[83] No comparison has been made with the educational theories of Froebel. Though his *Education of Man* was published in 1826, it had no influence on Wilderspin or the infant school movement, and the kindergarten was not transplanted to England until the 1850s.

[84] *Infant System* (1852), p. 16.

which he correctly defined as "the ability to comprehend the powers of numbers, without either visible objects or signs", when the whole school was chanting the multiplication tables, numerous examples of fractions or verses embodying tables of measure.[85] He saw little anomaly in combining antithetical methods in the teaching of the same subject; he familiarised children with the four quarters of the globe by the use of the four corners of the playground, but designated London as the capital city by having the children repeatedly chant "London is the capital, the capital, London is the capital, the capital of England".[86] Yet he could ridicule the constant repetition practised in monitorial schools, which allowed the understanding to lie in "a state of torpid inactivity".[87]

The other was a failure to reconcile the system he had devised in the early 1820s — which he characterised mainly in terms of pictures, apparatus and classroom arrangements[88] — with the theory he developed in the 1830s. A thorough evaluation of the implications of his theory would certainly have led to serious modifications of the system whose elements he tried to preserve; the gallery, monitors, even some uses of the arithmeticon could hardly have survived. His apparent inability to decide whether the purpose of intellectual education was the development of the mental powers or the communication of knowledge (or, to use David Stow's terminology, whether education should be "training" or "instruction") can also be seen as reluctance to abandon the didacticism of his *Infant Education* of 1825, despite protests to the contrary.[89]

Despite his shortcomings, however, Wilderspin placed the child at the centre of the educational process. Instead of putting all pupils through an identical mill, irrespective of the aptitudes of the individual or the nature of the subject, as was done in the monitorial schools, he strove to adapt instruction to the nature of the child, to provide different approaches to the teaching of each subject and also to vary the methods within each discipline. He had an acute awareness of individual differences, and was endlessly inventive in making learning amusing and interesting, and this perhaps was his greatest strength, though the vast numbers of children often found in infant schools sometimes defeated his efforts.

Two other characteristics distinguished him from his contemporaries and gave his model of the infant school a unique place in the educational world of the 1830s. First he endeavoured to teach the whole child; man, he believed, was a "compound being",[90] and "the faculties...the physical, the intellectual and the

---

[85] *Infant System* (1834), pp. 199-201; cf. also *Scotsman*, 15 Oct., 8 and 29 Nov. 1828.

[86] *Infant System* (1834), p. 222.

[87] *Infant Education* (1825), p. 277; *Infant Education* (1829), pp. 275-76.

[88] *Educational Magazine*, Vol. II, Aug. 1835, p. 149.

[89] At the end of his career, he asserted that he preferred training to instruction because he was against cramming the head with knowledge (*Hull Rockingham Gazette*, 24 Feb. 1844).

[90] *Cheltenham Looker-On*, 4 Oct. 1837.

spiritual, were united by nature, and they could not be separated by art".[91] Second, while bearing this in mind, he gave especial importance to the education of the feelings and affections; he applied the term "heart education" to his system,[92] and felt that a teacher could not begin too early in giving "safe scope" to the feelings of his charges, cultivating the better and subduing the worse.[93] To this extent he was at one with the nature educationists; but the roots of his pedagogy lay not in the idealisation of the peasant family and rural life that characterised Rousseau, Pestalozzi and Froebel, but in the realities of working-class life of the new cities of the Industrial Revolution. Swedenborg, we should remember, had been a mining engineer and scientist in the first half of his life, and was pre-eminently a man of the city.[94]

Whether or not Wilderspin's teaching fulfilled his aims and helped to produce the type of working man he had in mind is impossible to document, but his system, if followed, would logically have had an outcome different from that of the charity, dame or monitorial school; his pedagogy had an intellectual content that those of other systems almost entirely lacked. It was this that gave a sense of uniqueness to the infant school that it maintained long after the Wilderspin era. Despite the flaws in his work — if eclecticism sometimes triumphed when synthesis was needed; if he could condemn the work of dame and monitorial schools while utilising some of their practices; if he misread, on occasion, the logic of his own theory — nonetheless his achievement was great and those features of his pedagogy which were far in advance of his contemporaries and which appear amazingly "modern" to us, outweighed in the long run the negative aspects of his contribution.

[91] *Hull Rockingham Gazette,* 24 Feb. 1839.

[92] *Cheltenham Magazine of Science, Literature and Miscellaneous Intelligence,* Vol. I, 1837, p. 221.

[93] *Scotsman,* 28 Apr. 1830.

[94] Born in Stockholm and dying in London, he spent much of his life visiting or living in the major European cities. (G. Trobridge, *Swedenborg: Life and Teaching* (London, 4th. ed., 1945), *passim*).

CHAPTER 10

THE INFANT SCHOOL MOVEMENT
IN THE 1830s: CRISIS

By the mid-1830s the infant school was firmly established on the educational map of Britain. The pattern had been developed by Buchanan, Goyder and Wilderspin, and the Infant School Society, in endorsing this type of school and employing Wilderspin to popularise it, had given a powerful impetus to its diffusion throughout the British Isles. Even the growing number of infant schools organised by Evangelicals, and those sponsored by High Church clergy, were recognisable as greater or lesser modifications of the generally-accepted model. By 1836 Wilderspin estimated that no fewer than two hundred and seventy infant schools had been established in Great Britain — a hundred and fifty in England, seventy in Scotland and fifty in Ireland.[1] The greatest concentration, he stated, was in the large cities and the manufacturing districts and it was here also that there existed a recognition of the need to increase the provision still further.[2]

The bitter opposition of the 1820s had largely died away and the new institutions could now count on powerful and eloquent supporters. In a paean of praise to infant schools, Brougham, as Lord Chancellor, told the House of Lords in 1835 that "their manifest good effects have roused the attention of the community to the sacredness of the trust reposed in their hands".[3] Economic and educational treatises recognised the utility of infant schools,[4] newspapers and journals in England, Ireland and Scotland supported Wilderspin's labours,[5] and the indefatigable educational publicist James Simpson rarely lost an opportunity of publicising "the most powerful instrument of moral elevation yet invented by man".[6]

The characteristics of Wilderspin's initial model of the infant school have

---

[1] Wilderspin gave these figures in a letter to Frederic Hill (F. Hill, *National Education: Its Present State and Prospects* (London, 2 vol., 1836), I, pp. 169-70). Wilderspin almost certainly had in mind schools approximating to his own model. In his evidence to the Select Committee in 1835 he stated that there were "about 2,000" infant schools in the U.K., but added that "some of them were little better than dame schools". (P.P. 1835 VII, Report from the Select Committee on Education in England and Wales, p. 13). He probably took the latter figure from Brougham's speech in the Lords made four weeks earlier (Parl. Deb. 1835 XXVII, 21 May 1835, 1318). Wilderspin appeared to be inflating the figures for the purpose of making the infant school movement, and his contribution to it, seem greater than it actually was. It seems unlikely that he was unaware of the smaller and more accurate figure in June 1835.

[2] P.P. 1835 VII, Report from the Select Committee on Education in England and Wales, pp. 13-15, *passim.*

[3] Parl. Deb. 1835 XXVII, 21 May 1835, 1309.

[4] E.g., P. Gaskell, *The Manufacturing Population of England* (London 1833), p. 276 ff; S. Smiles, *Physical Education, or the Nurture and Management of Children* (Edinburgh 1838), p. 101; pp. 198-200.

[5] Particularly the *Lincoln, Rutland and Stamford Mercury,* the *Newry Commercial Telegraph,* and the *Scotsman* (Edinburgh). Cf. also the *Phrenological Journal,* Vol. VII, No. XXVIII, 1831, pp. 108-116.

[6] J. Simpson, *The Necessity of Popular Education* (Edinburgh 1834), p. 149.

been delineated in previous chapters; by the mid-1830s, after a decade of active involvement with the movement in all parts of the British Isles, acquaintance with sophisticated educationists, and the greater prominence he gave to Swedenborgian principles in his writings, he was able to augment and refine his original conception. The main features of his ideal school of this period may quickly be summarised. First, the basis of the school was the combination of building and playground; the former contained a sizeable schoolroom, a small classroom (for group work) and a gallery sufficiently large to seat all the pupils; the latter was furnished with swings and other apparatus and planted with trees and flowers. Second, the school taught a wide curriculum, consisting of at least half-a-dozen subjects. Third, an explicit theory of education was adopted, based on Swedenborgian principles, with Pestalozzian and phrenological additions; this theoretical approach emphasised the primacy of the senses and pointed towards a developmental approach to learning. Fourth, the methods used were a mixture of small group work, question-and-answer gallery lessons and monitorial instruction in the alphabet, spelling and reading. Fifth, a great deal of apparatus was used — the arithmeticon, the gonigraph, tangible objects of all kinds, coloured pictures, lesson cards, maps, globes, etc. Sixth, a flexible form of organisation was adopted, with short lessons and frequent breaks according to the mood of the children. Seventh, amusement, play and exercise — hand and arm movements, marching and singing — were an integral part of the daily routine. Finally, rewards were not given, corporal punishment reduced to a minimum and a jury system used to settle disputes.[7]

The outstanding features of the school were the inculcation of an ethical form of morals, in which the playground played the most important part, the inclusion in the curriculum of a relatively large number of subjects (both Wilderspin and Simpson believed this to be possible without undue strain on the pupil)[8] and the non-denominational religious instruction. A superintendent of Wilderspin's calibre — "a good gallery teacher", according to Brougham,[9] and also endowed with exceptional energy and resourcefulness — would be able to give due attention to each aspect of the system and to cultivate the physical, intellectual and moral faculties in turn.

The key question was — were others able to do it? Could the schools Wilderspin founded and the teachers he trained maintain the standards set in his books and lectures? Could schools outside his influence also be expected to do

---

[7]This outline is based on *The Infant System* (1834), *passim,* and *A System of Education* (1840), "Description of the Plates", xi-xvi.

[8]P.P. 1835 VII, Education, p. 21, for Wilderspin's position. Simpson believed that "a skilful teacher, upon the true principles of the system, can in the course of the four years they attend, without an effort of theirs, give them a great deal of very useful knowledge" (P.P. 1836, XIII, Report from the Select Committee on Education in Ireland, Pt. I, p. 251.)

[9]H. Brougham, "Education of the People", *Westminster and Foreign Quarterly Review,* Vol. XLVI, No. 1, Oct. 1846, p. 221.

so? Or would fissures appear in the model along the lines of weakness indicated in Chapter 9? The evidence, unfortunately, points to an affirmative answer to the last question. As early as 1830 there were signs that teachers in some schools were allowing errors and distortions to creep into their work. Edward Biber, in his *Christian Education,* made some disturbing allegations concerning the introduction of purely *memoriter* methods in alphabet and table learning, the indiscriminate singing of everything that could be put to music and unimaginative indoctrination in Scripture Knowledge.[10] The following year the *Lincoln, Rutland and Stamford Mercury,* a strong supporter of Wilderspin's system, more soberly hinted that directors of infant schools had in many cases failed to understand the system and aroused prejudice against their schools.[11]

Wilderspin himself, by 1832, had realised that failures and mistakes were beginning to beset many schools. He recognised, as always, that the lack of a central model school was at the root of the trouble, but apart from this, he felt that some committees had failed to avail themselves of knowledge from the best (presumably Wilderspinian) sources, that many schools lacked playgrounds and suitable apparatus and that teachers were often badly trained, wayward and inefficient and apt to introduce novelties and indulge in showy methods rather than to concentrate on sound teaching.[12]

If defects were noticeable in some infant schools at the beginning of the 1830s, the situation had deteriorated rapidly by 1835. The evidence for this comes almost entirely from those favourably disposed towards the movement, and their criticism was directed not against the concept of the infant school but against the distortions which directors and teachers had introduced, or allowed to creep in, because of inexperience or indolence. In February 1835 the *Educational Magazine,* whose editor William Martin became a friend of Wilderspin and sympathetic to his educational outlook, published a long article on the infant system in which a sober assessment of the position was made. In many places, the article pointed out, the infant system had "wholly failed, from the inefficiency and want of intelligence in the teachers, few of whom understand at all the principles under which they should teach"; many schools, in charge of frail or under-trained females, "are degenerating into the veriest dame schools".[13]

These charges were borne out, and supplemented, by an article in the *Scotsman* some months later. Under the editorship of Charles MacLaren, the *Scotsman* had become the most respected supporter of the Wilderspin system in the British Isles; surveying the situation in the schools in September 1835 it was alarmed to find that "a great and mischievous change in their management has,

[10]E. Biber, *Christian Education, in a Course of Lectures* (London 1830), pp. 174-75.

[11]*Lincoln, Rutland and Stamford Mercury,* 8 July 1831.

[12]*Early Discipline* (1832), p. 245 ff.

[13]"Education in England, No. 1. The Infant System", *Educational Magazine,* Vol. I, Feb. 1835, pp. 65-78.

in many instances, taken place". Exercise and amusement had virtually been abandoned, many schools had no playgrounds, classrooms were inadequately ventilated and the children were put through "an almost constant succession of tasks in spelling, pronouncing, reading and learning by heart hymns, psalms, texts, problems in arithmetic and geometry, lessons in Natural History and other most useful branches of knowledge..." No one would deny the value of these studies, the article continued, but it was possible to teach them on "a more humane and effective plan". If the trend continued there was danger of infant schools degenerating into places of "early and hurtful imprisonment for mind and body", and it would be better to see them extinguished altogether than to see them converted into snares for entrapping infants into "the toils of an ordinary school".[14] Further criticism along the same lines came from the *Phrenological Journal,* which felt that the American surgeon Amariah Brigham's allegations of overpressure in infant schools were in many cases well-founded; "long lessons, tasks and laborious repetitions", the *Journal* stated, had superseded moral and physical education and as a result teachers had departed from "the essential principles of legitimate infant training".[15]

Similar criticisms were made by Horace Grant of the Central Society of Education, particularly with regard to the rote learning of "dry and senseless verbiage"and arithmetical tables;[16] by the publicist J. Lalor, a strong admirer of Wilderspin;[17] and by the agent of the Manchester Statistical Society, J.R. Wood, whose strictures were based on the observation of a large number of infant schools in Manchester, Birmingham and Liverpool, and thus carried great weight.[18] He found the schools, whose principles he admired, to be overcrowded (which hampered moral training, "the one beauty of the infant school system") and their teachers dedicated to gallery lessons and exhibitions and to the inculcation of knowledge by rote learning and singing; the apt and quick were over-stimulated and the development of the intellect fostered at the expense of the character and the affections.[19]

The evidence points to the inescapable conclusion that by the late 1830s the infant school movement had, for several years, been in a state of crisis. Wilderspin himself, looking back in anger, gave examples of the "parrot system" of rote learning, the repetition of incomprehensible Scripture texts and creeds,

[14]*Scotsman,* 22 Aug. 1835.

[15]*Phrenological Journal,* Vol. IX, No. XLV, 1835, pp. 424-35. Cf. A. Brigham, *Remarks on the Influence of Mental Cultivation and Mental Excitement on Health* (Boston, 2nd ed., 1833).

[16]Grant's criticisms were cited in "Schools for the Industrious Classes", Central Society of Education. *Second Publication* (London 1838), p. 384.

[17]J. Lalor, "The Social Position of Educators", in *The Educator. Prize Essays* (London 1839), p. 101.

[18]For Wood's activities, cf. M.J. Cullen, *The Statistical Movement in Early Victorian Britain* (Hassocks, Sussex 1975), p. 112; pp. 115-16; p. 125.

[19]P.P. 1838 VII, Report from the Select Committee on the Education of the Poorer Classes, pp. 118-22.

the replacement of hand and arm movements by "ridiculous antics", and the degeneration of singing into perpetual squalling, which characterised the infant schools of the mid-30s;[20] In many cases the teaching had been made to harmonise with the dull, monotonous, sleepy, heavy system" of the National Schools.[21] He was forced to the conclusion that where the spirit had been neglected and only the mechanical parts retained, the infant system was "a complete and unhappy failure".[22]

How did this situation arise? The most obvious reason, as Charles Baker of the Central Society of Education pointed out, was the rapid expansion of the movement.[23] On the basis of Wilderspin's figures the average rate of increase was just under twenty schools per year between 1820 and 1835, and this did not include those which had closed during this period. Only the "new" monitorial schools, in the first twenty years of their existence, had expanded at a faster rate.[24] As infant schools were, however, considerably more sophisticated educational institutions than those of Bell and Lancaster, their proliferation in a period when experience, pedagogical expertise and adequate means of inducting teachers into the system were all at a premium, was bound to lead to problems. These were compounded by the deficiencies in Wilderspin's own theory and practice, analysed in Chapter 9. Wilderspin's penchant for conveying inert knowledge, and his tendency to put it in the form of rhyme, undoubtedly constituted an invitation to the lazy or incompetent teacher to extend the method to other areas of teaching. As J.R. Wood pointed out, teachers were sent to Wilderspin for a month or six weeks and came away with "the worst parts of the system, the noise and confusion of singing and so on", and the really valuable points of the method were overlooked.[25]

Teachers and their training were the crux of the problem. If the infant school movement, as Wilderspin had urged, had possessed a central organisational and teaching institution (or satisfactory local model schools) which could have selected recruits, superintended their training and enforced minimum standards, the inexperience and inefficiency of local committees — the other great weakness of the system — would have been offset or overcome. As it was, one weakness reinforced the other. In 1830 Biber had given an amusing picture of a group of well-meaning citizens of a small community who, wishing to found an infant school and converting an old barn or coach house for the purpose, were faced with the problem of choosing a teacher. Each of the

---

[20]*System of Education* (1840), p. 12; *Infant System* (1852), p. 14; p. 315; p. 325.

[21]*Infant System* (1852), pp. 10-11.

[22]*Infant System* (1840), p. 158.

[23]C. Baker, "Infants' Schools", Central Society of Education. *Third Publication* (London 1839), p. 18.

[24]PP. 1820 XII, "A General Table Showing the State of Education in England", p. 343. The rate of increase of these schools was, on average, 56 per year.

[25]P.P. 1838 VII, Education, p. 121.

patrons had a client in view; in the event the candidate of the most influential party would get the job. As the school might be advertised to open in a fortnight, the new teacher could not be sent to London to be trained in an established infant school; so he or she would be sent to the nearest school to "catch" the system. What would strike the trainee most favourably would be "the singing of the tables, the distribution in classes, the marching around the room, the clapping of hands, and all the other machinery". Returning to open the school, the teacher would attempt to reproduce this, with the result that the school became "a treadmill for the minds of the poor children".[26]

Biber's picture was undeniably accurate, possibly somewhat underpainted. Surviving records of infant schools show a startling lack of principle in the selection and training of teachers. Archdeacon Watson, on becoming chairman of Hackney Infant School Committee, felt it perfectly natural to nominate a Mrs. Haswell as the teacher of the school merely because he was acquainted with her; she was sent to the London Infant School Society's school for two months before taking up her duties.[27] A casual inquiry by the local vicar or committee secretary was sometimes the only investigation of eligibility to teach thought necessary.[28] Lack of teaching experience was no disqualification; Duncan Street Infant School, Liverpool, was satisfied to obtain "a healthy active person of good plain sense orderly habit and agreeable temper and manners and tolerable education".[29] A committee member in Shoreditch solemnly recommended a Miss Kirkcaldy, who he felt was well qualified for the situation "with the exception of practical acquaintance with the work of managing infant schools".[30]

There were two reasons for this state of affairs. First, schools of the Buchanan-Goyder-Wilderspin type were expensive to build, equip and operate. The modification of an old building might cost up to £200, the construction of a new one twice as much or more;[31] Pound Hill School, Cambridge, for instance,

---

[26]Biber, *Christian Education,* pp. 176-77. Cf. Wilderspin: "Infant schools...are generally copies of the schools nearest to them, which may be very badly conducted". (P.P. 1835 VII, Education, p. 15)

[27]Minute Book of the Hackney Infant School, Bridge Street, Homerton, 1826-1880, Minutes, 20 July, 14 Sept. 1826.

[28]G.L. Ms. 7509, St. Leonard Shoreditch Infant School Society, Minutes, 1837-1854, Minutes, 15 Oct. 1838; 24 Oct. 1839.

[29]Cited in J. Murphy, "The Rise of Public Elementary Education in Liverpool: Part Two, 1819-35", *Transactions of the Historic Society of Lancashire and Cheshire,* Vol. 118, 1966, pp. 105-36. The "Infant School Minute Book 1824-33" of the Society of Friends, from which this extract is taken, is now lost, but Murphy quotes it extensively.

[30]St. Leonard Shoreditch Infant School Society, Minutes, 6 Mar. 1848. Cf. a similarly-worded advertisement in the *Lincoln, Rutland and Stamford Mercury,* 27 Jan. 1832.

[31]P.P. 1846 XXXII, Minutes of the Committee of Council on Education 1845, J. Fletcher, "Report on Infant Schools on the Principles of the British and Foreign School Society", p. 356. Government grants covered only one-quarter of the initial cost (*Ibid.*).

cost £432 to build and equip.[32] The average cost of a National School, which could hold more than twice as many pupils, was only £340.[33] Once built, the infant school of 100 pupils cost something like £100 per year to operate.[34] Teachers of the calibre of Mr. and Mrs. Wilderspin and Mr. and Mrs. Goyder would expect £80 or £90 per annum plus a house, though something under £70 was the more usual figure.[35] Apparatus and lessons recommended by Wilderspin cost the Birmingham Society £40,[36] though most schools managed on much less.

Second, the sources of income of the majority of schools were uncertain and fluctuating. Those not attached to schools for older children derived their regular income from private subscriptions and children's pence in almost equal proportions.[37] Neither source could be relied upon. The money from fees fluctuated according to attendance and in any case had to be kept as low as possible, usually 2d per week. An attempt by Birmingham Infant School Society to make one of its schools self-supporting by raising the fees to 3d per week had to be abandoned in face of opposition from parents,[38] and Bolton Infant School tried but failed to make children's pence alone cover all expenditure.[39] Nearly all schools found that the zeal of committees and subscribers tended to wane after the first flush of enthusiasm. The Birmingham Society announced a continued fall in subscriptions and the piling up of debts in the mid-30s.[40] By 1829 Temple Infant School in Bristol, established in 1826, found its funds in "a depressed state" and new subscriptions urgently necessary.[41] Similar complaints were made by the committee of Hackney Infant School in 1837.[42] Subscriptions to Louth Infant School, founded in 1834, fell by over a third in the first five years of its existence.[43] St. Leonard Shoreditch Infant School, founded in 1837, was troubled by an "extensive falling-off" of subscriptions as early as November 1840.[44]

The result was that the committees were under pressure to cut expenses and

---

[32] P.P. 1837-38 XXIV, Report of the Commissioners for Inquiry Concerning Charity Schools, Vol. 31, Cambridge, p. 34.

[33] According to the table in M. Seaborne, *The English School* (London 1971), p. 141.

[34] F. Hill, *National Education: Its Present State and Prospects* (London, 2 vol., 1836), I, p. 173.

[35] P.P. 1846 XXXII, Fletcher, "Report", p. 357.

[36] Third Annual Report of the Birmingham Infant School Society (Birmingham 1828), p. 7; p. 12.

[37] P.P. 1846 XXXII, Fletcher, "Report", p. 357.

[38] Fourth Annual Report of the Birmingham Infant School Society (Birmingham 1829), p. 6.

[39] "The Rev. Prebendary Slade's Infant School, Bolton-le-Moor, Lancashire", *Educational Magazine*, N.S., Vol. II, Sept. 1840, pp. 178-79.

[40] Birmingham Infant School Society. Tenth Anniversary Meeting (Birmingham 1835), p. 6; Eleventh Annual Report, (1836), p. 10.

[41] B.R.O. Temple Infant School, Minute Book 1825-1868, Minutes, 11 May 1829.

[42] Hackney Infant School, Minutes, 20 Feb. 1837.

[43] Louth Infants' School: Report 1834 (Louth 1834), p. 7; Report 1839, p. 7.

[44] St. Leonard Shoreditch Infant School Society, Minutes, 9 Nov. 1840.

the axe fell on the obvious place — teachers' salaries. The general tendency in the 1820s had been to engage a man and wife; by the 30s women were increasingly taken on, mainly because they could be offered the lowest possible salaries, but also because the large number of single, lower middle-class women on the market enabled committees to lower the wages of women teachers or to dismiss them with impunity. When Hackney School advertised for a mistress in 1829 they had 60 applications for the post.[45]

Women teachers' salaries were usually fifty per cent or more lower than those offered to a man and wife. When the Goyders left Duncan Street Infant School in Liverpool in March 1828, the post was offered to a woman at half the salary; her training, perhaps not surprisingly, consisted of visits to "several Infant Schools".[46] Mothers with young daughters (who could act as assistants) were especially favoured. Mrs. Haswell, at Hackney, was assisted by her daughter aged twelve; her successor, Mrs. Camraux, though untrained, obtained the post in face of competition of eleven others solely because she had a daughter aged twenty who would act as her assistant. She was given £30 per annum, £20 less than Mrs. Haswell.[47] Similar salary cuts are recorded at Birmingham (Islington School) in 1831[48] and in the two schools at St. Leonard Shoreditch in 1844 and 1845.[49] In keeping with the situation, "a Lady" could write to the *Record* in 1837 inquiring if £10 per annum would be sufficient salary for the mistress of her proposed school.[50] But basic salary could go even lower than this. At the Curtain Road School, Shoreditch, in 1848, Miss Yarrow's salary was reduced to £5 per annum; the children's pence, which she was allowed to add, sank to a mere £1.13s in November.[51] It is hardly surprising to find that infant school minute books reveal something like a state of guerilla warfare between teachers and management; the latter cutting salaries or refusing to raise them, the former in retaliation letting children leave school early, neglecting their duties or threatening to resign.[52] Few things are more ironical than the spectacle of infant school committees, ostensibly devoted to running a school on the purest of Christian principles, cutting the already low wages of its teachers

---

[45]Hackney Infant School, Minutes, 12 Jan. 1829.

[46]Cited in Murphy, "Elementary Education in Liverpool", *loc. cit.,* p. 135.

[47]Hackney Infant School, Minutes, 15 and 17 Jan. 1829.

[48]Birmingham Infant School, afterwards Birmingham Infant School Society, Minute Books 1825-1831, Minutes, 26 Dec. 1831.

[49]St. Leonard Shoreditch Infant School Society, Minutes, 9 Feb. 1844; 24 Mar. 1845.

[50]*Record,* 15 May 1837.

[51]St. Leonard Shoreditch Infant School Society, Minutes, 6 Nov., 4 Dec. 1848.

[52]Hackney Infant School, Minutes, 8 Oct. 1827; Birmingham Infant School Society, Minutes, 24 Dec. 1827; 25 July 1831; Temple Infant School Minutes, 6 Sept., 9 Nov. 1830 (a rare case of the dismissal of a male teacher for inefficiency following a salary cut); St. Leonard Shoreditch Infant School Society, Minutes, 9 July, 30 Sept. 1842; 4 Dec. 1848; 5 Nov. 1849; 4 Aug. 1851.

and in general treating them with the scantest of consideration. "In England", lamented Wilderspin, "the teacher is treated more like a menial servant than an educator of youth".[53]

* * * * *

Wilderspin had certainly not envisaged this state of affairs when he began his missionary work. In the first place, he was convinced that men made the best infant school teachers, a conviction rooted in his experience of the first English infant schools and strengthened by what he had seen in Scotland.[54] A man's position as head of his family, he felt, enabled him to exercise a greater degree of authority over children, partly because he felt that women had neither the physical strength ("the intention of nature") nor "at present" the intellectual powers ("the defect of education") to manage an infant school. He recognised, however, that the minds of both men and women were capable of much greater activity than supposed and that education, while it had done little enough for men, had done even less for women.[55]

In addition, his conception of the ideal infant school teacher was in stark contrast to the type of person who was normally engaged by committees in the early 1830s. Wilderspin was opposed to the popular view that almost any person could do the job. In the first place, physical appearance was important; an infant school teacher, he believed, should have "a tenor voice, a good deal of vivacity, and a pleasant countenance".[56] This was important because children tended to imitate disabilities. "I know, for instance", he wrote, "a master who had a cast in his eye, and all the young children squinted; and another who had a club foot, in imitation of whom all the children limped".[57] Second, the teacher had to practise the ideals he wished to inculcate in his pupils. Precepts which he uttered ought to "shine forth" in his own conduct; He should not expect children to be honest if he himself were not honest in his own dealings with children; saying one thing to a child and meaning another, or promising what one was not able to perform were equally reprehensible.[58] Third, he should be patient, consistent and just, for things that were trifling to adults might appear of great importance to children.[59]

---

[53] Ms. Revisions, *Early Discipline* (1840), p. 139.

[54] *Infant System* (1840), p. 96; p. 176.

[55] *Infant System* (1834), pp. 109-11.

[56] P.P. 1835 VII, Education, p. 29.

[57] *Early Discipline* (1832), pp. 57-8.

[58] *Infant Poor* (1823), pp. 149-51; *Infant Education* (1825), p. 171 ff; *Infant System* (1834), pp. 106-07.

[59] *Infant System* (1834), p. 108; *System of Education* (1840), pp. 43-4.

Finally, he should not put children under too much restraint but be sensitive to their moods and encourage them to make him their confidant.[60]

In the 1830s these views, as Alice Paterson rightly pointed out, were completely new and very advanced.[61] Wilderspin, in fact, was in this as in other fields, a pioneer who was generations ahead of his time. This was also true of his conception of the status of the teacher. Infant teachers, he argued, were equal in all respects to other teachers and it would soon be realised that "his office and his responsibilities are greater and more important than the teaching at any other period".[62] Teachers in general, he maintained, should be more highly paid, greater efforts should be made to train and educate them and they should undergo an examination — "the same sort of examination that a medical man has to undergo" — before being allowed to teach.[63]

The misfortune of the infant school movement at this period was that its teaching force almost totally lacked the professional attributes and standing which Wilderspin advocated; the salaries and conditions, since the mid-1820s, had been driven down so far that the recruits to the profession were mainly women who lacked the educational background, and in some cases the personal qualities, which would enable them to become the kind of teacher Wilderspin envisaged. As Charles Baker pointed out in a Central Society of Education publication, after listing the qualities needed in an infant teacher, "few, very few persons with these endowments have been practically employed as teachers of Infant Schools".[64] Though the average recruit was unlikely to have been "a poor fellow, a tailor, a shoemaker, or a fiddler...an old dame...an old servant", as Bibler had alleged,[65] he or she was as likely as not to know little or nothing of education in general or infant education in particular when beginning to teach. Of the nineteen teachers about whom information was given in three surveys of the Manchester Statistical Society in the mid-1830s — Manchester, Salford and Liverpool — only three had been trained for infant school work.[66] The Rev. Horace Powys was accustomed to staff his three Warrington Infant Schools by choosing factory girls who taught in his Sunday Schools; "they soon acquire the art of managing an infant school", wrote an observer, "by visiting some older established one, or by the instructions of Mr. Wilderspin..."[67]

[60]*Infant System* (1834), pp. 108-09; *System of Education* (1840), p. 44.

[61]Alice Paterson, Samuel Wilderspin and The Infant System, Ph.D. thesis, Jena 1906, p. 79.

[62]*System of Education* (1840), p. 43.

[63]*Infant System* (1840), p. 97; p. 144; P.P. 1835 VII, Education, p. 36.

[64]C. Baker "Infants' Schools", *loc. cit.*, p. 19.

[65]Biber, *Christian Education,* p. 176.

[66]Report of the State of Education in Manchester in 1834 (London 1835), *passim;* Report of the State of Education in Salford in 1835 (London 1836), *passim;* Report of the State of Education in Liverpool in 1835-36 (London 1836), *passim.*

[67]"Slade's Infant School, Bolton-le-Moor", *loc. cit.*, p. 179.

But how well did they acquire this "art"? The question brings into focus the important issue of the training of infant teachers. Could Wilderspin organise a school and give adequate training to a teacher within the five or six weeks he normally allotted to the task, assuming that he could, in the first place, find a person with the necessary psychological and physical characteristics? In other words, could his method of instructing teachers solve the problems posed by the circumstances outlined above? T. Bilby and R.B. Ridgway, the two Evangelical teachers who emerged in the early 30s as Wilderspin's foremost critics, were convinced that the task was impossible. Their criticisms of existing practices, entitled "Some Causes of the Failure of Infant Schools", included as an appendix to the third (1833) edition of their manual *The Infant Teacher's Assistant,* included as the third point, "Employing a person to organise the school and instruct teachers in the system at the same time", which they called "decidedly bad".[68] What kind of experience, they asked, could a person obtain "in five or six weeks attendance at the mere organisation of a school?" No matter how well-qualified the instructor might be, the mechanical part of the system had first to be acquired, and if further progress were to be made (which was seldom the case) then it must be based on "the very elements of simplicity itself". The agent having departed, the teacher was left to proceed alone and not having witnessed the system in all its bearings, became bewildered and "riot and confusion" resulted. Their suggestion was to send the prospective teacher to a well-conducted school for five or six weeks, let him or her take a practical part in the teaching process, observe the system "in all its bearing on the infant mind" and then open and organise a school.[69]

This was a valid, if somewhat limited, alternative. But Wilderspin, with a combative zeal that was becoming characteristic, refused to countenance the argument and strongly defended his own method. Though he admitted *(apropos* his work at St. John's Infant School, Baldwin's Gardens) that "it was not to be expected I could bring the children, or the teachers, in six weeks, to the same state as those which had been practised for years", he contended that if the teachers had continued to base their teaching on "the *principles* laid down in *my* book", they would not have needed the additional advice and instruction to which Bilby and Ridgway alleged they had had recourse. These principles were couched in simple language (which he defended) and based on a knowledge of "*human nature, sound philosophy* and the *word of the living God*".[70] Teachers who followed these prescriptions, Wilderspin argued, had a course worked out for them "from which they can only wilfully depart"; the best teachers in the

---

[68]T. Bilby and R.B. Ridgway, *The Infant Teacher's Assistant* (London, 3rd. ed., 1833), App., p. 166.

[69]*Educational Magazine,* Vol. II, July 1835, p. 58; Bilby and Ridgway, *Infant Teacher's Assistant,* p. 166.

[70]*Educational Magazine,* Vol. II, Aug. 1835, pp. 150-51; p. 153.

kingdom had been trained in precisely this way.[71]

Wilderspin was attempting to defend the indefensible. Though he made the training in schools as thorough as possible — punctuality and regular attendance were stressed and students had to satisfy him that they had mastered all the different aspects of the system in turn[72] — two things were obvious to others: that though six weeks training might prove sufficient for some teachers, many would fail to learn the system thoroughly in that time; and that few of the latter would attempt to make up deficiencies by a study of the *Infant System*. J.R. Wood, for instance, was aware that many teachers left Wilderspin's care in the belief that the scope he gave to children's natural energy and a desire for noise and movement constituted the whole of the system, not realising that Wilderspin used this as a means of tuition and kept it strictly within limits.[73] George Combe put his finger on the weakness inherent in the whole situation:

> altho' men of peculiar talent like Wilderspin may devise and practically carry into effect an improved system of education under the mere inspiration of their own faculties, yet that, altho' they do their best, by precept and example, to communicate their knowledge and power, they cannot succeed in enabling *average* men to carry forward their improvements; but must find *superior* men like themselves, or allow the whole to die a natural death.[74]

It was a difficulty peculiar to the infant school movement and one which the National and British Societies, with their central training schools, did not have to face. In any case their teachers were not expected to be much more than managers of monitors. The infant system, with its more complex intellectual and moral education, depended almost entirely on "the peculiar qualifications of the teacher".[75] In practice, "average" teachers, inadequately trained (or not trained at all) were, in many schools, debasing the principles Wilderspin had pioneered.

* * * * *

Such a situation could hardly continue without the infant school movement falling into desuetude. Revival and reorganisation were imperative, but who was to take the initiative? The well-disposed, though critical, supporters of the movement might well have been amenable to mobilisation, and Wilderspin, by 1835 virtually a household name in educational circles, would have been the obvious person to take the lead in the reconquest of lost ground. A fresh start for the movement would, however, have involved a reconsideration of the crucial

---

[71] *Early Discipline* (1832), pp. 253-54.

[72] *System of Education* (1840), p. 457.

[73] P.P. 1838 VII, Education, p. 121.

[74] N.L.S. Add. Mss., 7381, ff. 26-7, G. Combe to A. Combe, 28 May 1846.

[75] P.P. 1835 VII, Education, p. 29.

question of the education and training of teachers, and it was on this issue that Wilderspin's position was at its weakest. He would have had to abandon or seriously restructure his method of instructing teachers, or take over the direction of a new model school. The latter move, of course, was one he had always looked forward to; but a great deal of preparatory work, not to mention some skilled diplomacy, would have been necessary before the supporters of his system could be organised to set on foot a project of this nature.

There is, however, no evidence that Wilderspin even considered such a step. He continued to pursue his travels, defend his system and denigrate those — supporters and opponents alike — who ventured to criticise his work. Ideally suited to the task of struggling alone against odds, of pioneering in virgin territory, he had many of the qualities of a missionary, though his energies were largely expended in secular concerns. He was less fitted for the tasks of diplomacy, of reconciling differences, or of conciliating opponents. His separation from his parents when young and the necessity of fending for himself in London during his childhood and adolescence, had given him an independent and self-reliant spirit, and he possessed physical courage that verged on the foolhardy; though small in stature, he drove off with a stick no fewer than eleven men who attempted to rob him and his wife in Manchester in 1826,[76] and his public denunciation of the Rev. Hugh McNeile in 1837 showed moral courage of an equally high order.[77]

These qualities, however, can often form the groundwork for obstinate self-righteousness which sees opposition where none really exists and views all criticism as inspired by malice. Late in life, looking back to the early part of his career, he declared that though he had known his own intentions, the world did not; "obloquy and persecution" merely made him "careless of the opinion of mankind", so long as he felt he was in the right, and "the more I was opposed, the more were my energies lighted up and strengthened".[78] Though far from having the "craze for being despised" of his contemporary de Quincey, he undoubtedly found fresh energies in opposition. This aspect of his character was criticised by his son-in-law Thomas Terrington in 1845; in the course of settling an argument by correspondence, he chided Wilderspin on his overbearing manner and his "immovable" attitude on certain issues:

> You say you "care but little for the opinions of mankind" — here I think lies *your error*. You have dared them and set them at defiance too much. If a man's opinions are wrong, to dogmatically tell him yours, or to force them upon him is not the way to put him right. Quietly to set him on the right track, to elevate

[76] *Early Discipline* (1832), p. 51.

[77] Cf. Chapter 13.

[78] *Infant System* (1852), pp. 9-10.

his low notions, and to place something higher before him is the proper way!...Why my dear Wilderspin, I have told you and will tell you again, that at times when you have suddenly and (?) in *your fiery manner* let out to me, you have filled me with astonishment, dismay, and doubt...[79]

Terrington could have had in mind Wilderspin's activities of the previous decade. In June 1835 he had taken Brougham to task for suggesting, in the recently-published report of the 1834 Select Committee on Education that Westminster Infant School was the first in Britain or the world.[80] A few weeks later, still indignant, he told the 1835 Select Committee that Owen had no system and that the New Lanark institution was an assembly of infants rather than a school.[81] In the same month he complained to Simpson that William Wilson, in his manuals, had taken over without acknowledgement the ideas he had pioneered at Spitalfields.[82] The following year, in an epistolary battle with Brougham and Owen in the pages of the *New Moral World,* he entered a controversy about the origin of infant schools which was to continue into the 1840s. Wilderspin's contribution was to declare that he had never been under Buchanan's or Owen's instruction and that "neither practically nor theoretically did I get a grain of information from Owen or his works", nor did he have "frequent visits" from Owen at Spitalfields, where the Infant System was first developed.[83] In a debate with Owen at Liverpool the following year he demanded recognition of his own role in initiating the Infant System.[84]

Wilderspin was often inconsistent when recalling the past, and statements of this kind, made under the pressure of argument or in hasty defence of his system, did not always represent his considered opinions. In August 1835, for instance, in the exchange of letters with Bilby and Ridgway, he paid a warm tribute to the value of Buchanan's friendship and assistance in the early days at Spitalfields.[85] Some of his more extreme statements, however, brought justified criticism. James Simpson felt obliged to set the record straight with regard to Owen,[86] and the author of "Schools for the Industrious Classes" was constrained to remark that "Mr. Wilderspin claims so much, that many persons have been

[79] Wilderspin Papers, T. Terrington to Wilderspin, 20 Nov. 1845.

[80] U.C.L. Brougham Mss., 27836, Wilderspin to Brougham, 1 June 1835.

[81] P.P. 1835 VII, Education, p. 16.

[82] Archives of W. and R. Chambers, Wilderspin to Simpson, 25 June 1835.

[83] *New Moral World,* Vol. II, N.S., No. 103, 15 Oct. 1836.

[84] *Early Discipline* (1840), pp. 331-32.

[85] *Educational Magazine,* Vol. II, Aug. 1835, p. 148.

[86] J. Simpson, *The Philosophy of Education* (Edinburgh, 2nd ed., 1836), p. 109n. "...Mr. Wilderspin did not first *invent* Infant Schools", wrote Simpson, "This boon mankind owes to the talent and benevolence of Robert Owen; who, whatever may be his errors it is gross injustice, as well as indiscriminating bigotry to deny, his large claims on the gratitude of his species. Mr. Wilderspin, however, has to a great extent improved infant schools in their details and practice..."

led to refuse him that degree of credit to which he is fairly entitled".[87] The pamphlet was published by the Central Society of Education, founded in 1837, and in that organisation, if anywhere, Wilderspin could have found support against the claims of the Home and Colonial Infant School Society, established by Evangelicals the previous year; indeed he was briefly to join the Central Society's campaign for national education in the autumn of 1837. But a few reasonable criticisms in the above work led him to denounce the pamphlet as "full of spleen", "illiberal and sectarian", and "partial and unjust" and allege that the society existed merely to "find fault with the doings of others". He lumped both the Central and the Home and Colonial Societies together as equally obnoxious:

> I distinctly charge both...with doing me great injustice; the one society complains of my plans without knowing them, the other adopts them without acknowledgement, and both have sprung up fungus-like, after the Infant System had been in existence many years...[88]

Wilderspin's opposition to the Evangelicals was as much territorial as doctrinal, though as a Swedenborgian he had no room for other denominations in his theological scheme. But he failed to realise that the Home and Colonial Society had "sprung up fungus-like" largely because no other group had taken the initiative to end the widely-recognised crisis in the movement. Even after 1836, a less combative individual might have inspired a movement which would have neutralised the Evangelicals' action and led to the formation of a more broadly-based and representative organisation, or achieved a *modus vivendi* which would have enabled any new organisation to make use of his talents. But Wilderspin had isolated himself and, as events turned out, he was to see those whom he regarded as his enemies take much of the credit for ideas and practices that he himself had pioneered.

---

[87]"Schools for the Industrious Classes", *loc. cit.,* p. 377n.

[88]*Infant System* (1840), p. 181; p. 183; p. 227; p. 243.

CHAPTER 11

THE INFANT SCHOOL MOVEMENT: NEW DIRECTIONS

So it was the Evangelicals and not Wilderspin who assumed the leadership of reform in the infant school movement. Ironically, the methods practised in the schools under their control — methods which sprang directly from their theological position — had contributed to the very crisis which they were concerned to solve. Evangelical doctrine demanded the inclusion in the curriculum of a large amount of Scriptural knowledge, and this in turn necessitated the introduction of rote-learning practices on a fairly large scale. Whereas malformations in the Wilderspin-type infant school could be accounted for by human weakness, the exigencies of Wilderspin's peripatetic work-habits or the voluntary system of management and finance, the Evangelicals modified the Wilderspin model on principle, in conformity with the imperatives of Evangelical ecclesiastical policy.

The Evangelicals of the mid-1830s were a very different group from that of fifteen or twenty years earlier. The outlook of Thomas Babington, Zachary Macaulay and their Claphamite associates, who had been willing to work with Quakers, Philosophical Radicals and others in broad schemes of social and educational improvement, including the promotion of Owenite enterprises, had given way to a narrower and more dogmatic conservatism. The "constitutional revolution" of 1828-35 (as Professor Best has termed it) which set aside legal disabilities on Catholics and Dissenters and reformed the political basis of national and local government, appeared to conservatives and Churchmen to threaten the very basis of the constitution.[1]

These changes provoked what today we would call a right-wing backlash, of which one of the most obvious manifestations was the Tractarian Movement. More significant for the development of education in general and the infant school movement in particular was the move towards an extreme Tory, pro-constitutional, pro-Church and anti-Catholic position by the Evangelicals. C.E. Trevelyan, Zachary Macaulay's son-in-law, returning to England in the late 1830s after a long sojourn in India, was struck by the fact that "most of the Low Church people had become High Church, and many of the High Church people had become Newmanites".[2] Recent research has suggested that this move to the right by the Evangelicals was under way by the middle 1820s,[3] and it was certainly complete by the middle 1830s when, with one exception, all

---

[1]G.F.A. Best, "The Constitutional Revolution, 1828-32 and its Consequences for the Established Church", *Theology*, Vol. LXII, No. 468, June 1959, pp. 226-34.

[2]C.E. Trevelyan, *The No-Popery Agitation* (London, 4th ed., 1840), pp. 4-5.

[3]I.S. Rennie, Evangelicalism and English Public Life, unpublished Ph.D. thesis, University of Toronto 1962, *passim*.

Evangelicals in Parliament were Tories, and the *Record* newspaper united serious Christians behind an uncompromising and militant Protestantism.[4] They put themselves forward as resolute defenders of the Christian state, the political prosperity of which, they asserted, rested on a popular spirit guided by "the principles of intelligent piety, of firm and constitutional order".[5] "The safety of England", following the Reform Act, depended upon the prevalence of "real vital Christianity" and that could best be ensured by the spread of "religious as well as general education".[6] In the infant school movement an Evangelical grouping began to gain strength in the late 1820s inspired, as we have suggested, by the foundation of the London Infant School Society. Manuals were written, teachers were trained and a coherent body of principles gradually formed.

The best known of the infant teachers who constituted the Evangelical group were the aforementioned Thomas Bilby and R.B. Ridgway. Their *Infant Teacher's Assistant* went through four editions between 1831 and 1835 and was to be found, they claimed, "in the hands of almost every National, British and Foreign, Infant, Sunday-School, and Nursery teacher, throughout the United Kingdom".[7] Bilby, a protege of Buchanan,[8] conducted Chelsea Infant School, which was opened in 1825 and moved to new premises in Markham Street, off the King's Road, three years later; it was patronised by ladies of the nobility and gentry of Chelsea and Kensington, and William Wilson preached a very Evangelical sermon on its behalf in 1826.[9] Ridgway was the master of the Hart Street Infant School, Long Acre, also a venue for Evangelical sermons.[10] Both schools served as training establishments for infant teachers; 133 had been trained at Hart Street during the early 1830s and Chelsea, it was claimed, had sent forth over 300 during the first ten years of its existence.[11]

James Rodgers we have met as the first master of Cheltenham Infant School and author of *A Practical Treatise on Infant Education,* published in the early 1830s. James Brown, husband of Wilderspin's first wife's sister, and a former Methodist preacher, was described by a visitor to his school as "a jolly, good-natured looking man, with a good head, plain manners and a shabby coat", with a tendency to make the children pray.[12] His *Essay on the Cultivation*

[4]*Ibid.,* p. 90. The lone Liberal Evangelical was T. Fowell Buxton.

[5]J.C. Colquhoun, *The Moral Character of Britain the Cause of Its Political Eminence* (Glasgow 1832), p. 6; pp. 23-4; p. 27.

[6]Rev. T.V. Short, *National Education, and the Means of Improving It* (London 1835), pp. 4-9, *passim.*

[7]*Educational Magazine,* Vol. II, Sept. 1835, p. 225.

[8]B.I. Buchanan, *Buchanan Family Records* (Cape Town 1923), p. 9.

[9]*Record,* 16 May 1828; Rev. W. Wilson, *A Sermon Preached in the New Church Chelsea...In Aid of the Funds of the Infants' School of that Parish* (London 1826).

[10]*Record,* 18 May 1837.

[11]*Educational Magazine,* Vol. II, Sept. 1835, pp. 225-26.

[12]J.M.D. Meiklejohn, *Life and Letters of William Ballantyne Hodgson* (Edinburgh 1883), p. 253.

of the Infant Mind was published in 1826. The most widely-known Evangelical writers on infant education were, however, Dr. Charles Mayo and his sister Elizabeth, whose names were associated with the organisation of the Home and Colonial Infant School Society; their *Practical Remarks on Infant Education* appeared in 1837. In Scotland David Stow had made Bible training the leading feature of the Model School of the Glasgow Infant School Society and given the Society as a whole a definite Evangelical orientation[13]; its successor, the Glasgow Educational Society, was an ultra-Protestant body which took its educational and religious attitudes from the Rev. Hugh McNeile, the most militant of the Evangelical leaders.[14]

The first open clash between Wilderspin and the Evangelicals occurred, as we have seen, in the summer of 1835. The acrimonious exchange of letters between him and the "two Goliaths" (as they signed themselves) in the pages of the *Educational Magazine* ranged over questions of teachers and teaching, the history of infant education and the existing state of the schools, and no quarter was spared on either side. Bilby and Ridgway's communications were spiced with personal allegations of a near-libellous kind, which would have roused a nature considerably less contentious than Wilderspin's. He was accused of personal ambition, hasty improvisation and various malpractices from financial chicanery to bad spelling; in his turn he charged Bilby and Ridgway with mendacity, incompetence and crude self-display, finally declaring that "my principles *will live* when you, and your names, and your principles, if you have any, will be entirely forgotten".[15] Bilby and Ridgway riposted with a declaration that infant schools should teach children to believe in "the holy and blessed Trinity — Three Persons in One God — the Father, the Son and the Holy Ghost", and a condemnation of Wilderspin's support of "the mystic doctrines of Baron Swedenborg on the Trinity, Atonement, Human Soul as being in a human form, etc., etc.", which beliefs, they felt, raised the question of his fitness to have charge of the education of young children.[16]

The "Two Goliaths" had undoubtedly pinpointed the basic theological differences between Swedenborgians and "Athanasian trinitarians" (as Christians outside the New Church were dubbed by a writer in the *Intellectual Repository*)[17], though whether this justified the exclusion of supporters of the New Church from participation in the infant school movement was, of course, another matter. Wilderspin's religious views — particularly when defined in

[13] *The Glasgow Infant School Magazine* (Glasgow, 2nd ed., 1834), v; A.D. Bache, *Report on Education in Europe* (Philadelphia 1839), p. 160.

[14] *Scottish Guardian,* 14 Oct. 1836.

[15] *Educational Magazine,* Vol. II, Aug. 1835, p. 151. The correspondence began in the June issue and continued to September.

[16] *Educational Magazine,* Vol. II, Sept. 1835, p. 225. They also stated (probably correctly) that Wilderspin's criticism of Spitalfields Infant School made in the 1834 edition of *Infant Education* (p. 66) was due to Brown's Evangelical attitude.

[17] "On Spiritual Freedom", *Intellectual Repository,* No. XIV, Apr.-June 1815, p. 235.

relation to religious teaching in infant schools — were closely in accord with the Swedenborgian canon. He defined religion in the active sense, as "a living principle, which must influence the life and conduct"; if we were "to love God, to love truth, and to love goodness" we should begin to love each other, and then "we should like to do to others as we would be done unto".[18] Love of God and love of Man, in fact, effectively summarises Wilderspin's religious *credo,* echoing Swedenborg's dictum that "love to the Lord and love towards the neighbour include in themselves all Divine truths. . ."[19]

The definition of religion in ethical-social terms was inspired by the Swedenborgian Doctrine of Use, which postulated human actions inspired by an active spiritual principle and religious activity infused with a humanitarian spirit. A high value was thus placed on the social uses to which a person applied his faculties and attributes and on the content of religion rather than the outward form.[20] "Uses are the goods of love and charity", affirmed Swedenborg,[21] and to members of the New Church, charity, in the form of general good-neighbourly relations, was an important part of their creed.[22]

Wilderspin's religious teaching rejected verbal formulations in favour of a practical humanism. He denounced the teaching of creeds and catechisms in schools; "the nature of the infant mind" made it impossible for children to understand "what they are made to say they believe", and in allowing a child "to say he believes in that which we must know he cannot understand" the way was paved for "his initiation into falsehood".[23] He rejected "particular doctrines" and the "externals and trappings" for "the simple and beautiful truths which form the spirit of religion".[24] "The pupils" Wilderspin insisted, "are not only to *say* but to *do* good things".[25] Prominence should be given

to those fundamental truths of love and goodness which Christianity inculcates. Let the first sounds of religion which salute the ears of infancy be that heavenly proclamation. . .'Peace on earth and goodwill towards men'.[26]

But mere exhortation was insufficient. The teacher, by his kindness towards children, could direct the will and the affections. Children should see in the teacher "no stern pedagogue to terrify him (sic) into religion, no frowning countenance, no uplifted hand to flog them into good rules and religious principles", but appreciate "the delights of mutual kindness towards their

[18]*System'of Education* (1840), p. 321; p. 324.

[19]E. Swedenborg, *A Treatise Concerning Heaven and Hell* (London 1778), 19.

[20]Rev. B.A.H. Boysen, *The Doctrine of Use* (London 1969), pp. 2-7.

[21]Swedenborg, *Heaven and Hell,* 402.

[22]E. Swedenborg, *The True Christian Religion* (London, 2 vol., 1781), 394-458.

[23]*System of Education* (1840), p. 22.

[24]*Infant Education* (1829), p. 279; *System of Education* (1840), p. 324.

[25]*System of Education* (1840), p. 324.

[26]*Infant Education* (1829), pp. 278-79.

teacher, and their teacher towards them". Furthermore, the development of moral sympathy would establish a bond of love between the children themselves, so that they would feel "the advantages and delights of giving and partaking kindness, not taught merely by *words* that it *should* be so"; in the best infant schools the children exhibited "continual displays of kindness towards each other, of forgiveness of injuries, acknowledgement and contrition for error".[27]

It was a conception of religion — and of childhood — fundamentally different from that of the Evangelicals. They saw evil and immorality as inherent in the nature of the child, whose salvation could be secured only by means of "education for eternity" — in practice, the subjection to Scriptural education at its most verbal from the earliest age. Wilderspin viewed children as beings of primal innocence, capable of responding to love and affection; if they displayed tendencies toward evil and immorality — of which juvenile delinquency was the most obvious manifestation — one should look to society for the cause:

> How many children are fed with evil influences, street associations, and are thus poisoned at every pore, until their being is thoroughly contaminated through neglect, public and private, and when not orphans, even parental neglect also; and thus after having increased our county rates, enlarged our prisons, and built union workhouses (with respect to morals and training for the young, I say pest-houses) we add ragged schools. We allow them to become contaminated, and when that is accomplished, we go to work to undo what has been done. If this does not succeed we punish by law the poor neglected beings for taking the poisons we really offered them![28]

The similarity of these views to the formulations of Owen hardly needs stressing, though they stemmed from the social aspects of Swedenborgian theology rather than from Owen's concept of character formation or his doctrine of circumstance.[29] It was a position that set Wilderspin further at odds with the Evangelicals, who showed a marked tendency to abstract children from their social context or transform the reality in which they lived with cloudy rhetoric; "as she approaches these dungeons of human depravity and woe", intoned Dr. Charles Mayo, "charity falters on the heavenly errand, and turns sighing from the threshold".[30] Evil resided in the child rather than in society. To the Rev. Francis Close the infant was "a fallen, corrupt and guilty child of Adam";[31] the Rev. William Wilson believed that children were "transgressors of the law of God, and, like ourselves, have sins to be pardoned and grace to receive".[32]

[27]*System of Education* (1840), pp. 22-3.

[28]*Infant System* (1852), p. 13; cf. also P.P. 1835 VII, Report from the Select Committee on Education in England and Wales, pp. 34-5.

[29]For Owen's theoretical exposition of the formation of human character through the influence of the objects of the external world, cf. *New View of Society*, Third Essay, Owen, *Life*, 1, p. 301.

[30]Rev. C. Mayo, *Observations on Infants' Schools* (London 1827), p. 6.

[31]Rev. F. Close, *Substance of a Lecture, Delivered in the Infants' School Room, at Cheltenham...*(Cheltenham 1832), p. 6.

[32]Wilson, *Sermon*, p. 22.

These beliefs shaped the aims of infant schools. The Evangelicals saw infant education in terms of the preparation of young children for God and Jesus; "let the school of infancy be as the gate of heaven", urged Dr. Mayo,[33] and Wilson argued for an infant education "whose aim is to discipline the soul for eternity, and to honour the work of the Saviour by extending his kingdom among men".[34] Close was more specific:

> ...the object of such schools...was certainly not to produce young philosophers, politicians, or legislators, or to impart a smattering of the world's shallow wisdom, but to afford such a religious education as might fit them to discharge the duties of life, and give them a good hope beyond the grave. Viewing all these little children as immortal beings, and as sinners...they would...educate them for eternity.[35]

Believing that only "spiritual and scriptural education" could lead to a child's salvation, they gave more space in the curriculum to Biblical knowledge and correspondingly less to the study of the world of nature.[36] Wilderspin's belief that children "seemed delighted to be led up to God through his works...the Creator has given us two books to learn from, His Holy Word and His book of nature"[37], was a position that was tantamount to infidelity in the eyes of Evangelicals.[38] In 1832 Close admitted that "geometry and the sciences, and many things totally unsuited to the infants' age and station in life...are excluded from the Cheltenham Schools",[39] and William Wilson stated in his evidence to the 1834 Committee on Education that "if the acquirement of Knowledge be the only end proposed by education, then the result may be questionable, and, at the best, partial", and revealed that only the 3Rs, Scripture history and music formed the curriculum at his Walthamstow school.[40]

The manuals written by Evangelical infant teachers confirmed that the curriculum they recommended was overloaded with Biblical knowledge, often of the most recondite kind. In the third and fourth editions of Bilby and Ridgway's book, 68 of the 168 pages were devoted to Scripture lessons, the remainder to tables, moral lessons and poems, mostly of a religious nature. Pages 32-55 of Brown's work consisted of Scripture lessons, a collection of

[33]Rev. Dr. Mayo and Miss Mayo, *Practical Remarks on Infant Education* (London 1837), p. 7.

[34]Wilson, *Sermon,* p. 22.

[35]*Cheltenham Journal,* 30 Oct. 1837.

[36]In 1825, however, in the more liberal period of Evangelical policy, William Wilson had advocated that the infant should learn from "the book of nature which lies at all times before him" (Rev. W. Wilson, *A Letter on Infants' Schools* (London 1825), p. 12).

[37]P.P. 1835 VII, Education, p. 17.

[38]One of the dangers of the time, according to the Rev. Hugh McNeile (speaking at a public meeting on education in 1839) was the presence of a lurking, concealed infidelity "which placed nature and the Bible as parallel revelations of the Divine Will" (*The Times,* 12 Feb. 1839).

[39]Close, *Substance of a Lecture,* p. 10.

[40]P.P. 1834 IX, Report from Select Committee on the State of Education, pp. 167-70; p. 173.

undigested matter on the Creation, Prophecies, Miracles, the Love of God, the Advent of Christ, and the Preaching of Paul, followed by 62 pages of hymns, prayers, religious anecdotes and rhymes. The content of the Mayos' *Practical Remarks* somewhat belied the title; in a book of over a hundred pages all except thirty-two (on Intellectual and Physical Education) were devoted to religious education. Rodgers was the only writer of the four to attempt to give advice on the way in which the day's work in an infant school should actually be conducted, but he made clear that his school was "strictly Biblical" in character, and that Scripture lessons were "all-important"; he included model lessons on the nature of sin, a collection of instances which proved Jesus to be both a God and a Man, lists of prophecies and the names of Jesus, and a large collection of hymns and moral songs.

The manuals, and the type of education based on them, were widely criticised. James Simpson described the Glasgow infant schools as "Schools of Infant Theology" and deprecated the continual reference to the Bible, whatever subject was being taught; the infant brain, he felt, was being overworked and even injured by "an excess of religious instruction".[41] F. B. Barton of Cheltenham, after witnessing an examination by Close at the local infant school, was moved to protest to the local press that the religious instruction there — mainly "controverted points and abstruse dogmas" — was "merely a teaching to repeat certain expressions *by rote*".[42] The author of "Schools for the Industrious Classes", in a lengthy analysis of the curriculum advocated by Bilby and Ridgway, James Brown and the Glasgow Infant School Society, demonstrated that repetition and rote-learning were the recommended methods — indeed the only possible methods — of learning the masses of Biblical knowledge with which the curriculum was loaded.[43] Charles Baker, writing in the Central Society of Education's *Third Publication,* was less trenchant in his approach, but was also opposed to the use of verbal memory in learning the "abstract truths" and "historical facts" of religion.[44] Wilderspin, after filling three pages of the 1840 edition of the *Infant System* with criticism of the religious rote-learning advocated by Bilby and Ridgway, felt it was his duty "solemnly to protest against this method of infant teaching".[45]

Though these criticisms date from the later 1830s, it is obvious that the methods they described had been in operation for some time, though whether the group of clergy and professional men who founded the Home and Colonial Infant School Society early in 1836 were aware of them is a moot point; if they

[41] J. Simpson, *The Philosophy of Education* (Edinburgh, 2nd ed., 1836), p. 196n.; P.P. 1836 XIII, Report from the Select Committee on Education in Ireland, Pt. 1, pp. 269-70.

[42] *Cheltenham Free Press,* 28 Oct. 1837.

[43] "Schools for the Industrious Classes", Central Society of Education. *Second Publication* (London 1828), pp. 379-85.

[44] C. Baker, "Infants' Schools", Central Society of Education. *Third Publication* (London 1839), pp. 16-17.

[45] *Infant System* (1840), pp. 177-80.

were, it is clear that they were unable or unwilling to make immediate changes in the schools in question. As we shall show, the sharp edge of the new society's policy was to be turned against the non-denominational ethic and the play and amusement practices of the Wilderspinian infant school; re-organisation of the movement was a means to this end.

* * * * *

As early as 1835 there had been several indications in educational circles that some rationalisation and improvement of the infant school system was considered necessary. The *Educational Magazine* and the *Quarterly Journal of Education* had both argued for the institutionalisation of teacher training, the former urging the immediate formation of "a central committee".[46] J.R. Wilson, agent of the Evangelically-inclined Sunday School Union had advocated the formation of a society in a letter to the *Patriot*,[47] and the Rev. T.V. Short, in a pamphlet, had maintained that the infant school system appeared "to require some decided organisation", though he felt this could best be done by adding lay members to the recently-formed infant teachers' society rather than by the formation of "a totally fresh society".[48]

The Home and Colonial Infant School Society was founded on 23 February 1836 at "a meeting of gentlemen" in London.[49] The inaugural meeting formulated three objectives which were to remain the basic purposes of the Society in its early years. First, "the improvement and extension of the Infant School system on Christian principles", in the colonies and other countries as well as Britain; second, the training of persons of "character and piety" who were "apt to teach"; third, to afford existing teachers the means of improvement. The provision of printed lessons and pedagogical material, and, as soon as funds permitted, the establishment of a model school, were to be the chief means to the fulfilment of these aims.[50] The Society's diagnosis of the situation which justified these steps was remarkably similar to that of Wilderspin and his supporters. The lack of a central, guiding authority had led to a situation in which different schools had different plans, the engagement of inferior and unsuitable teachers had resulted in the good parts of the system falling into disuse, and the system of training teachers by means of attendance for a few weeks at another school had

---

[46]"Education in England, No. 1. The Infant System", *Educational Magazine,* Vol. 1, Feb. 1835, p. 78; *Quarterly Journal of Education,* Vol. IX, No. XVIII, 1835, pp. 228-29.

[47]*Patriot,* 22 Apr. 1835.

[48]Short, *National Education,* p. 31. Short's reference was possibly to a pro-Evangelical group of infant teachers, formed in opposition to an older Infant Teachers' Union founded by J.P. Greaves c. 1830 (*Early Discipline* (1834), p. 299). According to J.S. Reynolds there were "two parties" among the London infant teachers in 1836 (*Record,* 9 June 1836).

[49]*Record,* 17 Mar. 1836.

[50]*Ibid.*

compounded the difficulties until it had "become difficult to say what is the established system of infant education".[51] Recognising that "everything in the way of infant instruction mainly depends on the teacher",[52] the Society admitted that few candidates for the profession possessed even the minimum qualifications and requirements;[53] the aim, therefore, was to provide an institution wherein teachers could learn to impart to the infant mind "solid and useful knowledge — knowledge suitable to their situation in life, which may be valuable in this world, and valuable with reference to the world to come".[54]

The Society was, from the beginning, "serious" about its religion. The list of qualifications for teachers entering training stated that the cultivation of religious principles and moral sentiments was the "primary object" of early education, and the sentiments outlined were indisputably those of the Evangelical variety.[55] Whether we consider the Society's leaders, its bankers, its meetings or its speakers and publicists, it is clear that it was an out-and-out Evangelical organisation. Lord Chichester, an Evangelical, presided at the early annual meetings and six of the nine Vice-Presidents were prominent Evangelical peers — Lords Clarendon, Glenelg, Barham, Calthorpe, Teignmouth and Henley, plus Sir Thomas Baring, the pro-Evangelical banker who had also been a member of the Infant School Society committee. At least twelve members of the thirty-strong General Committee can be identified as Evangelicals, including Fowell Buxton, M.P., Sir Oswald Mosley, M.P., John Hardy, M.P., and J.P. Plumptre, M.P.[56] The treasurer was the Evangelical lawyer John Bridges and the secretary J.S. Reynolds, a close friend of Dr. Charles Mayo.[57] Reynolds, born in Manchester in 1791, had made a career in the Audit Office until 1835. He had been converted to Evangelicalism — and also to an interest in infant education — while serving as secretary to the Irish Revenue Commission in Dublin in 1822-23. Thereafter he was active in missionary work, assisted in founding the *Record*, and helped to establish infant schools in various parts of the country.[58]

Subscriptions to the Society could be sent to Williams, Deacon's Bank, Hatchards the publishers, Suter's of Cheapside or the *Record* offices,[59] all Evangelical organisations or institutions. Speakers at its early meetings were almost all Evangelical M.P.'s or clergymen; the latter included the Rev. Daniel Wilson, the Rev. Baptist Noel, the Rev. John Cumming and the Rev. J.H.

[51]J.S. Reynolds, speech at a meeting to celebrate the opening of premises in Bloomsbury (*Record,* 9 June 1836).

[52]*Record,* 17 Mar. 1836.

[53]These were listed by Reynolds as proficiency in the 3Rs, some knowledge of geography, natural history and singing and a competent knowledge of the Bible and its history (*Record,* 9 June 1836).

[54]Reynolds' speech (*Record,* 9 June 1836).

[55]P.P. 1847 XLV, Minutes of the Committee of Council on Education 1846, "Report on the School of the Home and Colonial Infant and Junior School Society", by E.C. Tufnell, Esq., pp. 555-56.

[56]The list of vice-presidents and committee members is given on the flyleaf of the Mayos' *Practical Remarks* (1837).

[57]K. Silber, *Pestalozzi: The Man and His Work* (London 1960), App. I, p. 302.

[58]*Record,* 15 May 1874.

[59]*Record,* 27 June 1836.

Woodward, secretary of the Church Missionary Society. On 10 May 1837 a special meeting was convened at Exeter Hall, the temple of Evangelicalism, as part of the "May meetings", the annual jamboree of the Evangelical and allied societies, for the purpose of offering an explanation of the nature and objects of the Society to "the clergy and other friends of education at this time in town".[60]

Like the head of Janus, the Society faced two different ways, at least in the first half-dozen years of its existence. Publicly it presented an image of militant Evangelicalism, presumably with a view to securing the maximum support from the faithful. Privately it was concerned with the elaboration of methods of teacher training and the theory and practice of infant education, an aim often obscured by the anti-intellectual rhetoric of its public speakers. Unlike its predecessor the Infant School Society, the Home and Colonial Society saw the infant primarily as a sinner to be saved rather than as a delinquent who needed an improved environment and sympathetic instruction. The emphasis on Scriptural education led the clergymen and M.P.s who dominated the public meetings to place the inculcation of the spirit of vital religion above instruction in useful knowledge. The Rev. Baptist Noel pointed to the danger of allowing teachers to become "inflated" with the idea of possessing more knowledge than those around them and advocated simplicity in imparting "the elements of useful knowledge"; children leaving an infant school should have "a deep sense of piety".[61] "Children must have their wills conquered", insisted the Rev. Crabbe of Southampton "and be directed to the Saviour".[62] J. Hardy, M.P., had "no confidence whatever in that system of education in which the wit of man was substituted for the word of God".[63] The chief trumpeter of the Evangelical band was, however, the Rev. John Cumming, remembered today only as the subject of George Eliot's essay, the most devastating critique of Evangelicalism in nineteenth century literature. Master not only of the striking metaphor, the colourful anecdote and the apposite Biblical reference but also of the subtle non-sequitur, the false alternative and the irrelevant hyperbole, Cumming's style bore out George Eliot's perspicacious insight that his talent was as much journalistic as theological.[64] He regularly used his eloquence to instil in his hearers fear and dread of the "accumulation of knowledge" unleavened by Biblical truth. "I would rather that millions should descend to the grave ignorant of all but Christ", he cried, "than that millions should master and acquire every species of wisdom save that which is 'unto salvation'".[65]

---

[60] Record, 18 May 1837.

[61] Record, 9 June 1836.

[62] Ibid.

[63] Record, 6 Mar. 1837.

[64] [George Eliot], "Evangelical Teaching: Dr. Cumming", in T. Pinney (Ed.), Essays of George Eliot (London 1963), pp. 158-89. The article originally appeared in the Westminster Review in October 1855.

[65] Record, 18 May 1837; 5 Mar. 1838.

This zealous prosecution of the Holy War in the infant school movement rapidly resulted in the isolation of the Home and Colonial Society. Its policy was classed as narrow and sectarian by the author of "Schools for the Industrious Classes";[66] the *Educational Magazine* protested at one of Cummings' bizarre condemnations of Rousseau and Fellenberg;[67] and a large group of London infant teachers (one of whose leaders was J. Chalklen, a Swedenborgian) strongly criticised the Society for its attitude to the profession, the nature of the lectures at its Grays Inn Road headquarters, and the assumption that its method of training teachers was the only valid one. Though they did not mention Wilderspin by name, it was evident that they approved of and supported his methods.[68]

More serious for the future of the Society was a marked lack of co-operation from the Established Church. As an Evangelical body, the Home and Colonial Society could not identify too closely with High or Broad Church principles. At the same time it could not afford to appear as if it were in opposition to the Establishment, or give the impression that it was relying solely on Dissent for support. Accordingly, the Committee of the Society attempted to tread a middle path. Hastening to assert that they "venerate and love the Established Church", they nevertheless asserted that they were convinced that the promotion of infant education "is a work in which all who hold the fundamental truths of the Bible and love the Lord Jesus Christ in sincerity, may cordially unite"; the institution would therefore educate people of different religious denominations, provided they were of "decided piety".[69]

This statement failed to provide a basis of unity with the Church or the National Society. In February 1837 the latter announced that arrangements had been completed for the conversion of St. Margaret's and St. John's Infant School in Tufton Street, Westminster, to a Model School for training female teachers.[70] Nor did the statement have any significant effect on the numbers of Anglicans who wished to avail themselves of the services of the Society. The first Annual Report, of February 1837, referred to the "considerable difficulty" experienced in obtaining Anglican candidates for training; of the first 120 applicants, only 11 were members of the Established Church, and a special circular had been sent to clergymen "earnestly requesting their attention to the subject". Three months later, though the number of Anglican applicants had increased, there was still a "great want" in this area.[71]

---

[66]"Schools for the Industrious Classes", *loc.cit.*, pp. 377-78.

[67]*Educational Magazine*, N.S., Vol. II, pp. 176-77. Cumming had alleged that the only monuments to the theory of Rousseau, citing the pupils of Fellenberg as examples, were "gibbets and early graves" (*Record*, 25 Mar. 1839).

[68]*Record*, 12 Sept. 1836; *Educational Magazine*, N.S., Vol. II, July 1839, pp. 250-55.

[69]*Record*, 2 Nov. 1836.

[70]Twenty-Fifth Annual Report of the National Society (London 1836), p. 14; *Record*, 26 Dec. 1836; 20 Feb. 1837.

[71]*Record*, 6 Mar. 1837; 18 May 1837.

The Evangelicals had to face the fact that, despite their energetic preaching, the organisation of a multitude of societies and the distribution of myriads of tracts, they were still a minority within the Established Church and regarded with distaste, if not hostility, by High Church opinion, particularly the Tractarian Wing.[72] Attracting Anglican teachers was uphill work; of the 419 trained by the beginning of 1840, only 57% had been members of the Establishment.[73]

The antipathy of the Church towards the Society in its early days undoubtedly affected its finances. In its first year it received only £383 in subscriptions[74] and was described by its supporters as "struggling for existence".[75] A debt of £300 was still unpaid in 1841, despite strenuous efforts to liquidate it, and the following year the Society admitted that "everything is flourishing but the finances".[76] One reason for this was that wealthy Anglicans outside the Evangelical party simply refused to have anything to do with the Society. As far as can be ascertained, no orthodox Anglican clergyman and certainly no bishop or prominent Church of England layman supported the Society financially or in any other way during the first years of its existence.

It finally recognised the adverse effects that its policy was having. In 1841, at the instigation of the Rev. Edward Bickersteth, it made an important change in its rules. The objects of the Society were henceforward to be

> ...the improvement and general extension of the Infant-school system, on Christian principles, *as such principles are set forth and embodied in the doctrinal Articles of the Church of England.*[77]

This step marked the beginning of the Society's climb to acceptance by Church and State. The number of Anglicans under training increased,[78] the income rose steadily from 1843 onwards,[79] and two favourable inspections were made by Seymour Tremenheere in 1843 and by Carleton Tufnell in 1847. "In promoting a system of education...wholly drawn from, based in, or illumined

---

[72] I. Bradley, *The Call to Seriousness: The Evangelical Impact on the Victorians* (London 1976), pp. 72-3. In 1860, at the height of their influence, Evangelicals numbered only something over a third of Church membership, mostly at parish level.

[73] *Record,* 23 Apr. 1840.

[74] *Record,* 6 Mar. 1837. The figure is taken from the Annual Report.

[75] *Christian Lady's Magazine,* June 1837, p. 504.

[76] *Record,* 15 July 1841; 17 Jan. 1842.

[77] *Record,* 15 July 1841; the change was announced at the annual meeting.

[78] By 1847, two-thirds of the intake of teachers were Anglicans (P.P. 1847 XLV, Tufnell, "Report", p. 558).

[79] In 1843 the income reached £2,260 and in 1847 £3,246. (P.P. 1847 XLV, Tufnell, "Report", p. 558).

by the words of Holy Writ", wrote another H.M.I., Joseph Fletcher, in 1846, "the friends of the infant schools certainly establish a tacit claim to every aid and assistance which the State can render them".[80]

* * * * *

One other factor contributed to this transformation. This was the increasing attention devoted to the formulation of a viable pedagogical theory and, in the light of this, the elaboration of a teacher-training programme which would occupy months rather than weeks. The practice of giving precedence, in the press and public meetings, to "the wisdom unto salvation" was gradually superseded by exposition of the theory and practice of infant education. In doing this, the society had to come to terms with the realities of the situation in which it found itself; first, that the only Evangelicals with any pretensions to a knowledge of infant education were the Mayos, whose theory was based upon that of Pestalozzi; second, that if it were to accomplish its aim of purifying the movement, then beneath the dross to be cleared away lay the model Wilderspin had devised. In other words, it could not in any serious way ignore or repudiate the tradition which stemmed from Owen, Buchanan, Wilderspin, Goyder, Greaves and Simpson.

It could, however, make Pestalozzi an honorary Evangelical and remove Wilderspin's name from history. The Swiss reformer, who had been condemned by Evangelicals in the early 1820s as unsound on religious matters because of his evident belief in the goodness of the child,[81] was given a halo and transformed into "good old Pestalozzi".[82] Wilderspin's theories and practices were appropriated without acknowledgement and all mention of his name avoided; anyone studying the infant school movement from the records of the Home and Colonial School Society would conclude that Wilderspin had never existed. The employment by the Society of both Bilby and Ridgway in the early 1840s no doubt contributed to this attitude,[83] but the decision, obviously a conscious one, had been taken earlier.

Nevertheless, the pedagogical work of the Society bore a close resemblance to that of Wilderspin. This was evident in *Practical Remarks on Infant Education,* the first publication, in which Elizabeth Mayo glibly explained that

[80]P.P. 1846 XXXII, Minutes of the Committee of Council on Education 1845, J. Fletcher, "Report on Infant Schools on the Principles of the British and Foreign School Society", p. 356. In September 1847 infant schools were "admitted on the usual terms to Government inspection and aid" (*The Times,* 13 Sept. 1847).

[81]Cf. Chapter 4.

[82]In the annual report for 1840 (*Record,* 23 Apr. 1840).

[83]Bilby became Inspector of Schools for the Society in 1841 (*Record,* 20 Dec. 1841); Ridgway was employed in the depot for books and apparatus and also in devising lessons for teachers (*Record,* 3 Dec. 1840; 31 Mar. 1842).

education was divided into Religious, Moral, Intellectual and Physical aspects, that it should commence with the senses, utilise objects, lead to the formation of correct perceptions, and so on, in the manner of the sixth edition of the *Infant System*.[84] It was also evident in J.S. Reynolds' public advocacy of the importance of love in moral education, the stimulation of the child's natural curiosity, the need to form habits of observation, and to furnish the mind with clear ideas, very much in the words of Wilderspin's interpretation of Pestalozzian principles.[85] It was further evident in the advice of the staff to teachers at a half-yearly meeting in 1842, when they argued for kindness, patience, affection, persuasion and an understanding of human nature in dealing with infants, and when Dunning, the headmaster, (who was in a sense a protegé of Wilderspin) summed up the object of the infant school as the formation of character.[86]

It was evident above all in the curriculum eventually adopted in the Model School of the Society. In 1843 this included Scriptural instruction (given primary place), lessons on objects and toys, the use of coloured pictures, and instruction in human physiology, natural history, form and colour, number (with the aid of a ball frame) geography and drawing. Gallery work was carried out in groups according to age and some monitorial work was done on Wilderspinian lines, and marching and exercise in the playground was also undertaken.[87] The utilisation, by teachers, of the playground as a moral laboratory, and injunctions against cruelty to animals also appeared as part of the Society's repertoire.[88]

Wilderspin dismissed the Society as a mere collection of plagiarists who, coming together after the infant system had been "twenty years in practice", suppressed his works and boosted those by members of the Society, though the latter contained "page after page" of material he could "justly claim...as my own".[89] Was he correct? There were undoubtedly many features of the Society's theory and practice, particularly in the work of Elizabeth Mayo, which echoed Wilderspin's formulations, and on the whole, there were many more similarities than differences. In fact, the Society could do little else but follow in Wilderspin's footsteps; no other viable path was possible. But this did not necessarily imply that the Mayos, for instance, nor Dunning, the headmaster, lacked a theoretical position of their own. The Mayos were followers of Pestalozzi, and in applying his theories to infant education, as Wilderspin had

---

[84] Mayo, *Practical Remarks*, p. 34ff.

[85] *Record*, 15 July 1841.

[86] *Record*, 31 Mar. 1842.

[87] P.P. 1843 XL, Minutes of the Committee of Council on Education 1842-43, S. Tremenheere, "Report on the Model Schools of the Home and Colonial Infant School Society", July 1843, pp. 159-61; *Record*, 23 Apr. 1840; 15 July 1841.

[88] *Record*, 31 Mar. 1842; P.P. 1847 XLV, Tufnell, "Report", App., citing Course of Instruction, p. 573.

[89] *Infant System* (1840), p. 98.

done, were bound to arrive at fairly similar conclusions. Dunning was a student of the Scottish philosophers John Abercrombie and Dugald Stewart;[90] the latter's work on the mind furnished much useful material on perception.[91]

There were, of course, some important differences between the Society and Wilderspin, and the greatest single difference concerned religious and moral education. Where Wilderspin had seen moral education largely in ethical and secular terms, the Society identified moral education with vital Christianity and made religious instruction the prime subject in the curriculum. Though the excesses of the Bilby-Ridgway approach were avoided, religious teaching involved a large amount of verbalism and memory work — Biblical narratives, scripture geography and natural history, the learning of doctrines and precepts, e.g., sin, its consequences and its remedy by the sacrifice of the Saviour.[92] Questions and answers on Biblical pictures were conspicuously absent. One also gains the impression that the Society attempted to infuse the infant classroom with a more solemn and serious tone than Wilderspin was wont to do.[93] It certainly had a social and political outlook very different from his. Where he had included in his books extracts from and praise of Whig leaders' works, encomia of Lancaster and non-denominational education[94] and had generally taken a liberal and at times radical and anti-clerical position, the Society embraced a policy of conservatism and reaction. Brougham, Wyse and Simpson were attacked, Rousseau and Fellenberg condemned, and a "patriotic" stance adopted; an attempt was made to revive "the dying embers of English loyalty" by having infants sing the national anthem, "national airs" and crudely royalist songs, with the express aim of combating Owenism and Chartism.[95]

In the field of teacher training, however, the Home and Colonial Society was undoubtedly very advanced. The course was given in the Model School, which opened in October 1837 under the patronage of the young Queen Victoria, and which superseded the temporary arrangements of the training establishment at Bloomsbury.[96] The period of training, which had lasted only twelve weeks at the beginning of the Society's work, was increased by stages until it reached twenty-four weeks in 1845.[97] By 1847 the Society had trained 1,443 teachers,

[90]P.P. 1843 XL, Tremenheere, "Report", p. 154.

[91]D. Stewart, *Elements of the Philosophy of the Human Mind* (London 1792). Abercrombie's works included *The Culture and Discipline of the Mind* (Edinburgh, 4th ed., 1837) and *Inquiries Concerning the Intellectual Powers* (Edinburgh, 8th ed., 1838).

[92]P.P. 1843 XL, Tremenheere, "Report", App. I., p. 159.

[93]In 1837 Dr. Mayo had argued that "ingenious machinery, amusing pictures, well-combined evolutions and half-ludicrous amusements", dexterity in the application of the principles of numbers and exhibitions for the benefit of visitors and parents could have only a subordinate use in the infant school. The primary role of the teacher was to inculcate morals and religion in a solemn voice and with a devout manner (Mayo, *Practical Remarks,* p. 6; pp. 8-9).

[94]For Wilderspin's praise of Lancaster, cf. *Early Discipline* (1834), p. 202.

[95]*Record,* 5 Mar. 1838; 25 Mar. 1839; 15 July 1841; *Christian Lady's Magazine,* July 1838, pp. 68-9.

[96]*Record,* 18 Jan. 1838.

[97]P.P. 1847 XLV, Tufnell, "Report", p. 558.

mostly single women; some married couples were trained, but no single men.[98] The essential requirements of candidates were "sound moral and religious principles"; before entering training candidates were subject to "the most rigid scrutiny" and, if approved, to "strict moral control" during training.[99] The students worked a 56-hour week during the six months of their course and their studies were divided into three. First, academic work, which occupied 36 hours of the week and largely consisted of the subjects they were to teach; more than one-sixth of this time was devoted to the study of the Scriptures. Second, the principles and practice of education, to which 9¾ hours were devoted. Third, teaching practice in schools for 10¼ hours. This part of the course included observation of other students' teaching, practice lessons which were criticised by other students and by the headmaster, assisting in a school and taking charge of a school under inspection.[100]

The tripartite division of the training course into academic work, the theory of education and teaching practice has endured to this day. The Home and Colonial Society, despite the difficulties it faced with regard to the low educational level of entrants, was far ahead of the National and British Societies (whose training was largely concerned with method) and it preceded by two years the infant training establishment in Dublin set up by Wilderspin. Yet it found that even an extended course was insufficient and that at least half the teachers reverted to the old methods in the course of a year.[101]

But on the whole the teacher training scheme was successful, and to the extent that the Society succeeded in eliminating the major weaknesses of the mid-1830s — the peripatetic training methods and exhibition mania associated with Wilderspin and the excesses of scriptural verbalism inseparable from the Bilby and Ridgway approach — it can be credited with providing a positive solution to the crisis. But the year 1836 marked the end of the era of popular progressivism and individual enterprise in the infant school movement and the beginning of the age of standardisation, central organisation and ultimately of state intervention. Wilderspin was yet to play a role in education for older children in both Liverpool and Dublin and to publish an important work on the subject; but, despite some further activity in infant education in the early 1840s, his career as an infant school missionary, on which he had based his name and fame, was over.

* * * * *

[98]*Ibid.*, pp. 557-58.

[99]*Ibid.*, p. 554; *Record,* 5 Mar. 1838.

[100]P.P. 1847 XLV, Tufnell, "Report", pp. 564-65; App., p. 570.

[101]*Record,* 23 Apr. 1840.

Wilderspin and the progressives in the movement could, however, take some satisfaction from the fact that their methods and principles had not by any means been submerged. In fact, as we have seen, the manuals and treatises of Charles and Elizabeth Mayo added little that was fundamentally new to the established theory and practice of infant education; their main departure from Wilderspin's ideals was on the religious issue. When the Committee of Council on Education, the first government body on education, was formed in 1839, infant education was recognised as having a significant place in the national educational structure. Kay-Shuttleworth, the first secretary of the Council, earlier had been impressed by the infant school of Stow's Glasgow Normal Seminary, particularly the gallery work and the concept of the sympathy of numbers — both originally developed by Wilderspin — and felt that the methods of moral training and playground activity were important enough to be applied to larger schools and older children.[102] When, in the first year of the Council's existence, plans for infant schools were published, the schoolhouse-playground concept was preserved, and the "Special Questions on Infant Schools" issued to Inspectors covered the main lines of the methods established by Wilderspin. The Inspectors were required to look for the number of times periods of recreation occurred, to take note of the exercises, amusement and games of the children and the incidence of singing, drawing, and lessons on natural objects in the curriculum, the degree of affection shown to the teacher, and whether rewards and punishments were employed; awareness of possible abuses of gallery teaching was shown by the question, "Are the replies of the children made intelligently or mechanically or by rote?"[103]

In the first six or seven years of its existence the Home and Colonial Society, because of its strident Evangelicalism and isolation from the Church, made little impact on public life. The Whig-Liberal leaders — Brougham, Russell and Lansdowne — paid virtually no attention to it and continued to view infant education in terms of the Owen-Buchanan-Wilderspin model.[104] Brougham's *Letter on Education to the Duke of Bedford* (1839) did not mention the Society in its section on infant schools, and the inclusion of infant training in the Whig government's scheme for a Normal School, issued in the same year,[105] can be traced to the involvement of Brougham and Lansdowne with the movement over the previous two decades.

[102]P.P. 1838 VII, Education, pp. 4-5.

[103]P.P. 1840 XL, Minutes of the Committee of Council on Education 1839-40. "Plans of School Houses", p. 10ff; P.P. 1841 XX, Minutes of the Committee of Council on Education 1840-41, pp. 11-12.

[104]Cf. Chapters 14 and 16.

[105]P.P. 1839 XL, "Minute of Proceedings of the Committee of the Privy Council on Education of the 11th April 1839", p. 1.

In the mid-1840s Joseph Fletcher, an Inspector who strongly supported the Home and Colonial Society, described what he termed "the theory of the modern infant school". It embraced the physical, intellectual, industrial, moral and religious domains; the child's activities were directed to each in turn, with the aim of implanting good habits of body, heart and mind. Faculties would be developed in natural succession; observation and curiosity were the foundations and the comparison and naming of objects followed. Qualities and colours would then be distinguished, by which means the child would acquire the concepts of space, division and distance, and discover the coincidence and sequence of ideas. Manual exercises, marching and songs, and exercise in the playground (which also had a moral function) completed the scheme.[106] The pedigree of these principles and practices does not need elaboration.

The uniqueness of the infant school, with a theory and practice entirely distinct from the rigid and mechanical practices of the voluntary schools, was thus established in the public mind. Becoming part of the state system, infant schools endured the rigours of the Revised Code of the 1860s, flourished under the School Boards during the last third of the century and despite many difficulties survived to form the basis of the progressive primary schools of the twentieth century. A direct link can thus be traced between the theory and practice of the infant school in the Owen-Buchanan-Wilderspin era and the much admired primary schools of the present day.[107]

[106]P.P. 1846 XXXII, Fletcher, "Report", p. 353ff.

[107]For an elaboration of the points made in this paragraph, cf. D.A. Turner, "1870: The State and the Infant School System", *British Journal of Educational Studies*, Vol. XVIII, No. 2, June 1970, pp. 151-65.

CHAPTER 12

THE LIVERPOOL CORPORATION SCHOOLS 1836-1837

In August 1836 Wilderspin gave up his career as an itinerant educational missionary and accepted an engagement with the Corporation of Liverpool to organise the infant departments of its two non-denominational schools. He was probably chosen by the Corporation as much for his belief in non-denominational education as for his expertise in the infant sphere. With participation in the newly-formed Home and Colonial Infant School Society closed to him, the Liverpool opening offered a chance to put his principles into action in a new and exciting experimental situation.

The new Liverpool Town Council, swept to power in the election following the Municipal Corporations Act of 1835, was almost wholly a Liberal body, with a Unitarian mayor, William Rathbone, and several Dissenters among its members.[1] It had taken the unprecedented step of setting up a committee of twelve of its members (containing eleven Liberals) "to promote the Improvement and Education of the Poorer Classes".[2] Rathbone, a member of a long-established Liverpool family noted for its interest in progressive education,[3] was its chairman. On 29 March 1836 a report of a special sub-committee of the Education Committee, after criticising the facilities of the schools set up by the former council (which were run on strict Church of England lines), recommended extensions to the buildings and the addition of playgrounds. More importantly, the committee added that it would immediately inquire into "what plans have been found most effectual for the Physical Intellectual Moral and Religious improvement of the pupils in similar schools, particularly those adopted by the Irish Education Board"; anything "sectarian" or "exclusive" in the religious instruction should be avoided "in order that the schools may be open to and sought by all".[4] The existing regulations for the North and South Corporation schools, according to a contemporary observer, "amounted to a practical denial of education to Dissenters and Roman Catholics".[5] This was most keenly felt in the North school, situated in one of the

---

[1]J. Murphy, *The Religious Problem in English Education: the Crucial Experiment* (Liverpool 1959), p. 13. This, the standard work on the Liverpool Corporation Schools, is indispensable to an understanding of the situation, both locally and nationally.

[2]L.R.O. 352 MIN/COU II 1/1, Minutes of the Liverpool Town Council, 1835-1838, Minutes 8 Jan. 1836.

[3]Rathbone sent his son to Dr. Mayo's Pestalozzian school at Cheam, Surrey (E.F. Rathbone, *William Rathbone: A Memoir* (London 1905), p. 59). His sister and his daughter were members of the committee of Duncan Street Infant School (J. Murphy, "The Rise of Public Elementary Education in Liverpool: Part Two, 1819-1835", *Transactions of the Historic Society of Lancashire and Cheshire,* Vol. 118, 1966, p. 131).

[4]L.R.O. MIN/EDU I 1/1 Education Committee Minute Book 1836-48, "Report of a Sub-Committee appointed to prepare a General Report of the State of the Schools", Minutes, 29 Mar. 1836.

[5]C.E. Trevelyan, *The Liverpool Corporation Schools* (Liverpool 1840), p. 3.

poorest quarters of Liverpool, where the local population was nearly three-fourths Catholic; about half of the remaining Protestants were Dissenters. The population of Liverpool itself, a sprawling seaport on the north bank of the Mersey, was some quarter of a million, of whom 80,000 were said to be Catholics.[6]

The regulations regarding religious instruction were finally adopted by the Education Committee on 5 July 1836 and ratified at a Town Council meeting the following day. Protestant and Catholic children were to be assembled in the morning for the singing of hymns and the reading of the Irish Scripture Lessons, and one hour of each day was to be set aside for denominational religious instruction (normally to be undertaken by Catholic or Anglican clergy). There followed a phrase which was to be the cause of more opposition to the Education Committee and Council than all the others put together — "and that such hour be in the afternoon after the school has closed".[7]

Though it was followed by the explanation that for this purpose the school would be "considered as closed at 3 o'clock in winter and at 4 in summer" (i.e. one hour before the usual closing time in similar schools), the wording of the regulations gave an opportunity to the Tory and Anglican opponents of the Council, led by the fiery Evangelical Hugh McNeile, perpetual curate of St. Jude's, to whip up a fierce campaign against the Council and its educational policy.[8] The Council's regulations regarding religious education were similar to those of the Irish Board, except that in Ireland a whole day was set aside for religious instruction; what the two systems had in common was the exclusion of the Bible from the hours of literary instruction.[9] This, and the use of Scripture Extracts as a reading book, was sufficient to allow the Evangelicals and their supporters to cry that the Bible was "excluded" from the schools or used in a "mutilated" form.

This opposition to non-denominational education was part of a wider Protestant crusade against the machinations of "Popery"; the main enemy was the Irish Catholic hierarchy, but equally guilty were their allies among the Dissenters and "infidels", who allowed Catholic children into schools and refused to instruct them in the Authorised Version of the Bible. The agitation, which began in 1834 over the Repeal issue, was carried on throughout Ireland, England, Scotland and the Colonies during the late 30s and early 40s by a variously-assorted grouping: the Dublin Conservative Society, the Orange Society, the Protestant Association, the Evangelical wing of the Church, Irish

---

[6]*Ibid.*, pp. 3-4.

[7]Education Committee Minutes, 5 July 1836.

[8]This opposition was in no way lessened after the Education Committee, at the end of the year, had extended the school day by one hour so that religious instruction could be given during the last hour of the school day (Education Committee Minutes, 20 Dec. 1836).

[9]Cf. Chapter 14.

members of the House of Lords and the Tory press.[10] Mass meetings were an important part of the campaign, and in Liverpool on 13 July 1836, a gathering of 5,000, which included almost the whole of the Anglican clergy of the diocese, pledged to withdraw support from the Corporation schools and build schools of their own, wherein free use might be made of "the unmutilated word of God". £3,000 was collected at the meeting for this purpose, increased to £11,000 very soon after.[11]

McNeile, a forty-one year old Irishman, became the chief opponent of the Corporation, assailing it in a series of open letters; using a variety of arguments, notable more for their ingenuity than their truth, he attempted to convince the people of Liverpool that the Bible was excluded from the Corporation schools. Even after a visit to the schools where he saw the Bible being read, he could still maintain:

> *Till three o'clock* the Bible is not, and must not be read. *After three o'clock* it may or may not be read, according to circumstances...The system excludes the Bible, except for one hour. We cannot, by attending during that hour, give our sanction to this system; so that, as far as we are concerned, the system excludes the Bible altogether.[12]

On another occasion he argued that because the Catholic children did not read the Authorised Version of the Bible (though the Protestant children admittedly did), then all children did not read the Bible, and, as a school consisted of all the children and not part of them, he felt justified in maintaining that the Bible was "excluded from the schools".[13]

Thomas Blackburn, a member of the Council, wrote a spirited defence of the system in force in the schools, stressing that religious teaching was offered to all and that it was a "contemptible sophism" to maintain that the Bible was excluded because the school could not be said to exist during the hour when the Bible teaching was given.[14] Despite Blackburn's arguments, and numerous proofs that the children spent an hour a day studying the Authorised or Douai

---

[10]For this campaign, cf. G.A. Cahill, "Comment" on E. Larkin, "The Quarrel Among the Roman Catholic Hierarchy over the National System of Education in Ireland, 1838-41", in R.B. Browne, W.J. Roscelli and R. Loftus (Eds.), *The Celtic Cross* (Purdue 1964), pp. 147-52; cf. also G.F.A. Best, "Popular Protestantism in Victorian Britain", in R. Robson (Ed.), *Ideas and Institutions of Victorian Britain* (London 1967), pp. 115-42, and "Popery in the Colonies", *Protestant Magazine*, Vol. I, Mar. 1839, pp. 33-7.

[11]*A Full Report of the Speeches and Proceedings at the Meeting Held at the Amphitheatre on Wednesday, July 13, 1836, for the Promotion of Scriptural Education in Liverpool* (Liverpool n.d.), *passim.*

[12]Rev. H. McNeile, *Letters on National Education: Addressed to the Town Council of Liverpool* (London 1837), Letter II, 28 Nov. 1836, p. 31. McNeile's statement that the Bible "may or may not be read according to circumstances" referred to the fact that on his visit the Catholic priest due to take the Bible class was late.

[13]Murphy, *Religious Problem,* p. 73, citing a report of a speech by McNeile given on 11 July 1837.

[14]T. Blackburn, *A Defence of the System Adopted in the Corporation Schools of Liverpool* (Liverpool 1836), pp. 29-30; p. 36.

Versions[15], including a public statement by Wilderspin[16], McNeile and the clergy continued to maintain their exclusion thesis. Their efforts were almost successful and they came near to forcing the closure of the Corporation schools. The Anglican clergy (save one, the Rev. J. Aspinall) were refusing to co-operate in religious instruction, and several teachers had resigned. Nearly all the parents, following a poster campaign in the town, had withdrawn their children. On 14 July only 31 boys and 13 girls answered the registers at the North Corporation School.[17] Furthermore, the Church had begun to build schools of its own — "North" and "South" Church of England Schools — to attract Anglican children from the Corporation Schools.[18]

* * * * *

On 5 July 1836 Wilderspin had settled the terms of his engagement with the Liverpool Education Committee. It was agreed that he should have (as he had insisted) a completely free hand for one month, that he should be paid £40 for his services and that he should in addition engage a master or mistress for the North infant school; the committee also decided to order £15 worth of his apparatus for each school.[19] Arriving in the city at the end of August with the prestige of royal patronage behind him,[20] he immediately plunged into the task of assisting the resolute efforts of the Committee to get the schools on their feet again.

Dissenters, Roman Catholic priests and catechists, and members of the Education Committee and their wives were all rallying to the task of teaching and religious instruction, not without danger to themselves.[21] Violence, both verbal and physical, was suffered by children, teachers and committee members alike. Joshua Walmsley, a member of the Committee, recalled:

[15]The timetable for religious instruction for Protestant children in the North School was given by Walmsley in a speech to the Council in October 1836 (*Liverpool Mercury*, 14 Oct. 1836). Wilderspin gives a more detailed timetable for the four classes into which both Protestant and Catholic children were divided in *System of Education* (1840), pp. 250-51.

[16]In a letter to the *Chronicle* he stated that he had observed that every day a Catholic priest read a chapter of St. Luke to the Catholic children and questioned them upon it (*Liverpool Chronicle*, 8 Apr. 1837). Wilderspin, however, was not impressed with the clergy as teachers and felt that this would not answer as a permanent solution (*System of Education* (1840), p. 217; p. 482).

[17]Murphy, *Religious Problem*, p. 67.

[18]*Ibid.*, p. 93. According to Wilderspin these had stone Bibles above the entrance (Cf. Chapter 13).

[19]Education Committee Minutes, 5 and 12 July 1836.

[20]Education Committee Minutes, 24 Aug. 1836; "Mr. Wilderspin is just returned from Windsor", the *Liverpool Times* informed its readers, "where he has been arranging infant schools for her Majesty" (*Liverpool Times*, 9 Aug. 1836).

[21]Murphy, *Religious Problem*, pp. 69-70.

Some of the lower classes maltreated children on their way to the schools, pelted and hooted members of the committee as they passed. The characters of Mr. Blackburn, Mr. Rathbone and my own were daily assailed in pulpits and social gatherings.[22]

Wilderspin himself saw a great number of children from other schools waylay pupils from the Corporation schools "and beat them unmercifully: the little girls even did not escape".[23] On another occasion he himself was "very much hurt" when, with his usual courage, he attempted to turn out of the playground of one of the schools some men who had come to show their opposition to the new system by "using the most improper language".[24]

Gradually, however, the children returned. New teachers were engaged and posters put up advertising that the schools were open to all religious denominations. By November there were 435 children in the boys' and girls' departments of the South school, 133 of whom were Protestant, and the rest Catholic.[25] Despite this, McNeile maintained that the Corporation schools were "Roman Catholic Schools supported entirely by the corporate funds".[26]

In this sort of situation, it must have been heartening to the Committee to have had a nationally-known educationist assisting their efforts at reorganisation. Wilderspin himself was not content to confine his efforts to classroom work. Within a week of his arrival he had begun two series of public lectures; the first, commencing on 31 August, he gave at the Liverpool Mechanics' Institute.[27] The initial lecture was well attended and the *Albion* reported that "the dry humour with which the lecturer treated his subject convulsed the audience with laughter throughout".[28] Another paper reported that the series had excited "great interest" and that at the last lecture more money had been taken at the doors "than on any former occasion".[29] At this gathering, before an audience of some 500, of whom 100 were women, Wilderspin examined a group of children from the Corporation schools, urged the establishment of infant schools in connection with the Institute and concluded with a strong plea for the improved education of working-class women.[30] On the

[22]H.M. Walmsley, *Life of Sir Joshua Walmsley* (London 1879), p. 90.

[23]*System of Education* (1840), p. 323.

[24]*Liverpool Mercury* 23 Sept. 1836.

[25]Murphy, *Religious Problem*, p. 68; p. 89.

[26]McNeile, *Letters on National Education*, Letter VII, 13 Dec. 1836.

[27]*Liverpool Chronicle*, 3 Sept. 1836.

[28]*Albion*, 5 Sept. 1836.

[29]*Liverpool Chronicle*, 17 Sept. 1836.

[30]*Liverpool Mercury*, 23 Sept. 1836.

following day, 1 September, at the Royal Institution, Wilderspin started a second course of lectures on "Developing and Training the Infant Faculties", addressed specifically to "mothers of the middle and upper classes", with an admission fee of 3 shillings per lecture.[31]

Apparently impressed by Wilderspin's activities during the four weeks of his engagement, the Education Committee, at its meeting on 24 September, made two decisions. First, to extend Wilderspin's contract to the end of October and to increase his fee to £100. Second, to invite him to give an exhibition of his system on 13 October. For this purpose application was made to the Finance Committee of the Council for the use of the large ballroom in the Town Hall.[32] The Town Council, however, when the proposal was referred to them by the Finance Committee at the end of September, were by no means favourable to the proposal; there were objections on the grounds that the room might be damaged, and that Wilderspin himself might make something out of the shilling admission charge. After "considerable discussion" and after Rathbone had undertaken to be personally responsible for damage to the rooms, the Finance Committee's resolution was put to the vote and carried by a majority of one.[33]

Up to this time Wilderspin's activities had attracted little notice in the Tory papers. But when they learned that he was to lead an invasion of the ballroom of the Town Hall by the children of the Irish poor he was greeted with a verbal hailstorm that left him no doubt as to where he stood with the Committee's enemies. "Who this Mr. Wilderspin is", thundered the *Mail* in an editorial ten days before the event, "...is no concern of ours. But it strikes us that the ballroom of the Town Hall is not a convenient place for any such nursery for experimenting on infantine ideas..."; if the hall were to be "open to every caper, or at the service of every travelling empiric", then use of it could be claimed for "Mr. Atkin's menagerie of monkeys, and an exhibition of mental development of his blue baboon, and his astonishing elephant..."[34] A week later the *Mail,* in the meantime having identified Wilderspin as a "cockney lecturer on infant education", returned to the attack in a piece entitled "Infant Education Quackery".

The essence of the quackery, in the editor's opinion, lay in "grinding poor little brats in...scientific requirements"; teaching anything more than the minimum necessary to their future role in life was "not only useless but positively vicious".[35] Wilderspin, always ready to defend the right of the poor to education,

---

[31]*Liverpool Journal,* 27 Aug. 1836; cf. also a leaflet entitled "Mr. Wilderspin, the Originator of the Infant System, Will Deliver a Course of Four Lectures on His Method of Developing and Training the Infant Faculties..." (Wilderspin Papers). Wilderspin also gave some private lectures at Gateacre, residence of the Unitarian divine Dr. William Shepherd, a supporter of the Corporation schools (*Early Discipline,* (1840), p. 331).

[32]Education Committee Minutes, 24 Sept. 1836.

[33]*Early Discipline* (1840), p. 327; Town Council Minutes, 30 Sept. 1836; *Albion,* 3 Oct. 1835, reporting Town Council meeting.

[34]*Liverpool Mail,* 4 Oct. 1836.

[35]*Liverpool Mail,* 11 Oct. 1836.

was stung to the quick, and defended his position in two long and impassioned letters to the *Albion* and the *Telegraph.* He pointed out that most of the children in question lived on bread and potatoes, and that there was usually only one room for the whole family to eat, cook, sleep and play in. Yet those who were "eternally prating about the church, the Bible, and religion" compared the children to animals and denounced those who supported the principle of teaching the child of poor parents:

> Never mind if it does not know a pink from a mushroom, or a sunflower from a cow cabbage; it is a species of knowledge which must be reserved for the rich, because, forsooth, the poor child may have to get his living, when he becomes a man, by the sweat of his brow. Is this religion, to deny any of God's creatures information because they are poor? Did He give His book of nature for the rich only to read?

The elements of geometry, geography and other sciences, he argued, would benefit the children of Liverpool in every way. "The poor are greater fools than I take them to be", he concluded, "if they sit contented and allow the learned fools to make fools of them and their offspring many years longer".[36]

These exchanges roused to fever heat the interest in the exhibition of children at the Town Hall. At 10:30 a.m. on the morning of Thursday, members of the Education Committee were receiving guests at the door of the Town Hall;[37] by 11:00 a.m. the ballroom, which could hold 1,000 people, was reported to be "crowded to excess by a highly respectable assemblage, of whom the greater number were ladies". In the orchestra recess were the Mayor and other members of the Council, and at one end of the hall, in the specially-erected gallery, sat some 300 children between the ages of 3-5 years. Before Wilderspin commenced, Mr. Rathbone who (it was reported) took "great interest in the arrangement of the children, the success of the exhibition, and the comfort of the spectators", announced that because of the great crowd, those who could not get in or chose to retire might have their tickets returned and come to another exhibition to be given by Wilderspin on the following Saturday.[38] The room was "excessively crowded" according to the *Standard,* and the proceedings commenced "in the midst of pushing, and squeezing, and tip-toe jostlings of short ladies".[39]

Wilderspin informed the audience that he did not stand there as a theorist, but as one "who had made experiment of what he asserted"; he begged them to judge the actions of the infants as those of children, for however ridiculous or silly their motions might be to adults, they were sensible to young children. Everything the children would demonstrate had been learned by them in five or

---

[36]*Liverpool Telegraph,* 12 Oct. 1836; *Albion,* 17 Oct. 1836.

[37]Education Committee Minutes, 11 Oct. 1836.

[38]*Liverpool Chronicle,* 15 Oct. 1836.

[39]*Liverpool Standard,* 14 Oct. 1836.

six weeks and great credit was due to the teachers "who had faithfully followed his directions".[40] At both exhibitions Wilderspin put the children through the routines of singing and chanting, question and answer and arm and body movements.[41] At the conclusion the children were provided with buns and the teachers with wine (which Wilderspin paid for himself) and then the infants were transported back home in omnibuses specially provided by Mrs. Rathbone, mother of the chairman of the Education Committee.[42]

The whole performance, and particularly the omnibuses, proved too much for the opponents of the schools. "I found waiting on one side of the Town-hall", wrote an incensed citizen to the *Mail*, "four omnibuses which were about to convey the little darlings from the splendid saloon of the Town-hall to their bare school-rooms and dirty homes. Truly this is the age of quackery and humbug".[43] The letter was one of several printed in Conservative newspapers, all critical in various ways of Wilderspin's exhibitions, which undoubtedly were an obvious target for opponents of the system. He had never before, however, been assailed in such a scurrilous manner. The performances of the children at the exhibitions were likened to a whole menagerie of birds and beasts. Blue baboons and elephants having already been claimed by the editor of the *Mail*, "well trained dancing dogs and learned pigs" were preferred by "Democritus". Birds were the choice of the *Standard*, the answers of the children being compared with "a parrot's loquacity" or the effect possible to obtain "from a bullfinch by repeated trainings, which, when the first bar of a tune which it has been taught is whistled, will repeat the whole".[44]

Shortly after the exhibitions, the children of both the schools were taken on a visit to "the splendid and well-stocked gardens" of the Liverpool Zoological Society. The proprietors, however, fearing injury to the animals, flowers and shrubs, refused to allow the children to enter without a monetary deposit against damage. Wilderspin handed over the required amount without hesitation, knowing "the effects of moral training; long experience had taught me that in this I could scarcely err". Ever alert to observe the effects of his teaching, he noticed that those children who he had instructed in the elements of natural history and to whom he had shown coloured pictures of animals, stood before them with "a bold front and confident air", observing "with delight and pleasure, without any mixture of fear", whereas those who had just joined the school and lacked such teaching "shrunk, cowering and terrified behind their better taught companions". Needless to say, Wilderspin pocketed his deposit as they left the gardens amid complimentary remarks on the behaviour of the children.[45]

[40]*Liverpool Chronicle*, 15 Oct. 1836.

[41]*Liverpool Chronicle*, 15 Oct. 1836; *Albion*, 17 Oct. 1836; *Liverpool Times*, 18 Oct. 1836.

[42]*Early Discipline* (1840), pp. 327-28.

[43]Letter signed "Democritus" in *Liverpool Mail*, 18 Oct. 1836.

[44]*Liverpool Standard*, 14 Oct. 1836.

[45]*Early Discipline* (1840), pp. 328-30.

The middle-class supporters of the Corporation schools were commonly used to seeing poor children dirty, badly dressed, mouthing profanities and running around the streets. Their decorous behaviour in exhibitions and public places provided a model of the urban working-class child that the middle class wanted to see;[46] it also confirmed their belief that what the Council was doing was correct, and strengthened their resolve to continue their support. In this sense, Wilderspin's exhibitions — quite apart from his work in the schools — served a useful purpose in reconciling the Council and the public. The Conservatives were not unaware of this. The *Standard* felt that the exhibitions were a "ruse" on the part of the Education Committee to bring the Corporation schools "again into favourable notice".[47]

Of Wilderspin's actual work in reorganising the infant schools there are few accounts. The American educationist A.D. Bache made the cryptic remark that the schools "offered me an example for inspection, though not of the most favourable kind".[48] C.E. Trevelyan, civil servant and educationist, and a son-in-law of Zachary Macaulay, who wrote a pamphlet on the Corporation schools following a visit some two years after Wilderspin had left the Council's employment, was more positive, though he confined most of his observations to the religious instruction. No distinctions of any kind were allowed in the infant schools, he wrote; girls and boys, Protestant and Catholic, were united in prayer in the mornings (a practice which did not take place in the upper schools).[49] The religious instruction Trevelyan described as "peculiarly Christian" in the broadest sense; its aim was to foster the love of God and the love of man.[50] Wilderspin, it might be said, had left his trade-mark on the schools. He had, he recalled later, in his only reference to the teaching there, confined religious instruction to questions and answers on Scripture pictures and taken care to see that no catechisms were used.[51] For the rest there is silence, apart from Trevelyan's general conclusion that "the Corporation Infant Schools differ in no respect from other infant schools, except that they are in higher order than most others".[52]

* * * * *

[46] A Liberal paper significantly remarked of the second exhibition, "If they had been the best-bred children in the town, their behaviour could not have been more exemplary" (*Liverpool Times,* 18 Oct. 1836).

[47] *Liverpool Standard,* 14 Oct. 1836.

[48] A.D. Bache, *Report on Education in Europe* (Philadelphia 1839), p. 158. Bache may have had scruples about the religious teaching. He appeared to favour the model infant school of the Glasgow Evangelicals. (*Ibid.,* pp. 159-66).

[49] The Roman Catholic priests refused to allow Catholic children in the upper schools to join with Protestants for prayer (Murphy, *Religious Problem,* p. 212.) They did allow, of course, Catholic children to receive non-denominational religious instruction (from the Irish Scripture Extracts) at the hands of Protestant teachers.

[50] C.E. Trevelyan, *The Liverpool Corporation Schools* (Liverpool 1840), p. 6.

[51] *System of Education* (1840), p. 221.

[52] Trevelyan, *Corporation Schools,* p. 6.

The Council and the Education Committee, despite their admirable intention of opening their schools to children of all creeds, had begun their work with a somewhat narrow and restricted view of the scope and content of education for the poor. The first report of the Education Committee in May 1836 had, not uncharacteristically for middle-class Liberals (even advanced ones), recommended economy as a most important consideration in any plans for the benefit of the poor,[53] and the Ladies' Committee had also been instructed to practise a similar economy and to limit education to what would fit the girls to become "domestic servants, wives or mothers".[54] Once their work had begun, however, the Liberals found the experiment an education in itself. Rathbone was on friendly terms with Wyse and Simpson and an admirer of Combe,[55] so it was not surprising to find these educationists lecturing in Liverpool during 1836 and 1837.[56] The Liberals' conception of education was enlarged, and Wilderspin's own lectures and his activity in the infant schools furthered the process.

As the Council began to make changes in the schools, expenditure rose, which angered their opponents. Undoubtedly the Liberals' most significant forward step was their decision, in January 1837, to request Wilderspin to return to Liverpool "to undertake the arrangements of the Corporation Schools for Three Months at a remuneration of one hundred and fifty pounds",[57] and later to extend this engagement till the end of August.[58] Wilderspin's salary — a notional £600 per annum — was five or six times that of even the most highly paid teacher. His appointment led to even greater expenditure, for the virtual abandonment of the monitorial system at his instigation led the Council to engage highly qualified teachers at high salaries;[59] Robert Neilson, the headmaster of the North School, had a degree and was paid £110 per annum; the other teachers were also well paid, the women teachers' salaries being equal to those of the men.[60]

---

[53]"Report of a Sub-Committee", *loc. cit.*

[54]Education Committee Minutes, 7 Apr. 1836, "General Instructions to the Ladies' Committee".

[55]Rathbone attended a dinner in honour of James Simpson at Manchester on 25 May 1836, at which Wyse presided. Rathbone proposed a toast to George Combe (Murphy, *Religious Problem*, pp. 40-41).

[56]Simpson lectured on education in Liverpool in May 1836 (*Liverpool Mercury*, 6 May 1836), Combe in April 1837 (*Liverpool Chronicle*, 29 Apr. 1837) and Wyse in September 1837 (T. Wyse, M.P., *Speech Delivered at the Opening of the New Mechanics' Institution, Mount Street, Liverpool, on the 15th of September, 1837* (Liverpool 1837).

[57]Education Committee Minutes, 14 Jan. 1837.

[58]*Ibid.*, 28 Apr. 1837.

[59]In 1840 Rathbone made this point to a critic. The total salaries in the two schools in 1840 amounted to £1,350; in 1828, under the old Council, it has been £370 (Murphy, *Religious Problem*, p. 216).

[60]Neilson appears as "Robert J. Nelson (sic), A.M". on a letter which Wilderspin used in the national education campaign in Cheltenham in November 1837 (Cf. Chapter 13). Neilson received £110 per annum, an increase of £18 on the salary of his predecessor ("Report of a Sub-Committee", *loc. cit.*; North Corporation Schools, Committee Minutes, Dec. 1837). The female teachers received £70 per annum each, the same sum as Emanuel Morris, the infant teacher at the North School (North Corporation Schools, Committee Minutes, 1 May 1837). Wilderspin was impressed with the quality of the teaching. "I never met with children in *any* school, or under *any* circumstances, who were better taught than the children in these schools" (*System of Education* (1840), p. 222).

For nearly eight months Wilderspin was to be engaged in reorganising and improving the practices in the schools for older children, a field in which he had little direct experience. He was on record, however, as having declared that some of his principles and methods could with advantage be introduced into schools of this kind,[61] and he obviously welcomed the opportunity to put his belief into practice. As part of his duties he submitted, in March, a memorandum containing suggestions for the running of the schools and an outline of the policies which he felt the Education Committee should pursue.[62]

As was usual with Wilderspin's writing, the arrangement of the material was somewhat haphazard, but many of the points he made were interesting and valid, though his own particular prejudices surfaced here and there. His acceptance of a high teacher-pupil ratio was evident in the suggestion that two mistresses and three masters in each school was sufficient staffing; more would be "in the way" and "quite unnecessary". His concern for morality led him to suggest that a residence for one or more teachers be attached to the premises, so that the children might at all times be under the eye of some responsible person, particularly if the children should want to use the playground out of school hours. Moral education — and "respect for private property" — would also be furthered if each school had a garden planted in the playground. His long-held belief about the need for male teachers found expression in his recommendation for the infant schools: a master in charge would better carry out the essentials of the infant school system, avoiding the fatigue (and recourse to "the parrot system") to which he felt female teachers were liable; this would be the more desirable as it was the intention to make the infant schools into model schools. Finally, the schools should be free; this would increase attendance, thus taking potential juvenile delinquents off the streets and bringing in more Protestants.

This touched upon wider issues, and in this area Wilderspin's latent anti-Catholicism asserted itself. Though he disliked bigoted Protestant clergymen, he was opposed to Catholicism *tout court*. It was necessary for the Committee to attempt to get equal numbers of Protestant and Catholic children in the schools, to be firm in their policy and to keep power in their own hands, for to please both parties would require the utmost firmness and wisdom. The Committee knew the worst the Protestant clergy could do, but were perhaps unaware of the power of the Catholic priest over his flock. The Catholics should have no power in the infant schools, as these were not run on the lines of the Irish system, and Wilderspin warned against the possibility of the Catholics obtaining control of the Corporation schools as a whole; this would lead to "the destruction of the schools, united opposition from the Protestants of Great Britain and much injury to the cause of liberality".

---

[61] *Infant Education* (1829), p. 277; P.P. 1835 VII, Report from the Select Committee on Education in England and Wales, p. 21: "I would introduce some of the principles of development we adopt, and a method of teaching the child to think".

[62] Wilderspin Papers, "Subjects Worth the Attention of the Committee of Corporation Schools in order to follow up their proposed plan of Education" (31 Mar. 1837).

He saw the whole experiment as something wider in significance than a storm in a teacup in a provincial city. The Corporation schools of Liverpool, he pointed out, were the first of their kind in Britain, and "if we succeed, it will be one of the greatest moral triumphs in Education which has ever been made in this kingdom". Whichever of his suggestions (and those of the masters) the Committee put into operation, he concluded, they would be "steps so far gained towards *uniformity, a National System of education, from infancy to completion,* and which really will combine a system of religious, moral, physical, and intellectual education which I believe does not at present exist in this country".

Wilderspin's view of the schools as the forerunners of a national undenominational network followed that of the more radical members of the Council. One of the first acts of Rathbone when appointed chairman of the Education Committee had been to write to Brougham to inquire if he had any immediate intention of bringing forward a measure of national education which might serve as a guide to the Committee.[63] The national context of the experiment was further emphasised when Rathbone circularised the Council in November 1836, reminding them that it had been planned to make the schools into model training institutions once they were better organised. This would extend their benefits over the country and prove "the practicability of a National System which should include a religious education *for all";* at the subsequent Council meeting Thomas Blackburn made a similar statement.[64]

Wilderspin's understanding of the revolutionary nature of the project impelled him to make greater changes than perhaps he otherwise would have done. He faced a somewhat difficult situation in that he was an outsider brought in to instruct established teachers in methods of his own devising. Reserving only the teaching of singing for himself, he concentrated on initiating the teachers of the junior classes into teaching with pictures, and assisted them "to enter into the spirit of the playground arrangements". On the whole, he felt, "we jogged on tolerably well together"; but he sensed a certain unease on the part of one or two of them at being instructed by someone who had previously directed almost all his attention to infants.[65]

He must, however, have got on exceedingly well with one of the female teachers at the South Corporation School, Mary Dowding, a young widow, for he married her a year later.[66] Perhaps this explained the rebuke which the management of the North Corporation School found it necessary to record in their minutes on 1 May:

---

[63]U.C.L. Brougham Mss., 23033, Rathbone to Brougham, 2 Feb. 1836.

[64]Murphy, *Religious Problem,* p. 86; p. 89.

[65]*Early Discipline* (1840), p. 330.

[66]Cf. Chapter 14.

Mr. Wilderspin was informed by the Committee that they considered the North School to have a claim upon him for a larger measure of his attention than it has hitherto enjoyed — and he was empowered to carry his plans into operation in conjunction with the Masters and Mistresses of the Schools — reporting to the Committee from time to time his progress.[67]

Whichever way he divided his time, Wilderspin was making sweeping changes in the organisation of the schools. This is clear from the complaints of a hostile critic, a former teacher in the schools named Alexander Farrill. "The passion for change and experiment had free scope", he wrote, "the children were to be educated, as it were, by *steam*...things were to be done at a *rail-road rate*". The monitorial system of Dr. Bell, inherited from pre-Education Committee days was abandoned; there were "Systems from Ireland, Models from London, and Methods from Edinburgh...every pretender to some new discovery in the *art* and *mystery* of School Teaching was sure of being entertained, if not well paid, by the Corporation School Committee..." The school resounded to "the *chanting, reciting, singing, clapping* and *marching* processes", to the neglect, Farrill alleged, of their *"spelling, reading, writing, sewing* and *knitting"*, which, he felt, "must of necessity continue (notwithstanding the march of intellect) to be the essentials of female education at school". The result of "the new experiments", he concluded, was a dramatic fall in attendance.[68]

Wilderspin, inevitably, took up the challenge. He began by offering to meet Farrill in public debate "within twenty-four hours".[69] When this was not taken up, he wrote a long letter to the *Chronicle,* couched in the highly-coloured style in which he excelled, with the object of preventing "an undue prejudice being excited against the schools". He insisted that his system had "succeeded admirably", claimed superiority for his methods of singing (in Farrill's school he observed boys sang "through the nose") and condemned the old system, in which "sit still" was the constant command, for its exclusion of movement and physical exercise. Many of Farrill's charges were false, he maintained, particularly that concerning the drop in attendance; this was due partly to the cold winter weather, partly to the opening of a new Church school but mainly, he implied, to the conduct of the opponents of the schools. "We are going on swimmingly now", he concluded.[70] In fact, the North Corporation School, when Wilderspin wrote the letter, had an attendance of 235 boys, 175 girls and 110 infants.[71]

[67]L.R.O. 352 EDU 1/5/1 North Corporation Schools Bevington Bush Sub-Committee Minute Book, Vol. I, 1837-1849, Minutes, 1 May 1837.

[68]A. Farrill, *The Schoolmaster's Appeal to Public Candour* (Liverpool 1837), p. 14 ff.

[69]*Albion,* 27 Mar. 1837.

[70]*Liverpool Chronicle,* 8 Apr. 1837.

[71]North Corporation Schools, Committee Minutes, 1 May 1837.

A more oblique attack on Wilderspin's educational theories was made by no less a person than McNeile himself. In the first week of January 1837 McNeile had given a lecture to young persons on "present modes of education". In an obvious reference to Wilderspin and those who thought like him, he had pointed out that the meaning of education was said to be the drawing out of the reasoning faculties and the communication at any one time of only as much as the youthful mind could understand. This sounded plausible but it was wrong. Why? "The first and crowning reason is that it is not God's plan in the Bible". God spoke words man did not and cannot understand, and prophets did not fully understand what they were saying:

> This is God's mode of teaching. The modern fashionable system reverses this mode: it simplifies the language, so that the human mind is enabled to comprehend every step as it goes along. See the mischief. The mind becomes habituated to make its own comprehension the standard of truth.

A man so instructed, asserted McNeile, leaping over a large gap in logic, can never know God. Furthermore the new system, he continued in his well-known syllogistic manner, would get rid of "mystery"; the Bible, however, is full of mysteries; therefore the new system will eventually get rid of the Bible. "Let them therefore call our old system the parrot system. . .the new system, which goes synthetically to work, putting one proposition after another — not asking the mind to receive one till it has comprehended the preceding, and so carrying it up to the highest elevation the intellect can reach, is an infidel system".[72]

This farrago of nonsense hardly needed a reply and there is no evidence that Wilderspin made one. The specific complaints of both McNeile and Farrill were, however, the strongest evidence that Wilderspin was introducing some important innovations. He was making what was almost certainly the first conscious attempt to dismantle the monitorial or "parrot" system on grounds of principle; and he was attempting to put in its place a mode of education which was based to a large extent on the theoretical ideas set out in Chapter 9.

This is confirmed by Trevelyan's description of the upper schools, in which we may recognise some typical Wilderspinian features. First, the use of monitors was confined to "management" and the best parts of other systems had been adopted, particularly "the methods recommended by Pestalozzi, Wood, etc., for sharpening and quickening the intellect, and communicating a variety of useful information". The great object was "to teach the children to think correctly and to understand everything as they go on. The variety of aspects in which the same thing is presented to them, until they have thoroughly appropriated it, is quite extraordinary". Tangible objects, pictures and Wilderspin's arithmeticon were in constant use, and much attention was paid to the structure of the language and its Latin and Saxon roots.[73]

[72]*Liverpool Courier*, 4 and 18 Jan. 1837.

[73]Trevelyan, *Corporation Schools*, pp. 7-8.

Second, the curriculum had been greatly widened; in addition to the 3Rs, lessons were given to both boys and girls in natural history, geography and astronomy, illustrated by maps, globes and simple experiments.[74] Much of this was apparently due to the influence of Neilson who, in August 1838, had memorialised the North School Committee on the importance of providing varied apparatus for mechanical, chemical, geographical and astronomical studies.[75]

Third, playgrounds had become an integral part of the educational process. Whenever a class began to get weary, it was turned into the playground to enjoy itself for a few minutes. The masters were always present in the playground, took part in the games and lost no opportunity to recommend honesty and humanity and to discountenance their opposites; "Scripture texts of the most practical tendency", which adorned the playground, assisted their efforts.[76] The boys' playground was equipped with "swinging poles", and, according to Wilderspin, all were laid out with flowers and trees in knot gardens, the borders of which the children surrounded with shells gathered from the nearby shore.[77]

Fourth, the jury system, "the public administration of justice", had been introduced. In all cases of offences against morality or loss of personal articles, an assembly of the whole school heard evidence for and against and passed their own judgment.[78] Finally, there were many out-of-school and extra-curricular activities: visits to scientific demonstrations or the zoo, the provision of libraries in each school, and in the South school the establishment of a choir and a museum (largely stocked by sailor fathers). Gymnastic apparatus was also provided for the boys, and they became so expert in its use that they could, as Wilderspin later recalled, "jump eight feet high, and would be pleased to see a tall gentleman come to visit them, over whom they might jump with his hat on".[79]

In a relatively short time the Corporation schools had become the most advanced of their kind in the country, giving a wider range of subjects and introducing more healthful and creative practices than almost any other schools for the poor. "I believe", said Wilderspin, "they are the only schools in this kingdom for poor children in which are to be found a system of religious — moral — intellectual and physical education united".[80] James Simpson,

[74]*Ibid.*, p. 9.

[75]North Corporation Schools, Committee Minutes, 8 Aug. 1838.

[76]Trevelyan, *Corporation Schools,* p. 8.

[77]North Corporation Schools, Committee Minutes, 22 June 1837; *Cheltenham Chronicle,* 26 Oct. 1837, reporting a speech by Wilderspin.

[78]Trevelyan, *Corporation Schools,* pp. 7-8.

[79]Trevelyan, *Corporation Schools,* p. 9; *Cheltenham Chronicle,* 26 Oct. 1837.

[80]*National Education* (1837), p. 32.

impressed in particular by the liberal religious teaching, enthusiastically informed Brougham that he considered the schools "as immortalising William Rathbone"; they were "not only the best schools in Liverpool but are not exceeded by any I have seen".[81]

They stood in sharp contrast to the average monitorial school with its emphasis (in Professor Perkin's words) "on self-help and emulation, the constant tests and examinations and striving for place in the class, the concentration on work and discipline to the exclusion of play and physical exercise, [which] made the school a microcosm of the competitive, authoritarian, class-ridden world outside".[82] The Liverpool schools, however, were not only a moral indictment of the average school for the poor; they functioned as centres for the diffusion of the new education. Young people came to the schools to be trained and these teachers carried ideas away with them. The teacher training was carried out in a thorough fashion. Before gaining their certificate the candidates had to demonstrate that they could manage each division of the school in turn, both in schoolroom and playground. The regular teachers were requested to impress on the trainees "the new and distinguishing features...in the institution, viz., physical and moral education", and to give special attention to this aspect of the training. Work in the playground was considered of particular importance and the students had to attend there every day, to see that no injury was done to the flowers and shrubs and "anxiously to watch for the manifestations of character in all the pupils, so that the duty may become habitual to them when they get to their own schools".[83]

* * * * *

The Corporation schools, though too short-lived to form the nucleus of a country-wide system, did have some impact on national policy. In October 1838, Lord John Russell, Home Secretary in Melbourne's Whig administration, visited the schools, and their harmonious arrangements helped to persuade the government that religious instruction should be given to pupils of all denominations when they issued their plans for national Model and Normal Schools in April 1839.[84] This proposal had to be abandoned in face of pressure from the Church and Conservative opinion. In Liverpool also the Liberals were feeling the pressure from this powerful alliance. The Conservatives, influenced by McNeile's continuing opposition and his cynical manipulation of Protestant forces, particularly the Protestant Operative Association, whittled away the Liberals' majority in successive elections until a Conservative Council was

---

[81] U.C.L. Brougham Mss., 15919, Simpson to Brougham, 24 Nov. 1837.

[82] H. Perkin, *The Origins of Modern English Society* (London 1969), p. 295.

[83] *System of Education* (1840), pp. 251-52.

[84] This is Dr. Murphy's view; for the background to the relationship between the Liverpool experiment and national policy, cf. *Religious Problem,* Chapters 8 and 9.

installed at the end of 1841. One of their first acts was to issue a new set of rules for the Corporation schools which virtually turned them into Anglican institutions. Though all children were required to read the Authorised Version and join in prayer twice a day, the Conservatives apparently believed that Catholic children would continue to attend. Almost all Catholic children were withdrawn, however; the two headmasters Neilson and Buchanan resigned, and in January 1842 the Liverpool experiment came to an end.[85]

Wilderspin's last act for the Council had been to hold, in August 1837, public examinations of the children under his charge. These, coming after the notorious Bible election of July in which the Conservatives had used the exclusion issue in a violent campaign which unseated the Liberal incumbent, were largely intended to convince the public that the charges of the Council's opponents were false. The examinations were announced as commencing with "the Scriptural examination of the children"; the older children, in fact, were questioned about little else. The Rev. James Aspinall and the Rev. George Stokes, the only two Anglican clergymen to support the Education Committee, examined the Protestant children, assisted by J.J. Carruthers, "a minister of the Independent denomination" who was in no way connected with the schools and who felt that "the amount and accuracy of Bible knowledge possessed is astonishing".[87] The theological tenor was decidedly Evangelical, which suggests that Aspinall and Stokes did not differ greatly from their colleagues in this respect. Trevelyan also noticed this tendency in the religious instruction in the upper schools.[88]

It is possible that the exhibition had once again been used as a public relations exercise, making use of Wilderspin's talents to impress the public.[89] The Education Committee appeared to have little faith in the exhibition as an educational instrument, for it abandoned it on Wilderspin's departure. According to Trevelyan, these displays "always depressed timidity and encouraged self-conceit, and they are really no test at all, as no school is so badly conducted that it may not be shown to advantage on such occasions".[90] This had not been the view of the popular press in Wilderspin's heyday. In fact, until he came to Liverpool his public examinations had excited nothing but wonder and praise in the newspapers. In that city, however, for the first time, his methods received serious criticism. As a coda to his Liverpool experiences, it is

[85]Murphy, *Religious Problem*, Chapter 11, for the details.

[86]*Ibid.*, pp. 95-8.

[87]Walmsley, *Life of Walmsley*, p. 94.

[88]Trevelyan, *Corporation Schools*, p. 10, "With regard to the nature of this instruction, I shall perhaps describe it best, by saying that it is strictly of the kind usually termed 'Evangelical'".

[89]*Albion*, 28 Aug. 1837; *Liverpool Telegraph*, 30 Aug. 1837, for descriptions of the exhibitions.

[90]Trevelyan, *Corporation Schools*, p. 10.

worthwhile examining the controversy, for though there was an element of *parti pris* in the attacks of his opponents, they also laid bare some of the weaknesses of this form of educational display and, by extension, in Wilderspin's role as an educational entrepreneur.

Before doing so, it will be instructive briefly to examine the purpose and content of the exhibition. The object, quite simply, was to advertise the system;[91] the methods usually employed are summed up in an (uncritical) description by the *Caledonian Mercury* of Wilderspin's Edinburgh exhibition of April 1829:

> Whether the exercise was reading, spelling, explaining in natural and Scripture history, mental calculation, rapid enumeration of little balls shown by one of their monitors, and sung very sweetly — geometrical figures, illustrated by objects pointed out by the infants in the room, such as five circles in the lustres, a perpendicular in the chain, a horizontal in the floor, & c. — the compass — the clock — whether they sat, or rose, or faced, by whistle, beat time, sung, or marched, showing by signs as they moved with measured step to their own song, how they sow the corn, and reap the corn, and thrash the corn — they were equally at home.[92]

However superficially attractive to the untutored eye all this might be, it was virtually a negation of the spirit of the infant system, founded as it was on the provision of healthful exercise, the inculcation of moral behaviour and the promotion of individual mental activity. The system, as the *Stamford Mercury* pointed out, had to be seen in operation many times, both in the schoolroom and the playground, properly to be appreciated.[93] The *Scotsman,* likewise a supporter of Wilderspin, did not hesitate to assert that the "real gems" of the system were lost among "the rubbish" of the antics of the children on the platform.[94]

Wilderspin himself was also constrained to admit that his exhibitions gave but an imperfect view of his system[95]; but the logic of his position compelled him to hold them. As long as he had to earn his living as an independent educator, he was forced to advertise his wares to the public in the most attractive way, even though the method contradicted his theoretical aims. In normal cicumstances, during a brief visit to a city, this went unnoticed or received muted criticism. But in the maelstrom of Liverpool educational politics Wilderspin experienced sustained opposition for the first time and the weak points of his armoury were mercilessly exposed. The verbatim account in the Tory *Liverpool Standard* of the Town Hall exhibition of October 1836 and the accompanying commentary

[91]Cf. *Extracts on Infant Schools* (Bury 1835.), a pamphlet containing accounts of several of Wilderspin's Scottish exhibitions. The same pamphlet was later reprinted under the title *Extracts on the Advantages of Mr. Wilderspin's Training System* (London 1840).

[92]*Caledonian Mercury,* 27 Apr. 1829.

[93]*Lincoln, Rutland and Stamford Mercury,* 23 Mar. 1832.

[94]*Scotsman,* 22 Aug. 1835.

was a salutary departure from previous paeans of praise. Many of the children, according to the *Standard,* repeated in "a semi-shout...the words which had been drilled into them by frequent lessons"; others, however, were "gaping in wonder at the gilt ornamental ceiling...looking this way and...that, their attention evidently engaged with the novel scene around them". After some allegedly mechanical answers to arithmetical question, the children sang songs, imitated movements and chanted rhymes before moving on to general knowledge:

"Now, my dears, let me see if you can't think; automatons can't think, you know. How much is twenty pence?" "One shilling and eight pence". "How much is twice two and one over?" "Three", replied one young urchin in a corner, and was, of course, followed by "Three" from half the number of children. "Think, you there now; you don't think. You shall have time to rest a bit; now, try again. How much is three times one and a half of two?" "Twelve", "Think, my dears. Now, then, how much is it?" "Twelve, nine, seven, sixteen", immediately answered a hundred different voices. "No, my dears, you don't think. How much is five times two?" "Twelve". No, my dears, you don't think; try again?" "Seven, thirteen, six, ten". "Very well". Then, repeating the lesson in rotation, the children got into the beaten track and answered readily. "Now, my dears, what is the capital of England?" "London". "Of France?" "Paris". "Of Switzerland?" "Berne". I have a great, large, big basket of buns. Do you like buns?" "Iss". "Will you eat 'em fair, and not pick the currants off?" "Iss". "Now, what is the capital of Germany?" "Scotland?" "Some boy says Scotland. Don't you think you ought to have two buns for that?"

According to the reporter, the children then answered, "with the glibness of a well-trained parrot", questions on rhomboids, spheroids and equilateral triangles which "Euclid has deemed worthy of elaborate problems to explain".[96] A correspondent in the *Mail* felt that the production of a few unmeaning phrases, at the call of a dexterous instructor, in a context of "excitement and false notoriety" unfitted children for "the humble drudgery which the poverty of their homes necessarily imposes on them".[97] A writer in the *Courier,* not unsympathetic to Wilderspin's intentions, asked, "Is this the proper way to deal with the infant mind?" A knowledge of octagons and pentagons, obtuse and equilateral triangles, or of the capitals of Corsica, Iceland, Saxony and Switzerland was learned before the infant could have "any notion of the face of the globe" or understand what the word "capital" meant. "Is it not evident", the writer went on, "that these are mere parrot sounds, suggested by the association of words, without any definite idea of the thing signified?" Wilderspin, the writer pointed out, constantly appealed to the child's imitative ability, and thus the

[95] *Early Discipline* (1832), p. 245.

[96] *Liverpool Standard,* 14 Oct. 1836.

[97] Letter signed "Democritus" in *Liverpool Mail,* 18 Oct. 1836.

children, in repeating that Dresden was the capital of Saxony, were merely imitating the teacher. Not only was this "a very near approach to the old drill system"; it was also a "forcing process" and "hot-house education", and "more than the nervous energy of a child of three, four or five years of age is capable of sustaining".[98]

Little more need be said. Further criticisms of the exhibition were made by J.R. Wood of Manchester in 1838,[99] by Cruikshank in his *Comic Almanack* in 1843[100] and by H.M.I. Joseph Fletcher two years later. "It is possible to contemplate it with forbearance", wrote Fletcher,"...only as a first unsteady step in search of a right path. Happily its prints are fast disappearing".[101] Wilderspin himself, then on the eve of retirement, had ceased to use it and there is no evidence that any other educator had adopted it. So a peculiar feature of the early days of popular education came to an end; the initial strike against it had undoubtedly been made in Liverpool, though Wilderspin himself was characteristically unable to admit it.[102] The Merseyside experience did, however, have some positive effects on his fortunes. It gave him an interest in government support for education which was to involve him in a new role as a national campaigner; it also brought him an offer of a post with the Board of National Education in Ireland which was to have a decisive effect on his future career.

[98]*Liverpool Courier*, 19 Oct. 1836.

[99]P.P. 1838 VII, Report from the Select Committee on the Education of the Poorer Classes, p. 118.

[100]"Infant Education. Baby-Lonian University", *Comic Almanack, 1843.* (London 1843), pp. 39-40.

[101]P.P. 1846 XXXII, Minutes of the Committee of Council on Education 1845, J. Fletcher, "Report on Infant Schools on the Principles of the British and Foreign School Society", p. 353.

[102]Despite the charge that children in exhibitions acted like automata, Wilderspin maintained that it was the "old plan" of teaching which made children act thus and that he had been trying for many years to eradicate this defect (*Albion,* 17 Oct. 1836).

CHAPTER 13

NATIONAL EDUCATION:
WILDERSPIN VERSUS THE EVANGELICALS

When Wilderspin returned to Cheltenham from Dublin at the beginning of October 1837, after advising the Board of National Education on the organisation of their projected Model Infant School, he had no thoughts of any further involvement in the national education question. He was waiting to be recalled by the Irish Board and intended to spend his time in rest and recuperation, having been away from Alpha House for nine months.[1] Within a matter of weeks, however, he was caught up in one of the most violent controversies of his career, the ultimate outcome of which was profoundly to affect his future prospects.

By a strange coincidence, Thomas Wyse, M.P. for Waterford and chairman of the Central Society for Education, also happened to be in Cheltenham at the same time, on a visit to his mother.[2] Before his arrival in Cheltenham Wyse had spoken at a meeting on national education in Salford with James Simpson,[3] and they were due to speak in Manchester later in October.[4] Wyse and Simpson, the main speakers on this educational tour[5], were the most active of a group of liberal, middle-class intellectuals, aptly dubbed "experts", who in various ways and with different degrees of commitment, advocated a system of state education in the 1830s. They included J.P. Kay, later James Kay-Shuttleworth, first secretary of the Committee of Council on Education; R.A. Slaney, M.P., chairman of the Select Committee on Education of 1838; the factory inspector, Leonard Horner; Seymour Tremenheere, an H.M.I.; and, among independent educationists, B.S. Duppa, secretary of the Central Society of Education, W.E. Hickson and Frederic Hill. Active on commissions, committees and social inquiries, many of them had links with the statistical societies of the provincial cities. The first generation of intellectuals to accept the fact of the Industrial Revolution, they campaigned for an educational programme which they felt would suit the needs of developing industrial capitalism: a system of unsectarian education for all, established, financed and inspected by a government Board or Commission, with a wide curriculum that would include the physical sciences and modern languages, and taught by methods based on the most up-to-date British and continental practices.[6] The Central Society of Education, founded in

---

[1] *National Education* (1837), p. 39.

[2] According to Lieut. R.J. Morrison, in a letter to the *Cheltenham Free Press,* 9 Dec. 1837.

[3] *Manchester Guardian,* 27 Sept. 1837.

[4] *Manchester Times,* 30 Sept. 1837; *Manchester Guardian,* 7 and 14 Oct. 1837.

[5] For the educational tour, cf. J. Murphy, *The Religious Problem in English Education: the Crucial Experiment* (Liverpool 1959), p. 107ff.

[6] This paragraph relies on R. Johnson, "Educating the Educators: 'Experts' and the State 1833-39", in A.P. Donajgrodzki, *Social Control in Nineteenth Century Britain* (London 1977), pp. 77-107.

1837, was a radical pressure group organised to fight for these aims.[7]

The presence of the Society's chairman in Cheltenham was, for at least one citizen, too good an opportunity to miss. A certain Lieut. R.A. Morrison of the Royal Navy drafted a petition in favour of more extensive government support for national education; it also requested Wyse to chair a meeting of "the friends of popular education".[8] Cheltenham hardly would have suggested itself to the Central Society of Education as an ideal place for such a meeting. Whether or not its population consisted of "East India plunderers, West India floggers, English tax-gorgons. . .gluttons, drunkards and debauchees", as Cobbett had alleged,[9] it was, as we have seen, a solidly Anglican town which acknowledged the leadership, in social, moral and educational matters, of the Rev. Francis Close, the epitome of conservative Evangelicalism. By the late 1830s this "parish Pope" had established an ascendancy in Cheltenham that few other clergymen could rival; "in the bosom of hundreds and thousands of households", stated *The Times,* "his social decrees were accepted without a thought of the possibility of opposition".[10]

Wilderspin, with his feelings in favour of national education strengthened by his sojourn in Liverpool, was the first to sign Morrison's petition; about thirty others followed him, mostly professional men, including half-a-dozen doctors and surgeons.[11] He also agreed to speak at the meeting, which took place on 18 October at the Literary and Philosophical Institution, with Wyse in the chair. He commenced the proceedings, however, by handing over the chairmanship to C.F. Berkely, the local member of Parliament, in order to be free to express at length his views on national education. Following a general introductory speech by a local man, Mr. R. Winterbotham, Wyse began with a definition of a good education; in his view it was one which combined the mental, the moral and the physical. He then went on to query the quality of education given in National Schools (which, by denying access to Dissenters, belied their name), Sunday Schools and infant schools (numbers of which travestied, by ignorance or design, many of Wilderspin's "most judicious views"). He then alleged that half the youth of the country were in want of education, and called for a Board of Commissioners to finance, control and inspect schools, precisely because the system of "leaving things to take care of themselves had not succeeded".[12] Wyse's speech was a judicious and unsensational exposition of the general policy of the Society and those associated with it, and, though he had drawn attention to the sectarian nature of National Schools he had carefully avoided giving any

[7] R. Parkin, *The Central Society of Education.* Educational Administration and History: Monograph No. 3 (Leeds 1975).

[8] *Cheltenham Free Press,* 9 Dec. 1837.

[9] W. Cobbett, *Rural Rides* (London, 3 vol., 1930), II, p. 446. The date of the visit was 1826.

[10] *The Times,* 22 Dec. 1882, cited in *Memorials of Dean Close* (London 1885), p. 10.

[11] *Cheltenham Free Press,* 9 Dec. 1837.

[12] *Cheltenham Free Press,* 21 Oct. 1837.

detailed proposals for the solution of the religious problem or any mention of the situation in Liverpool, which he had recently visited.[13]

In contrast, Wilderspin's contribution was racy, anecdotal and amusing; though he moved a rather curious resolution calling for the establishment of a Government Board of Education to "guide the outlay" of the "vast wealth" bequeathed by benevolent individuals for educational purposes,[14] he confined his speech to some of his favourite topics — reminiscences of his early teaching days, the extent of crime, destitution and degradation in the cities, the backward state of girls' education, and the generally low quality of schools and teachers. "Such facts as these", he cried, "were enough to bring a blush into the face of Englishmen, and shame them into an effort to ameliorate the system". Then, with characteristic impetuosity, he went on to declare that "a splendid exception existed in the case of the schools under the protection of the Corporation and Town Council of Liverpool". After giving details of the system there he continued with an attack on its opponents in a manner virtually guaranteed to rouse the ire of Churchmen:

> A party in Liverpool which had said that education ought to be overthrown, had since built four schools at an expense of at least £2,000 each, with a stone Bible in front, which luckily for them had its back turned outside — as, he supposed, the internal arrangements were just in the spirit and of a piece with the position of the emblematic stone Bible outside.

Wilderspin then proceeded to allege that a master of one of the "Bible schools" had abetted his scholars in an unprovoked attack on Corporation boys, which proved that "a Christian is one not who professes a reverence for the Bible, but a follower of Christ".[15]

Wyse's advocacy of a Board of Commissioners to superintend an improved national system of education, no less than Wilderspin's barbed criticisms of Evangelical churchmen, aroused the anger of their opponents to an extraordinary degree. The *Record* directed its readers' attention to "a rich feast, provided...by certain Roman Catholics, Swedenborgians and Unitarians".[16] "These schemers", alleged the local *Journal,* wanted to substitute "vain deceit" and "false philosophy" for the revealed will of God, and to set up yet another Board "to satisfy the hungry cravings of their liberal supporters for the sweets of office".[17] But it was Wilderspin's introduction of the Liverpool issue which provided the major issue in the controversy and led to further attacks on the

[13]Cf. T. Wyse M.P., *Speech Delivered at the Opening of the New Mechanics' Institution, Mount Street, Liverpool, on the 15th of September, 1837* (Liverpool 1837).

[14]*Cheltenham Free Press,* 28 Oct. 1837.

[15]*Cheltenham Free Press,* 21 Oct. 1837.

[16]*Record,* 30 Oct. 1837.

[17]*Cheltenham Journal,* 30 Oct. 1837.

Liverpool Council and its schools, and the arrival of McNeile himself in Cheltenham to give his version of the story.

* * * * *

Before this happened, however, the meeting at Manchester took place and Wilderspin was invited to speak. In many ways he was the perfect foil to Wyse, who was a master of the art of the long, carefully argued and well-documented speech. Wilderspin was a raconteur with a ready fund of amusing anecdotes and, unlike most middle-class educational reformers, he had an extensive first-hand knowledge of educational and social conditions in many parts of the country. As something of a character, or "card", he would go down well with the popular audience the organisers of the meeting were hoping to attract. Richard Cobden was a member of the planning committee of a hundred, which included Dissenters, professional men, "several individuals of scientific and literary attainments", and "the most wealthy, intelligent, and influential, among the bankers, merchants and manufacturers of Manchester".[18] The meeting was held on the evening of Thursday 26 October, at the Theatre Royal, and was described in the Manchester Times as a "Great Festival of National Education"; pink and white draperies on the walls and pillars, a transparency on one of the walls bearing the words "National Education", and a brightly-illuminated star above the chairman's seat gave the hall a "brilliant and imposing appearance".[19]

At the chairman's table Wilderspin sat with Thomas Wyse, Dr. Jerrard of London University, and a number of local M.P.s. At a nearby table "assigned to distinguished friends of education" sat James Simpson; years later, in a letter to Wilderspin, he was to recall "the stirring time...when I met you in the theatre in Manchester, at that striking festival".[20] The theatre was packed with an audience of over 2,000, the boxes were placed at the disposal of "fair and intelligent townswomen", and the gallery was filled with members of the Mechanics' Institute. At 7 o'clock a flourish of trumpets was sounded and Mark Phillips, M.P., rose to open the proceedings, reading letters of apology for absence from Lord Brougham and the Bishop of Norwich, toasting the health of the Queen (received with "rapturous acclamation" and applause lasting several minutes) and calling on a male voice choir to render the National Anthem. The chairman then introduced Wilderspin as "the able and indefatigable advocate of infant school education".

Standing on top of the table (at the request of the audience), Wilderspin spoke in his most impassioned and radical manner; infancy, he began, was the seed-time of life, and it was a "vital error" to believe that children could not be

[18] According to Cobden, in a letter to the Manchester Guardian, 25 Oct. 1837.

[19] Manchester Times, 28 Oct. 1837. The following account is based on this report.

[20] Wilderspin Papers, Simpson to Wilderspin, 13 Oct. 1845.

educated at the age of eighteen months or even earlier. But what was education? Not rote-learning but the drawing out of the faculties, and he hoped to see the day when "the study of the infant mind would not be considered a degrading study even to the wisest philosophers." Unless they had a conception of what a human being really was, how was it likely they could ever have a proper system of national education? Children, he continued, ought to be managed by love, not fear, a principle he would recommend to "the attention of our legislators", who wasted too much time passing laws to preserve "hares, pheasants and partridges"; both Houses, he urged, should begin to legislate on "the best method of preventing crime instead of spending millions on punishing people by banishment (cheers)". Condemning existing schooling, particularly that of girls, he declared that "England is disgraced as a nation by her schools and system of education". He would suggest that education include physical, intellectual and religious elements; but religious education should concern itself with the essence and not the form. What were "prayers and forms of prayer, or worship, and creeds and catechisms", he asked in conclusion, to the cheers of the audience, "...if the heartfelt desire of universal love for all mankind was wanting?"

It was Wilderspin's finest hour. Described by the following speaker as "the distinguished and excellent individual who had honoured that festival with his presence", whose speech was "amusing, highly instructive and truly philosophical", Wilderspin found himself temporarily in the position of one of the leaders of the campaign for national education. The general aims of the campaign were made clear by Wyse. Addressing himself to "the Englishmen who live in the epoch of steam, of gas, and of railway communication", he held out the possibility of an alliance of the middle-class, who wished to diffuse intelligence among all, and the working-class, "the base on which this great commonwealth is founded", and on which "the safety of the whole depends"; together they would act against the aristocracy, who feared and opposed the spread of education. Whatever might be the situation in Manchester, it was an alliance which, on a national scale, did not materialise in sufficient strength to carry the educational programme of the "experts".[21] But Wyse had his finger on the pulse of Cottonopolis when he quoted from the reports of the Manchester Statistical Society to demonstrate that half the children of the country lacked education, and advocated study of the educational provision in continental countries "in order that we might learn how it was that they were enabled to rival us in our commerce".

* * * * *

---

[21] For the reasons for this, cf. Johnson, "Educating the Educators", *loc cit.*, p. 97 ff.

The Manchester gathering was the largest addressed by Wyse on his tour. But it was the meeting at Cheltenham seven days earlier which had aroused the greatest opposition, and the local clergy lost little time in gathering their forces for a counter-attack. On 27 October, the day following the Manchester meeting, "the friends of exclusive scriptural education", who included the High Sheriff of the County, all the clergy of the town, several of the magistrates, the great body of the resident gentry and visitors, and many "Ladies of Distinction", met at the Cheltenham Assembly Rooms.[22] The meeting was chaired by the Rev. Francis Close, who presented the Evangelical case in an eloquent and forcible manner. He was glad, he stated, that the Wyse meeting had been held for it enabled them to learn something of the plans recommended and to oppose "the dangerous and insidious character of...modern education". He would, he declared, demonstrate three propositions: first, that Bible schools had been "travestied, calumniated and falsified"; second, that a system had been recommended which was "unscriptural, tyrannical, oppressive and Utopian"; third, that his audience should bestir themselves to preserve the word of God and drive out the dangerous doctrines which infested the country.

This he proceeded to do at great length and in considerable detail, objecting in particular to Wyse's criticism of National Schools, the lack of religion in the kind of education the latter had proposed, the tyrannical nature of Boards, the folly of learning from other countries — "come back to Old England, and say, with all your stupidity and ignorance, I think you are the best and safest after all! (Cheers)". Close sneered at the possibility of "the clowns of Gloucestershire" being taught to reason on the spirit and operation of the laws, "mechanics and ploughmen" being taught astronomy and geography, and "the natives of Pantile Row and Magpie Alley" the sciences and philosophy ("Roars of laughter").

He did not fail to pick up Wilderspin's allegations about the church party in Liverpool. He asserted that Wilderspin's jibe at a body which spent £2,000 on each of four schools was self-refuting, that the Town Council had introduced the Irish Lessons and compelled children to read a mutilated Bible "with Popish notes and references". He referred to Wilderspin merely as "this person", who "seemed to think the Irish system was "the very *beau ideal* of all good systems of education"; he commended to his audience McNeile's *Letters on National Education,* which exposed its "abominations". Of the clergy who spoke after Close, little need be said. They reiterated many of Close's points and indulged in blood-curdling generalisations about the character and aims of the national education campaign: "a march of evil things" (Rev. J. Browne); "the restoration of Popish ascendancy" (Rev. C.G. Davies); "a deeply-laid scheme for the destruction of our Church and of our constitution" (Rev. W. Kinsey).

A number of resolutions were passed at the meeting, proclaiming faith in Scriptural education and warning against the introduction of the Irish system

[22] *Cheltenham Journal,* 30 Oct. 1837, on which the following account is based.

into England. The second resolution perfectly expressed the position of the Evangelicals with regard to popular education:

> That any system of Education which does not recognize the Supreme Authority of the Word of God, which gives prominence to human rather than to divine knowledge, and which aims at cultivating the mind rather than reinstating the heart, is unsuited to the state of man as a sinner needing a Saviour, and is unworthy of the support of a Christian people.[23]

The meeting also launched two petitions, one to the young Queen Victoria praying that she would never sanction the introduction of a general system of non-scriptural education into the country, and another to the House of Lords in a similar vein.[24]

Wilderspin had left Manchester to visit Liverpool and was not aware of the Cheltenham meeting until he read reports of it in the local press. Incensed at what he felt were untrue allegations about the Corporation and its schools, he reacted immediately. He obtained the signatures of all the teachers at the two schools to a statement that the Authorised Version of the Bible was read daily, attached it to a declaration of his own accusing Close and Davies of "false statements", had them printed as posters, and placarded the streets of Cheltenham with them.[25] It was an unusual action and probably the first time that Close had been publicly challenged, let alone accused of issuing falsehoods.

Close and Davies hit back with placards of their own. The former, accused of what he called "one of the gravest crimes of which a Minister of the Gospel of Truth can be guilty", denied that he had spoken of the exclusion of the Bible from the Liverpool schools and claimed he had referred to the "garbled extracts...substituted for the Bible during school hours"; the disclaimer of the masters was, therefore, "a denial of that which was never said". He subjoined the relevant extract from his speech with a quotation from McNeile's *Letters on National Education* in support. Davies reprinted the words he had spoken:

> "It is a system which *excludes* from the Schools, as *a book to be used in the Schools, the Bible as a whole".* Again; —"*A system,* from which the Bible, as a book to be used in the schools, by which I mean, *in what are considered school hours,* is *excluded".*[26]

Like Close, he added extracts from McNeile's *Letters* to his own statement.

Undaunted by the clergymen's action, Wilderspin addressed a letter to them which was published in the *Cheltenham Journal*. Several persons present at the meeting, he stated, had declared to him that Close and Davies had indeed claimed the exclusion of the Bible; now, said Wilderspin, they were trying to shift

[23]*Cheltenham Chronicle,* 2 Nov. 1837.

[24]*Ibid.*

[25]*National Education* (1837), pp. 40-41. The teachers' placard was reprinted in the *Cheltenham Free Press,* 4 Nov. 1837.

[26]*Cheltenham Journal,* 6 Nov. 1837.

their ground and maintain that they meant it was not read in school hours. Further, to say that "garbled extracts" were "substituted" was effectively to state the Bible was not read, for "a *substitute* is another thing".[27]

Much of the controversy centered on the semantic quibbles which had bedevilled the issue in Liverpool. The statements of Close and Davies were worded in such a way that they were capable of more than one interpretation. Close was correct in claiming that he had not stated in so many words that the Bible was excluded from the Liverpool Corporation Schools, but his statement on the substitution of the extracts could have borne the interpretation Wilderspin gave it. Davies' qualifying phrase re the Bible — "as a book to be used in the schools" — enabled him to make his point against the Corporation and also to deny that Wilderspin was correct. Both Close and Davies took it for granted, of course, that the Bible study from 3-4 p.m. had nothing at all to do with the daily business of the Schools.

Wilderspin dismissed Davies's lengthy disclaimer as an "elegant specimen...of clerical composition", which appeared to him and "to everyone who would have the patience to read such jargon, a lame story". Quoting from McNeile was not equivalent to proof:

> You seem, gentlemen, to think that an extract made from an obscure pamphlet, written by a violent political partisan a year ago, is to be put in competition with the evidence of thirteen highly respectable teachers, daily employed in the schools, and also with *my* evidence, who daily inspected these schools for more than eight months, and have only just left them![28]

Close did not let the matter rest. The following Sunday he began to preach a series of sermons in his church, directed against "a newly projected system of National Education" which he described as "anti-Christian in its fundamental principles, infidel in its tendency, and highly derogatory to the truth and integrity of God's holy word". In order to make himself perfectly clear he named Wyse, Simpson and Wilderspin as its principal advocates. On the Monday he accused Wilderspin of attempting to deceive the public.[29]

Assailed in press and pulpit, Wilderspin was preparing his defence. Immediately after putting up the placards, he had composed an extended reply to the speeches at the meeting in the Assembly Rooms, which was in the press by 6 November.[30] Wilderspin seemed determined to fight the issue to the end. In this instance his almost arrogant belief in his own powers stood him in good stead. The charisma and prestige exercised by ministers in early Victorian times was very great; private criticism was muted and public criticism of the kind

---

[27] *Ibid.*

[28] *Ibid.* The Ms. of this letter is preserved in the Wilderspin Papers. Wilderspin annotated it with the words "Copy of Placard in answer to Falsehoods of the Cheltenham clergy".

[29] F. Close, *Sermons for the Times* (London 1837), iii. The first sermon was preached on Sunday, 12 Nov. 1837. The charge of deceit was made in a letter to the *Cheltenham Journal*, 13 Nov. 1837.

[30] *Cheltenham Journal*, 6 Nov. 1837.

Wilderspin employed almost unknown. In the Tory spa, where Close was all-powerful, the consequences could be serious. Close was not above exercising temporal chastisement in cases where he felt religion had been brought into disrepute. He had offered a reward of £5 for the identity of, and threatened legal proceedings against, the author of another (anonymous) handbill issued on 27 October which criticised the use of the Bible in religious instruction;[31] five years later he was alleged to be behind the arrest and imprisonment for blasphemy of George Jacob Holyoake.[32]

Wilderspin probably felt himself safe from anything but verbal opposition and sufficiently self-confident in his new status as a consultant to the Irish Board of Education to give full rein to his accumulated anger at the attitude of the Evangelicals, both towards himself (the Bilby and Ridgway criticism and the exclusion from the Home and Colonial Infant School Society) and towards the education of the poor. The Evangelicals' growing tendency to give priority to Protestant theology in any general system of education was, he felt, tantamount to depriving children of instruction in useful knowledge. He was to be given the opportunity of stating this in a spectacularly public fashion with the arrival in Cheltenham of the most militant Evangelical of them all, the Rev. Hugh McNeile.

* * * * *

McNeile's presence in Cheltenham, ostensibly fortuitous[33], could not have been entirely unconnected with the controversy over national education and the issue of the Liverpool schools. A second meeting on Scriptural education was announced for 10 November, principally, according to the *Chronicle,* to allow McNeile to establish the truth concerning the charges made against the Liverpool schools; "handbills, by no means complimentary to the Reverend Gentleman's character for veracity", the *Chronicle* reminded its readers, "have recently been plentifully circulated amongst us".[34] This oblique reference to Wilderspin's placards was probably fair warning that his particular allegations would not go unremarked. When McNeile spoke at the meeting, it was evident that despite the apparent intransigence of the Evangelicals, Wilderspin's efforts as unofficial publicity officer for the Liverpool Corporation Schools had not been without effect. Though McNeile made a long criticism of the Irish Scripture Selections (4,688 variations from the Authorised Version and capable of

---

[31] The handbill was the work of F.B. Barton, a Unitarian, who considered that parts of the Bible were improper and unfit for youthful instruction. The incident is described in a pamphlet by Barton entitled *A Letter to the Rev. Francis Close, M.A.* (Cheltenham 1837).

[32] *Memorials of Dean Close,* p. 11 ff.

[33] He stated, at the meeting of 10 November, that he had come to Cheltenham "on the occasion of the sickness of one of my children" (*Cheltenham Chronicle,* 16 Nov. 1837).

[34] *Cheltenham Chronicle,* 16 Nov. 1837. The report of the meeting is mainly from this source.

"Popish" interpretations) and reiterated in tedious detail his opposition to the Liverpool Council and its alleged effects, he also made two significant concessions. First, he admitted that the Bible was "not positively, peremptorily and all day long excluded from the schoolroom", and that for one hour he had the right to instruct children in the Bible. His grounds for opposition now turned on the "Popery" argument; instruction of the children sanctioned "a system which presents to my view on the other side of the room the peculiar dogmas of the Church of Rome". Second, in contradiction to his defence of rote-learning of the previous January, he now urged "let us put an end forever, if we can, to that cold, careless, and parrot-like mode of instruction which has given these men a handle against us".

He also showed he was sensitive to Wilderspin's barbs. He thundered against the references to his "obscure pamphlet" and to himself as a violent political partisan. Later in his speech, after his allegations that all children in the schools were taught the Irish Selections, a denial was shouted from the floor, possibly by Wilderspin; further interruptions followed, and, according to the *Chronicle*, "during the confusion Mr. Wilderspin claimed a right to be heard". Wilderspin was probably one of the few people in the country with the courage to face McNeile in public, and McNeile, angered by this unusual treatment, seized his chance to even the score:

> I will not consent to be called in question by any obscure individual — neither will I consent, though it is said the schoolmaster is abroad, that a clergyman of the Church of England should stand to compete with a schoolmaster. The Irish extracts are taught to all the children.

Though McNeile continued his speech without further interruption, the meeting ended in disorder and confusion. Immediately after McNeile sat down a Mr. Spencer, of Liverpool, attempted to speak, "but the uproar was so great", reported the *Free Press*, "we could not catch a word".[35] After R.B. Cooper had moved a vote of thanks another member of the audience tried to gain a hearing but failed. "Let the proceedings go on; never mind these talkers", snapped Close. Then Wilderspin again tried to speak and declared he would put it to the chair or to the vote of the meeting whether he should be heard. ("Cries of 'hear, hear' and great confusion"). It was a courageous but futile attempt. Cooper, in a stentorian voice, shouted "we shan't hear you, Sir; there's no use in your persisting", and Close, determined to get the last word, declared that if Mr. Wilderspin wished to call a meeting to prove him and the clergy of Cheltenham liars, he was at liberty to do so, but he should not address that meeting.[36]

Furious at the treatment he had received, Wilderspin went home, dashed off a denunciation of McNeile and sent it to be added to the criticism of Close

[35] *Cheltenham Free Press*, 11 Nov. 1837.
[36] *Ibid.*

already in the press.[37] It was published before the end of November as a *A Reply to the Various Speeches Delivered at a Meeting, held at the Assembly Rooms, Cheltenham, on Friday, October 27th, on the Subject of National Education.*[38] It is doubtful if McNeile had ever been assailed by such angry eloquence, or had his own brand of invective turned against him. He was denounced as "a master of sophistry", "a narrow-minded bigot", "a political preacher" and "an arch-agitator"; his presence in Cheltenham, Wilderspin alleged, had not been accidental, but engineered by Close. His speech had been nothing more than a series of insults to Catholics, Dissenters and the Town Council of Liverpool, from the moment he suggested that the meeting should be opened by prayer:

> Gracious God — Supreme Governor of the Universe! that thou shouldst be so mocked! and thy Sacred Name so profaned by those who profess, and whose office it unfortunately is, to teach the Holy Word — that they should pray to Thee to assist them to do the thing which is right, and immediately afterwards proceed to violate every Christian rule, by defaming, maligning, and insulting every conscientious Christian, who differed with them![39]

Wilderspin's chief complaint, however, was that McNeile's impressions of Liverpool schools had been gained on a visit of only fifteen minutes, and that with this credential he had been allowed to speak for an hour and a half, whereas Wilderspin himself, who had devoted his life to education and spent a year in the Liverpool schools, had not been allowed to speak at all, on the grounds that McNeile would not compete with a schoolmaster:

> It was not likely, after the Town Council of Liverpool had been vilified, their motives impugned by a fanatic, their schools misrepresented and the teachers libelled, that they would hear the man who had *organized* these schools — of course it would not *do* — I was in the way — the party *dared not hear me* — so took the only method they had in their power, which was, to *stop my mouth.*[40]

To buttress his arguments that the Bible was not excluded from the Liverpool schools, Wilderspin quoted in full letters of four Liverpool clergymen (the Revs. Carruthers, Spence, Kelly and Godwin) the Unitarian Dr. Shepherd and William Rathbone, all of whom wrote from first-hand experience.[41]

Wilderspin's treatment of Close, the clergy and the Church in the first part of the pamphlet was less heated but equally uncompromising. In fact, the theme of the book could well have been the sentence on page five — "When anything is proposed for the benefit of the human race the alarm bell is sure to be sounded by

---

[37] This is deduced from the pages devoted to the McNeile meeting in the latter part of the book; these could not have been written prior to 10 November, at which date the book was at the printers.

[38] The exact date of publication has not been ascertained, but it was reviewed in the *Cheltenham Journal*, 27 Nov. 1837.

[39] *National Education* (1837), p. 43.

[40] *Ibid.*, pp. 44-5.

[41] *Ibid.*, pp. 18-28.

the Clergy". He cited their opposition to Joseph Lancaster, the Bible Society, Sunday Schools, London University, and last but not least, to the first infant schools. "If we wish to educate the people", he complained bitterly, "we are told we want to pull down the establishment, no matter what the subject may be, the church, the church, is perpetually thrust forward".[42]

The speakers at the Wyse meeting were called enemies of the Bible, religion and the church; but no speaker, argued Wilderspin, disapproved of Bible education; they merely wanted more of the essence and less of the form. No speaker maintained that existing schools were productive of no good; they merely pointed out that they could not, with propriety, be called national schools or serve as the basis for a national system. The Irish system was not introduced into the Liverpool schools — "many of the plans adopted there were suggested by myself".[43] The speakers were correct in maintaining that education was lacking in many parts of the country, and Wilderspin cited reports of the Manchester Statistical Society to prove it. As for Close's laughter-making derision at the possibility of teaching the sciences to ploughmen and mechanics:

> How truly laughable; yes, and how very clerical; these hints speak but too plainly what sort of education we are to expect from you — because a poor Girl or a poor Boy happens to be born in Pantile-row, or whose parents may reside in Magpie-alley, they forsooth must be outcasts — aliens — and of, course, kept in the most profound ignorance.[44]

The concluding paragraphs of the pamphlet (written, of course, following the McNeile meeting) again attacked the clergy for their attitude to education, sparing neither words nor feelings: "narrow-minded zealots"; men blinded by "party spirit, bigotry and fanaticism"; "mock-Christians" who wanted "good water in their own wells...leaving their fellow men to die of thirst". Were these, he cried, fit and proper persons to take enlightened and comprehensive views on the question of national education?[45] The present system was a stain on the national character, and all practical men were determined it should exist no longer.

> We bid defiance to the ignorant, narrow-minded bigots of the age, and tell them plainly, that they cannot, and they shall not prevent it. The vituperation of such men may retard it for a time, but in the end they will be vanquished.[46]

As a defence of the Liverpool schools and an exposure of Evangelical educational policy, *National Education* was an effective piece of partisan literature. It reads as strongly today as it must have done in 1837 and reveals that

[42] *Ibid.*, pp. 5-6. The punctuation follows the original.

[43] *Ibid.*, p. 4; pp. 10-14; p. 32.

[44] *Ibid.*, p. 30.

[45] *Ibid.*, pp. 45-6.

[46] *Ibid.*, p. 46. The punctation follows the original.

Wilderspin had an unexpected talent for pamphleteering; in fact, the sharpness of his language was redolent of the rhetoric of the radical press. It was hardly accidental that a reviewer of Close's *Sermons for the Times* in the *Journal* of 4 December linked phrenologists, Dissenters and the Working Men's Association as supporters of national education.[47] The Address on National Education of the W.M.A. had been published in the *Free Press* of 25 November, and despite misgivings about the role of the state, the line of the document had many similarities to the Central Society's policy. Its references to infant schools bore an unmistakable affinity to Wilderspin's prescriptions for infant education: infant schools should be open to all children between three and six years; cleanliness and punctual attendance should be insisted upon, to amalgamate class distinctions and preserve children from corrupting influences; the children should not be confined in close atmospheres or compelled to sit still for hours — the air and exercise of the playground and garden are the first essentials at this early stage, where the teachers should as carefully watch over them as in the schoolroom and infuse them with principles of justice and kindness necessary to form their character; they should be taught knowledge of things rather than words and learn about objects through the senses; principles of morality should be explained, not learned by rote.[48]

It was a case of Wilderspin influencing the Chartists rather than the other way round. But it was a measure of the radical tenor of his views at this time that even a tenuous link should be made between his policies and those of the Working Men's Association. The Tories of Cheltenham had little doubt where he stood. The *Journal,* after dismissing his pamphlet as "an aggregation of mud", and its author as "a moral quack" who had associated so much with children and Papists that "one half of his intellect is babyish and the other Jesuitical", rejoiced that the plans of the "Catholics, Infidels and *political* Dissenters" had been routed:

> The efforts of the powerful triumvirate of Wyse, Wilderspin, and Winterbotham have proved unavailing; they have agitated, but only for the benefit of their opponents; they have called on the inhabitants of the town to aid them, but they have answered, no; and they are now exposed to all the galling feelings of an ignominious defeat, brought on by their own recklessness in needlessly making this the scene of their politico-religious exploits.[49]

The "defeat" was measured in terms of the number of signatures to the rival petitions: 13,054 signatures to those of the Evangelicals,[50] only 348 to the

---

[47]*Cheltenham Journal,* 4 Dec. 1837.

[48]"The Working Men's Association to the Working Classes, on the Subject of National Education", *Cheltenham Free Press,* 25 Nov. 1837. The address was signed by the Committee, whose secretary was William Lovett. The Committee included such well-known Chartists as Robert Hartwell, John Cleave and Henry Hetherington.

[49]*Cheltenham Journal,* 27 Nov. 1837.

[50]Vide Close in a letter to the *Record,* 30 Nov. 1837. The *Free Press* alleged that "the numbers were obtained in a very great measure from children" (*Cheltenham Free Press,* 9 Dec. 1837).

petition of Lieut. Morrison which had begun the whole controversy.[51] But Wilderspin's efforts had succeeded in stirring up interest in and publicising the Liverpool Schools question, and the liberals of Cheltenham took up the cause of the Corporation; the *Free Press* printed letters from James Buchanan, headmaster of the South Corporation school and from the Revs. Buck and Aspinall of Liverpool, as well as giving other coverage to proceedings there.[52] Wilderspin's placards and letters, his pamphlet in reply to the clergy and his speeches at the two meetings added fuel to the national campaign. As he wrote later, the meetings "made a great deal of noise at the time and...have been the means of effecting a great deal of good",[53] and his earthy brand of populism might well have been utilised more widely in the national agitation. The campaign led by Wyse and Simpson was, in fact, sharp enough to push the government into introducing proposals for a Committee of Council on Education, an inspectorate and a state normal school, but it lacked the power to withstand the subsequent campaign of the Church and the Conservatives, which whittled away the last two measures.[54]

Essentially, the struggle was between two different conceptions of education, each the product of different social forces. On the one side were the liberal intelligentsia, with strong links with provincial industrialists, who were eager to introduce a modern, non-sectarian type of popular education, but convinced it was too important a subject to be left to the free play of the market. Opposed to them were the Evangelicals, orthodox Churchmen and the Conservatives, who saw in the Monarchy, the Church and the Bible the bulwarks of the Constitution and the social order against the new forces in society, whose educational policies, they were convinced, could lead to the ultimate horror of revolutionary change. With Liverpool in mind, Close could ask, in 1838:

> Shall our National, Infant and Sunday Schools, instead of being identified with the clergy and the Church, be placed under the absolute sway of the *civic political councils,* to be educated in a hot-bed of Universalism, and be taught that church or chapel, Jew and Turk, are all alike — Jehovah, Jove, or Lord?[55]

The Church, its educational influence thus weakened, would be unable to counter a further threat — the spread of revolutionary ideas among the working class:

---

[51]This figure was given by Lieut. Morrison in his letter to the *Cheltenham Free Press,* 9 Dec. 1837.

[52]*Cheltenham Free Press,* 4, 11 and 25 Nov. 1837; cf. Murphy, *Religious Problem,* p. 117.

[53]*Early Discipline* (1840), p. 323.

[54]Cf. Johnson, *"Educating the Educators",* loc. cit., p. 95 ff., for an analysis of the campaign. One of the weaknesses of the agitation for national education was the hostility of orthodox Dissent to state education.

[55]Rev. F. Close, *National Education and Lord Brougham's Bill Considered; in a Series of Nine Letters* (Cheltenham 1838), pp. 50-51.

The great barrier against the progress of revolutionary principles among the working classes, is the salutary influence of the clergy, greatly exercised through the medium of the children; and therefore it is sought to remove those children from that wholesome influence, and so to weaken the hold which the Church has upon the population.[56]

In a previous paragraph Close had shown, in a reference to the zealous support of secular education by "Unitarians, Arians, Swedenborgians and all that unhappy class of our deluded fellow creatures. . ." that he had not forgotten Wilderspin's role in the events of the previous year. Wilderspin himself, when the first flush of his anger was over, must have known the Church would never forgive him. At the time it was scarcely a problem, for on 20 November he received an urgent summons to Ireland, and a new career in the Model Schools in Dublin seemed to be opening up. But later on, in different circumstances, he was to find his former role as the hammer of the Church a shackle on his advancement.

[56] *Ibid.*, pp. 51-2.

CHAPTER 14

THE DUBLIN MODEL SCHOOLS 1837-1839

The initial request for Wilderspin's services in Ireland — to advise on the construction and appointment of the proposed Model School and playground of the Board of National Education — had been made by one of the Board's Commissioners shortly after the termination of the Liverpool engagement in the last week of August 1837. Wilderspin went over to Dublin, probably during the last two or three weeks of September, and gave "the necessary instructions to the surveyor and set the principal parties in a proper position to begin the undertaking". He left with the understanding that he would be advised of the time when his services would again be required.[1] Then followed the events described in the last chapter.

During that period he was engaged in further negotiations with the Irish National Board. Two days before the great Manchester rally he had received a letter from the Rev. James Carlile, one of the Commissioners. Evidently Wilderspin, when in Ireland, had suggested his eldest daughter, Sarah Anne, and her fiancé Thomas Young, as teachers for the Model Infant School; the Board, wrote Carlile, had confirmed this appointment and offered them a salary of £200 per year plus the rent of a house. Wilderspin himself, Carlile added, would not need to come over to Dublin until greater progress had been made in fitting up the Model Infant School.[2]

Nearly a month later, shortly after he had dashed off his final denunciation of McNeile, Wilderspin received an urgent letter, dated 20 November, from Thomas Kelly, secretary of the National Board, urging him to travel to Dublin "as quickly as possible".[3] Wilderspin left immediately, but how long he stayed is not clear, nor the precise nature of his work. The Fifth Report of the Commissioners states that towards the end of 1837 he was employed by the Board in a temporary capacity "to assist in founding infant schools",[4] but this may have been a reference to his work in connection with the preparation of the Model School. Subsequent events suggest that at this period also he entered into an agreement with the Board to oversee the opening and establishment of the model school when its construction was completed.

He was almost certainly back home before 20 December, for on that day his daughter Sarah Anne and Thomas Young were married in Cheltenham.[5]

---

[1] *Early Discipline* (1840), pp. 332-33.

[2] Wilderspin Papers, Carlile to Wilderspin, 24 Oct. 1837. That Wilderspin had advocated the appointment of the Youngs was confirmed in a letter from Thomas Young to his father-in-law eight years later (Young papers, T.U. Young to Wilderspin, Dec. 1845).

[3] *Early Discipline* (1840), p. 333, Kelly to Wilderspin, 20 Nov. 1837.

[4] P.P. 1839 XVI, Fifth Report of the Commissioners of National Education in Ireland for the Year Ending 31 March, 1838, App. No. 1, p. 16.

[5] *Cheltenham Journal,* 25 Dec. 1837.

Shortly afterwards the young couple left for Ireland to take up their appointment at the infant school, which was to begin on 1 January 1838.[6] They were well received, largely on account of their connection with Wilderspin; during their first week in Dublin they took tea with Carlile.[7] Shortly afterwards Wilderspin was in Liverpool endeavouring to recruit teachers for the Board's schools. Carlile was particularly anxious to secure the services of J. Buchanan, Wilderspin's former ally in the North Corporation School, as head of the Board's boys' school; but though he suggested that Buchanan name his own salary, he was unsuccessful in persuading him to move.[8]

Wilderspin, however, had other business in Liverpool besides interviewing teachers; he was making preparation for his own marriage to Mary Dowding, a twenty-nine year old widow with two children. He had met her, as we have seen, during his service with the Corporation schools. The wedding took place at St. David's Church, Liverpool, on Sunday 25 February.[9] The Wilderspins went over to Dublin, taking with them the former Mrs. Dowding's two daughters and Wilderspin's youngest child Emma, then a girl of sixteen. They settled in Drumcondra Hill, a fashionable suburb, and Wilderspin, with nostalgic memories of Cheltenham, named the residence Alpha House.[10]

* * * * *

He was familiar with the Irish scene — he had made seven journeys there to establish infant schools[11] — and had, in fact, publicly advocated the establishment of a Dublin Infant School Society and a model infant school on lecture tours in 1833 and 1834.[12] Ireland, he had declared, was peculiarly favourable to the spread of infant education because "her children are the quickest I have ever met with".[13] He realised, however, that Ireland presented peculiar problems to the educationist, manifested most obviously in the religious sphere. On previous visits he had been impressed by the awe in which the Catholic priest was held by his flock and the virtually absolute power which he exercised over his parishoners. He was therefore disposed to think that a direct attack on the Catholic Church would be "exceedingly impolitic" and would hamper the spread of the infant system, particularly if it were in any way

[6]P.P. 1870 XXVIII, Royal Commission of Inquiry into Primary Education (Ireland), I, VII, p. 51.

[7]Wilderspin Papers, Carlile to Wilderspin, 10 Jan. 1838.

[8]Ibid. Buchanan remained at Liverpool until 1841, when he took up a post as head of the English Department in Dr. Bell's Institution, Inverness (Wilderspin Papers, Buchanan to Wilderspin, 5 Sept. 1841).

[9]General Register Office, Marriage Certificate dated 25 Feb. 1838.

[10]Young Papers, T.U. Young, "Memoir of My Family" (Ms.).

[11]So he informed Brougham in a letter of 1835 (U.C.L. Brougham Mss., 27836, Wilderspin to Brougham, 1 June 1835).

[12]Saunders's News-Letter, 19 Sept. 1833; Cork Evening Herald, 6 Oct. 1834.

[13]Saunders's News-Letter, 19 Sept. 1833.

associated with the advocacy of Protestantism, which the Catholics abhorred. Infant education in Ireland, he felt, could contribute to the eradication of "turbulence" from the Irish character and help the promotion of peace and order by giving "the mental ascendancy over the physical".[14]

His views did not conflict with traditional English policy. Education in Ireland during imperial rule had always had as its main function the control and Anglicisation of a subject population. From the earliest educational legislation of the sixteenth century, which attempted to Anglicise the inhabitants of the Pale, via the multiplicity of schools established in the succeeding centuries — Diocesan, Royal, Charter and others — to the largely Evangelical proselytising societies of the late eighteenth and early nineteenth centuries,[15] the purpose had broadly been the same — the maintenance of colonial rule, *de jure* or *de facto*, by the spread of the English language and the Protestant religion.[16] Many of the schools and societies received government subsidies; the largest Protestant body, the Society for Promoting Education among the Poor of Ireland (usually known as the Kildare Place Society) had received £6,000 per annum as early as 1816 and was receiving no less than £30,000 in 1831.[17] All the societies, declared Thomas Wyse, expressing a widespread nationalistic sentiment, were but "joint stock companys, for the curing of Catholic souls, rather than the instruction of Catholic minds".[18]

By the middle 1820s it was obvious that the societies were less than successful; they aroused Catholic opposition, spearheaded by O'Connell and the Catholic Association, without influencing any appreciable fraction of the Catholic children, whose education was largely gained in the hedge schools.[19] A new policy was called for, and in preparing it the government was able to draw on a large number of previous proposals, ranging from those of Thomas Orde in 1787 to Spring Rice's Select Committee of 1828.[20] A similarity of purpose existed — in essence the attraction of Catholic children into "national schools" by modification of the regulations for religious instruction while maintaining ultimate control in the hands of the British government.

The policy which inaugurated the Irish National System of Education was put forward by Edward Stanley (later Earl of Derby), Chief Secretary for Ireland, in the debate on the vote of supply for Irish education in September

---

[14] *Early Discipline* (1832), pp. 64-7.

[15] The most important were the Association for Discountenancing Vice (1792), the London Hibernian Society (1806), the Baptist Society (1814) and the Irish Society (1818).

[16] D.H. Akenson, *The Irish Education Experiment* (London 1970), pp. 17-39; pp. 80-91.

[17] *Ibid.*, pp. 86-7.

[18] T. Wyse, *Education (Ireland): Speech of Th. Wyse, Esq., M.P., in The House of Commons on Tuesday, May 19, 1835* (London 1835), p. 16.

[19] In 1825 the schools of the societies contained less than 12% of the Catholic children (P.P. 1826-27 XIII, Ninth Report of the Commissioners of Irish Education Inquiry, App. No. 5, p. 60.)

[20] Akenson, *Irish Education*, pp. 61-80; pp. 94-107.

1831; the details were elaborated in a letter to the Duke of Leinster. Stanley's proposals, when put into operation, established an inter-denominational Board of National Education, a model school for the training of teachers and a school system open to children of all creeds.[21] In the schools, literary and moral instruction were "combined" and undertaken for a minimum of four hours per day, for four days per week; Bible reading and religious controversy were excluded, though a book of Scripture Extracts prepared by the Commissioners was allowed to be used and a "general lesson" on Christian ethics was printed and hung in every school. Religious instruction was "separate" and held on a day of the week set aside for it and before or after the school hours on days of combined instruction, if the parents desired it. It was undertaken by the clergy of every faith of which there were children in school.[22]

The creation of a national system of education was the continuation of the time-honoured policy of using Ireland as a proving ground for measures of social reform, a strategy which underlined Ireland's subordinate status.[23] In the more particular sense, national education, as R.B. McDowell has argued, was part of the Whig plan of "devitalising the repeal movement by removing Irish grievances"; reform, good administration and a break-up of the Protestant monopoly of power would make the Union viable, unfold to Catholics the benefits of Emancipation and close the gap between the people and the administration.[24] The role envisaged for the Board's national schools exactly fitted this conception; if Protestant schools had excited in Catholics "feelings of discontent towards the State, and of alienation from it", the Board would henceforward train a race of teachers who would be "identified in interest with the State", who would promote "morality, harmony and good order...a spirit of obedience to lawful authority" and bring about "civilisation and peace".[25]

The Board itself, though it had no legal status (having been created on the instructions of a Chief Secretary) paradoxically possessed great power; it had absolute control over educational funds, had the right to dismiss teachers, and also controlled the issue and use of all textbooks and lesson materials in the schools. The Board consisted of seven members, known as the Commissioners of National Education and in the early years they had virtually a free hand to run the system. When Wilderspin arrived in Dublin the original members were still in office. In addition to the resident Commissioner James Carlile, a Scottish Presbyterian, there were four other Protestants: the Duke of Leinster, the nominal President, who attended irregularly; Archbishop Whately, the *de facto*

[21] *Ibid.*, pp. 120-21; App., pp. 392-402.

[22] *Ibid.*, pp. 159-60.

[23] *Ibid.*, pp. 17-20; pp. 37-9. Cf. also E. Strauss, *Irish Nationalism and British Democracy* (London 1951), p. 71; G. Kitson Clark, *Churchmen and the Condition of England 1832-1885* (London 1973), pp. 21-2.

[24] R.B. McDowell, *Public Opinion and Government Policy in Ireland 1801-1846* (London 1952), p. 178; p. 203.

[25] P.P. 1835 XXXV, Second Report of the Commissioners of National Education in Ireland, for the Year Ending 31 March 1835, pp. 4-5.

President; Dr. Sadleir, Provost of Trinity College Dublin, and Robert Holmes, a Unitarian barrister. The only two Catholics were Dr. Murray, Archbishop of Dublin, and Richard Antony Blake, Chief Remembrancer of the Treasury and an important educational figure; he had been one of the Commissioners of the Educational Inquiry of 1824-27 and gave evidence to the Select Committee of 1837.[26] The presence of Murray and Blake and the preponderance of Protestants on the Board did nothing to enhance its image in the eyes of Catholic nationalists. Wilderspin, however, could count on two Commissioners, Carlile and Whately (a friend of George Combe), as his supporters.

* * * * *

When Wilderspin arrived in Dublin with his family, final preparations were being made to open the Model Infant School, part of a complex which occupied a site in Marlborough Street near the centre of the city. The buildings, which still exist and are in use today, largely as education offices, were solid structures set in spacious grounds, and included the Training Department and Model Schools for older boys and girls. The Infant Model School opened for the reception of children on 5 March 1838[27] with Wilderspin as superintendent, a post which gave him a free hand (which he secured by a specific agreement with the Board)[28] to oversee all aspects of the work, including the teaching of his daughter and son-in-law. It was a measure of his prestige and the esteem in which he was held that his salary was £600 per annum,[29] the same rate of pay that he had received in Liverpool and double the official salary of James Carlile, the resident Commissioner.[30] The contract, however, was apparently of an informal nature, for it was to continue, Wilderspin wrote, "as long as my services were required".[31]

The main schoolroom of the Model Infant School was 64' long, 31' wide and 25' high, with three classrooms opening off it,[32] and the rules were very similar to those which Wilderspin had promulgated in Spitalfields eighteen years earlier, including injunctions to parents to send their children to school clean, washed, combed and properly clad.[33] Within a short time Wilderspin was satisfied that he had "a suitable model infant school established". The institution

[26]Akenson, *Irish Education*, p. 3; p. 111n.; pp. 127-28; pp. 133-39.

[27]*Dublin Evening Mail*, 2 Mar. 1838.

[28]*Early Discipline* (1840), p. 333.

[29]*Ibid.*, p. 334.

[30]Carlile, however, was also granted a residence and horse and carriage worth £100 and was allowed to keep his parish income (Akenson, *Irish Education*, p. 140).

[31]*Early Discipline* (1840), p. 334.

[32]P.P. 1856 XXVII, Twenty-Second Report of the Commissioners of National Education in Ireland, for the Year 1855, Vol. II, App. G., IV, "Professor McGauley's Report on the Training and Central Model Schools...", p. 186.

[33]*Dublin Evening Mail*, 2 Mar. 1838.

"excited much attention" and he felt that the Board recognised that the arrangements for mental and moral education were "novel and striking" and that they could not but perceive the superiority of his system to anything formerly attempted.[34]

Little evidence of the organisation, curriculum and teaching methods in the Model Infant School have survived, but a glimpse of the activities of a typical day may be seen in Thomas Young's rather light-hearted description of his duties:

> ...to do gallery work twice a day, attend to marching, reading, spelling, singing, etc., etc., etc. To be at once judge and advocate in all disputes, to be Magistrate to keep the peace and correct abuses, Parent to soothe, comfort and cherish. To be an intellectual being, to excite, and feed, the children's minds, a moral being, to repress their evil passions, and bring forth latent good, and lastly to direct and control their physical development, rousing the dull child out of its inactivity, and checking the active, that they may not break their arms, or heads or necks.[35]

According to a memorandum prepared by McGauley and Rintoul, two of the staff of the Training Department, the infant school was divided into twelve classes, under monitors. The older children were taken to do group work in the smaller classrooms while the younger had lessons on objects. There were gallery lessons on geography, arithmetic and natural history and plenty of singing, chanting of tables and rhymes, marching and playground exercise. Apart from an opening and closing hymn and a "moral address" at the end, there was apparently no formal religious observance or religious instruction. The playgrounds — there was one attached to each of the three schools — were, the memorandum continued "very important appendages to the schools"; "various species of gymnastics" took place there and "propriety of conduct and moral restraint" were inculcated, principally by the media of fruit and flower borders, which the children learned not to touch.[36]

* * * * *

Sometime during Wilderspin's first months in Dublin an event occurred which was to have a decisive influence on his future — Dr. McArthur, the superintendent of the three model schools, was afflicted with mental illness and had to be relieved of his post. The Board's choice of successor fell on Wilderspin.[37] From the sources available it is not possible to date these events

[34] *Early Discipline* (1840), pp. 333-34.

[35] Young Papers, T.U. Young to Wilderspin, 22 Jan. 1843.

[36] B.M. Add. Mss. Peel Papers, 40612, ff. 110-13; the memorandum is untitled and undated.

[37] *Early Discipline* (1840), p. 334. Wilderspin was justifiably annoyed when Lord Morpeth, Chief Secretary for Ireland, referring to the incident in the House of Lords a year later, omitted to mention that Wilderspin had been appointed in McArthur's place. (*Ibid.*, p. 334n.). For Morpeth's account, cf. Parl. Deb., 3rd Sers., XLVI, 19 Mar. 1839, 891.

with any accuracy. In an account of the incident written years later Wilderspin stated that he had requested a little time to consider the offer and had suggested that in the meantime he might give a course of six lectures on infant and juvenile education. The lectures were advertised as being "for the benefit of the masters of Primary Schools" then under training at Marlborough Street, but they were also attended by "some authorities from the Castle", Archbishops Whately and Murray and some of the other Commissioners; admission was by ticket only, "with the seal of the Commissioners on each ticket".[38] In the first two lectures Wilderspin explained, in his usual fashion, that he based his educational programme on the three-fold nature of man — moral, intellectual and physical. He devoted the third, fourth and fifth lectures to a fairly general exposition of physical, mental and moral education, stressing the importance of the playground as both a moral and physical training area, the desirability of stimulating the child's curiosity and love of knowledge, the need for intellectual instruction to be graded from the simple to the complex and the importance of love as a moral agent.[39]

Though the content of the lectures marked little progression on the ideas of the sixth edition of the *Infant System,* it was sufficiently "advanced" to compel attention. Only in the sixth lecture, in which he advocated that boys and girls be educated with reference to their respective duties in later life did he bow to the conventions. At the conclusion of the series Dr. Whately moved a vote of thanks "in such complimentary terms as need not be stated", and Dr. Murray seconded.[40] The lectures served several purposes. They enlightened the student teachers; they secured Wilderspin the support of several important Commissioners; above all they served as a public declaration of the principles which Wilderspin would put into practice should he accept the post with the Board.[41]

He was not seeking the office; he wrote later that "it was given entirely of their own free will, without solicitation on my part, either directly or indirectly".[42] Nor did he consider it without some heart searching; unlike the situation at the Model Infant School, the post involved becoming a permanent official of the Board, and Wilderspin, accustomed to *ad hoc* engagements, was loth to lose his independence, preferring the life of the free-lance educationist. "As long as I lived and could work, I could find plenty to do and be my own master", he maintained, but after a renewed request, which followed the lectures,

---

[38] Ms. Revisions, *Early Discipline* (1840), p. 334-35.

[39] Wilderspin Papers, leaflet entitled "Six Lectures on the Elements of Popular Education" (n.d.).

[40] Ms. Revisions, *Early Discipline* (1840), pp. 335-36.

[41] The dates of the lectures present some problems. The syllabus in the Wilderspin Papers assigns the first lecture to 27 February, two days after his wedding in Liverpool, and the last to 15 March. These dates, though not impossible, do not harmonise with the sequence of events outlined in *Early Discipline* (1840), nor the Ms. Revisions to this text, which sequence has been followed. It is possible that the lectures were given on dates other than those advertised. The Ms. Revisions mention eight lectures, but this is probably a slip.

[42] *Early Discipline* (1840), p. 334n.

he accepted the invitation.[43] A letter from the secretary of the Board, dated 25 May, informed him of his salary; to his great surprise, though he had been promoted, his salary was cut by £100. "I undertook all the additional labour", he remarked ruefully, "at a smaller salary than I had received when superintending the infant department alone". Only his perennial conviction that opportunities to extend the scope of his work were of greater importance than monetary reward allowed him to accept the situation.[44]

His appointment came at a critical period in the history of the national system. The Presbyterians, organised in the Synod of Ulster under the leadership of Dr. Henry Cooke, a demagogic Evangelical, had withdrawn a number of their schools from the system four years earlier and continued to attack it (as MacNeile had attacked the system in Liverpool) on the grounds that the Bible was barred from the schools and that the Scripture Extracts were a "mutilation".[45] At the beginning of 1838 the relations of the Board with the Synod were still in a delicate state, despite the former's concession on religious instruction of the previous October, which paved the way for ultimate reconciliation.[46] The Established Church of Ireland, also dominated by Evangelicals and conservatives, constantly attacked the system on the same grounds as the Presbyterians and on 17 May 1838 took the first steps to form the Church Education Society;[47] this society established its own schools and seriously upset the "mixed" nature of the national schools, especially in the South.[48]

The Catholics, who formed some eighty per cent of the population, had initially supported the system on the pragmatic grounds that it made inroads into illiteracy. But at the beginning of 1838, John MacHale, Archbishop of Tuam, began to attack it in a series of widely-published letters to Lord John Russell, which continued throughout the year. MacHale was an ultra-nationalist with an appetite for polemical politics, who saw little difference between Whig and Tory policies, but placed the cause of all Ireland's miseries and discontents at the door of the Protestant English.[49] The "foreign functionaries" of the Board, he thundered, were men "of alien countries and alien creed", the agents of an English legislature whose policy was "to sap the

[43]Ms. Revisions, *Early Discipline* (1840), p. 334; p. 336.

[44]*Early Discipline* (1840), pp. 334-35.

[45]Akenson, *Irish Education,* pp. 161-68.

[46]*Ibid.,* p. 183. The managers of the schools were allowed to set the time for religious instruction at any time of the day instead of at the beginning or end of the day, provided the arrangement was publicly announced to interested parents in advance.

[47]P.P. 1854 XV, Report from the Select Committee of the House of Lords Appointed to Inquire into the Practical Working of the System of National Education in Ireland, Pt. II, p. 1255.

[48]Akenson, *Irish Education,* pp. 197-99.

[49]For MacHale's politics, cf. N. Costello, *John MacHale, Archbishop of Tuam* (Dublin 1939), *passim;* O. MacDonagh, "The Politicization of the Irish Catholic Bishops, 1800-1850", *Historical Journal,* Vol. XVIII, No. 1, 1975, pp. 37-53.

religion of the people under the specious guise of liberal education". He objected to the use of the Scriptures as a textbook, to the Board's right to choose books for Catholic children, to the alleged waste and extravagance at Marlborough Street, which had "as many schools for infants and academies for adults as your taste may indulge..." "Get rid at once of the useless humbug of a metropolitan model school", he cried to Russell, "and the long suite of clerks and inspectors — an invention which our *liberal* theorists have imported from Prussia".[50] MacHale succeeded in winning over ten of the twenty-six bishops, but the majority, led by Murray, who had a reputation as a "Castle Bishop" among the nationalists, upheld the work of the Board. The matter was brought to the attention of Rome, which on 2 May 1838 asked both MacHale and Murray for an account of the system.[51]

May 1838 thus marked the beginning of a critical period in the Board's history, for if the Vatican were to pronounce against the system the Irish educational experiment was at an end. For the next three years, in fact, until the compromise worked out with the Presbyterians in 1840,[52] and the Vatican's decision in January 1841 to leave approval of the national system to individual bishops,[53] the fate of the Board hung in the balance. To compound the difficulties, Carlile resigned his post as Commissioner sometime in May; his duties, he complained, had become almost entirely concerned with finance, and he wished to return to more academic pursuits. At his own request he was appointed Professor of Education in the Education Department, "in which", he stated, "there was some danger of disorder arising",[54] possibly a reference to the transfer of superintendence from McArthur to Wilderspin.

The conditions under which Wilderspin entered upon his duties were far from ideal. Prudence would have suggested a gradual approach and an attempt to win the teachers over to his point of view; he was, after all, an outsider. But with characteristic haste he began a course of what a critic later called "theorising" and "experiments".[55] Wilderspin found a lack of flexibility in the teaching in the upper schools; the masters always put the same questions to the pupils and received the same answers and, on inquiry, he was told that they were not allowed to ask any questions except those that were written down. The

---

[50]This paragraph is based on the letters of MacHale to Russell between 12 February 1838 and 18 January 1839, in *The Letters of the Most Reverend John MacHale, D.D.* (Dublin 1847), pp. 392-496, *passim.*

[51]For a detailed account, cf. E. Larkin, "The Quarrel Among the Roman Catholic Hierarchy over the National System of Education in Ireland, 1838-41", in R.B. Browne, W.J. Roscelli, and R. Loftus (Eds.), *The Celtic Cross* (Purdue 1964), pp. 121-46.

[52]Akenson, *Irish Education,* pp. 183-87. In non-vested schools (i.e. those receiving annual grants for books and teachers' salaries only) the Presbyterians were allowed to draw up their own rules; these, in Akenson's view, turned them into "denominational schools with a conscience clause".

[53]Larkin, "Roman Catholic Hierarchy", *loc. cit.,* p. 141.

[54]Carlile's letter of resignation from his post as Professor, printed in *Dublin Evening Mail,* 28 Dec. 1838.

[55]D. Dunlop, *A Review of the Administration of the Board of National Education, in Ireland* (London 1843), p. 15.

[56]*System of Education* (1840), p. 231.

monitorial system was also in use to some extent. "So I found that the 'parrot system' had been revived", he complained, "which I thought had been consigned to the tomb of the Capulets".[56] Lacking the diplomatic talents which might have persuaded the teachers to modify their methods, he tried precipitately to introduce his own conceptions of teaching; the methods were probably similar to those he had found it easy to persuade the Liverpool teachers to adopt. But the situation in the Dublin Model Schools was vastly different from that which existed in the Liverpool Corporation Schools. The Irish teachers considered his plans "a gross innovation (sic) upon their rights and privileges" and he found that "several cabals were raised against me". Unwisely, perhaps, he went over their heads and sought the aid of "the chief and practical members of the Board" (probably Whately and Murray) who sent orders to the teachers that the schools were to be entirely under Wilderspin's control.[57]

Again there is a dearth of information regarding the kind of changes which Wilderspin brought about. A report on the boys' school in 1840, however, referred to class teaching, Pestalozzian methods in reading and linear drawing and the importance of moral training in the playground;[58] these were probably Wilderspinian innovations which had survived. In any case it would appear that Wilderspin was able to make some changes, for within a few months he had the schools in what he considered "a fair and workable condition".[59] He had every reason to believe, by the end of the summer of 1838, that his position was satisfactory and secure, and that he had at last found a position in which, despite difficulties, he could bring his life's work to fruition.

* * * * *

Sometime in early September, however, Wilderspin was involved in another altercation; this time it was to have a disastrous and lasting effect on his career. Antony Blake happened to be visiting the schools and observing that the masters were preparing the pupils to march out of the classroom ten minutes before dismissal time, apparently a custom introduced by McArthur, reproved them in front of the pupils and of Wilderspin himself. Wilderspin, according to Blake, reacted angrily and "betrayed intemperance. . .and disrespect towards him". Wilderspin's version of the story (in a letter to the Lord Lieutenant, Viscount Ebrington) was that Blake had broken the rule that all orders respecting the schools should come through him as chief superintendent; Blake had treated him "in a manner in which I had never been treated before", and had

---

[57] *Early Discipline* (1840), p. 335.

[58] P.P. 1842 XXIII, Seventh Report of the Commissioners of National Education in Ireland for the Year 1840, Professor Sullivan, "An Outline of the General Regulations and Methods of Teaching in the Male National Model Schools. . .", pp. 106-20.

[59] *Early Discipline* (1840), p. 335.

rendered the master "a mere cypher in the eyes of his pupils and myself as superintendent a mere cypher in the eyes of all".[60]

Blake brought the incident to the notice of the other members of the Board; their immediate reaction was that "Mr. Wilderspin be strictly admonished as to his future conduct while in the employment of the Board". Two days later he was summoned to a Board meeting, where it was recorded in the minutes that "Mr. Wilderspin expressing himself conscious of having acted improperly on the occasion, and his regret for the same, the Commissioners expressed themselves satisfied". At the earlier meeting the Board had directed that Wilderspin "forthwith proceed to Belfast" to report on the infant school there and to assist in effecting any necessary changes. They also decided that they were "uncertain" whether his services would be required after the end of his contract year, which, according to the Board, expired on 21 March 1839. Should they require his services, they concluded, and were Wilderspin disposed to render them, they would then enter into a new arrangement with him.[61]

According to Wilderspin's account, this was not made known to him immediately — an "abrupt hint" was given later.[62] Probably not very much later, for the Fifth Report of the Board, published in early 1839, contained the report of an economy committee which stated that the decision had been "notified to him in September last". This committee, no doubt interpreting the Board's wishes correctly, was quite certain that the necessity for Wilderspin's services had ceased; it added that his successor as superintendent would be Mr. Lawton, a teacher in the Model School, at a salary of £120. This move, the committee did not fail to point out, would effect a saving of £380 per year.[63]

Wilderspin duly proceeded to Belfast where he set in order the infant department of Frederick Street School to the satisfaction of the committee.[64] It was ironical that the master of this school, Robert Dunning, was a year or so later made head of the Home and Colonial Infant School Society's school in Gray's Inn Road.[65] On his return from Belfast Wilderspin found that "the whole tone of the Board changed towards me", but apparently he remained in his post as superintendent during the remainder of the year of his contract, for he stated

[60]This account is derived from a copy of the Minutes of the Board of National Education for 27 and 29 September 1838 and a letter of Wilderspin to the Lord Lieutenant, Viscount Ebrington, of July 1939 (S.P.O.D. 48/5091 P. 493, "Extract from Board's Minutes dated 27th September 1838; Adjourned Meeting — 29 September 1838"; S.P.O.D. 48/5091 P. 443, Wilderspin to Ebrington, 8 July 1839).

[61]S.P.O.D. 48/5091 P. 493, Minutes 27 and 29 Sept. 1838. The date suggests that his contract began on 21 March 1838. This was after the conclusion of the lecture series (if the dates were correct) but only sixteen days after the opening of the Infant Model School. On March 16 Whately stated that Wilderspin "is engaged to superintend our national infant Schools" (N.L.S. Add. Mss., 7248, f. 168, Whately to Combe, 16 Mar. 1838).

[62]S.P.O.D. 48/5091 P.443 , Wilderspin to Ebrington, 8 July 1839.

[63]P.P. 1839 XVI, Fifth Report of the Commissioners, "Report of a Committee to Inquire into Establishments and Advise on Reductions", App. No. 1, p. 16.

[64]*Early Discipline* (1840), p. 337-38.

[65]*The Schoolmasters' Magazine and Educational Inquirer* (Armagh), Vol I, No. VII, Mar. 1840, pp. 217-18.

explicitly that the schools at Dublin and Belfast were the only ones he organised for the Board.[66] As the expiry date of his contract approached, he made a number of attempts to enlist the aid of public figures to secure redress of his grievances with the Board.

In March he wrote to Archbishop Whately, though he was unwise enough to accompany his request for support with hints of further action. Not unnaturally Whately reacted strongly against what he termed "a threat, or something — to say the least — which may be easily understood as a threat, of resorting to some plans of agitation, in the event of your not obtaining what you consider as fair play", and declined to see Wilderspin on these terms without "a very distinct explanation...on this point".[67] Immediately on receipt of Whately's reply he addressed a letter to Lord Brougham, requesting his aid in securing him a post in England under the newly-formed Committee of Council on Education.[68]

In May he sought the help of Lord Lansdowne, in June that of Lord John Russell; and in July he wrote the letter to Lord Ebrington, the Lord Lieutenant, already referred to. Without exception the noble lords declined to interfere.[69] What had started out as the long-awaited opportunity to further the infant system through the agency of a model school ended in a humiliating and fruitless series of supplicatory letters. Wilderspin remained in Ireland until the beginning of August, when, leaving his family in Dublin, he returned to England.[70]

The conflict with Blake went deeper than a quarrel over regulations between an over-zealous official and a contentious superintendent, though personal antipathies and national-religious animosities were undoubtedly present. Thomas Young later referred to Blake as Wilderspin's "enemy", who had been "relentless" in chasing him out of his situation.[71] Wilderspin, on his part, thought Blake had shown "zeal without discretion" and the kind of "overbearing conduct without the necessary prudence to guide it" which he had seen too often in Ireland. How easily such feelings could assume a politico-religious colouring was evident in Wilderspin's next remark (in the letter to

[66] S.P.O.D. 48/5091 P. 443, Wilderspin to Ebrington, 8 July 1839; *Early Discipline* (1840), p. 337.

[67] Wilderspin Papers, Whately to Wilderspin, 4 Mar. 1839. This incident did not permanently affect his friendly relationship with Whately. (Young Papers, T.U. Young to Wilderspin, 22 Dec. 1843). A few weeks after the brush with Wilderspin, Whately was asked by George Combe, then in the U.S.A., "whether your Irish Board is done with him, and whether he could be induced to come to the United States for a season". (N.L.S. Add. Mss., 7396, f. 46., Combe to Whately, 30 Mar. 1839). It is not known whether Whately informed Wilderspin of this.

[68] U.C.L. Brougham Mss., 29076, Wilderspin to Brougham, 7 Mar. 1839.

[69] Wilderspin Papers, Lansdowne to Wilderspin, 24 May 1839; Russell to Wilderspin, 21 June 1839. Wilderspin's letter to Ebrington in the State Paper Office, Dublin, is endorsed with a secretary's note, "His Excellency has uniformly made it a rule not to interfere in such cases".

[70] *Early Discipline* (1840), p. 345. The date is deduced from the endorsement on the Ebrington letter, which records a reply sent to Wilderspin on 2 August. It is assumed that Wilderspin remained at Alpha House, from which the letter was sent, until he received a reply. A series of advertisements for his "Lessons and Apparatus" in the *Dublin Evening Mail* continued until 2 August.

[71] Young Papers, T.U. Young to Wilderspin, 8 Apr. 1849.

Ebrington), "Englishmen are not accustomed to such treatment, and there are some who will not tamely submit to it".[72] But more was involved. Blake was a vital link between the government and the Catholic Church — an "official Catholic",[73] exercising power on behalf of the government in a highly-sensitive experiment with the minds and hearts of Irish children. In antagonising Blake Wilderspin was, in effect, challenging the whole enterprise, and the consequences were correspondingly serious.[74]

On his return to England Wilderspin lost little time in putting his views on his recent experiences into print. He incorporated some strong criticisms of Ireland and the national system of education in new editions of the *Infant System* and *Early Discipline* and in *A System of Education for the Young,* all written in late 1839 and early 1840.[75] His remarks were scattered and repetitive, but could be reduced to three main allegations. First, he felt that conditions in Ireland were conducive to jobbery and chicanery; "the plan usually adopted is, to talk much and do little, and make a wonderful noise with few results". Though the National Board had spent half a million pounds "raised from the English taxation", there was not a solitary instance of their having organised a good school, mainly because men who were "totally destitute of practical knowledge" and unfit for the duties required were put into positions of responsibility.[76]

Second, the teaching at the training schools was of too abstract a nature for the comprehension of the teachers in training; "...the idea of appointing a professor of belle lettre(sic) to teach Irish schoolmasters, many of whom only receive eight pounds per annum, and scarcely any above five and twenty, is...truly laughable". What the Irish teacher needed, he thought, was "plain education on plain and useful matters", plus moral training and perhaps some instruction in the teaching of girls.[77]

Third, the Irish educational system was falling into the hands of the Catholics. The Whig government's policy of liberalisation of the Irish administrative machine by appointing Catholics and liberal Protestants to vacancies as they occurred,[78] evident in the Board's appointment of a Catholic and Protestant as joint secretaries in December 1838 and some changes in personnel favourable to the Catholics,[79] was critically received by Wilderspin. It was clear evidence of the Catholic domination of Marlborough Street; training masters, monitors and students were overwhelmingly of that faith. Under

---

[72]S.P.O.D. 48/5091 P. 443, Wilderspin to Ebrington, 8 July 1839.

[73]The phrase is Akenson's (*Irish Education,* p. 111 n.).

[74]We are indebted to Susan Parkes for an elaboration of this point.

[75]Wilderspin Papers, J. Hodson to Wilderspin, 10 Sept. 1839, for evidence of dating.

[76]*System of Education* (1840), pp. 226-27.

[77]*Ibid.,* pp. 231-33.

[78]J.C. Beckett, *The Making of Modern Ireland* (London 1969), pp. 315-17; G.O. Tuathaigh, *Ireland Before the Famine 1798-1848* (Dublin 1972), pp. 183-84.

[79]*Dublin Evening Mail,* 7 Nov. 1838; *Freemans's Journal,* 5 Dec. 1838.

pressure from the nationalists — "a party. . .who can defeat the best intentions of any government" — the Irish experiment in non-denominational education was "a most complete and decided failure".[80] Though he had somewhat exaggerated the situation as it existed in 1839, there was no doubt that Wilderspin had put his finger on the general trend; by the mid-century the national system had become "undenominational in theory but denominational in practice", largely because of the demographic situation, but also partly due to the Board's failure to insist upon school managers of mixed faiths.[81]

Though he took a broad view of trends within the system, he was unable to see his own role in a larger context. He persisted in depicting himself as a victim of intrigue:

> . . .if perchance a man should be determined to do his duty, and also to insist that those placed under him should do the same, he will become exceedingly unpopular, be dubbed with the character of a busybody, and no means will be left untried which falsehood, double-dealing, hypocrisy and deceit can accomplish, finally to victimize him.[82]

The independent progressive educator hampered by the conservatism of his colleagues and entangled in the meshes of bureaucracy? Or the imported pedagogue, inculcating policies and methods developed in a politico-religious situation foreign to that in which he was working? Wilderspin saw the situation almost entirely in terms of the first model, and though he sincerely believed that the more creative and flexible methods he advocated were superior to those he criticised, he showed himself less than aware of the fact that representatives of emerging Catholic nationalism might see the situation in a different light; that what to him was an up-to-date system eminently suited to benefit the Irish people within the structure of a national system of education might appear to a large body of Catholic opinion as a foreign import, part and parcel of what an eloquent nationalist called "that worst of tyrannies — Protestant ascendancy in a Catholic country".[83]

Brougham, who alleged that Wilderspin's qualifications were of "too humble a character" to allow of his retaining the appointment under the Board,[84] missed the point. Wilderspin's failure in Ireland was fundamentally due to the fact that he found himself occupying a sensitive outpost in the Anglo-Irish conflict and was unable, because of his outlook and personality, to transcend the

---

[80]*System of Education* (1840), p. 225; p. 482. Wilderspin also hinted that "certain parties" had more or less deliberately mismanaged a visit of Lord John Russell to Marlborough Street in September 1838, which resulted in Russell receiving an unfavourable impression of his own work (*System of Education* (1840), pp. 254-55).

[81]Akenson, *Irish Education,* pp. 214-24.

[82]*System of Education* (1840), p. 226.

[83]Letter signed "Camillus" in *Freeman's Journal,* 18 Dec. 1838. The writer was a fairly frequent contributor to the Catholic press and was praised by MacHale for his nationalism (MacHale to Russell, 2 May 1838 (MacHale, *Letters,* p. 430)).

[84][H. Brougham], "Education of the People", *Westminster and Foreign Quarterly Review,* Vol XLVI, No. 1, Oct. 1846, p. 221.

situation. But the issue cannot be seen entirely in personal terms; it was part of a wider failure of the British administration to solve the "Irish problem" in a manner acceptable to the whole Irish people.

* * * * *

Wilderspin left two legacies to Ireland. The first was the Model Infant School, in charge of his daughter and son-in-law. The Youngs were, in the best sense, disciples of Wilderspin. They kept a bust of him in their sitting-room,[85] shared his interest in the principles of Swedenborg and Pestalozzi[86] and consistently tried to put into practice the Wilderspinian system of infant education. They inhabited a very different mental universe from those among whom they worked, and sometimes they felt that they were fighting a continual battle against "the prejudices, the passions, and the selfishness of those around us";[87] on one occasion Young wrote to his father-in-law, "We who are here in close contact with unfortunate and misguided Paddy almost envy you your honest comfortable neighbour John Bull".[88] In 1843 he was seriously considering quitting his Dublin post for a position in an Orphan School in London.[89]

The Youngs remained in Dublin, however, coping as best they could with the ever-present problem of great numbers of children (attendance fluctuated around the 300 mark during the early 1840s)[90], the constant stream of visitors, and the presence each day of some thirty teachers in training.[91] By the mid-40s certain improvements made their task easier and more pleasant. A gallery to hold fifty children was constructed in one of the classrooms, writing desks were installed, and the playground paved, surrounded by a wall and re-stocked with flowers; "a handsome pair of twelve inch globes" was also provided for each school.[92] In 1850 Sarah Anne informed her father:

> We have a very large school now, but having the three classrooms is a great convenience and help, for we divide the numbers whenever we can, such as at reading, arithmetic and at lunch time, so that the children are only altogether a short time, the first thing in the morning and at marching being the only time

[85]Young Papers, T.U. Young to Wilderspin, 22 Dec. 1843.

[86]Sarah Anne Young, in particular, was a devoted follower of Swedenborg throughout her life and a student of his works. (Young Papers, T.U. Young to Wilderspin, Dec. 1849; S.A. Young to Wilderspin, 8 Mar. 1857). Her husband wrote to Wilderspin in 1851 praising Pestalozzi, "who had the true spirit of the educator in him" (Young Papers, T.U. Young to Wilderspin, 22 Nov. 1851).

[87]Young Papers, T.U. Young to Wilderspin, 22 Dec. 1843.

[88]Young Papers, T.U. Young to Wilderspin, 22 Dec. 1848.

[89]Young Papers, T.U. Young to Wilderspin, 22 July 1843.

[90]P.R.O.I. 2C.57.31. Registers, National Schools Co. Dublin, Vol. I, 1835-45.

[91]Young Papers, S.A. Wilderspin to Wilderspin, July 1845; T.U. Young to Wilderspin, Dec. 1849.

[92]Young Papers, S.A. Young to Wilderspin, July 1845; T.U. Young to Wilderspin, Dec. 1845; 21 Mar. 1850.

the whole number are together, and of course at play, for we do not divide them then.[93]

The school received a measure of international acclaim, being visited and praised by W.E. Hickson, Professor Pillans of Edinburgh, W. Cooke-Taylor and the American feminist and abolitionist Lucretia Mott.[94] At the end of the 1840s the Board was opening District Model Infant Schools, on the pattern of the one in Dublin, in various parts of Ireland; the methods and practices of Wilderspin, as developed by the Youngs, thus spread well beyond the confines of the capital.[95]

In the Dublin school, Wilderspin's ideals and the spirit of his system were exemplified in the teaching of his daughter Sarah Anne. Her personality and outlook, her husband recalled in later life, were admirably suited to her task. Her fundamental principle with regard to infants was "draw them to you by love". If you began by putting their will in opposition to yours, she would exclaim, it was impossible to teach them; "you cannot use force with infants". "Catholic, Protestant and Jew alike experienced her kindly care", her husband wrote, "and were ever treated with equal love". In formal teaching she believed in simplicity in the early stages and the need for the teacher to bring herself down to the level of the pupils if they were to benefit by the lessons. She herself was adept at this; "her own manner in teaching was characterised by a wise playfulness; so that while her lesson was to the pupil a pleasant game it conveyed much instruction".[96]

What might be called Wilderspin's second legacy to Ireland was Thomas Young's *The Teacher's Manual for Infant Schools and Preparatory Classes,* written at the request of the Board and published in 1852; an extremely popular work, it sold 30,000 copies within the first decade of its publication.[97] Composed in conscious opposition to the Home and Colonial Infant School Society's manuals, it was intended to be an exposition of Wilderspin's ideas; Young informed his father-in-law that he had kept as close as possible to "your principles" and had followed "your system only". He had originally intended to make it a purely secular work, but on showing the proofs to Archbishop Whately, who remarked that there was no more Christianity in it than if it had

[93]Young Papers, S.A. Young to Wilderspin, 21 Mar. 1850.

[94]Cf. W.E. Hickson, *Dutch and German Schools* (London 1840), p. 38; Young Papers, R. Wilderspin (?) to Wilderspin, 19 June 1845; W. Cooke-Taylor, *Notes of a Visit to the Model Schools in Dublin* (Dublin 1847); F.B. Tolles (Ed.), *Slavery and "The Woman Question". Lucretia Mott's Diary of Her Visit to Great Britain to Attend the World's Anti-Slavery Convention of 1840* (Haverford and London 1952), p. 64.

[95]Young Papers, T.U. Young to Wilderspin, 8 Apr. 1849. For some interesting glimpses of the Wilderspin system at work, cf. P.P. 1850 XXV, The Sixteenth Report of the Commissioners of National Education in Ireland (for the year 1849), App. XLIII, p. 244-80.

[96]Young Papers, T.U. Young, "Memoir of the Late Mrs. Young" (Ms. II). Worn out with the burdens of teaching and child-bearing (she was the mother of ten children) Mrs. Young died in 1860 at the early age of forty-six.

[97]T.U. Young, *The Teacher's Manual for Infant Schools and Preparatory Classes* (Dublin 1852). The third (1860) edition had "30th thousand" on its title page.

been written by a Jew or a Mohammedan, he introduced "some more direct Christianity".[98]

Even so, the completed work was remarkable for the separation of religion from morality, and for the contention that morality itself should be based upon the development of the reasoning and intellectual faculties, thus making it an outcome of the educational process. Apart from this, the text displayed all the usual Wilderspinian features — exercise, play, amusement, singing, gallery work; a wide curriculum — sacred history, reading, spelling, grammar, writing, drawing, arithmetic, geography, natural history and poetry; the need for well-qualified teachers, able without severity or ridicule to inspire in children habits of willing obedience, truth, gentleness, generosity and mutual love, was also brought out. In many ways it was a clearer and more highly theoretical exposition of Wilderpin's principles than Wilderspin himself had ever achieved, particularly in the treatment of ideas derived from Pestalozzi; Young was one of the few British educationists who understood Pestalozzi's concept of "intuition" and who attempted to apply it to infant teaching.

The *Manual* was the most advanced work on infant education of the mid-nineteenth century and could not but have exercised a beneficial influence on the Irish schools. In the final analysis, however, it is not possible to ignore the Irish context. The spread of Wilderspin's ideas could not be seen as a means of enlightenment *tout court*. On the one hand it was desirable, as Thomas Young wrote, "to see the system established generally in Ireland as part of the common school education of the people".[99] On the other hand, it could not be separated from the British apparatus of social control; one of the functions of education, Young pointed out, was to arm the Irish people against becoming "a prey to the designing demagogue and bigoted priest".[100] Not surprisingly, Irish nationalists never became reconciled to the work of the Youngs. In 1859, J.W. Kavanagh, formerly a Head Inspector, wrote *Mixed Education. The Catholic Case Stated,* a work which became "the educational source book of the Catholic hierarchy";[101] he criticised certain "anti-Catholic" features of the *Manual* and lamented the fact that for twenty years the training of the infancy and tender childhood of Irish Catholics had been directed by the daughter and son-in-law of "Mr. Wilderspin, an Englishman".[102]

[98] Young Papers, T.U. Young to Wilderspin, 22 Nov. 1851; Dec. 1851.

[99] Young Papers, T.U. Young to Wilderspin, Dec. 1849.

[100] Young Papers, T.U. Young to Wilderspin, 23 Dec. 1846.

[101] Akenson, *Irish Education,* p. 301.

[102] [J.W. Kavanagh], *Mixed Education. The Catholic Case Stated; or, Principles, Working and Results of the System of National Education* (Dublin 1859), pp. 45-6.

CHAPTER 15

YEARS OF ADVERSITY

When Wilderspin returned from Ireland in the late summer of 1839, he took up residence in Warrington in the belief that his services might be of more use in a densely-populated manufacturing district than in any other part of the country.[1] The proximity of Warrington to Liverpool, the port of disembarkation from Ireland and territory familiar to him, might also have been a consideration. From September onwards he attempted to resume his career as a lecturer and organiser of infant schools that he had broken off three years earlier.

At the beginning of September he opened a school in Warrington for the Hon. and Rev. Horace Powys.[2] On 16, 18 and 20 September he gave three lectures, to moderately-sized audiences, at the Court House, Stockport, which led to the opening of an infant school (with "moderate" fees and a restricted entry) and the formation of the Victoria Infant School Society on the principles of his system.[3] Further lectures in Warrington at the end of the month were, however, "very badly attended",[4] and shortly afterwards an agent lecturing on Wilderspin's behalf at Middlewich found himself addressing an audience of one. A subsequent lecture at Northwich by Wilderspin himself attracted only twelve listeners. Other engagements involving the organisation of schools followed, concluding with an examination of the infants at Warrington during the last week of October.[5]

The number of engagements could be considered satisfactory; but it was clear that his name was no longer a magnet which drew people to lectures. "What a falling off is here", he had cause to complain, "from the splendid auditories I have recently addressed".[6] He noticed, in fact, "a marked difference" in the manner of his reception from that to which he had formerly been accustomed; the engagement in Ireland, he wrote, "has injured me very seriously".[7]

Anxious to re-establish his position, Wilderspin turned to writing as a means of bringing his name once more before the public, the enforced leisure-time towards the end of the year providing him with ample opportunity. He revised the sixth edition of the *Infant System,* putting in an extra chapter on gallery work and adding here and there some sharply-worded criticisms of

[1] *Early Discipline* (1840), xvii.

[2] *Ibid.,* p. 338.

[3] *Ibid.,* p. 345; *Stockport Advertiser,* 13 and 27 Sept., 11 Oct. 1839; *North Cheshire Reformer,* 20 and 27 Sept. 1839; *Manchester Guardian,* 28 Sept. 1839; *Manchester Chronicle,* 28 Sept. 1839.

[4] *Early Discipline* (1840), p. 339; *Manchester Times,* 28 Sept. 1839; *Manchester Guardian,* 5 Oct. 1839.

[5] *Early Discipline* (1840), pp. 339-42; pp. 344-45; *North Cheshire Reformer,* 1 Nov. 1839.

[6] *Early Discipline* (1840), p. 340.

[7] *Ibid.,* p. 338.

various opponents. He also prepared a third edition of *Early Discipline,* and brought it up to date with a section on his experiences in the previous half-dozen years. Both were published in the first months of 1840.[8]

His major preoccupation, however, was the composition of a new work entitled *A System of Education for the Young,* which appeared some six months later.[9] This was plainly intended to be his *magnum opus* and though its impact was smaller than its contents warranted, it had many virtues and would repay study by teachers and educators today. The book was intended both as a statement of Wilderspin's mature educational wisdom and as a contribution to the debate on education which had been raging during the years following the Reform Act. Unfortunately, it appeared a year or so too late, at a time when the major confrontations over the Whig government's reform proposals had ceased and something of a lull in the educational battle had set in.

A System of Education reflected, in the first place, much of the experience Wilderspin had gained in organising schools for older children in Liverpool and Dublin. It was an attempt to propound in detail the system of education "from infancy to completion" which he had advocated at Liverpool; it also obviously owed much to the work of Wyse and Simpson.[10] The system, Wilderspin felt, should be run by a national Board of Education, preferably staffed by paid commissioners, and with representation from Churchmen and Dissenters in due proportion. An inspectorate and normal school would be welcome, provided they were in the hands of "practical men". The religious question could be solved by the inclusion of the Bible in schools; once this was done "the chief and main difficulty" was over. The Bible, he pointedly added, should certainly not be excluded to please the Roman Catholics. Wilderspin believed that the National Society and the British and Foreign School Society would co-operate — both had introduced the Bible into schools — but he looked to "liberal Churchmen" to recognise that the Church could not monopolise the education of the people. The school, he insisted, was the province of the schoolmaster, who should confine himself to moral and non-dogmatic religious education; the church was the place for the clergyman and for spiritual teaching. Neither should encroach on the domain of the other. The content of religious instruction which Wilderspin proposed was in no way different from his previous formulations; it should be a living principle, influencing life and conduct and producing harmonious relations between teacher and pupil and among pupils themselves.

The greater part of the work was devoted to the teaching of boys and girls aged six and over, which he felt should be carried out in separate schools. The sections on infant education dealt largely with its aims and purposes and a

---

[8]The exact date of publication is not recorded, but the preface of each is dated January 1840.

[9]The preface is dated May 1840.

[10]The following paragraphs are based on the text of the book (pp. 1-471). Most of Wilderspin's proposals regarding the structure and religious arrangements of a national system were made in his comments on Lord John Russell's speech on education to the House of Commons on 12 February 1839 and included as an Appendix (pp. 472-87).

general survey of its methods and effects; though some refinements of previous formulations were included, the Pestalozzian and phrenological concepts of the later editions of *Infant Education* were omitted. The most striking aspect of the work concerned the education of girls; the neglect of their education, he felt, was "appalling" and nothing less than an education similar to that of boys would do them justice. His suggestions, both as to content and method, were far in advance of anything practised in even the most advanced monitorial schools and, in fact, were not put into operation in elementary, or even grammar schools, until the twentieth century. In the first place he stressed the importance of health and the need for both physical education in the playground (which should include exercise, marching, singing and playing on swings) and the study of physiology. The academic curriculum was wide: the 3Rs; geography, taught with the aid of maps (including large ones drawn on the floor and in the playground), water trays with cork islands and model boats and people, and some question and answer periods; botany, utilising the plants of the playground and of gardens; natural history, by means of pictures; object lessons; geometry, taught by means of the gonigraph and pictures of shapes; music and singing; grammar, by means of the elliptical system, rhymes and question and answer; and religious instruction of an undenominational and undogmatic nature. There was a notable absence of "girls' subjects". The curriculum for boys was similar, with the addition of zoology and astronomy, taught by observation of the heavens and the diagrams of the stars and planets. The whole curriculum, with its orientation towards the world of nature, had unmistakable affinities with the work of the progressive educators of the Enlightenment and, more precisely, with the type of education advocated by George Combe.

Wilderspin's *System of Education* can take its place with other works on the subject produced in the same period. More closely concerned with pedagogical practice than Frederic Hill's panoramic survey of 1836[11], more liberal and wide-ranging than Henry Dunn's Anglican tract,[12] it was closest in spirit to Wyse's *Education Reform* and Simpson's *National Education,* and had the same preoccupation with the role of education in forming the character of an industrious, sober, thrifty and intelligent working man that was particularly evident in Wyse's book.[13] Unlike all the other significant works on national education of the post-Reform period, however, it was the product of a practising teacher of long experience and this offset its crudities of style and clumsiness of construction, typical of Wilderspin's excursions into print.

The book also served the purpose of announcing that Wilderspin had abandoned his attitude of hostility to the Church in general and to Evangelicals in particular and that politically he had reverted to support of the moderate

---

[11]F. Hill, *National Education: Its Present State and Prospects* (London, 2 vol., 1836).

[12]H. Dunn, *National Education* (London 1839).

[13]T. Wyse, *Education Reform* (London 1836), pp. 213-23; *System of Education* (1840), pp. 4-7.

Whigs. The inclusion of favourable references to and long extracts from Lord John Russell's speech on education of 12 February and Brougham's *Letter on National Education to the Duke of Bedford* (not to mention a severe condemnation of Owen's social theory) leaves us in no doubt that he was trying to lose the radical reputation he had gained in the mid-thirties.[14] His attitude to the Church shows a dramatic change compared with his *National Education* of 1837. There was no overt criticism of the Establishment; he hoped the Archbishop of Canterbury might become permanent president of any new Board of Education, he looked to the National Society to co-operate with the British and Foreign Society, he appealed, as we have seen, to "liberal Churchmen" and was not above some criticism of Roman Catholics.[15] In the *Infant System,* revised during the same period, he went further, praising the Church's formation of Diocesan Education Societies and Normal Schools, commending the Church of England Prayer Book to infant schools and stating that "if I had my choice, I would train the infants, as far as practicable, into a knowledge of the Church of England principles".[16]

These violent shifts of opinion lay Wilderspin open to charges of inconsistency at best and trimming at worst, and there is no doubt that he was often willing to identify himself with views or principles which might gain him some immediate advantage, particularly if his future seemed at risk. When his position was secure, as in 1836-37, he felt free to advocate radical and anti-clerical views; in 1939-40, however, with the Irish fiasco only recently behind him, almost completely isolated from developments in the world of infant education and faced with the discovery that his name no longer attracted a sizeable audience at every lecture, he felt he could not afford to be overly critical of those whose good will he might yet have to seek.

* * * * *

Early in 1840, before the manuscript of *A System of Education* was completed, and with little prospect of further work in sight, Wilderspin was forced into a course of action that was both new and distasteful — soliciting employment by letter. Swallowing his pride, he began to send out a series of letters to important public figures, inquiring about posts in government or Church organisations. In January 1840 he began at the obvious point by writing to James Kay-Shuttleworth, the recently-appointed secretary of the Committee of Council on Education, presumably seeking a post under the government. Kay-Shuttleworth acknowledged the letter, but nothing came of the application.[17] Wilderspin then turned his attention to the Church. He addressed

---

[14]*System of Education* (1840), p. 338ff; p. 472ff. By this time Brougham had adopted the position that no scheme of national education could exclude the Church.

[15]*Ibid.,* pp. 473-75; p. 483; p. 485.

[16]*Infant System* (1840), p. 75; pp. 326-27.

[17]Wilderspin Papers, J. Kay-Shuttleworth to Wilderspin, 13 Jan. 1840.

a series of letters to leading churchmen who had shown some interest in education and might have known of his work — the bishops of Durham, Gloucester, Chester and Exeter — offering to give a series of lectures on infant education in their dioceses, perhaps as an initial step to more permanent employment. None acceded to his request, but the Bishop of Gloucester and Bristol advised him to apply to the National Society, of which the Archbishop of Canterbury was President, assuring him that "any recommendations sanctioned by approval from that quarter will probably be cheerfully adopted by members of the Church of England".[18] Wilderspin hastened to address a letter to the Society, but John Sinclair, the Secretary, replied that the Society's Committee, while sensible "of your services as a promoter of the infant school system...do not wish at present to avail themselves of your obliging offer".[19]

Rebuffed by Church and State he turned his attention to the working class and sought lecturing engagements with the Mechanics' Institutes. These had sprung up in most of the industrial towns of England on the model of those established by Birkbeck, Brougham and others in London in the early 1820s. Many of these institutes had, by the 40s, members from the lower middle-class, as well as from the working-class, and offered lectures on a wide range of subjects. In March 1840 Wilderspin had addressed a letter to the Mechanics' Institutes in Birmingham, Manchester, Liverpool and Leeds, as well as to those in Sheffield, Dublin and Chester, offering to lecture on "Education and the Art of Teaching" upon the usual terms. "I have long seen", he wrote, "the advantages of Mechanics' Institutes in teaching the different sciences to the working classes". But there was one science, he pointed out, that had never been fully appreciated and discussed — the science of the art of teaching. "I know by experience", he assured his correspondents, "that lectures on the art of teaching may be made highly interesting to the working classes".[20]

The only immediate result was an engagement to lecture in March and April at the flourishing Manchester Mechanics' Institution in Cooper Street. Advertising the course widely,[21] he adapted his earlier lectures to his audience with good effect, urging the universal education of the people and calling for the erection of a central Normal School in Manchester in order to improve the quality of infant schools in the district.[22]

---

[18] Wilderspin Papers, Bishop of Durham to Wilderspin, 24 Apr. 1840; Bishop of Gloucester and Bristol to Wilderspin, 25 Apr. 1840; Bishop of Chester to Wilderspin, 30 Apr. 1840; Bishop of Exeter to Wilderspin, n.d.(? 1840).

[19] Wilderspin Papers, J. Sinclair to Wilderspin, 13 May 1840.

[20] Wilderspin Papers, draft of a letter to Mechanics' Institutes, 8 Mar. 1840.

[21] Cf. ten advertisements in *Manchester Guardian, Manchester Times, Manchester Courier, Manchester Chronicle, Manchester and Salford Advertiser*, 21 Mar. — 18 Apr. 1840, *passim*.

[22] Wilderspin Papers, folder entitled "Four Lectures on Education and the Art of Teaching" (Apr. 1840); *Manchester Guardian*, 18 Apr. 1840.

No other offers were forthcoming and Wilderspin began to realise that the northern industrial districts at the beginning of the Hungry Forties offered little hope for the re-establishment of his fortunes. The worsening economic conditions, the unemployment, poverty and industrial unrest which formed the background to the upsurge of Chartism, militated against his efforts to re-establish a position in infant education. So in the early summer of 1840 he moved to London, taking up residence at 4 Factory Cottage, Tottenham.[23] Thus in the space of a year he had exchanged the position of a gentleman in a fashionable suburb of Dublin for the standard of living and accommodation of a member of the artisan class. The wheel had turned full circle and he was now in circumstances comparable to those of his life before starting at Spitalfields twenty years earlier.

Hardly surprisingly, his thoughts turned once again to the possibility of employment in America. The occasion came shortly after his move to Tottenham. Lucretia Mott, the American anti-slavery campaigner, was visiting England to attend the World Anti-Slavery Convention; having discussed the question of female education with Sarah Anne Young in Dublin in July, she met Wilderspin himself a few weeks later when visiting Robert Forster, the Quaker philanthropist, in Tottenham.[24] After tea, faced with the company of the sisters of the family, she sent for Wilderspin (who presumably was living nearby). She recorded the conversation cryptically in her diary: "had talk with him of Infant Schools — visiting America..."[25] Whether this was significant of Wilderspin's intention or merely of his interest is a moot point; but eleven days later he wrote to George Combe, who had met Mrs. Mott and her husband in the United States earlier in the year,[26] "I am greatly obliged to you for mentioning my humble name in the United States... How odd it is that when my Glasgow friends try to knock me down, my Edinburgh friends are sure to lift me up".[27] Combe replied, "...I endeavoured to get up a subscription of £100 in Philadelphia to pay your passage out and home to induce you to come to that city to institute an infant school, but the money was not forthcoming". Combe asserted that Wilderspin was "very much wanted in the United States" and assured him that he would find there "abundance of employment and good remuneration"; he added, however, that "no individual will invite you, lest they should give offence".[28] In

---

[23]The date and place are deduced from addresses on his correspondence at this period. He later moved to 8 St. James' Place, Hackney and then to 4 Gwynne's Place, Hackney Road.

[24]F.B. Tolles (Ed.), *Slavery and "The Woman Question". Lucretia Mott's Diary of Her Visit to Great Britain to Attend the World's Anti-Slavery Convention of 1840* (Haverford and London 1952), p. 64; p. 75.

[25]*Ibid.,* p. 75, entry dated 20 Aug. 1840.

[26]*Ibid.,* p. 37.

[27]N.L.S. Add. Mss., 7257, f. 161, Wilderspin to Combe, 31 Aug. 1840. The "Glasgow friends" were David Stow and his associates who, according to Wilderspin, were claiming credit for his work of the late 1820s.

[28]N.L.S. Add. Mss., 7388, f. 209, Combe to Wilderspin, 27 Sept. 1840.

Wilderspin's straitened circumstances there was no question of his finding the money himself and for the second time his hope of employment in the New World was dashed. Combe, however, added at the end of his letter, "I regret to hear that the Government is doing you an injustice. They will not do so intentionally, and if you write to Sir Thomas Wyse, H.M. Treasury Chambers, London, he will not allow you to be wronged". Whether or not Wilderspin wrote to Wyse is not recorded, but if he did it became clear that nothing positive transpired.

1841 saw little improvement in Wilderspin's prospects. In May Edward Herford, Secretary of the Manchester District Association of Literary and Scientific Institutions, reported that he was unable to arrange for a single engagement since "all the Institutions about here are so low on funds and the working classes generally discouraged with the badness of the times".[29] Later in the year Thomas Plint wrote on behalf of the Literary Institution in Leeds that it would be useless to attempt a lecture on education there. "There is a remarkable apathy on the subject just now — in fact the public can have only one great subject before it at one time, and it has such a subject now".[30] That, presumably, was the social and economic condition of the country. There was, however, a flurry of activity as the year closed — a lecture in the Library of the Parish of St. Bride's in Fetter Lane in November or December; a lecture on "Education" before the Richmond Mechanics' Institution on 20 December; and a course of four lectures for the Greenwich Society for the Acquisition and Diffusion of Knowledge in late December 1841 and early January 1842.[31]

This was followed by a course of lectures on "Education for the Children of the Respectable Classes", which he delivered on 19 and 26 January and 2 and 9 February 1842 in the North London Juvenile Training Seminary in Liverpool Street, the London outpost of Stow's Glasgow training institution. It was a measure of his desperation that he felt it necessary to address this body and to advertise in the *Record,* the Evangelical newspaper, which was the main publicity agent for the Home and Colonial Infant School Society.[32] He kept some of his self respect by describing himself as the "inventor of the Infant and Training System", apparently without objection from his hosts.[33] This was followed by a flying visit to Scotland to lecture at the Watt Institution, Dundee, in early March.[34]

[29] Wilderspin Papers, E. Herford to Wilderspin, 20 May 1841.

[30] Wilderspin Papers, T. Plint to Wilderspin, 20 Nov. 1841.

[31] Wilderspin Papers, T. Dale to Wilderspin, 15 Nov. 1841; poster entitled "Richmond Mechanics' Institution. . .S. Wilderspin, Esq. . ." (1841); poster entitled "Greenwich Society. . .Mr. Samuel Wilderspin. . ." (1841).

[32] *Record,* 17 Jan. 1842.

[33] Wilderspin Papers, leaflet entitled "Lectures on Education, by Mr. Wilderspin. . ." (n.d.).

[34] Wilderspin Papers, leaflet entitled "Dundee Watt Institution. Syllabus of a Course of Four Practical Lectures by Mr. Wilderspin" (1842).

An indication of the manner in which economic depression was affecting both the schooling of children and public interest in education was afforded by Wilderspin's engagements in the Potteries, where he lectured in late May and early June on "The Education of Children".[35] He found Hanley Infant School had been given up and that the local British school had also closed "in consequence of the debt upon it and the badness of the times".[36] Wilderspin's lectures also suffered. Though both the content and presentation of his first lecture were as good as ever — a local newspaper described it as "forcible, graphic and humorous...a rich fund of anecdote and amusing narrative being blended with instruction" — the audience was small.[37] In fact, there were so few present that a group of "influential inhabitants" felt it necessary to remunerate Wilderspin privately so that the remaining lectures could be thrown open to the public without an admission fee.[38]

Further engagements to work in infant schools in Dudley, Bloxwich, and Haggerston (London), during the autumn helped Wilderspin to survive a difficult year.[39] In September, however, he received a crushing blow — a letter from Hodson reporting that his printing firm had been forced into bankruptcy and that all his equipment and effects in Fleet Street, including his stock of Wilderspin's three books, had been seized. Hodson tried to soften the blow by saying that he had managed to hold on to the plates made for illustrating the books, without which the books were incomplete, and that already the new owners had asked to make use of them.[40] Wilderspin may have salvaged something by keeping control over the plates, but the principal asset represented by the books was gone.

In September 1841 he had been encouraged to make another approach to the government. J. Milnes Gaskell, a nephew of Daniel Gaskell of Wakefield, received an appointment to the Treasury Board under the new Peelite administration, and Wilderspin wrote to him with an eye to a post in the government's educational service. On the grounds that he had no claim to interfere in the appointments, Gaskell declined to intercede.[41] Wilderspin also wrote to Lord Lansdowne and Lord Leinster, but with similar negative results.[42] Almost a year later, Wilderspin made a last bid for a government position. This

[35] Wilderspin Papers, leaflet entitled "... Syllabus of a Course of four practical lectures by Mr. Wilderspin..." (n.d.); *North Staffordshire Mercury*, 21 May 1842.

[36] Ms. Revisions, *Early Discipline* (1840), p. 110.

[37] *North Staffordshire Mercury*, 4 June 1842.

[38] *North Staffordshire Mercury*, 11 June 1842.

[39] Wilderspin Papers, C. Cameron to Wilderspin, 19 Sept. 1842; P. Gilbert to Wilderspin, 22 Sept. 1842; C. Baylie to Wilderspin, 7 Oct. 1842.

[40] Wilderspin Papers, J.S. Hodson to Wilderspin, 19 Sept. 1842.

[41] Wilderspin Papers, J. Milnes Gaskell to Wilderspin, 8 Nov. 1841.

[42] Wilderspin Papers, Lord Lansdowne to Wilderspin, 8 Nov. 1841; Lord Leinster to Wilderspin, n.d. (?1841).

time his intercessor was Sir Francis MacKenzie, a titled supporter. After a full discussion of Wilderspin's situation, it was decided that in view of his long experience in working with the poor, his best hope was to apply for a post with the Poor Law Commissioners. Sir Francis agreed to forward Wilderspin's letter of application to Edwin Chadwick, with a short but strong recommendation of his own. When Chadwick replied more favourably than not, Sir Francis wrote Wilderspin advising him to call upon Chadwick "as soon as convenient, and if he cannot see you then, for I never saw anyone who appears to have his *minutes* so completely occupied, ask when you can see him".[43] Early in 1843 a final, almost desperate, appeal for employment to the Bishop of Norwich (who had visited the Liverpool Corporation schools) was made. "Pray my Lord do not refuse this request of a member of the Church", wrote Wilderspin, but it is evident that the Bishop must have done so, for like the interview with Chadwick, nothing more was recorded of the incident.[44]

Wilderspin had by this time been back in England over three years and the negative or evasive replies he had received to his letters of inquiry made it obvious that all avenues to employment, whether under the Committee of Council, the Church, the National Society, the Poor Law Commission or in any other organisation or institution, were closed to him. He obviously felt that his experience as an educator could best be utilised as one of Her Majesty's Inspectors. No doubt with himself in mind he insisted that the Inspectorate should consist of "practical men", and the unflattering picture he painted of the type of Inspector he feared would be appointed, and the consequences which might ensue, is eloquent of his feelings on the matter:

> ...if the inspector was to come with a high sounding title, and a number of letters attached to his name, such as LL.D. and F.R.S., D.D., B.A., and so on, with a corresponding amount of buckram and pomposity in his behaviour, and probably with all these titles, totally ignorant of the essential qualities necessary in a master, as well as the necessary facts to be developed in a school, with regard to physical, intellectual, moral and religious education; then I say, such a man could not do a master justice; he could not report properly, and of course the master would be disgusted, and become miserable in his office.[45]

No doubt Wilderspin as an Inspector would have shaken the complacency of some people, but few would have been able to bring to the post such a range of experience or such an advanced knowledge of the theory and practice of education, and English education was the poorer for his absence. If he could salvage any comfort from the situation it was the knowledge that all the other progressive educationists of the 1830s — Greaves, Combe, Wyse, Simpson —

---

[43] Wilderspin Papers, F. MacKenzie to Wilderspin, 19 and 26 Sept., 5 Oct., 2 and 10 Nov. 1842.

[44] Wilderspin Papers, Bishop of Norwich to Wilderspin, 17 Feb. 1843.

[45] *System of Education* (1840), p. 484. The passage occurs in the Appendix, Wilderspin's commentary on Lord John Russell's speech of 12 February 1839.

were also denied the opportunity to use their talents and experience in government service. Simpson's country-wide campaign, in the late 1830s, for an advanced system of state education lost him the chance of the post of Secretary of the Education Department, a position he was very desirous of obtaining.[46]

* * * * *

Wilderspin, on his return from Ireland, had made great efforts to present himself to the public as a moderate reformer and a friend of the Church of England. He had also felt it necessary to undertake the humiliating task of importuning leading Churchmen and politicians on the question of employment. Privately, however, his independent nature asserted itself and he turned for friendship and intellectual stimulation to liberal and radical intellectuals and reformers, as he had done in the 1830s.

He continued, for instance, to maintain his friendship with Simpson and Greaves, as his correspondence testifies. Greaves, in July 1840, was urging Wilderspin to expose in his lectures "the real error" of education — impure marriage relationships.[47] Through Greaves, Wilderspin made the acquaintance of Mrs. S.C. Chichester of Ebworth Park, a wealthy middle-class patroness of reformers and their causes. Mrs. Chichester had settled an annuity of £100 per annum on Greaves, which enabled him to live in moderate comfort in London and to spend the season at Cheltenham.[48] She espoused various causes, from the co-operative schemes of Fourier and St. Simon (whose pamphlets she pressed on Wilderspin with a plea for the their circulation),[49] to the British and Foreign Society for the Promotion of Humanity and Abstinence from Animal Food.[50] She was also one of the founders and benefactors of Alcott House, where Greaves and his disciples opened a quasi-Pestalozzian private school for children of both sexes, an institution not unlike Wilderspin's at Alpha House, with which both Greaves and Mrs. Chichester were familiar.[51] With characteristic disdain for public opinion, she supported G.J. Holyoake, the Owenite and secularist, during his imprisonment in Gloucester jail on a charge of blasphemy, instigated by Wilderspin's old opponent, the Rev. Francis Close of Cheltenham.[52]

---

[46]R. Johnson, "Educating the Educators: 'Experts' and the State 1833-9", in A.P. Donajgrodzki (Ed.), *Social Control in Nineteenth Century Britain* (London 1977), p. 99.

[47]Wilderspin Papers, J.P. Greaves to Wilderspin, 16 July 1840.

[48]Fruitlands Museum, Mass., W. Harland, "Bronson Alcott's English Friends" (Ms.), p. 5.

[49]Wilderspin Papers, S.C. Chichester to Wilderspin, ? Nov. 1841.

[50]*New Age and Concordium Gazette,* Vol. I, No. XII, 1 Dec. 1843, p. 138.

[51]Greaves and Mrs. Chichester kept in touch for many years with Mrs. Cuff, who, as noted earlier, had taught for a time at Alpha House School.

[52]G.J. Holyoake, *Sixty Years of an Agitator's Life* (London, 2 vol., 1892), I, p. 162.

When Wilderspin was struggling to keep his head above water, Mrs. Chichester wrote to offer him encouragement. In January 1840, she assured him that she and her friend Mrs. Welch were "quite as much, I may say, even more impressed with the value and importance of the work you are engaged in, than when we last had the pleasure of seeing and conversing with you".[53] She enclosed a prospectus of the Alcott House School, saying that she and Mrs. Welch were much interested in it and observing that the "address made to the spirit within is found indeed to be responded to". Early in 1842, when Wilderspin was going through a particularly stringent period, Mrs. Chichester sent him a donation of £5.[54]

It seems likely that Wilderspin's friendship with Mrs. Chichester enabled him to meet some of the coterie of *avant-garde* literary and reformist intellectuals who formed part of her circle. We know of two in particular: Goodwyn Barmby, who founded the Universal Communitarian Society under the banner of "Common Love, Common Property and Common Enjoyment",[55] and to whom Wilderspin later sent an inscribed copy of *Infant Education;*[56] and Dr. John Epps, physician, lecturer, phrenologist and one of the founders of the Common Good Society.[57] Epps was an admirer of Wilderspin's theories; he found himself "highly delighted" with a lecture he attended in February 1840,[58] and later put work in his way.[59]

The new conception of education which Wilderspin propounded was, of course, always more likely to attract the attention of reformers and radicals than that of the Establishment in Church and State. It is not surprising, therefore, to find that many of his proposals were once again favourably received by Chartists in the great upsurge of Chartist activity in the late 1830s and early 40s. William Lovett and John Collins, in their *Chartism: A New Organisation of the People,* (1840), based the long section on infant schools largely on the sixth edition of Wilderspin's *Infant System. Chartism,* written in Warwick Gaol, was as much an educational as a political tract. Pedagogically it was a crystallisation of the best work of the advanced educationists of the 1830s — Wilderspin, Simpson, Combe, and the Pestalozzians — transformed by a vision of social change which aimed to procure for the people *"equality of political rights"* and to place them in "such a *social condition* as shall best develope and preserve all their faculties, physical, moral, and intellectual".[60] Almost all Wilderspin's formulations and

[53] Wilderspin Papers, S.C. Chichester to Wilderspin, 14 Jan. 1840.

[54] Wilderspin Papers, S.C. Chichester to Wilderspin, 20 Feb. 1842.

[55] *Educational Circular and Communist Apostle,* No. VI, N.S., May 1842, p. 47.

[56] The copy is in Dr. Williams' Library, London.

[57] Mrs. Epps (Ed.), *Diary of the Late John Epps, M.D. Edin.* (London n.d.), p. 241 ff.

[58] *Ibid.,* p. 328, entry for 29 Feb. 1840.

[59] Wilderspin Papers, J. Epps to Wilderspin, 4 Dec. 1840. The letter was sealed with an anti-Corn Law stamp.

[60] J. Lovett and W. Collins, *Chartism: A New Organisation of the People* (London 1840; Victorian Library ed., 1969), v.

prescriptions, from his use of the playground to his advocacy of exercising the perceptive powers by the use of objects, from his teaching by apparatus and pictures to the inculcation of moral duties, were fairly closely reproduced.[61] If *Chartism* can stand as one of the finest educational productions of the British labour movement, it owes not a little of its merit to "Mr. Wilderspin", as the authors called him. Lovett and Collins were not, however, the only Chartists who appreciated his work. The following year, the Chartist newspaper the *Illuminator,* discussing "The Education of the People", declared that "the only real commencement in public education made in our own times, — the Infant School system, — was made by the revered Wilderspin, one of the people's own".[62]

The late 30s and early 40s saw a revival of Owenism as well as that of Chartism. The Universal Community of Rational Religionists had been formed in 1839, under the leadership of Owen; it adopted a socialist programme (which included universal education) and by the beginning of the 1840s had over three thousand members organised in sixty-five branches.[63] Wilderspin, once again, was drawn into conflict with his erstwhile mentor. At Manchester and Stockport, at the end of 1839, he had heard Owenite speakers lecturing on social questions, and he was disturbed by the good reception which Owen's doctrines received. "The greatest wonders", he wrote harshly, "are to be accomplished by the mighty genius and unwearied philanthropy of this individual and his followers, and woe be to those who dare stand up and call any of these nostrums in question; they settle the matter at once by calling him an ignorant fool".[64] He regarded their views on religion and marriage "with the utmost abhorrence", and was so shocked at the propagation of the doctrines of the Owenites in their own schools that he urged everyone to redouble his efforts to produce a suitable system of education for the poor.[65]

This diatribe carried more than a hint of the antagonism that had, since the late 1820s, characterised his attitude to Owen and his theories. Consistency, however, was not Wilderspin's strong suit, and having condemned the Manchester Owenites in print at the beginning of 1840, he made preparation to lecture to their London comrades at its end. The economic necessity of accepting any engagement offered no doubt played a part in the decision; but his attitude to the Owenites may have been mollified by an article in the *New Moral World* in June. This praised Wilderspin as one "to whom the system owes so much for his persevering exertions in making it known". What seemed to impress them most,

---

[61] *Ibid.,* pp. 77-92, *passim.*

[62] *Midland Counties Illuminator,* 20 Mar. 1841. We owe this reference to Dr. R.J.B. Johnson.

[63] W.A.C. Stewart and W.P. McCann, *The Educational Innovators 1750-1880* (London 1967), p. 83 ff., for the growth and educational policy of the Rational Religionists.

[64] *System of Education* (1840), pp. 310-11.

[65] *Ibid.,* p. 312.

however, was Wilderspin's success in teaching "the little Highland children, whose parents spoke only Gaelic, the English language in the same manner as if they were children from the heart of England". This was a reference to his teaching in the Highlands of Scotland in the first months of 1832; to the *New Moral World* it was further evidence of the efficacy of Owen's "noble discovery" and "its incalculable influence as a means of human regeneration".[66]

The engagement specified that Wilderspin give four lectures to Branch A1 of the Rational Religionists at John Street, Tottenham Court Road, London. In the first lecture he did something to modify his repudiation of Owen's place in the history of infant education made a few years earlier. "With regard to the system of infant schools, such as I propose", he stated, "I have always maintained, and always will maintain, that their germ originated with Mr. Robert Owen, of New Lanark". Again contradicting his rash assertions of previous years he described Westminster as the first infant school to be established in England. The remainder of his speech was mainly an anecdotal account of his career, graphic and amusing, which suggests Wilderspin was at home with his audience.[67]

His battles with Owen himself were not yet over, however. At the end of 1842, delivering the fourth of a series of lectures on infant education at the Literary Institution in the Hackney Road, he was interrupted by the appearance of Owen himself, accompanied by a number of followers. Owen walked to the platform and sat in the lecturer's chair behind Wilderspin "amid the cheers, and congratulations of his friends". Wilderspin continued the lecture as if nothing had happened, but, he alleged, "Mr. Owen impertinently desired me to make haste, as *He* wished to address the meeting". A debate on the origin of infant schools developed and Wilderspin felt he had pressed his case to the satisfaction of Owen's friends, who later apologised for the interruption.[68]

* * * * *

The lectures at Hackney were among the last of 1842, and 1843 opened with little prospect of further work; if his fortunes were to improve, he needed responsible and remunerative employment or the aid of a wealthy patron. The early 1840s were probably just about the last period when such patronage could be secured, and Wilderspin was fortunate to find it. His benefactors were friends of long standing — the wealthy, radical, religiously-unorthodox and philanthropic Gaskells of Wakefield, Yorkshire. Mary and Daniel Gaskell, when they realised how badly Wilderspin was faring, began to offer him support and encouragement, and ultimately they initiated measures which secured for him a comfortable and financially-secure retirement. In addition they offered

[66] *New Moral World*, Vol. VII, No. 88, 27 June 1840, p. 1358.

[67] *New Moral World*, Vol. I, 3rd Sers. No. 19, 7 Nov. 1840, pp. 291-92.

[68] Archives of W. and R. Chambers, Wilderspin to W. and R. Chambers, 28 Feb. 1845.

him rest and relaxation at Lupset Hall, their country seat, a handsome, red-brick building set in parkland sweeping down to the River Calder.

Mary Gaskell was a Heywood, cousin of the Manchester banker Sir Benjamin Heywood and a distant relative of Moncton Milnes, M.P., later Lord Houghton. Her husband Daniel was the uncle of J. Milnes Gaskell, M.P. The Gaskell's circle of acquaintances took in many members of the liberal intelligentsia, including John Minter Morgan, Mr. and Mrs. Howitt, Mrs. Leman Gillies, George Searle Phillips ("January Searle") and James Silk Buckingham.[69] The outlook of this circle has aptly been described by J.F.C. Harrison:

> ...that peculiar ethos compounded of undenominational Christianity and Owenite-Rationalist, Radical Temperance influences which pervaded the pages of *Howitt's Journal, The Truth Seeker, The Reasoner* and *The People,* and which was at the root of so many schemes for social improvement. It was an intellectual climate favourable to all kinds of social reform, but especially to education and mental and moral improvement...[70]

Although the Gaskells were "kinderlos", as Mary Gaskell was wont to say, both loved children and provided support for several schools in the Wakefield area. Not piously inclined, they based their lives on the principle of love and charity to one's neighbour while holding at least a nominal membership in the Unitarian Chapel in Wakefield's Westgate Common. They respected Wilderspin's more confident religious faith, even though they did not fully share it, and admired his freedom from bigotry, concern for human welfare and originality of mind. Their political views were congenial to those of Wilderspin, Daniel Gaskell having been elected to Parliament as the radical member for Wakefield after the 1832 Reform Act. Before his election, his nephew Milnes Gaskell had written:

> Seriously I should be very sorry to see my Uncle Member for Wakefield, not because I would not like to see 'him' in Parliament; I would canvass for him and vote for him most heartily, but because it is, in fact, my Aunt that would be Member of Parliament and I do not quite like the notoriety in which she would bring the name of Gaskell...[71]

There is no evidence, however, that his fears were realised. Although a born organiser, Mrs. Gaskell was wise enough to turn to others for advice, deferring, for example, to Wilderspin's judgment in the direction of her Horbury school. As time went on, her relationship with Wilderspin acquired what might be called a slight romantic tinge, but there is no evidence whatsoever in their long and intimate correspondence that the proprieties were in any way disregarded; the hospitality of Lupset Hall was as freely offered to Mrs. Wilderspin and her daughters as to Wilderspin himself.

[69]S.T. Hall, *Biographical Sketches of Remarkable People* (London 1873), p. 207.

[70]J.F.C. Harrison, *Social Reform in Victorian Leeds* (Leeds 1954), p. 54.

[71]C.M. Gaskell (Ed.), *An Eton Boy* (London 1939), p. 85.

Though Wilderspin had known the Gaskells since the early 1830s,[72] he appears to have lost touch with them during the remainder of the decade. In fact, not until 1843 is there any evidence that they were making any special efforts on his behalf. In February Mrs. Gaskell began making plans for him to lecture at Wakefield Mechanics' Institute in the spring. At the beginning of the year Wilderspin had sent his circulars to a score of institutions from Bath to Barnsley and from Wisbech to Worthing — his most intensive solicitation to date — but the results had been meagre. Only Kingston and Blackheath accepted his offer, although Scarborough asked for his terms, and Ipswich offered their rooms free for lectures at Wilderspin's risk.[73] In this atmosphere of gloom, a letter from Wakefield radiated optimism. "Mr. Cameron, our energetic Minister and President", Mrs. Gaskell wrote, "recommends decidedly your lecturing at the Mechanics' Institute *twice*... Shall it be given out for Tuesday and Wednesday, you coming to us on Monday?" Two lectures would be best, she advised, as Wakefield "is depressed by the late awful failures. . .and as the subject is a grave one after the wand of the *necromancer* has been so exciting".[74]

Unfortunately, Wilderspin was engaged at Blackheath for the dates proposed and had to decline. Mrs. Gaskell was disappointed but not deterred. "I am sorry you cannot come sooner", she penned, "having something (not much, I hope) of Lady Macbeth in my nature, I like things done quickly....After your week's visit to us you could look after the schools. . .but everyone recommends your beginning at the Institute, making a flash there, it is the most flourishing in England in proportion to the population and the *Vox Populi* dominates amongst us". Mrs. Gaskell had made sure that the lectures would be a financial success. "The proceeds of the names I have got", she said, "will pay the expenses of the two nights, and the entrance money will surely be £8 or £10".[75]

The Wakefield lectures were finally scheduled for 15 and 16 March. Mrs. Gaskell was elated at the prospect. On 27 February she wrote to Wilderspin: "You see we abound in *Isms,* Pusey, Mesmer, Socialism — a Lady said 'well of them all I prefer Wilderspinism...' You will, I am sure, admire the beautiful school just finishing at Horbury under the auspices and sole expense of good Dan'l Gaskell".[76] On 5 March she sent a final note, "One more penny worth, good Mr. Wilderspin, and then I trust all is settled, and though not so

[72] J.R.U.L.M. English Ms. 386/3062, Wilderspin to M. Gaskell, 22 Dec. 1832. In this letter he gives a long account of his engagements in the north of England.

[73] Wilderspin Papers, C. Fricker to Wilderspin, 9 and 13 Feb. 1843; G.W. Bennett to Wilderspin, 23 Feb. 1843; W. Webster to Wilderspin, 22 Feb. 1843; R. Colton to Wilderspin, 24 Feb. 1843.

[74] Wilderspin Papers, M. Gaskell to Wilderspin, 15 Feb. 1843. The "necromancer" was a recent lecturer on mesmerism.

[75] Wilderspin Papers, M. Gaskell to Wilderspin, 17 Feb. 1843.

[76] Wilderspin Papers, M. Gaskell to Wilderspin, 27 Feb. 1843. The school at Horbury, which contained infants and older children, was built at Daniel Gaskell's expense. In his will he directed that a tablet be affixed to the front of the school: "School for all denominations, built and endowed by Daniel and Mary Gaskell of Lupset Hall". (P.P. LXVIII 1898, Endowed Charities (West Riding of York), pp. 150-52).

advantageously as I *wish,* as well as I *can.* I inquired about the 2 other Rooms, but then came back again to the old agreement. The Exchange Room lets for £6.6 a night and the old Mechanics' Institute is let to the Socialists. I trust we shall meet on Tuesday evening the 14th, hearing nothing we expect you".[77]

Before leaving for Wakefield, Wilderspin called upon Lord Ashley (better known as Lord Shaftesbury) to urge him to include infant schools in the proposals he was then making for popular education. A year earlier Wilderspin had followed with interest the Evangelical peer's speech in the Commons (7 June 1842) on women and child labour in the mining districts,[78] and now that Lord Ashley was prodding Parliament on national education, he felt he should speak up. His lectures at Blackheath gave him the opportunity, as one of his auditors was a friend of the peer, and able to arrange an interview. On 6 March, G.W. Bennett, the Secretary of the Blackheath Society for the Diffusion of Useful Knowledge, wrote Wilderspin saying that Lord Ashley had asked to see him and urging him to call at once.[79] The intermediary was "Charlotte Elizabeth", i.e. Mrs. Charlotte Elizabeth Tonna, the editor of the Evangelical *Christian Lady's Magazine* and a strong supporter of the Home and Colonial Infant School Society. Once again Wilderspin felt that the urgency of the situation demanded relationships with the Evangelicals.

Wilderspin followed up his interview with Lord Ashley with a letter putting his views on the record. "The appalling facts developed by the Commissioners", he wrote in part, "have long been known to me, but I had no means of placing them before the legislature". He then went on to give Lord Ashley the results of another one of his local research projects. "The enclosed documents will show your Lordship that I was in the mining districts at the time the disturbances occurred last year, and on a careful examination among the colliers I found that the average number among fathers of families of those who knew even the alphabet was only about one in ten and that they were proportionately ignorant on *all* religious subjects". His conclusion was characteristic of the dislike of "agitators" he had developed in the 1840s. "Had these poor people been better instructed, those persons who made it their business to agitate among them would not have been so successful in tempting them to disobey the laws".[80]

It is difficult today, on reading Lord Ashley's account of the inhuman treatment to which women and children in the mines were subjected, to condemn the "agitators" who urged the oppressed workers to cast off their chains, but Wilderspin, like most of his contemporaries, viewed them as malefactors and proposed to correct the intolerable conditions against which they protested by the slow processes of formal inquiry, legislation and education. On the other

[77]Wilderspin Papers, M. Gaskell to Wilderspin, 5 Mar. 1843.

[78]Wilderspin Papers, copy of Lord Ashley's speech, with numerous underlinings by Wilderspin.

[79]Wilderspin Papers, G.W. Bennett to Wilderspin, 5 Mar. 1843.

[80]Wilderspin Papers, Wilderspin to Lord Ashley, 8 Mar. 1843, a copy made by Emily Wilderspin.

hand, he pressed hard for reform through the established channels. After leaving for Wakefield he spent much of the spring and early summer of 1843 preparing petitions on infant and national education and obtaining signatures to be forwarded to Lord Ashley.[81]

* * * * *

The engagement at Wakefield in March 1843 marked the beginning of Wilderspin's dependence on the Gaskells, and their friends and relations, for much of his livelihood. At the end of March, for instance, The Rev. Edward Brooksbank of Tickhill, near Rotherham, a brother-in-law of Mrs. Gaskell, wrote a long letter to the *Doncaster Chronicle,* bringing to the notice of its readers the subject of infant education and the work of "the first leader and teacher and abettor of the system". Giving a brief resume of Wilderspin's principles, he argued that all classes of society could support infant education and that National Schools might well be enlarged to include an infant school. He urged local councils to throw open their Town Hall or Mansion House to Wilderspin, who, he added (not quite accurately) was "brought up within the pale and in the principles of the Established Church" and was an adherent and a communicant of that body. Brooksbank's letter was followed by an encomium of Wilderspin from "H" of Wakefield in the following week's *Chronicle.*[82]

This publicity resulted in a number of lectures in the Yorkshire area in the following three months: Tickhill on 17 April, Blythe shortly afterwards and Holmfirth (under the auspices of Anstonley Scientific Society) during the last week of the month.[84] Happy to be profitably employed again, Wilderspin crowded too much into his schedule. In between lectures in Huddersfield in late May (including two lectures to the pupils of Huddersfield College),[85] Pontefract (23 and 26 May)[86] and Ipswich (21, 23, 24 and 27 June),[87] he was bedridden for several days in Mr. Hale's lodging house in the Horse Fair, Pontefract. A local physician, Dr. Robert Buchanan, prescribed dinner pills, and drops to be taken "when pain at stomach is urgent",[88] a treatment suggesting that Wilderspin

---

[81] Wilderspin Papers, E. Brooksbank to Wilderspin, 25 Apr. 1843, "The petitions have gone to Lord Ashley"; J. Hirst to Wilderspin, 13 May 1843, "The petitions are prepared. . .we must get them signed and sent off as soon as possible".

[82] *Doncaster Chronicle,* 31 Mar., 7 Apr. 1843.

[83] Wilderspin Papers, leaflet entitled "Infant Schools" (n.d.).

[84] Wilderspin Papers, poster entitled "Mr. Wilderspin will again lecture. . .on the subject of Education. . ." (1843); *Doncaster Chronicle,* 14 Apr. 1843; Wilderspin Papers, H. Walker to Wilderspin, 10 Apr. 1843; J.B.H. Greenwood to Wilderspin, 25 Mar., 13 Apr. 1843.

[85] Wilderspin Papers, J. Moody to Wilderspin, 28 Apr., 10 May 1843. The lectures at the College were given on 31 May and 1 June (*Bradford Observer,* 1 June 1843).

[86] Wilderspin Papers, R. Stainforth to Wilderspin, 26 Apr., 16, 17, and 18 May 1843.

[87] Wilderspin Papers, poster entitled ". . .Mr. Wilderspin will commence his course of lectures on early education. . ." (n.d.).

[88] Wilderspin Papers, R. Buchanan to Wilderspin, ? May 1843.

might have had a chronic ulcer which flared up under stress.

Two events of the spring and summer of 1843 did little to lighten the stress. The first was an action for slander he had taken out against his old adversary R.B. Ridgway, the alleged offences going back several years. The details of the case are not known, but Wilderspin was under pressure from his lawyer William Haynes and his printer James Hodson to prepare evidence; when a young protegé of his named Paris Anderson was, however, unable to furnish any solid testimony, Wilderspin seems to have had second thoughts. Hodson remonstrated with him at the beginning of June for "being lukewarm about your forthcoming trial", and Wilderspin apparently decided not to proceed with the action.[89]

The second was the decision of his daughter Emma to become a teacher at Alcott House school at Ham Common in Surrey. Wilderspin's youngest daughter Emily, or Emma as she was called, had been placed as a governess with a wealthy family in Barnes. Unfortunately, her desire to please was exploited by her employers; she complained to her sisters of her drudgery, describing how she rose at six in the morning to begin a long day's labour, while she was often occupied until midnight in making the children's clothes. After Sarah Anne and Rebecca interceded with their father, he brought Emma home, but again a heavy burden of household cares devolved upon her and her situation was only slightly improved.[90] Mrs. Chichester had called at the Wilderspin home in the Hackney Road in September and found a despondent Emma tending the Dowding girls and managing affairs at home. Mrs. Chichester was perceptive enough to see, if Emma did not make it plain herself, that as the last of the Wilderspin daughters she had become the family drudge, whose situation in comparison with her sisters in Dublin was miserable indeed; taking pity on the girl, she offered her a position at Alcott House school. Emma, glad to escape from her unenviable situation, accepted immediately, and without telling her father she left home and joined the utopians at Ham Common.

Wilderspin reacted somewhat like a typical Victorian *paterfamilias* and received the news with mingled anger and resentment, feeling that Emma had deserted her post and committed the cardinal sin of disrespect for her father. In Dublin, however, there was rejoicing. Hearing from Emma that she had accepted Mrs. Chichester's offer, but not knowing she had done so without permission, Tom, Sarah Anne and Rebecca welcomed her liberation. When Wilderspin complained bitterly of Emma's defection, they strove to mollify him. "My dear father", implored Sarah Anne, "let me beseech you to look upon the thing in its right light...she had felt that she *must* provide for her own future support...and when the opportunity *did* offer, she (for fear of any opposition)

[89]Wilderspin Papers, P. Anderson to Wilderspin, 9 Apr. 1843; W. Haynes to Wilderspin, 23 Apr. 1843; J. Hodson to Wilderspin, 9 June 1843.

[90]Wilderspin Papers, S.A. Young to Wilderspin, 1 Sept. 1842; R. Wilderspin to Wilderspin, 8 Sept. 1842; G.W. Jones to Wilderspin, 4 Feb. 1843.

jumped at it with too much eagerness". Pleading for forgiveness on Emma's behalf, Sarah Anne added "She has unfortunately erred this time, yet my beloved Father, think of your own youth and do not judge her harshly... Do let me implore of you (and oh remember it is your first born child who humbly asks this of you) to banish all anger and resentment from your mind and freely give your consent to any arrangement Mrs. Chichester has made for her".[91] Predictably, Wilderspin's temper soon subsided and his better nature reasserted itself; relenting, he allowed Emma to remain at Alcott House.

Despite some intense solicitation in the summer of 1843, employment was proving even more difficult to find. Mrs. Gaskell, writing from the "Silent Library" at Lupset Hall, invited him to spend the last two weeks of July at the Horbury School, and engagements followed at Burton-on-Trent and Knottingley.[92] As autumn approached he had only one lecture in prospect — an invitation from John Cameron, Mrs. Gaskell's "extraordinary young Highlander", who preached from the Unitarian pulpit in Westgate Common, to lecture in Wakefield in October.[93]

As the time approached for his Wakefield lectures, Mrs. Wilderspin came up from London to join her husband, and together they took rooms in Mrs. Brown's lodging house in Wakefield Common. "We are glad to hear you are so near us", wrote Mrs. Gaskell, "and hope you can dine and stay the night on Friday next..."[94] Apparently she found temporary employment for Wilderspin to teach singing in local schools, leaving ample time for country excursions and fishing at Walton Hall, Charles Waterton's spacious estate along the Barnsley Canal.[95] It was a pleasant interlude, but Wilderspin's main problem — the lack of regular lecturing engagements — had not been solved. Moreover, the demand for his services in organising infant schools seemed almost to have ceased. It was a situation wich was to require extraordinary efforts on the part of the Gaskells and their friends to remedy.

[91]Wilderspin Papers, S.A. Young to Wilderspin, 17 Sept. 1843.

[92]Wilderspin Papers, D. Gaskell to Wilderspin, 7 Aug. 1843; W. Morley to Wilderspin, 11 Aug. 1843; W. Morehouse to Wilderspin, 11 Nov. 1843; R. Cotton and J. Edmond to Wilderspin, 18 Aug. 1843; M. Gaskell to Wilderspin, ? June 1843; R. Thornwell to Wilderspin, 17 July 1843.

[93]Wilderspin Papers, J. Cameron to Wilderspin, 7 Apr. 1843.

[94]Wilderspin Papers, M. Gaskell to Wilderspin, 13 Sept. 1843.

[95]Wilderspin Papers, C. Waterton to Wilderspin, 16 Sept. 1843.

CHAPTER 16

AN ACTIVE RETIREMENT

"It was predicted by many", wrote the *Morning Chronicle* of Wilderspin in 1846, "that unless his country remunerated him, his old age must be an old age of poverty: and the prediction is on the eve of fulfilment".[1] For the previous two years, in fact, Wilderspin had been facing a situation which offered little hope for the future. 1844 had begun bleakly. The only recorded engagement in the early part of the year was a lecture at Hull Mechanics' Institute at the end of February.[2] Though he informed the meeting that he intended to devote all the summer to instructing teachers and children in Yorkshire, little work was placed in his way. On 6 June, however, he conducted an examination of the children of two Hull infant schools, having spent the previous month training them. The exhibition, the first of its kind ever held in Hull, was a great success; hundreds were turned away from the hall and it was repeated the following evening.[3] Thomas Terrington, secretary of the Hull Infant School Society, who had contacted him a year earlier and was later to become his son-in-law,[4] followed the meeting with a eulogistic letter to the local press. If properly carried out, "Mr. Wilderspin's beautiful infant system", he wrote, "would effect a greater change for the better in the moral world than any of the discoveries of the last century have done in the physical or commercial worlds".[5]

It was evident, despite the success and consolidation of the Home and Colonial Infant School Society, now eight years old, that Wilderspin and his system still commanded respect and admiration in certain quarters. But fees from occasional engagements were no substitute for a steady income and in the early summer of 1844 Wilderspin decided to leave London and settle in Lincolnshire. The reasons were not far to seek. London was expensive, at too great a distance from the Midlands, the North and the Eastern counties where his system had flourished, and moreover was dominated by the Home and Colonial Society, who continued to act as if he had never existed. Barton-on-Humber, where he decided to settle, offered cheaper living, greater opportunities for employment, the support of the *Stamford Mercury,* and rural solitude in which he could pursue his hobbies of gardening and fishing. Not least, it was within reasonable distance of the residence of his friends and supporters the Gaskells, at Lupset Hall, near Wakefield. Barton was a market town of some 3,500 inhabitants situated in Lindsey, North Lincolnshire, at the foot of the

---

[1] *Morning Chronicle,* 27 Apr. 1846.

[2] *Hull Rockingham Gazette,* 24 Feb. 1844.

[3] *Hull Advertiser,* 24 and 31 May, 7 June 1844; *Hull Packet,* 7 June 1844.

[4] Wilderspin Papers, T. Terrington to Wilderspin, 17 Aug. 1843. Terrington married Rebecca Wilderspin three years later (*Hull Advertiser,* 8 Jan. 1847).

[5] *Hull Advertiser,* 14 June 1844.

Lincolnshire Wolds. The Wilderspins, as far as can be ascertained, arrived there at the beginning of June. The tax assessment described their house as having thirteen windows and they paid a rent of £16 per year.[6]

Soon after his arrival in Lincolnshire Wilderspin received welcome news from his old supporter, William Martin, former editor of the *Educational Magazine,* now launched on a career as an author of school texts and children's stories.[7] Martin had been in touch with Sir Robert Peel, the Prime Minister, with a view to obtaining an *ad hoc* grant to tide Wilderspin over his lean period. "Sir Robert Peel, to whom I mentioned your services and wants", wrote Martin, "has generously offered you aid by a donation of twenty pounds from the Royal Bounty which I can obtain for you at any time". He added that an appointment — "colonial or otherwise" — might also be in the offing and invited Wilderspin to London to discuss the situation.[8]

Martin had written to Peel on 10 June, commending Wilderspin as "one of those faithful public servants who deserve well of their country and to whom a small annuity might be judiciously granted". Infant schools, he pointed out, inculcated "those principles of order and obedience which induce by far the larger portions of the lower classes to look upon your administration with gratitude . . ." The success of the schools had been entirely due to the thirty-year labour of Wilderspin, who had now completely exhausted his resources. "I need only say", Martin concluded, "that on a recent occasion I found him without the common necessaries of life and his family without bread".[9]

Wilderspin received £20, part payment of a grant of £50, in mid-July, and in a letter of thanks to the Prime Minister offered his services to the government.[10] Peel passed the letter on to Kay-Shuttleworth, Secretary to the Committee of Council on Education, asking what he knew of Wilderspin and his possible usefulness to the Government.[11] Kay-Shuttleworth then wrote a tactful note to Wilderspin, marking it "Confidential". "I was glad", he disclosed, "to have an opportunity upon a reference from Sir Robert Peel of stating what I knew of you and of suggesting that you would be able to render service to the Government if they had an opportunity of employing you in one of our Colonial Dependencies". In England, he added, the government had no opportunity of promoting his views.[12]

---

[6]Wilderspin Papers, Assessed Taxes, No. 42, Book 39, Commissioners of Assessed Taxes, Barton-on-Humber, 24 Feb. 1849; *Manchester Guardian,* 30 Sept. 1846.

[7]According to the British Library catalogue, Martin wrote a dozen or so textbooks, several being reprinted many times, and ten stories for boys.

[8]Wilderspin Papers, W. Martin to Wilderspin, 16 and 22 June 1844.

[9]B.M. Add. Mss. Peel Papers, 40546, ff. 244-46, W. Martin to Peel, 10 June 1844.

[10]B.M. Add. Mss. Peel Papers, 40546, f. 247, Wilderspin to Peel, 15 July 1844.

[11]Peel's note on the cover of Wilderspin's letter.

[12]Wilderspin Papers, J. Kay-Shuttleworth to Wilderspin, 1 July 1844.

Wilderspin was less than satisfied with this answer and eight months later he wrote to W.H. Stephenson, Peel's private secretary, intimating that he still felt he might expect a post in the educational system. He could not resist adding, with a touch of self-pity, "Had I been as careful of my own interests and that of my family as I have been to the interests of the rising generation I should not now stand in need of assistance".[13] Stephenson replied that at present there was no opening of any kind, but that he still held the balance of Peel's grant and would remit it at once if necessary; but he cautioned Wilderspin not to expect "any further aid of *this nature*".[14] Occupied in Scarborough in March, Wilderspin acknowledged the receipt of the money on his return to Boston, asking, in addition, if Lady Peel would like his forthcoming collection of infant songs to be dedicated to her;[15] she replied, through Stephenson, that she would "rather on the whole decline of availing herself of the proposed compliment".[16] Wilderspin, however, promised to send her a copy when the book was published.[17]

A joint work with Terrington, who wrote most of the verses,[18] the volume was entitled *A Manual for the Religious and Moral Instruction of Young Children in the Nursery and Infant School*. Attempting to fill a need for instructional material of a religious and moral nature which could be read, memorised and sung, it was undistinguished from a literary or musical point of view. A few of Terrington's poems have an artless simplicity, but most bear a heavy weight of moralising. The music is also disappointing. Sarah Anne's reaction on receiving a copy of the book was critical. "I am afraid", she wrote to her father, "by what I have seen of the *musical part* that it is not what you could have done had you given more time and exerted your *own* natural good taste in music more. The tunes seem to me to be meagre and out of harmony".[19] The book did not sell well and added little or nothing to Wilderspin's reputation. He did, however, take the opportunity of stating in the preface that "I am a member of the Established Church, worship within her walls, communicate at her table, and am instructed by her ministers".[20] No doubt he felt that this was a necessary step if he were to continue to hope for employment by the government.

After their arrival at Barton, however, Wilderspin and his wife were mainly concerned with finding enough work to keep them alive. In mid-June 1844 he

---

[13]B.M. Add. Mss. Peel Papers, 40562, f. 276, Wilderspin to W.H. Stephenson, 12 Mar. 1845.

[14]Wilderspin Papers, Stephenson to Wilderspin, 17 Mar. 1845.

[15]B.M. Add. Mss. Peel Papers, 40562, f. 227, Wilderspin to Stephenson, 20 Mar. 1845; f. 280, Wilderspin to Stephenson, 3 Apr. 1845.

[16]Wilderspin Papers, Stephenson to Wilderspin, 11 Apr. 1845.

[17]B.M. Add. Mss. Peel Papers, 40562, f. 282, Wilderspin to Stephenson, 14 Apr. 1845.

[18]Terrington later published a number of serious, if undistinguished, poems; these included *Welton Dale* (London 1852), and *Christmas at the Hall* (London 1853).

[19]Wilderspin Papers, S.A. Young to Wilderspin, July 1845.

[20]*Manual of Instruction* (1845), vi.

organised a school at Barrow, Lincs., which was under the patronage of the local vicar; an advertisement for a second examination announced that "Mr. and Mrs. Wilderspin are ready to open Schools and instruct Teachers in any part of the country".[21] The only results, however, were courses of lectures at Beverley, Yorks., in October and at Market Rasen in December.[22] 1845 saw a definite improvement in fortune. He lectured at Winterton, Lincs., in January, then commenced an extended engagement in Scarborough, which included training a schoolmistress for the Rev. W.N. Miller, organising an infant school for the Rev. J.D. Hilton, and opening another school for St. Thomas' Church in nearby Tuthill in March. This was followed by a course of lectures in York three months later.[23]

In Barton itself both the Wilderspins obtained employment. An infant school opened there in January 1845,[24] and according to the recollection of a local resident, John Gee, in a letter to a local historian half-a-century later, Wilderspin became the master.[25] This is confirmed by the report of an Inspector, who described the school as "actively superintended by Mr. Wilderspin".[26] Mrs. Wilderspin also became a teacher at Barton Infant School at a salary of £40 per year.[27] She had admirable success in eliciting the best efforts and affections of the children. When she relinquished her position three years later, *The Mercury* reported that the children of the Church Infant School in their esteem and affection for their mistress presented her with a silver whistle, made in London for the occasion, richly chased and surrounded in high relief with rose, shamrock and thistle, and bearing the inscription, "Presented to Mrs. Wilderspin by the children of the Infant Church School, Barton-upon-Humber, as a token of their affection".[28]

Gee, who had known Wilderspin in 1846, gives an interesting picture of him at this period. He describes him as "rather below the middle stature" and as "a quiet, unassuming man; he had a mild intelligent countenance, and, using the word in its proper sense, his deportment was gentlemanly". Apparently he lived "a retired life" in Barton, with few friends or acquaintances. He was never seen, for instance, with the local worthies at the George Inn, but spent his time

[21] *Hull Advertiser,* 14 and 28 June 1844; *Lincoln, Rutland and Stamford Mercury,* 28 June 1844.

[22] *Hull Advertiser,* 25 Oct. 1844; *Hull Packet,* 25 Oct. 1844; *Lincoln, Rutland and Stamford Mercury,* 27 Dec. 1844.

[23] Wilderspin Papers, W. Miller to Wilderspin, 8 and 17 Feb. 1845; M. Gaskell to Wilderspin, 20 June 1845; J.D. Hilton to Wilderspin, 22 Sept. 1845; B.M. Add. Mss. Peel Papers, 40562, f. 278, leaflet entitled "The New Infant School, near St. Thomas' Church, Tuthill" (Mar. 1845).

[24] R.C. Russell, *A History of Schools and Education in Barton-on-Humber: Part One — 1800 to 1850* (Barton 1960), p. 14 of unnumbered pages.

[25] Hull Public Library, FL MISC/10/15/17, J. Gee to H.W. Ball, Sept. 1896.

[26] P.P. 1847-48 L, Minutes of the Committee of Council on Education. East Midland District; Report by ... Rev. J.J. Blandford, p. 257.

[27] *Manchester Guardian,* 30 Sept. 1846.

[28] *Lincoln, Rutland and Stamford Mercury,* 14 May 1847.

cultivating the garden of his cottage. He told Gee he loved flowers and was fond of gardening and Gee felt that the garden "bore evidence to his taste and skill". Wilderspin gave Gee an account of his early commitment to teaching, the opening of his first school, his travels and the spread of his system, and the young man, impressed, felt it "rather curious that a man living in the little town of Barton should receive intelligence that he was deemed worthy of a national pension".[29]

This was a reference to the government pension which Wilderspin was granted in 1846. This was followed by an annuity derived from the monies collected in a "National Tribute". To these activities of Wilderspin's friends and supporters we must now turn.

* * * * *

Daniel Gaskell had written to Wilderspin in September 1844, "Don't let your friend W.M. sleep upon the proposition he made to you. We are quite anxious to see a List with the name of Her Majesty at its head".[30] In November, Mrs. Gaskell referred to the "List" again. "You do well to bear in mind how much we love to hear of your being and doing, dear Mr. Wilderspin... How does the Queen's List advance? I want to hear of it".[31] Having succeeded in obtaining £50 as an honorarium from the government Martin was apparently probing the possibilities of a yearly pension for Wilderspin from the Queen's Civil List.

While the outcome of this was still in the balance, Mrs. Gaskell conceived the idea of a "National Tribute" as the most likely means of ensuring her friend a modicum of comfort and security in his old age. If a substantial fund were raised by public subscription, she reasoned, the interest would provide Wilderspin with a small annuity, leaving the principal to revert to his family at his death. Mrs. Gaskell lost little time in contacting relatives and friends. The wife of Benjamin Gaskell of Thornes was urged to approach a brother in the Church.[32] Samuel Gurney of Manchester received an urgent request. "We want to raise Mr. Wilderspin £100 a year", she told him. "Think you will do well if it reaches £70", he replied, "that will take a great deal of getting".[33]

Gurney was right. The inexperience of the campaigners made the task difficult. The appeal was launched in January 1846 with the aid of a three-page circular entitled "Testimonial to Mr. Wilderspin", with a short text which outlined Wilderspin's labours and suggested that a subscription to assist in

[29]Hull Public Library, FL MISC/10/15/17, J. Gee to H.W. Ball, Sept. 1896.

[30]Wilderspin Papers, D. Gaskell to Wilderspin, 17 Sept. 1844.

[31]Wilderspin Papers, M. Gaskell to Wilderspin, 25 Nov. 1844.

[32]Wilderspin Papers, M. Gaskell to Wilderspin, 26 Sept. 1845.

[33]Wilderspin Papers, M. Gaskell to Wilderspin, 8 July 1846.

securing a provision for himself and his family was "highly desirable".[34] It was hardly a stirring call and many of the sixty or so subscribers listed were the family and friends of the Gaskells, among whom the Heywoods of Manchester were prominent. James Simpson was amazed at the naivety of the organisers, who were unwilling to use any part of the subscriptions as expenses in the campaign. "A feeling must be aroused, by local Committees and circulars", he advised Wilderspin, "and the money expended will be returned many fold". He agreed to do his part by writing to various people. "Don't hurry the matter", he pleaded, "do it well — and don't despair at the beginning".[35]

Simpson himself became one of the secretaries of the appeal campaign, together with Thomas Terrington and E.P. Lamport, a Manchester Unitarian. Subsequent editions of the circular were much improved, possibly due to the help of Wilderspin's former printer, James Hodson.[36] The title was changed to "Wilderspin National Tribute Fund" and an extended text assigned to Wilderspin "the chief merit of developing and practically carrying out the System of Infant Training", gave details of his labours, and asked help in relieving his last days of "anxiety and privation". The recently-granted pension of £100 a year from the government, the circular concluded, did not supersede the necessity of a further subscription.[37]

The attempt to obtain a pension for Wilderspin had borne fruit in July 1846. Whatever William Martin's part had been, the final effort had been made by Moncton Milnes, Mrs. Gaskell's relative, who had been Peel's unofficial adviser on Civil List matters. On the fall of Peel's administration following the repeal of the Corn Laws, Milnes had changed his allegiance and joined Russell's Liberals on their taking office in July 1846.[38] Possibly Russell was merely carrying out an undertaking decided on by Peel at Milnes' suggestion, possibly he heeded the advice of his new recruit. In the event Russell wrote to Wilderspin in mid-July, "I have received Her Majesty's command to place your name on the lists of pensions to deserving persons charged upon the Queen's Civil List for a yearly sum of one hundred pounds. It gives me great pleasure to convey the Queen's gracious wish that you will accept this testimonial to your services as the founder and promoter of Infant Schools".[39]

---

[34] U.C.L. Brougham Mss., 24966, folder entitled "Testimonial to Mr. Wilderspin"; on the back is a letter from Mrs. Gaskell to Brougham, soliciting his support, dated 12 Feb. 1846.

[35] Wilderspin Papers, J. Simpson to Wilderspin, 27 Jan. and 2 Feb. 1846.

[36] A draft of one version of the circular in Hodson's hand is preserved in the Wilderspin Papers.

[37] Wakefield Metropolitan District Council Archives, Goodchild Loan Mss., Box M/55, circular entitled "Wilderspin National Tribute Fund" (1846).

[38] T. Wemyss Reid, *The Life, Letters, and Friendships of Richard Moncton Milnes, First Lord Houghton* (London, 2 vol., 1890), I, p. 295; p. 376.

[39] *Hull Advertiser,* 7 Aug. 1846, citing the letter of Russell to Wilderspin, 7 Aug. 1846; cf. P.P. 1847 XXXIV, Return of Pensions Granted on the Civil List, p. 358.

Russell's use of the term "founder" was shortly afterwards challenged by Brougham in the Lords. He was certain, he declared, that Robert Owen was the founder of infant schools and Wilderspin only the "active promoter"; Lord Lansdowne concurred.[40] This was too much for Wilderspin, who leaped in with a letter to *The Times,* claiming that the schools at Lanark and Westminster were mere asylums (until the latter was re-organised by him in 1827) and that the patent of the system was his.[41] It was the hair-splitting of the 1830s once again, and Wilderspin's friends became fearful that the controversy, which had spread to the pages of the *Atlas,* the *Athenaeum, Douglas Jerrold's Magazine,* the *Daily News* and the *Spectator,* would be harmful to the Tribute.[42] Mrs. Gaskell cautioned Wilderspin that "the Battle had better be fought by your Generals and you sit quietly fighting your fish".[43]

If the news of Wilderspin's pension was received with satisfaction in the Wilderspin camp, it aroused only dismay and anger among the family of Wilderspin's old colleague James Buchanan, who had emigrated to South Africa in 1839. The Colonial Office had made inquiries as to his whereabouts during 1846, requesting his son William to furnish information to the government. Despite a piece by Brougham on Buchanan's behalf in the *Westminster Review,* in which he stated that Wilderspin's claims to originality rested on nothing but "the modifications he has introduced into the system...and upon a wire-drawn distinction between infant schools and infant *asylums",* no pension was granted to Buchanan, which angered both his family and supporters such as Sarah Austin. According to his grand-daughter, however, he did receive an honorarium of £100 from the British government.[44]

Meanwhile, leaving his "generals" to carry on the campaign, Wilderspin had forsaken his fishing for more active pursuits. He lectured for the Manchester Athenaeum in April, for the Greenwich Society for the Acquisition and Diffusion of Useful Knowledge on 9 and 16 June, and for the Blackheath Society on 11 and 18 June. Later in the month he went to Aswanley Park, Falkingham, to open an infant school for Lady Whichcote.[45]

He returned to Barton to receive an enthusiastic letter from Mrs. Gaskell:

[40]Parl. Deb., 3rd Sers., LXXXVIII, 3 Aug. 1846, 274-75. Brougham repeated the statement on 14 Aug. (699).

[41]*The Times,* 8 Aug. 1846.

[42]Wilderspin Papers, E. Lamport to Wilderspin, 20 Aug. 1846. Lamport sent conciliatory letters to the journals concerned (*Manchester Guardian,* 10 Aug. 1846).

[43]Wilderspin Papers, M. Gaskell to Wilderspin, 21 Aug. 1846.

[44][H. Brougham], "Education of the People", *Westminster and Foreign Quarterly Review,* Vol. XLVI, No. 1, Oct. 1846, pp. 182-219, addendum, "Origin of Infant Schools", pp. 220-22; *Westminster and Foreign Quarterly Review,* Vol. XLVII, No. 2, July 1847, pp. 484-86; B.I. Buchanan, *Buchanan Family Records* (Cape Town 1923), pp. 8-9; U.C.L. Brougham Mss., 26554, W. Buchanan to Brougham, 2 May 1851; 2292, 2293, 26533, Sarah Austin to Brougham, 21 Feb. 1851; n.d. (? Mar. 1851); 19 Mar. 1851.

[45]Wilderspin Papers, E. Lamport to Wilderspin, 25 Apr. 1846; leaflet of Greenwich Society, entitled "Syllabus of Lectures, January-July 1846"; leaflet of Blackheath Society, entitled "Syllabus of Lectures, Quarter Ending June 21, 1946"; Lady Whichcote to Wilderspin, 17 June 1846.

The receipts are from Leicester £15-7, from Mr. Davidson 2-2; Mr. Baines, Leeds, 2-2, Archdeacon Musgrave £2. Lamport is busy in Manchester — glorious Manchester! He promises 60. We live, we move, cannot Mrs. W. send me some Hereford names, her native place ought to be productive, and York, too, *you* have friends there... The bright vision of £50 from Mr. Dawson's services is quite faded. Mr. L.H. sent 6 Circulars which he forwarded where he thought best... Kindest regards to Mrs. W. and love to Rosa, and now *good night,* dear friend, *good night.*[46]

Spurred on by articles in the *Morning Chronicle,* the *Spectator* and the *People's Journal,*[47] the fund rose to over £700 by July and topped the £1000 mark by August.[48] In Manchester in September a successful public meeting concluded with a donation of £50 by the Rev. T.H. Fisk of Cheltenham, who was reported as saying, "Wilderspin ought not now to have to labour for his living in his old age, but to enjoy that repose and those comforts which his exertions entitle him to, and which his age and state of health require".[49]

Wilderspin's health was, in fact, giving cause for concern. At the height of the campaign, it suddenly gave way, threatening an early end to the Tribute. Although he managed to give a course of lectures in the Stand Church near Manchester in August,[50] he was so much a sick man that his friends became alarmed. The Rev. E. Brooksbank wrote to caution him against depending upon his all-purpose remedy of brandy and salt "for fear of my Lord John finding an early opportunity to turn the stream of the Royal Bounty into some other channel".[51] The Gaskells were no less worried. "If you are suffering a serious attack of illness", Daniel Gaskell advised, "send for a physician without delay and follow his advice".[52] Tom Young, in his family memoir, stated that his father-in-law suffered "a partial paralysis".[53] In any case, recovery was slow, the *Leeds Mercury* reporting in September that Wilderspin was seriously ill.[54] He had, however, recovered sufficiently to resume lecturing in October, when he visited Ipswich. He then made an extended tour of the North West, lecturing at

[46]Wilderspin Papers, M. Gaskell to Wilderspin, 1 July 1846.

[47]"The Old Age of Wilderspin", *Morning Chronicle,* 27 Apr. 1846; *Spectator,* Vol. 19, April 1846, p. 395; Mary Leman Gillies, "Mr. Wilderspin, — The Friend of the People's Children", *People's Journal,* No. 18, 2 May 1846, pp. 245-46.

[48]Wakefield Metropolitan District Council Archives, Goodchild Loan Mss., Box M/55, Wilderspin Testimonial Account Book, entries for July and August 1846.

[49]*Manchester Guardian,* 8 and 30 Sept. 1846.

[50]Wilderspin Papers, syllabus of lectures at the Stand Church Sunday School (1846).

[51]Wilderspin Papers, E. Brooksbank to Wilderspin, 28 Aug. 1846.

[52]Wilderspin Papers, D. Gaskell to Wilderspin, 30 Aug. 1846.

[53]Young Papers, T.U. Young, "Memoir of My Father" (Ms.).

[54]*Leeds Mercury,* cited in *Lincoln, Rutland and Stamford Mercury,* 11 Sept. 1846; Wilderspin Papers, E. Lamport to Wilderspin, 18 Sept. 1846.

Manchester, Liverpool, Chester and Birkenhead in November and at Patricroft the following month.[55] Apparently he continued to supervise Barton Infant School during this period; it is obvious, however, that the demand for his services as an infant school organiser had dwindled to almost nothing, a circumstance which underlined the need for a regular source of income.

By the beginning of 1847 the amount in the fund was just short of £1,500, but contributions were beginning to lag.[56] Lamport conceived a plan to have J.R. Herbert, R.A., who he described as "perhaps the first portrait painter in England", paint a portrait of Wilderspin; the original would be presented to him and engraved copies could be sold to benefit the fund. Herbert, then in Manchester at work on a painting of members of the Anti-Corn Law League, undertook the commission for a fee of £50, half of which he returned as his contribution to the fund.[57] This had now to compete with a nation-wide collection to relieve the Irish potato famine and Mrs. Gaskell recognised that little more could be done. "Alas, everything comes to an end", she wrote to Wilderspin, "the sweetest as the bitterest. The portrait is our only hope . . ." She added, "My sovereigns are exhausted, but I am willing and pleased to ask for *pence*. How generous Lady Byron! She answered by saying her children had just been canvassed for the Irish; she would send £5 instead of applying to them again".[58]

In May 1847 she informed Wilderspin that Charles Dickens had sent "such a nice letter and £3.3", but that she now considered her "better class" applications at an end.[59] When the trustees closed their books on 1 July, the total in the fund was £1,817.16.11,[60] just short of the target figure of £2,000.[61] The money was invested in shares of the London and North Western Railway and produced dividends of something over £40 per year,[62] not a princely sum, but sufficient, with his pension, to keep him in reasonable comfort in his old age.

An examination of the contributors to the fund reveals some interesting points. As the *Spectator* pointed out, two significant classes of potential contributors were largely absent from the list — "our manufactory millionaires

[55]*Manchester Guardian*, 14 Nov. 1846; Wilderspin Papers, E. Lamport to Wilderspin, 1 Nov. 1846; T. Hogg to Wilderspin, 3 Nov. 1846; handbill of Liverpool lectures, in Welsh (1846); W. Hodgson to Wilderspin, 12 Nov. 1846.

[56]Wilderspin Testimonial Account Book, entries for January 1847; Wilderspin Papers, M. Gaskell to Wilderspin, n.d., (? Dec. 1846).

[57]Wilderspin Papers, E. Lamport to Wilderspin, 8 Nov. 1846; *Wakefield Journal*, 11 June 1847.

[58]Wilderspin Papers, M. Gaskell to Wilderspin, n.d. (? Feb. 1847); 28 Mar. 1847.

[59]Wilderspin Papers, M. Gaskell to Wilderspin, 8 May 1847.

[60]Wilderspin Papers, Report of the Trustees of the Wilderspin National Tribute, 1 July 1847.

[61]This figure was announced in the *Lincoln, Rutland and Stamford Mercury*, 4 Dec. 1846. A proposal to raise £1,000 by penny subscriptions from children seems not to have materialised (*Howitt's Journal*, Vol. 1, 1847, Weekly Record, p. 47).

[62]Wakefield District Council Archives, Goodchild Loan Mss., Box M/55, receipt for half-yearly dividend of £21.13.6 on L.N.W.R. stock, dated 25 Aug. 1864.

and merchant princes", and the Church.[63] Though the final list contained the names of the Archbishops of Canterbury and York, the Bishop of London and thirteen other members of the Bench, the parish clergy, apart from a handful of names, were conspicuously absent. The merchants and industrialists were represented almost entirely by philanthropic Nonconformists — the Marshall, Strutt, Rathbone, Loyd, Martineau, Gurney, Barclay and Darby families. There were few celebrities, apart from Dickens, Cobden and Bright. A handful of the aristocracy and a number of titled ladies added their mite.[64] If we remember that the three secretaries of the committee were respectively a phrenologist, a Swedenborgian and a Unitarian, and that Manchester contributed over £300, while London gave less than £50,[65] we are forced to the conclusion that Wilderspin's support had changed little over the years. It still lay among groups and classes outside the politico-religious mainstream, and was largely middle-class, nonconformist and provincial. Wilderspin had previously pointed out that the Quakers had been his most ardent assistants in his "peregrinations", and that Unitarians had been prominent in promoting education, his own efforts included.[66] The most notable absentees from the fund were the Evangelicals; the antagonisms arising from the events of the mid-30s were still alive and the virtual boycott of the Testimonial by the vital Christians undoubtedly reduced the total. Lord Calthorpe, Fowell Buxton, the Rev. Hugh Stowell of Manchester and Mrs. Chambers "of the Home and Colonial party", who Mrs. Gaskell had dragooned into contributing at a soirée, were the only prominent Evangelicals to give a donation.[67]

When the fund was closed, all that remained was to organise a ceremony for the presentation of the Tribute, the portrait and other gifts, and Mrs. Gaskell felt that their London residence in Strattŏn Street was a better venue than "Lupset or any country place". The ceremony was held on 7 June 1847 and widely reported in the press. The guests included Charles Dickens, Moncton Milnes, M.P., Thornton Hunt (son of Leigh Hunt) Mr. Gaskell (probably J. Milnes) of Thornes, and several of Mrs. Gaskell's lady friends and Wilderspin admirers, including Mrs. Gillies, Mrs. Loudon, Mrs. Marsh, Mrs. Heywood, Mrs. Thelwall and the Hon. Mrs. Denman. The portrait by Herbert was prominently displayed beside a continuous scroll of over 1,000 infant autographs reaching from ceiling to floor. In the centre of the table was a handsome silver clock and chimes, which had been made for the occasion by John Bennett, an old friend of Wilderspin and a prominent jeweller in Cheapside, and purchased by the penny gifts of infant-school teachers and children. It was ornamented with a finial

[63] *Spectator*, Vol. 19, Apr. 1846, p. 395.

[64] Wilderspin Testimonial Account Book, *passim*.

[65] *Patriot*, 10 Sept. 1846; Wilderspin Papers, folder entitled "Wilderspin National Tribute Fund", n.d. (? July 1846).

[66] *Early Discipline* (1834), p. 324; *System of Education* (1840), p. 482.

[67] Wilderspin Testimonial Account Book, *passim;* Wilderspin Papers, M. Gaskell to Wilderspin, 24 Oct. 1846.

representing a group of children at study and bore the inscription: "The Teachers' and Children's Gift to Samuel Wilderspin, Juventutis, Amator and Amor, June 7th, 1847". As the clock struck eleven, Daniel Gaskell arose and in a simple speech reported on the results of the subscriptions and made the presentations. Wilderspin was nearly overcome with emotion but managed to reply, thanking his benefactors and recounting some of the difficulties by which his path had been obstructed, particularly the prejudice against the education of all children, whether Jew, Catholic, Protestant, Baptist or other Dissenter. He then alluded to the time when Sir Robert Peel, by a timely gift of £50, sheltered him from utter destitution, bridging the gulf until his friends at whose table he now stood set in motion "the action which would rescue the remainder of his days from want and anxiety".

Other speakers followed. Moncton Milnes (with the power and ease of a practised speaker, said the reports) praised Wilderspin as a man of genius, whose catholic spirit was too seldom expressed in public and professional life. Milnes gave to the Gaskells the main credit for the success of the Tribute, and Mrs. Gaskell in turn passed the compliments on to Lamport and her other helpers in the cause. Dickens concluded the ceremony by speaking briefly, since he was suffering from a heavy cold. His remarks, chiefly addressed to the ladies, noted how appropriate it was than an enterprise so closely connected with the welfare of children should have originated with a woman and been carried forward "in the spirit of generous fervour which characterised the sex".[68]

After the ceremony, Mrs. Gaskell continued her efforts to add a few more pounds to the Testimonial fund.[69] The hoped-for income from the sale of engravings of the Herbert portrait apparently did not materialise, however, and the only large sum of money — £3 from James Simpson in Edinburgh — was received by Wilderspin as late as April 1850.[70] "I still hold my quiet rather than my *weary* way for the Testimonial", Mrs. Gaskell informed Wilderspin late in 1848.[71] Her unflagging efforts were appreciated by the Wilderspin family. "I cannot tell you the pleasure it would be to me to see dear Mrs. Gaskell and to thank her for all she has done for you", wrote Sarah Anne to her father from Dublin early in 1848, "I could never tell her half the gratitude that fills my heart".[72] Yet within three months Mrs. Gaskell was dead. On a visit to London in April, the Gaskells had stayed with friends in Hertfordshire where Mrs. Gaskell had suffered a stroke which proved fatal within less than a week.[73] With her

[68] *Wakefield Journal,* 11 June 1847; *Lincoln, Rutland and Stamford Mercury,* 18 June 1847; *People's Journal, Annals of Progress,* 18 June 1847, p. 50.

[69] Wilderspin Papers, M. Gaskell to Wilderspin, 21 Aug. 1847.

[70] Wilderspin Papers, E. Lamport to Wilderspin, 19 Aug. 1847; 1 Apr., 23 Aug. 1848; J. Simpson to Wilderspin, 9 Apr. 1850.

[71] Wilderspin Papers, M. Gaskell to Wilderspin, n.d. (? late 1847).

[72] Wilderspin Papers, S.A. Young to Wilderspin, 24 Jan. 1848.

[73] Wilderspin Papers, W. Hawkes to Wilderspin, 16 Apr. 1848.

death Wilderspin lost the warmest and most generous friend he ever had. During his years of adversity she had given him unfailing moral and material support. It was she who rescued him from poverty, revived his fading reputation, and restored his morale. In addition she had opened to him the gates of Lupset Hall with its material comforts and rural charm. She had provided "quiet social, serious evenings" at which religion, education and everything that was "important and interesting" was discussed.[74]

Less than five months after Mrs. Gaskell's fatal collapse, Wilderspin suffered another loss in the death of his daughter Emma, after a short life filled with disappointment and suffering. Leaving Alcott House within two years, following internal dissensions there, she took a post in the infant school at Darby's ironworks in Ebbw Vale, but for most of the time she was isolated, lonely, overworked and in poor health. Shrouded in the secrecy surrounding such episodes in respectable Victorian families, she formed an unfortunate liaison with a suitor who refused to acknowledge the son she bore him, leaving her to face her father's wrath a second time. But in this crisis he stood by her, provided money for placing the child in a foster home, and helped her find a new position in Salford, where she took charge of an infant school in Great George Street. But her health was collapsing and Wilderspin, newly arrived in Wakefield, brought her home. She died on 29 September 1848 at the early age of 26 and was buried in Thornes churchyard.[75]

As far as can be ascertained, Wilderspin had taken up residence in Wakefield in the summer of 1848. Shortly after Mrs. Gaskell's death her widower had inquired "What are you doing and what do you propose to do?"[76] It was a question Wilderspin had to face. Declining an offer from a friend to settle in Beverley, Yorks.,[77] his thoughts had turned to Wakefield as a permanent home. After initially refusing the offer of a cottage from Benjamin Gaskell because of the high rent and the cost of moving from Barton, he finally agreed to the transaction when, in June, Daniel Gaskell advanced him £50 on the security of the dividends of the railway stock.[78] Moor Cottage, Westgate Common, was a pleasant walk from the centre of Wakefield. The entrance to Thornes Park, the country seat of Benjamin Gaskell, was scarcely a stone's throw away. Lupset Hall was about a mile to the southwest, set in park-like surroundings just east of the Horbury Road, with a sweeping view of the Calder River and the rolling hills beyond. The countryside offered ample opportunities for fishing and other rural pursuits and Wilderspin remained in Moor Cottage until his death in 1866.

* * * * *

[74] Wilderspin Papers, M. Gaskell to Wilderspin, n.d. (? June 1847); 5 Aug. 1847; 7 Dec. 1847; n.d. (? Mar. 1848).

[75] Wilderspin Papers, A. Darby to Wilderspin, 26 May, 4 July 1845; E. Wilderspin to Wilderspin, 30 Nov. 1845; C. Richson to Wilderspin, 27 Sept. 1848; Register of Burials, District Chapelry of Thornes, No. 541.

[76] Wilderspin Papers, D. Gaskell to Wilderspin, 17 May 1848.

[77] Wilderspin Papers, J. Birtwhistle to Wilderspin, 24 Jan. 1848. Wilderspin assisted Birtwhistle to open a National School later in the year (*Hull Advertiser,* 11 Aug. 1848).

[78] Wilderspin Papers, D. Gaskell to Wilderspin, 25 May, 22, 27 and 28 June 1848.

He did not, however, devote himself entirely to his hobbies and the early years of his retirement were full of varied activity. He assisted in finding posts for teachers or advising on the methods and principles of education, a duty he had undertaken in Barton and which he continued in Wakefield.[79] He also kept a watching brief over Daniel Gaskell's Horbury school[80] and organised an infant school for Trinity Church[81]. He was secretary of the Committee of Wakefield Ragged School in 1849 and gave an address at the school's New Year celebrations three years later.[82]

Wilderspin's main activity in Wakefield, however, during the last ten active years of his life in the 1850s, was as a leading member of the Wakefield Mechanics' Institution, then at the height of its power and influence, though largely supported by the middle and lower-middle classes. During the 50s Britain was entering the high summer of Victorian prosperity, ushered in by the Repeal of the Corn Laws and marked by the International Exhibition at Crystal Palace in 1851. With the failure of the Chartist Petition of 1848, the majority of the working class turned towards the building of the New Unions and mutual improvement and self-help societies. The bitter industrial battles and trade union struggles of the first half of the century were now largely a memory and Lovett and Collins' *Chartism*, which had embodied many of Wilderspin's ideas, proved to be the last important radical educational manifesto of the labour movement. State education was advancing steadily, though not without opposition from the Church. Infant schools were becoming a recognised part of the state system and their propriety was no longer questioned. All in all the social and educational scene was calmer than when Wilderspin had been fighting the battles of infant education and he felt justified in devoting what today we would call an early retirement — he was fifty-seven when he moved to Wakefield — to speaking, writing, advising and encouraging from an honoured position in the town's leading cultural institution. With white hair and a newly-grown beard, he began to look the part of an elder statesman of education.

The first Wakefield Mechanics' Institution had been founded in 1825 with the object of diffusing "useful information among the operative classes" and of assisting its artisan members to patent their inventions. It was one of the many founded in the West Riding at the time with the general aim of taking science to the artisans. By the early 1830s it was clear that this policy was not successful and

---

[79]Wilderspin Papers, J. Hargreave to Wilderspin, 11 Jan. 1847; J. Simpson to Wilderspin, 14 Aug. 1847; G. Benson to Wilderspin, 14 July 1848; C. Payne to Wilderspin, 30 Aug. 1848; P. Anderson to Wilderspin, 25 Jan. 1850; 13 Feb. 1851; 14 June, 1 Sept. 1853; G. Fenton to Wilderspin, 3 June 1853; W. Tait to Wilderspin, 11 July 1854; J. Shepherd to Wilderspin, 18 Aug. 1856; W. Good to Wilderspin, 3 Oct. 1858.

[80]Wilderspin Papers, D. Gaskell to Wilderspin, 6 Aug. 1851.

[81]*Wakefield and West Riding Examiner*, 28 Nov. 1850; *Wakefield Journal*, 29 Nov. 1850; Wilderspin Papers, leaflet entitled "Syllabus of the Performance of the Children in the Trinity Church Infant School, 28 November 1850".

[82]Wilderspin Papers, report entitled "Committee of the Wakefield Ragged School" (Wakefield 1850), *passim; Wakefield Journal*, 3 Jan. 1852.

in 1836 the society was disbanded and its library and scientific apparatus sold to pay the rent. It was succeeded by a Literary and Philosophical Society and a Working Man's Educational Society. On the demise of these two bodies in 1841 the new Wakefield Mechanics' Institution had been formed. It offered intellectual and moral improvement to all the citizens of Wakefield and its weekly lectures were all on popular and literary subjects and in the late 40s concerts of classical music helped to form "a cultivated taste". Its lectures attracted an average attendance of 200, of whom two-thirds were female. The artisan membership was less than half the total and it is clear that the Institution drew much of its support from the lower middle class and its financial backing from the middle and upper classes; "liberal donations" from Daniel Gaskell and the Hon. W.S. Lascelles, it was reported, enabled the Institution to accumulate furniture, books and chemicals.[83]

Mechanics' Institutes, Wilderspin believed, were of "immense utility in the way of popular instruction", though more, he felt, might be done to attract the working man.[84] The Wakefield Institution certainly proved an ideal vehicle in which to put his views into practice. Elected to the committee in August 1849 and as a Vice-President the following year,[85] he was placed in charge of the direction of all classes[86] and also became president of the Discussion Class which met weekly to enable working men to acquire greater facility of speech and self-expression. Each member read a paper, after which the meeting was open for comment. The subjects ranged from juvenile delinquency to kindness to animals, from opposition to alcohol to state education, all typical Wilderspinian themes.[87]

He also undertook a certain amount of lecturing outside Wakefield. Though he ventured as far as Newport and Abercarn in Wales,[88] most of his visits were to Mechanics' Institutes in the Yorkshire area. Letters and leaflets in the Wilderspin Papers show that he gave some forty lectures of this kind during the 1850s, and that he was also in demand at soirées. These were an annual feature of the programme in most institutes, and between musical numbers distinguished guests were usually asked to contribute some informal remarks on

[83]This account is taken from Mabel Tylecote, *The Mechanics' Institutions of Lancashire and Yorkshire before 1851* (Manchester 1957), p. 57; pp. 273-74. J.F.C. Harrison, *Learning and Living 1790-1960* (London 1961), p. 59; p. 66; p. 68; pp. 70-71; "The Wakefield Mechanics' Institution and its Precursors", Wakefield Mechanics' Institution *Bazaar Gazette*, No. 6, 30 Oct. 1855.

[84]*Wakefield and West Riding Herald*, 14 Dec. 1850.

[85]Wakefield Metropolitan District Council Archives, Wakefield Mechanics' Institution Minute Book, Minutes, Annual Meeting, Aug. 1849; Minutes, Annual Meeting, 28 Aug. 1850.

[86]W.M.I., Committee Minutes, 20 Dec. 1849.

[87]Wilderspin Papers, folder entitled "Wakefield Mechanics' Institution Discussion Class. Subjects for Discussion" (n.d.).

[88]Wilderspin Papers, J. Jayne to Wilderspin, 27 Dec. 1849; leaflet entitled "Abercarn Scientific Institute...S. Wilderspin, Esq..." (30 Jan. 1850); handbill of the Newport lectures (n.d.).

topics of the day, a genre particularly suited to Wilderspin's abilities as an extemporaneous raconteur. He offered many variations on the theme of education — "The Human Mind", "Education and the Working Man" and so on, and was willing to try his hand at such recondite topics as "The Tombs and Remains of our Celtic Ancestors" and "The Impeachment of Warren Hastings".[89]

A study of the lectures and other material of this period reveals the interesting point that, despite his stated membership of the Church of England, Swedenborgian ideas and concepts still exercised an influence on his thinking. The impressions of his early life had been too strong to be eradicated and attitudes and turns of phrase show that his Swedenborgian roots were still evident during his retirement. Writing to the Youngs in Dublin at the end of 1848, he summed up his religious creed in Swedenborgian terms:

> You will, I trust, not fail to bring up your children in that which is good, and true, and just, and right. This is the basis, if not the sum and substance of Religion. Of all things guard them from being bigots, and let them see that Religion is based upon *Love:* love to God primarily and love to man universally, that any religion that sheds blood to support it, and prop it up, no matter what church it may belong to, its quality is bad, and it is from Hell and not from Heaven.[90]

In various speeches he referred to the will and the understanding in its Swedenborgian meaning, to his belief in man as a progressive being "to all eternity" (a form of words he had used in his early writings), and to the perusal of the book of nature as leading to an understanding of the Scriptures.[91] In 1855 he questioned the view that the creative faculty "existed purely in man", for "man was only a receptacle of light; and all that he had given him he had through God".[92] These undoubtedly Swedenborgian statements were, of course, made in the context of larger discourses, and would have escaped notice by all but a theologian. But it is significant that his daughters and sons-in-law, all of whom were followers of Swedenborg, took it for granted that Wilderspin was interested in the Writings; "we are reading an interesting life of Swedenborg by James John Garth Wilkinson", Rebecca wrote in 1853, "I think you would be pleased with it . . ."[93]

To assign all aspects of Wilderspin's general ideological orientation to Swedenborgian origins would be supererogatory. It is tempting to wonder, however, whether his view that in 1848 the working class wanted "good religious

[89] *Wakefield Express,* 11 Mar. 1854; 26 Mar. and 2 Apr. 1859.

[90] Young Papers, Wilderspin to T.U. and S.A. Young, 27 Dec. 1848.

[91] *Wakefield and West Riding Examiner,* 8 June 1850; *Hull Advertiser,* 17 Dec. 1852; *Wakefield Journal and Examiner,* 2 Dec. 1853.

[92] *Wakefield Journal and Examiner,* 16 Nov. 1855.

[93] Young Papers, R. Terrington to Wilderspin, 15 Apr. 1853.

290

teachers, not agitators",[94] or his declaration that Owen's plans were "impracticable",[95] had something to do with Swedenborg's ideas on polity;[96] perhaps there were more mundane explanations. No doubt Wilderspin's liberal populism led him to campaign against the taxes on knowledge,[97] to chair a meeting of the National Public School Association at Wakefield in 1851,[98] and to champion the right of the poor to education. In 1850 he was reported as saying "He would to God that every being had the chance which Providence intended him to have. The objection to the education of the poor sprang from a selfish motive. Some people say 'If you educate the son of the tinker he will be competing with my boy at college'. Why should he not?"[99] A lecture on "The Amusements of the People of England" led him to castigate the directing classes for their treatment of the people. If the amusements of the common people became brutal and cruel, it was because they were neglected by the upper classes; cock-fighting and bear-baiting were allowed, "to the eternal disgrace of nobility, magistrates, clergy and schoolmasters . . ." Later, playgrounds were stolen from the people while the Church stood idly by; the people were kept ignorant "that they might be the more easily fleeced, until at last the working population possessed no rights, but to labour and slave for those who were called their betters".[100]

Through all Wilderspin's thinking ran this vein of genuine concern for the rights of ordinary English people against the possible intrusions of Church and State. On occasion this could take, as we have seen in previous chapters, a sharply anti-clerical tone, be the cleric in question a High Churchman, Evangelical or Catholic priest. To some extent this may have been due to the Swedenborgian belief that all Churches were in process of being superseded and that all priestly dogma was suspect.[101] In Wakefield Wilderspin continued to harass Anglican clergy. In 1857 he contributed twenty-six column inches of invective against the Rev. H.B. Smyth, clerical secretary of the Church Institution, for his "illiberal, pharisaical and unchristian attitude" towards the Mechanics' Institution;[102] "religion was one thing and bigotry another",

[94] *Hull Advertiser,* 11 Aug. 1848.

[95] *Wakefield and West Riding Examiner,* 14 Dec. 1850.

[96] E. Swedenborg, *The New Jerusalem and Its Heavenly Doctrine* (London, 4th ed., 1792), 312; 320; 323; 325. Swedenborg generally enjoined obedience to the law.

[97] G.J. Holyoake, *Sixty Years of an Agitator's Life* (London, 2 vol., 1892), I, p. 292.

[98] Wilderspin Papers, poster entitled "National Public School Association. A Meeting...28 May 1851".

[99] *Wakefield and West Riding Examiner,* 8 June 1850.

[100] *Wakefield and West Riding Examiner,* 19 Jan. 1850.

[101] E. Swedenborg, *The Apocalypse Revealed* (Manchester, 2 vol., 1791), *passim;* E. Swedenborg, *The True Christian Religion* (London, 2 vol., 1781), *passim.*

[102] *Wakefield Journal,* 10 Oct. 1857.

Wilderspin declared, "and he hoped as long as he had eyes to see and ears to hear, he should continue to expose it, cost him what it might".[103]

In his belief in the rights of the people, verging at times towards a simple patriotism, combined with a hatred of Church hierarchies, must lie the explanation for his outburst against "priestly domination" from Rome in 1850.[104] If his opposition to Catholicism in 1840 had been muted, it now sprang forth in full vigour. The issue was first presented to the people of Wakefield when the *Wakefield Journal,* the voice of the local Establishment, reported in October 1850 that Pope Pius IX had divided England into twelve Catholic dioceses to be presided over by bishops appointed from Rome, Cardinal Nicholas Wiseman to be the primate as Archbishop of Westminster. This action, the *Journal* claimed, was viewed by most Anglicans as encroaching upon English law and practice, which held that the Sovereign, as head of the Established Church, exercised supreme spiritual as well as temporal authority and that all English bishops must be appointed by the Crown.[105]

A violent anti-Catholic campaign swept the country, with Wilderspin's old enemies the Evangelicals in the van. In Wakefield a public meeting was held on 29 November, with the Mayor in the chair, to consider an address to the Queen. Wilderspin, amid cries of "Well done, old cock!", poured fuel on the flames by raising the spectre of "foreign aggression", claiming that England's enemies were determined, if they could not beat her by fair means, to sow divisions among the people. Though he was willing, he insisted, to give his fellow citizens — "yea, to every man that breathed the breath of life" — the liberty to worship in whatever way he thought fit, yet at the same time he was firmly determined to oppose foreign enemies bent on subverting England's religion. Other speakers took up the theme, those who called for tolerance were shouted down and an Address to the Queen, protesting against the Pope's action, was adopted by acclamation.[106] The *Examiner,* which generally took a liberal line, was shocked by Wilderspin's intemperance. "Had any person with subordinate claims to public regard elaborated so monstrous a conceit as the one for which Mr. Wilderspin stood sponsor", it remonstrated, "we should have recommended him for the careful *surveillance* of his friends".[107]

Wilderspin, characteristically, was not deterred by this public rebuke and entered the lists again with a series of six long letters to the *Journal* and *Examiner,* in which he took on not only Charles Waterton, the noted naturalist and Catholic who resided near Wakefield, but also Joseph Wood, a retired army

[104]He used this phrase in a letter to the *Wakefield and West Riding Examiner,* 30 Nov. 1850.

[105]E.R. Norman, *Anti-Catholicism in Victorian England* (London 1968), pp. 52-79; pp. 159-85; *Wakefield Journal,* 25 Oct. 1850.

[106]*Wakefield Journal,* 29 Nov. 1850.

[107]*Wakefield and West Riding Examiner,* 7 Dec. 1850.

officer and prominent Catholic layman, and the Rev. Edward Higginson, his Unitarian friend and neighbour.[108] In all the letters, written in high-flown language, Wilderspin wrote as if the Pope were planning to lead an invasion of England to subvert the constitution and deprive Englishmen of their liberties. "Neither Italian Popes nor English cardinals shall ever again chain the faculties of the immortal soul in this Kingdom", he avowed, and he felt he could not blame the people for crying "No Popery" or wishing to repeal the Catholic Emancipation Act. Higginson replied calmly and reasonably, but Wilderspin continued to assign unrest in Ireland to the Catholic Emancipation Act, to relate horror stories of nunneries and the confessional, to accuse Catholic countries of tyranny, and to treat his opponents with scorn and to urge them not to descend to abuse.[109] Well might the *Examiner* suggest that he cease "hostilities", as he appeared "entirely to have lost sight of the real question in dispute, and mistaken abuse and ridicule of the Church of Rome for a sufficient reply to the demand of Roman Catholics for the full measure of religious liberty accorded to every other class of the Queen's subjects".[110]

The whole episode did Wilderspin no credit and must have pained his friends. It seems strangely inconsistent with his usual sense of fair play and can only be excused, if at all, by a mistaken belief, shared by many others, that fundamental English liberties were at stake. Perhaps for this reason his reputation in the town did not appear to suffer, and he continued to be active and effective in all spheres in the Mechanic's Institute. During the 1850s, in addition to his duties as lecturer and vice-president, he served on the important sub-committees for conducting soirées, engaging outside speakers (where he failed to secure the services of Charles Dickens)[111] and for promoting a Lancasterian day school.[112] Towards the end of the 1850s, however, his activities somewhat declined and in 1859 he failed to get elected to the committee or as vice-president.[113] His last activity in the Institution was to attend the 1861 soirée.[114] He could, however, look back on a decade of continuous work. Apart from his multifarious lecturing and speaking engagements, he had attended 72 of the 150 or so committee meetings held between 1849 and 1859, chairing 35 of them.[115]

[108]Waterton's letters appeared in the *Wakefield and West Riding Examiner*, 11, 18, and 26 Nov., 9 Dec. 1850. After his last letter he refused to contend with Wilderspin any further (*Wakefield and West Riding Examiner*, 21 Dec. 1850). For the letters of Wood and Higginson, cf. *Wakefield and West Riding Examiner*, 7, 21, and 25 Dec. 1850.

[109]*Wakefield and West Riding Examiner*, 30 Nov., 6, 14 and 21 Dec. 1850; 4 Jan. 1851; *Wakefield Journal*, 6 and 20 Dec. 1850.

[110]*Wakefield and West Riding Examiner*, 21 Dec. 1850.

[111]Wilderspin Papers, Dickens to Wilderspin, 22 Feb. 1855; Dickens "regrets that he cannot possibly comply with Mr. Wilderspin's request".

[112]W.M.I., Committee Minutes, 23 Aug. 1850; 5 June 1851; 13 Sept. 1855; H. Speak and J. Forrester, *Education in Wakefield* (Wakefield 1970), p. 11.

[113]W.M.I., Minutes, Annual Meeting, 31 Aug. 1859.

[114]W.M.I., Soirée Minutes, 19 Sept. 1861.

[115]W.M.I., Minute Books, 1849-1859, *passim*.

Perhaps the esteem in which he was held by his fellow members was best illustrated at the 1854 soirée, when his name was placed on a banner decorating the hall, together with those of Chaucer, Shakespeare, Bacon, Milton, Newton, Scott, Dickens, Birkbeck, Lancaster and other luminaries from the worlds of education, literature and science.[116]

* * * * *

During the last six years of his life, Wilderspin hardly stirred from Moor Cottage. The death of his eldest daughter Sarah in 1860 was a great blow and in the last year or two of his life he seems to have been ailing. The Wakefield Poll Book for 1865 lists him as an elector who was too ill to vote.[117] At the time of his death it was reported that he had not been out of the house for seven or eight months.[118] The end came a few days before his 75th birthday. On the afternoon of March 10, 1866 a telegram was delivered to the Young residence in Rathgar, Dublin. It was from Mrs. Wilderspin in Wakefield and said, "My husband died very peacefully at 10 mins. past 1 o'clock today".[119] He was buried beside his daughter Emily in Thornes Churchyard on Wednesday 14 March. An obituary notice in the *Wakefield Free Press* concluded:

> Although a plainspeaking man, and apt to fire up in an instant at aught that seemed to be unfair, his heart was made of kindness. Never in any other man have we found, as we found in him, such a gentle and child-like character, surviving long years of trials and adverse buffetings of opponents. He had all the impulsiveness of a child, but he was very generous and forgiving, and as docile as a child when kindly dealt with. He always wished everybody to do right; above all desiring to do right himself. If he failed to take a preferable course in his little contentions, he never willingly or knowingly hurt others by following the road he did.[120]

This praise of Wilderspin's personal qualities no doubt reflected the writer's desire to pay homage to a departed friend. But the esteem in which Wilderspin was held by the public, and which found expression in the National Tribute Fund, rested on a more solid foundation — his lasting contribution to British education. He was, of course, the principal advocate and organiser of a system of infant education that was well in advance of his time, and this has been recognised by educational historians. What is less generally appreciated is that Wilderspin greatly enlarged the views of his contemporaries on many aspects of education then poorly understood: on the nature of teaching and the status of

[116] *Wakefield Journal and Examiner,* 3 Nov. 1854.

[117] Wakefield Metropolitan District Council Archives, Wakefield Poll Books 1865.

[118] *Wakefield Free Press,* 17 Mar. 1866.

[119] Wilderspin Papers, telegram, M. Wilderspin to T.U. and S.A. Young, 10 Mar. 1866.

[120] *Wakefield Free Press,* 17 Mar. 1866.

the teacher; on the desirability of training them professionally and paying them a just reward; on the divisive nature of denominational education, the deficiencies of the voluntary system, and the need for the widest education of the children of the poor; above all on the nature of infancy, its importance as a crucial stage in human development and the need to develop a mode of education suited to the early childhood years.

APPENDIX I

Select List of Infant Schools in Britain 1816 - 1825

The following list of infant schools founded between 1816 and the end of 1825 does not pretend to be definitive. The sources are incomplete or defective and contemporary imprecision as to what constituted an infant school precludes an exact assessment. For these reasons, lists with retrospective dates such as the 1833 Education Returns or the Manchester Statistical Society surveys, have not been utilised. Reliance has been placed on the statements of Wilderspin and the Infant School Society, plus a few other trustworthy references, and these provide a reasonably accurate guide to the extent of infant school provision in the period under review. In fact, they understate the position, as schools mentioned in sources other than those given below may well have referred to genuine infant schools on the New Lanark — Westminster — Spitalfields — Bristol model.

The table is compiled from the following sources: (i) Wilderspin's list in *Infant Poor* (1824), pp. 23-4, made c. January 1824; (ii) Brougham's statement at the Infant School Society meeting, 7 June 1824 (*Morning Chronicle*, 8 June 1824), (iii) Infant School Society. Annual Report, 4 June 1825; (iv) Wilderspin's statement in *Infant Education* (1825), pp. 8-9, and list p. 284, compiled late 1825; (v) Wilderspin's statement in *Early Discipline* (1832), p. 9, (vi) various newspaper and journal reports and references in the text. After (i), schools appearing in previous lists have been omitted. The schools are given in the order in which they appear in the lists; a few schools have been more precisely dated by reference to the sources in (vi).

1816 (Jan.) New Lanark; **1819** (Feb.) Westminster; **1820** (July) Spitalfields; **1821** (June) Bristol (Meadow St.); **1822** (Apr.) Stoke Newington; **1822 or 1823:** Hackney, Peckham, Camberwell; **before Jan. 1824:** Whitechapel, Brampton (Hunts.), Blackfriars, Putney, Worthing, Liverpool, Wandsworth; **1824:** (Jan.) Brighton, (Mar.) Walthamstow, (Mar.) St. Luke's (Middlesex), Wellington (Somerset), Bath, Enniskerry (Ireland); **1824 (June) — 1825 (June):** (May 1825) Hereford, Shrewsbury, (May 1825) Worcester, (May 1825) Ross-on-Wye, Chelsea, Chelmsford, Wantage, Down, Farnborough, Ampton, Enfield, Sturminster, Clapham, Deddington, Banbury, Byfleet, Stratford (London), Wellington (Salop.), Brixton, Sutton (Beds.), Wapping, Battersea Rise, West Bromwich, Shipcombe, Battersea Fields, Palmer's Village (Westminster), Pudding Lane (London), Mill Hill (London), Bethnal Green (2 schools), (Sept. 1824) Glastonbury, (late 1824 or early 1825) Bath (2nd school), (Apr. 1825) Chelmsford (2nd school), (May 1825) Bristol (Temple); **1825 (after June):** Liverpool (two additional schools), Norwich, (first two c. July 1825) Durham (three schools), Devizes, Clifton (Bristol), Exeter, (June 1825) Newcastle, Greenstead, Boston, Wantage, Plymouth, (May 1825) Stockport, Lindfield, (July 1825) Manchester (Buxton St.), (June 1825) Kidderminster, Southampton, Woolwich, Lancaster, Stamford Rivers, Chilham, (Oct. 1825) Liverpool Street (London), Macclesfield.

APPENDIX II

Wilderspin's journeys to organise infant schools and to lecture
on education, 1825 - 1836: a select list.

The following table covers most of the journeys which Wilderspin made when travelling organiser for the Infant School Society from early 1825 to late 1828, and as an independent educational missionary from early 1829 to the summer of 1836. A separate section is devoted to his Scottish activities. The table includes details of schools founded or organised by Wilderspin or his agents, of lectures or exhibitions and, in a few cases, of sojourns in, or visits to, certain places. Only data for which documentary evidence is available has, however, been included. Thus the table omits the schools founded or visits made by Wilderspin (mostly in the 1820s) which are mentioned in the text, in the various editions of *Early Discipline*, or elsewhere, for which independent documentary evidence is non-existent, defective or doubtful. The dates in the left-hand margin are sometimes approximate and in certain cases cover the presumed length of stay in a town or district.

DATE	PLACE	SOURCE	NOTES
1825	**England, Ireland & Wales 1825-1828**		
Mar., Apr., May	Ross-on-Wye	*Hereford Journal*, 15 June 1825	Opened school c. 1 May; examination after 5 weeks.
Apr., May	Hereford	*Hereford Journal*, 1 June 1825	Opened school c. 15 May; examination later.
May	Bristol (Temple)	*Taunton Courier*, 31 May 1827	Opened by pupil & agent.
May	Stockport	*Stockport Chronicle*, 29 Apr. 1825	Opened school 16 May.
c. July	Durham (2 schools)	Report, Newcastle I.S.S., 1826, p.6; *Durham County Advertiser*, 12 Feb. 1825; 14 Jan. 1826	Organised & opened with agent & boy.

Date	Place	Source	Activity
June	Kidderminster	*Berrow's Worcester Journal, 30 June 1825*	Opened school c. 25 June.
June	Newcastle	Report, Newcastle I.S.S., 1826, p.6	Trained master.
July	Manchester (Buxton St.)	*Manchester Guardian, 26 June 1825*	Opened school.
1826			
Feb.	London	Marriage certificate	Marriage to Miss Peacock.
Feb. onwards	Manchester	*Chester Chronicle*, 29 Aug. 1826	A stay of several months.
May	Manchester	*Leeds Mercury*, 27 May 1826	
June	Manchester (Chorlton Row)	*Manchester Courier*, 24 June 1826	Examination, 26 June.
Late July	Chester (Kaleyard)	*Chester Chronicle*, 1 Aug. 1826; *Chester Courant*, 1 Aug. 1826	To superintend school & stay a few weeks.
End Aug.	Chester (Kaleyard)	*Chester Courant*, 29 Aug. 1826	Examination prior to departure.
Sept.	Manchester (Buxton St.)	*Manchester Guardian* 26 Aug. 1826	Examination, 1 Sept.
Early Sept.	Leeds	*Chester Chronicle*, 18 Aug. 1826	To promote school.
Sept.	Birmingham	Second Report, Birmingham, I.S.S., p. 17	Two visits.
Oct.	Dublin (Westland Row)	*Dublin Evening Mail*, 11 Oct. 1826	Organised & opened school.
Nov., Dec.	Ireland	*Early Discipline* (1832), pp. 63-70	Travelling & recuperating from illness.
1827			
Jan.	Derby (Siddals Lane)	*Derby Mercury*, 24 Jan. 1827	Examination.
Apr.	London (Wandsworth)	*Weekly Times*, 8 Apr. 1827	Spoke at meeting, first week of April.
May	Cheltenham (Alstone)	*Cheltenham Chronicle*, 24 May 1827	Examinations, 16 & 17 May.
End June	Melbourne (Derbys.)	*Derby Mercury*, 20 June & 4 July 1827	Examination.

Sept., Oct.	Westminster	*Educational Magazine*, Vol. II Aug. 1835, p. 149	Reorganised Westminster Infant School.
End Oct.	Taunton	*Taunton Courier*, 24 Oct. 1827	Spoke at meeting, 26 Oct.
Dec.	Aylesbury	*Bucks., Beds. & Herts. Chronicle*, 15 Dec. 1827; 5 Jan. 1828	Organised school.
1828			
Jan.	Aylesbury	*Bucks., Beds. & Herts. Chronicle*, 5, 19 & 26 Jan. 1828	Lectures & examination.
Jan., Mar.	?	*Early Discipline* (1832), p. 94	Affliction: no work for some weeks.
Sept.	Hanley (Staffs.)	*Staffordshire Mercury*, 13 & 27 Sept. 1828	Lecture, 22 Sept.
Dec.	Newcastle - under-Lyme	*Staffordshire Advertiser*, 20 Dec. 1828	Lecture, 15 Dec.
Dec.	Burslem	*Staffordshire Mercury*, 20 Dec. 1828	Lecture, 17 Dec.
Dec.	Hanley	*Staffordshire Mercury*, 20 & 27 Dec. 1828	Examination.

* * * *

Scotland 1828-1832

1828			
Apr.	Glasgow	*Glasgow Chronicle*, 28 Apr. 1828	Lecture, 30 Apr.
May	Glasgow	*Glasgow Herald*, 12 & 19 May 1828	Examination, Drygate school, 30 May.
May	Glasgow	*Glasgow Herald*, 19 May 1828	Lecture.
June, July	Paisley	First Report, G.I.S.S. App. III, p. 6; *Early Discipline* (1832), pp. 115-16	Lecture & exhibition.
Sept.	Greenock	*Scotsman*, 1 Oct. 1828	Arrived 28 Sept.
Nov.	Greenock	*Scotsman*, 8 Nov. 1828	Letter to *Scotsman*, 1 Nov.

Date	Place	Event	Source
Nov.	Perth	Examination, 19 Nov.	*Perthshire Courier, 13. Nov. 1828*
Nov.	Edinburgh	Lecture, 27 Nov.	*Scotsman, 2 Nov. 1828*
Dec.	Edinburgh	Lecture, 1 Dec.	*Scotsman, 29 Nov. 1828*
Dec.	Perth	Examination, 4 Dec.	*Perthshire Courier. 4 Dec. 1828*
1829			
Apr.	Edinburgh	Lectures, 22 & 23 Apr.	*Scotsman, 18 Apr. 1829*
Apr.	Aberdeen	Lectures, 28 & 29 Apr.	*Aberdeen Journal, 29 Apr. 1829*
May	Dundee	Lectures, 2 & 4 May.	*Dundee, Perth & Cupar Advertiser, 30 Apr. 1829*
1830			
Mar.	Dundee	Lectures, 3, 8 & 4 Mar.	*Dundee, Perth & Cupar Advertiser, 24 Feb., 4 Mar. 1830*
Mar.	Dundee	Exhibition, 24 Mar.	*Dundee, Perth & Cupar Advertiser, 18 Mar. 1830*
Mar.	Montrose	Lectures, 30 & 31 Mar.	*Montrose, Arbroath & Brechin Review, 26 Mar. 1830*
Apr.	Edinburgh	Lectures, 26, 28 & 30 Apr.	*Scotsman, 21 & 28 Apr. 1830*
May	Edinburgh	Exhibitions, 4 & 11 May.	*Edinburgh Weekly Journal. 5 May 1830; Scotsman, 12 May 1830*
May	Leith	Lectures, 7 & 10 May.	*Scotsman, 12 May 1830*
July	Dundee	Exhibition.	*Dundee, Perth & Cupar Advertiser, 15 July 1830*
Sept.	Dumfries	Lecture, last week in Sept.	*Glasgow Herald, 8 Oct. 1830*
Oct.	Glasgow	Lectures, 5 & 7 Oct.	*Glasgow Herald. 1 Oct. 1830*
Oct.	Glasgow	Lectures, 14 & 15 Oct.	*Glasgow Herald. 8 Oct. 1830*

1831

Nov.	Aberdeen	*Aberdeen Chronicle*, 5 Nov. 1831	Lectures 7, 8, 10 & 11 Nov.
Nov.	Aberdeen	*Aberdeen Observer*, 18 Nov. 1831; *Aberdeen Journal*, 23 Nov. 1831	Exhibitions, 17 & 21 Nov.
Nov.	Aberdeen	*Aberdeen Journal*, 23 Nov. 1831	4 lectures, week commencing 24 Nov.
Early Dec.	Inverness	Letter Book, 12 Dec. 1831	
Dec.	Dingwall	*Scotsman*, 7 Jan. 1832.	Spoke at meetings 8 & 22 Dec.
Late Dec.	Inverness	Letter Book, 24 Dec. 1831	

1832

Jan.	Banff	*Aberdeen Journal*, 18 Jan. 1832	Concluded course of lectures, 10 Jan.
Feb.	Inverness	*Aberdeen Journal*, 1 Feb. 1832	Exhibition, 1 Feb.
Sept.	Dingwall	Mackenzie to Brougham, 9 Sept. 1832	Organised school.

* * * * *

England, Ireland & Wales 1829-1836

1829

Jan., Feb., Mar.	Cheltenham	*Cheltenham Chronicle*, 19 Mar. 1829	Rented Alpha House.
Mar.	Cheltenham	*Cheltenham Chronicle*, 26 Mar., 2 Apr. 1829	Lectures, 27 & 28 Mar.
Sept.	Cheltenham	*Cheltenham Chronicle*, 3 Sept. 1829	Lectures 1, 3 & 5 Sept.

1830

Sept.	Whitehaven	*Cumberland Pacquet*, 31 Aug., 7 Sept. 1829	Lecture & examination, 3 Sept.
Sept.	Cockermouth	*Carlisle Journal*, 4 Sept. 1830; *Cumberland Pacquet*, 7 Sept. 1830	Lectures, 9 & 10 Sept.

Sept.	Whitehaven	*Cumberland Pacquet*, 7 & 14 Sept. 1830	Lectures, 13 & 14 Sept.
Sept.	Cockermouth	*Cumberland Pacquet*, 14 Sept. 1830	Exhibitions, 16 & 17 Sept.
Sept.	Workington	*Cumberland Pacquet*, 21 Sept. 1830	Lecture, 21 Sept.
Nov.	Kendal	*Westmoreland Gazette*, 13 Nov. 1830; *Westmoreland Advertiser & Kendal Chronicle*, 20 Nov. 1830	Lectures, 16 & 17 Nov.
1831			
Jan.	Llandovery	*Carmarthen Journal*, 14 Jan. 1831; Letter Book, 10 Jan. 1831	Lectures, organisation of school & exhibition.
Jan.	Lincoln	*Lincoln & Newark Times*, 22 Jan 1831	Lectures, c. 20 Jan.
Early Feb.	North of England		
Feb.	Evesham	*Berrow's Worcester Journal*, 24 Feb. 1831	Lectures, 23 & 25 Feb.
Feb.	Worcester	*Berrow's Worcester Journal*, 17 Feb. 1831	Lectures, 22, 23 & 24 Feb.
Feb.	Kidderminster	*Worcester Herald*, 26 Feb. 1831	Lecture, c. 28 Feb.
Mar.	Coventry.	*Coventry Herald*, 4 Mar. 1831; Letter Book, 5 Mar. 1831	Lectures, 9, 10 & 11 Mar.
Mar.	Sheffield.	*Sheffield Courant*, 11 & 18 Mar. 1831	Lectures & exhibition, 14, 16 & 17 Mar.
Mar.	Chesterfield	*Derbyshire Courier*, 19 & 26 Mar. 1831	Lectures, 21 Mar. ff.
Apr.	Reading	*Reading Mercury*, 4 Apr. 1831	Lectures, 6 & 7 Apr.
Apr.	Swansea	*Cambrian*, 9 Apr. 1831; Letter Book, 10 Apr. 1831	Lectures, 14, 15 & 18 Apr.
Apr.	Bath	*Keene's Bath Journal*, 18 Apr. 1831 Letter Book, 26 Apr. 1831	Lectures, 21, 22 & 23 Apr.
May	Cheltenham	*Cheltenham Chronicle*, 10 May 1831	Lecture, c. 7 May.
May	Bath	*Bath and Cheltenham Gazette, 3 May* 1831; Letter Book, 18 May 1831	Lectures, 9, 11 & 12 May.

May	Bath	*Bath Herald*, 14 May 1831; *Bath Journal*, 23 May 1831	Lectures & exhibition, 17, 19, 21 & 22 May.
June	Cheltenham	*Cheltenham Chronicle*, 21 June 1831	Lectures, 7, 9 & 11 June.
June	Lincoln	*Linc., Rutland & Stamford Mercury*, 10 June 1831	Lectures, 16, 17 & 20 June.
July	Newark	*Linc., Rutland & Stamford Mercury*, 8 July 1831; *Lincoln & Newark Times*, 6 July 1831; Letter Book, 28 June 1831	Lectures, c. 1 July ff.
July	Boston	*Boston Gazette*, 5 July 1831	Lecture, 4 July.
July	Louth.	*Linc., Rutland & Stamford Mercury*, 8 July 1831; Letter Book, 12 July 1831	Lectures, 11, 12 & 13 July.
July	Stamford	*Linc., Rutland & Stamford Mercury*, 15 July 1831	Lectures, 15, 16 & 18 July.
July	Cambridge	*Cambridgeshire & Hertfordshire Independent Press*, 23 July 1831; Letter Book, 27 July 1831	Lectures, 25, 26 & 19 July.
Aug.	Nottingham	*Nottingham Journal*, 20 Aug. 1831	Lectures, 22, 23, 29 & 30 Aug.
Sept.	Newark	*Linc., Rutland & Stamford Mercury*, 23 & 30 Sept. 1831	Exhibition, 27 Sept., after 4 weeks training.
Oct.	Newark	*Drakard's Stamford News*, 7 Oct. 1831	
1832			
Feb.	Lincoln	*Linc., Rutland & Stamford Mercury*, 17 & 24 Feb. 1832; *Boston Gazette*, 28 Feb. 1832	Opened school c. 16 Feb.
Mar.	Lincoln	*Linc., Rutland & Stamford Mercury*, 9, 16 & 23 Mar. 1832	Exhibitions, 15 & 19 Mar.
Nov.	Wakefield	*Wakefield & Halifax Journal*, 16 & 23 Nov. 1832	Lectures, 19, 20 & 26 Nov.

Date	Place	Source	Activity
Dec.	Huddersfield	*Halifax Guardian*, 29 Dec. 1832	Lecture, 27 Dec.
1833			
Jan.	Halifax	*Wakefield & Halifax Journal*, 18 Jan. 1833	Lectures, 15 Jan. ff.
Feb.	Doncaster	*Wakefield & Halifax Journal*, 22 Feb. 1833	Lectures, 15 Feb. ff.
Apr.	Belfast	*Belfast Newsletter*, 9 Apr. 1833	Lectures, 16, 18, 19 & 20 Apr.
May	Belfast	*Belfast Newsletter*, 14 May 1833	Exhibition, 20 May.
May	Warrenpoint	*Newry Commercial Telegraph*, 24 May 1833	Lectures, 28, 29 30 & 31 May.
June, July	England		Ill.
Aug.	Newry	*Newry Commercial Telegraph*, 31 May, 11 June & 2 Aug. 1833	Lectures, 5, 6,7 & 8 Aug.
Aug.	Dungannon	*Newry Commercial Telegraph*, 2, 6, 9 & 13 Aug. 1833	Lecture, c. 9 Aug.
Aug.	Monaghan	*Newry Commercial Telegraph*, 13 Aug. 1833	Lecture, 12 Aug.
Aug.	Dublin	*Newry Commercial Telegraph*, 13 Aug. 1833; *Dublin Evening Post*, 17 Aug. 1833; *Saunders's Newsletter*, 19 Aug. 1833	Lectures, 26, 27, 28 & 29 Aug.
Sept.	Dublin	*Saunders's Newsletter*, 4 Sept. 1833	Lectures, 4, 5, 6 & 7 Sept.
Sept.	Booterstown	*Saunders's Newsletter*, 4 Sept. 1833	4 lectures, c. 9-14 Sept.
Sept.	Kingstown	*Saunders's Newsletter*, 17 Sept. 1833	3 lectures & examination 18, 19, 20 & 21 Sept.
Sept.	Londonderry	*Londonderry Sentinel*, 21 & 28 Sept., 5 Oct. 1833	Lectures, 25, 26, 27 & 28 Sept.

1834

Jan.	Peterborough	*Linc., Rutland & Stamford Mercury,* 3 Jan. 1834	4 lectures, c. 5-9 Jan.
July, Aug.	Waterford	*Waterford Mirror,* 26 July, 2 Aug 1834	5 lectures, 29 July-6 Aug.
Sept.	Waterford	*Waterford Mirror,* 6 & 13 Sept. 1834	Exhibition, 10 Sept.
Sept., Oct.	Cork	*Cork Evening Herald,* 26 Sept., 6 Oct. 1834	Lectures, 24, 26 & 29 Sept., 1 Oct.
Oct.	Cork	*Cork Evening Herald,* 6 Oct. 1834	Lectures & examination.

1835

Jan.	Thetford	*Bury & Norwich Post,* 21 Jan., 4 Feb. 1835	Lectures, 26, 29 30 & 31 Jan.
Apr.	Bury	*Bolton Chronicle,* 18 Apr. 1835	Opened school, 13 Apr.
Apr., May	Bury	*Bolton Chronicle,* 2 & 9 May 1835	Lectures, 30 Apr., 1 May.
May	Bury	*Bolton Chronicle,* 16 May 1835	Exhibition, 8 May.
May	Wigan	*Bolton Chronicle,* 16 May 1835	Opened school, 18 May.
June	Wigan	*Bolton Chronicle,* 13 June 1835	Examination, 11 June.
June	London	P.P. 1835 VII, Select Com. on Educ.	Evidence, 18 June.
June	Cheltenham	Wilderspin to Simpson, 25 June 1835	At home, until c. 25 June.
June, July	Bromsgrove	Wilderspin to Simpson, 25 June 1835	Relieving daughter at school, c. 26 June onwards.
July	Bromsgrove	*Worcestershire Guardian,* 8 Aug.1835	Examination, 23 & 24 July.
Late July, early Aug.	Chorley	Wilderspin to Simpson, 25 June 1835	Opened school.

1836

Feb.	Swaffham	*Norwich Mercury*, 30 Jan. 1836	Lectures, 1, 3, 4 & 5 Feb.
Feb.	Wells	*Bury & Norwich Post*, 17 Feb. 1836	Lectures, 20 Feb. ff.
Mar.	Yarmouth	*Norwich Mercury*, 20 & 27 Feb. 1836	Lectures, 1, 2, 3, & 4 Mar.
Mar.	Norwich	*Norwich Mercury*, 5 Mar. 1836	Lectures, 8, 9, 10 & 11 Mar.
Mar.	Norwich	*Norwich Mercury*, 12 Mar. 1836	Lectures, 14 & 15 Mar.
Mar.	Norwich	*Norwich Mercury*, 19 Mar. 1836 / *Norfolk Chronicle*, 26 Mar. 1836	Examination, 22 Mar.
Apr.	Cheltenham	*Cheltenham Looker-On*, 23 & 30 Apr. 1836	Lectures, 22 & 29 Apr.
June, July	Windsor	*Windsor & Eton Express*, 25 June 1836	Lectures, 30 June, 1 July.
Aug.	Hereford	*Hereford Times*, 20 July 1836	Lectures, 1, 2, 4 & 5 Aug.
Aug.	Kington	*Hereford Times*, 6 Aug. 1836	Lectures, 8, 9, 11 & 12 Aug.
Aug.	Hereford	*Hereford Times*, 13 & 20 Aug. 1836	Examination, 18 Aug.

BIBLIOGRAPHY

The bibliography, because of contemporary printing costs, is limited to the unpublished manuscript sources utilised in this book. Printed secondary sources can be found in the footnote references.

MANUSCRIPT SOURCES

Wilderspin Papers (In the possession of John A. Young, Wolcott, Vermont, U.S.A.)

(i) 25 letters, drafts or copies of letters by Wilderspin; memoranda, notes, etc.

(ii) 430 letters to Wilderspin, including 88 from members of his family; 51 from Daniel and Mary Gaskell; 276 from various correspondents, including Brougham, Lansdowne, Kay-Shuttleworth, Dickens, James Simpson, George Combe, several bishops and other public figures and educators; 15 from institutes and societies.

(iii) Ms. entitled "Subjects Worth the Attention of the Committee of Corporation Schools in order to follow up their proposed plan of Education" (31 Mar. 1837).

(iv) Letter Book 1831-32, containing 191 entries of letters written by his office manager C.F. Lewis.

(v) *Early Discipline* (1840), interleaved with blank pages inscribed with Wilderspin's Ms. notes for additions to a future (unpublished) edition.

Young Papers (In the possession of John A. Young, Wolcott, Vermont, U.S.A.)

Approximately 200 items, including letters to and from Wilderspin, manuscripts, photographs, paintings and other memorabilia relating to the family of Sarah Anne and Thomas Urry Young, Wilderspin's daughter and son-in-law. The Mss. include T.U. Young's "Memoir of the Late Mrs. Young" (two versions); "Memoir of My Father's Family"; "Memoir of My Own Family".

Public Record Office

Register of Baptisms, Friar's Street New Jerusalem Church, 1787-1837; New Jerusalem Chapel, St. George's Fields, 1816-34.
Census 1851, returns for Alverthorpe with Thornes Parish.

Public Record Office Ireland

Registers, National Schools Co. Dublin, Vol. I, 1835-45.

State Paper Office Dublin

Extracts from minutes of the Board of National Education; letter of Wilderspin to Lord Ebrington.

British Museum

Peel Papers.

National Library of Scotland

Combe Papers.

Bristol Record Office

Temple Infant School, Minute Book, 1825-1868.

Hampshire Record Office

Calthorpe Papers.

Liverpool Record Office

Minutes of the Liverpool Town Council 1835-1838.
Education Committee Minute Book 1836-48.
North Corporation Schools Bevington Bush Sub-Committee Minute Book, Vol. I, 1837-1849.

Guildhall Library

London Weavers' Company, Court Minute Books 1786-1824.
St. Leonard Shoreditch Infant School Society, Minutes 1837-1854.

University College London

Brougham Mss.
Bentham Mss.

John Rylands University Library Manchester

Wilderspin correspondence.

Edinburgh City Council

Warrants of the Lord Dean of Guild and the Council, 1829.

Birmingham Central Library

Birmingham Infant School, afterwards Birmingham Infant School Society, Minutes Book 1825-1831.

Wakefield Metropolitan District Archives

Wakefield Mechanics' Institution Minute Books.
Wakefield Poll Books, 1865.
Wilderspin Testimonial Account Book (Goodchild Loan Mss.).

Hackney Libraries Archives Dept.

Hackney Charity School, Minute Book, Vols. 3 and 4, 1787-1834.

Hull Public Library

Letter of J. Gee.

National Society Library

Minute Book of the General Committee, Vol. III.

General Conference of the New Church

Minute Book of the Society for Promoting the Heavenly Doctrines of the New Jerusalem Church, East Cheap, London.
New Church Sunday School, Minute Book 1816.
Rules and Signatures of Members of the New Jerusalem Church, Waterloo Road, 1823.
The Committee of the New Jerusalem Church Free School in Account with Jervoise Bugby.

Fruitlands Museum, Mass.

Harland Mss.

Archives of W. and R. Chambers

Wilderspin correspondence.

Office of the Brechin Advertiser

Brechin Infant School Society, Minute Book, 1835-1873.
Brechin Infant School Society, Correspondence Book.

Hackney Free and Parochial Secondary School

Minute Book of the Hackney Infant School, Bridge Street, Homerton, 1826-1880.

Typescript

R. Russell, "The Lindsey Infant Schools and Samuel Wilderspin" (n.d.).
O. Vag, "The Spread of a New Type of Educational Institution: Public Pre-School Education" (1980).

Index

314

DATE DUE

GAYLORD	No. 2333		PRINTED IN U.S.A.